T0311492

# A HISTORY OF PUBLIC BANKING IN PORTUGAL IN THE 19TH AND 20TH CENTURIES

This book examines the history of what became one of Portugal's largest banks, the *Caixa Geral de Depósitos*. The bank was founded in 1876 by the state to run public deposits, and evolved into a savings bank, catering for both public and private deposits. Its history goes beyond the history of banking, as it ties in with the role of the state in the banking sector and financial markets.

The book weaves in and out of different political and international contexts, following the many changes of the Portuguese political regime and of its interactions with the national and international economy. The most important lesson from the study is that publicly owned institutions can compete successfully with the private sector when they simultaneously cater for the interests of policy makers as well as those of the public, in this case, the depositors. The history of the *Caixa Geral de Depósitos* therefore shows how the state of a peripheral economy is capable of successfully managing a large financial institution when the right set of incentives is in place.

This work will be a valuable resource for researchers and students of financial and economic history at both the advanced undergraduate and postgraduate levels. It will also provide interesting insights for practitioners in the financial sector.

**Pedro Lains** (Lisbon, December 1959 – May 2021) was Research Professor at the Instituto de Ciências Sociais, University of Lisbon. His main research interests were Portuguese and European economic history. He has published many books and journal articles in these fields, including a forthcoming edited volume on *The Economic History of the Iberian Peninsula, 711–2000*.

# FINANCIAL HISTORY

Edited by Farley Grubb and Anne L. Murphy

MONEY, POLITICS AND POWER
Banking and Public Finance in Wartime England, 1694–96
*Richard A. Kleer*

REGULATION OF THE LONDON STOCK EXCHANGE
Share Trading, Fraud and Reform 1914–1945
*Chris Swinson*

MONETARY PLURALITY IN LOCAL, REGIONAL
AND GLOBAL ECONOMIES
*Edited by Georgina M. Gómez*

SHARE TRADING, FRAUD AND THE CRASH OF 1929
A Biography of Clarence Hatry
*Chris Swinson*

THE ORIGINS OF MODERN BANKING IN SPAIN
Monetary Plurality and Local Monopolies
*Edited by Carles Sudrià and Yolanda Blasco-Martel*

EUROPEAN INVESTMENT IN GREECE
IN THE NINETEENTH CENTURY
A Behavioural Approach to Financial History
*Korinna Schönhärl*

A HISTORY OF PUBLIC BANKING IN PORTUGAL
IN THE 19TH AND 20TH CENTURIES
*Pedro Lains*

For more information about this series, please visit:
www.routledge.com/series/FINHIS

# A HISTORY OF PUBLIC BANKING IN PORTUGAL IN THE 19TH AND 20TH CENTURIES

*Pedro Lains*

Routledge
Taylor & Francis Group

LONDON AND NEW YORK

First published 2022
by Routledge
2 Park Square, Milton Park, Abingdon, Oxon OX14 4RN

and by Routledge
52 Vanderbilt Avenue, New York, NY 10017

*Routledge is an imprint of the Taylor & Francis Group, an informa business*

© 2022 Pedro Lains

*British Library Cataloguing-in-Publication Data*
A catalogue record for this book is available from the British Library

*Library of Congress Cataloging-in-Publication Data*
Names: Lains, Pedro, author.
Title: A history of public banking in Portugal in the 19th and
20th centuries / Pedro Lains.
Other titles: História da Caixa Geral de Depósitos, 1876-1910. English
Description: 1 Edition. | New York : Routledge, 2020. |
Series: Financial history | Includes bibliographical references and index.
Identifiers: LCCN 2020026880 (print) | LCCN 2020026881 (ebook)
Subjects: LCSH: Caixa Geral de Depósitos (Portugal)–History. |
Banks and banking–Portugal–History.
Classification: LCC HG3198.C35 L3513 2020 (print) | LCC HG3198.C35
(ebook) | DDC 332.109469–dc23
LC record available at https://lccn.loc.gov/2020026880
LC ebook record available at https://lccn.loc.gov/2020026881

ISBN: 978-1-138-38820-8 (hbk)
ISBN: 978-0-367-61222-1 (pbk)
ISBN: 978-0-429-42572-1 (ebk)

Typeset in Bembo
by Taylor & Francis Books

# CONTENTS

*Introduction*                                                                                    viii
*Acknowledgements*                                                                           xvii

1  The rise of public finance, 1820–1870                                            1

   *The Bank of Lisbon and the Public Credit Board, 1821–1846  2*
   *The 1846 financial crisis and the foundation of the Bank of Portugal  5*
   *1853: the new financial order  9*

2  Financial boom and crisis, 1870–1876                                          16

   *The liquidity boom, 1870–1876  16*
   *The 1876 crisis  19*
   *The Public Credit Board reformed once more  22*

3  The establishment of the *Caixa Geral de Depósitos*, 1876–1880   25

   *The Parliamentary debate  25*
   *The commencement  29*
   *How it worked  35*

4  The establishment of the *Caixa Económica Portuguesa*, 1880–1886   39

   *The debate on the public savings bank  39*
   *The plan for the establishment of the* Caixa Económica Portuguesa  *41*
   *The wider financial reforms, 1885–1886  45*

5  The financial reforms, 1886–1890                                               53

   *The Progressive financial revolution  54*

*A new statute for the Bank of Portugal 56*
*Government control 59*

6   The financial crisis, 1890–1892                                          66

*How it started 67*
*The radical solution 71*
*The progressives once more 77*

7   Back to the old order, 1892–1910                                         81

*The return of the* regeneradores *82*
*The 1896 reform 85*

8   The Republic, 1910–1926                                                  91

*The new political regime 92*
*The impact on the* Caixa *94*
*The second Republican reform 97*

9   The new order, 1926–1929                                                102

*Before Salazar 102*
*Salazar as finance minister 104*
*Beyond public bonds 106*
*The 1929 reform 108*
*The politics of regime change at the* Caixa *112*

10  The path consolidation of the Estado Novo, 1929–1935                    115

*Financial stability 115*
*Credit to the economy 116*
*Social housing and urban improvements 119*
Caixa *and the Empire 121*

11  Public investment, 1935–1950                                            129

*The new state and the economy 130*
*World War II 132*
*After the war 135*

12  Between the state and the market, 1950–1968                            141

*Financial concerns 142*

*The development plans 147*
*Housing 149*
*The new banking framework 150*

13  Staying behind, 1968–1974                                              156

*The technocratic dictator 157*
*The public company 163*
*Hard times 165*

14  The nationalisations and beyond, 1974–1992                             173

*Regime change and the banking sector 173*
*Remittances and construction 178*
*Normalisation 180*
*The Caixa and the government 181*
*The acquisition of the Banco Nacional Ultramarino 185*

15  Coping with the monetary union, 1992–2010                             191

*The fragile internationalisation 193*
*The Iberian ambition 196*
*Following the language 199*

Conclusion                                                               203

*References*                                                             213
*Index*                                                                  222

# INTRODUCTION

The expansion of the role of the state, an important feature of nineteenth century liberalism, in Portugal and elsewhere in Europe, implied the rise of public financial resources, achieved through the collection of indirect taxes, as well as taxes on trade, property and income, and credit in the domestic and international markets. To raise credit, the state sold bonds directly to the public or resorted to private financial institutions, namely investor's syndicates, to which it conceded special privileges, such as the monopoly of issuing bank notes at the regional or national level. The new institutional framework was at the root of the foundation of the Bank of Lisbon in 1821, its successor, the Bank of Portugal, in 1846, the confirmation of the monopolies for tobacco, soap, and other staples, and later on the restructuring of the Treasury. The same reason applies to the foundation of the Public Credit Board (*Junta do Crédito Público*) in 1837, the institution that was in charge of placing government securities on the market and managing the payment of interests. It also acted as the deposit bank for the funds owed to the state due to a number of legal and court obligations. The 'public deposits' had historically been managed by local institutions in an uncoordinated way, in contradistinction to the principles of the centrally run liberal state.

The definition of the boundaries between the functions of the Bank of Lisbon, the Public Credit Board, the Treasury, and the smaller financial institutions spread across the country was far from clear. It was thus necessary for the new liberal governments to rearrange the financial system in order to increase the control over resources and the efficiency of their collection and use. That task, however, took a long time to materialise because the evolution of the liberal state in nineteenth-century Portugal was relatively slow, as was the overall development of its economy and financial sector. Thus, it was only in 1876, following a series of political events that allowed the pacification of the country and the consolidation of the central state, that the *Caixa Geral de Depósitos* was funded and helped in the reorganisation of the collection of funds owed to the state.

The late creation of the *Caixa* was due to the turbulence of the first decades of liberalism in Portugal. The first half of the nineteenth century was particularly unstable, because of the impact in the country of French wars, the Napoleonic invasion, and the ensuing end of the *Ancien Regime* in the hands of the 1820 liberal revolution, which was followed by civil and military unrest for almost three decades. Political stability returned in a durable way only from the year 1851 on, when a further military insurgency managed to bring together the rival factions of the emerging liberalism. To understand the reasons behind the creation of the *Caixa Geral de Depósitos*, it is necessary to take into account the complex framework of the formation and servicing of the public debt. Effectively, the *Caixa* would take on functions belonging to other institutions and in the process of its development helped the reorganization of the public financial system. The process took a long time, however, because it implied that the new institution would take powers attributed to other existing institutions, particularly the Bank of Portugal.

The new institutional order included other significant changes in the financial and banking sectors. From those changes, we have to single out the adoption of the gold standard in 1854, a new statute for public accounting in 1863, the foundation of the *Banco Nacional Ultramarino* and the *Companhia Geral do Crédito Predial Português* both in 1864, public legislation on limited companies in 1867, and, finally, the new Civil Code in 1868. A period of rapid development of the banking system followed from 1870 and ended in a mild banking crisis in 1876. It was right before the outburst of the crisis that the government founded the *Caixa Geral de Depósitos*.

The foundation and further development of the *Caixa* was dependent on legislation produced by the Parliament or the governments, through its Finance Ministry. As such, the history of the institution necessarily reflects national political and financial history. In addition, the role that governments assigned to the *Caixa* in the national financial system was intrinsically connected to the development of the country's financial history. Therefore, the fact that the state of public finances shaped in a significant way the development of the *Caixa's* performance and institutional model implies that its history is a privileged field for the study of the mechanisms of interdependence between the state and the national financial system.

Before the *Caixa* was founded, different institutions scattered around the country received the public deposits. In the two main cities, the funds belonging to the state, in currency, gold, or silver, were kept by the Public Deposits of Lisbon and Porto, which dated from 1751 and 1774, and which received private deposits. These deposit houses paid no interest for the capital they received. The collection of public deposit funds was possibly an important business for some agents and in certain regions of the country, but as a whole it involved relatively modest amounts. In the rest of the country, the collection of public deposits remained the responsibility of the county tax offices, which were private entities.

By placing the *Caixa* under the administration of the Public Credit Board, the legislator was condemning the bank to slow development, as the Board would prove to be the main competitor of *Caixa*'s development. At its counters in the *Praça do Comércio* in Lisbon, the board sold securities, some of rather low face value, and small savers did not need recourse to the intermediation services of a bank as the *Caixa*. In other words, the Public Credit Board administered a financial service at the *Caixa Geral de Depósitos* few investors would be interested in, and which competed with other services of the same board.

In 1880, in order to push for an increasing role of the new institution, the government proposed and the Parliament approved the establishment of a savings bank in the structure of the *Caixa Geral de Depósitos*. The formal creation of a savings bank department was a response to the slow development of deposits in the public bank and in the country in general, a consequence of the weak development of the Portuguese banking system as a whole. For years, savings banks were seen as institutions apart from the rest of the banking system, with a focus on charity and education on savings for the less affluent classes. However, the history of such institutions in other European countries shows the extent to which they were in fact simply the first deposit banks catering to the smaller deposits of a larger section of the population. The fact that the *Caixa* was both a deposit bank and a state savings bank set it apart amongst its counterparts in western Europe, where the norm was the constitution of state-owned deposit banks to which converged the savings gathered in private savings banks, usually regional in scope and almost always grouped in national confederations. In some cases, deposit banks from other countries also created their own savings banks, but they never achieved the same degree of development as in Portugal.

The development of the Public Credit Board and consequently of the *Caixa* was affected by the political change imposed by the rise of the *Partido Progressista* government in 1886. The following year, the finance minister (Mariano de Carvalho) of a new left government imposed a new contract on the Bank of Portugal in 1887, which in the end implied the transfer of part of the functions of the Public Credit Board to the *Caixa*, and the board became a mere advisory institution with a substantial reduction in power. In 1891, a financial crisis broke which led to a partial default that ultimately would affect the *Caixa*'s accounts that by law had all its capital invested in state bonds. The period was particularly serious in the life of the institution to the extent that for a period of seven years it ceased to publish its annual accounts. The Public Credit Board restored partially its powers in 1893, but it did not recover the control of the *Caixa*, and it was left with the presidency of the then-created *Caixa*'s supervisory board. The Public Credit Board had a degree of autonomy from the government and was an important element of the credibility of public debt management and the partial demise of its powers meant an increase of the power of the government and in particular of the finance minister in what concerned the management of the public debt. In 1902 and 1905, the government reached an agreement with its external creditors as a first sign of the improvement in state finances, and the value of the *Caixa*'s assets recovered to previous levels. During the financial crisis, however, private deposits with the *Caixa Económica Portuguesa* experienced an exceptional growth, and it became the largest savings bank in outpacing its main competitor, the *Montepio Geral*'s savings bank. The rise of deposits in the public bank shows how, despite all difficulties, the state remained the main destination for individual savings. As the state financial situation improved and the level of deposits increased, the governments changed the legislation in order to allow the *Caixa* to concede credit to public works, as well as to agricultural and industrial investments, thus opening the doors for it to become a most relevant tool of economic policy. The most important change in those years was a new statute published in 1909.

The reform undertaken in 1909 gave the government greater power to appoint the institution's administration and thus to intervene more directly in its financial and investment policies, and it eventually turned the *Caixa* into a true state bank. By the time of the Republican revolution of 1910, the *Caixa* was again a major pillar of the Portuguese public financial system, alongside the Treasury and the Bank of Portugal. At the time, the Bank of Portugal was also under greater government control due to the statutes from 1887, but it was not yet a regulator of the banking sector, a responsibility it would acquire only through the statute revision of 1925, and it kept some functions typical of private banks.

The importance the *Caixa* had acquired in 1909 was mostly due to its ability to secure a large share of the national deposit market, and governments got increasingly interested in using the institution for conduct their policies. This was an unexpected outcome. Most of the time, the influence of governments on the running of the institution tended to be discreet, in order not to repel the private depositors. Yet when times were less favourable, the influence of governments became more visible, but this was not necessarily taken as negative by the public, as the state managed to keep its reputation as one of the safest destinations for private savings. The *Caixa*'s main depositors were middle- or lower-middle income earners and it was not a 'bank of the poor', similar to what happened in the rest of Europe, as the poor did not resort to financial intermediation services, given the cost they represented. In addition, for the small saver there were few alternatives, as few banks offered services similar to those of the *Caixa Económica Portuguesa*, the second-best alternative being the Treasury, where the public could buy government securities directly, albeit under less favourable conditions. Thus, the history of the *Caixa* reflects the history of the modes of operation of governments, mainly in the financial and banking spheres.

With the instauration of the Republican regime, a new period of financial distress returned to the *Caixa*, and that was due mainly from the high financial and monetary instability that followed Portugal's entry into World War I and the consequences of the war on international markets. In fact, from 1917, the Portuguese economy entered a spiral of monetary depreciation and inflation due to difficulties in international payments related to the decline of exports, the sharp reduction of remittances from emigrants in Brazil, as well as the outflow of large sums of capital. Financial instability further aggravated with the rise of public debt and the increase in money issuance needed to finance the war effort and the current account balance. The financial problems were such that the governments of the Republic had to intervene in the *Caixa*'s management. On the other hand, the deposits from the public continued to increase, as well as investments in central and local government bodies. The legislation for the institution also evolved in a favourable way as it gained more autonomy. The relative tranquillity of the relations between the *Caixa* and the governments of the Republic shows the political care with which the institution was dealt. The financial and monetary instability of the period at national and international levels did not reflect in the economic activity, which expanded at a rapid and unprecedented pace. Such positive trends reflected favourably on the life of the *Caixa*. Major problems would soon return to the institution, again for pure political reasons, as the Republic ended with another military coup in May 1926.

The years following the 1926 coup were again rife with political turmoil and civil unrest that lasted for more than a decade despite the tough grip imposed by the fascist dictatorship that emerged from it. Once more, the history of the *Caixa* closely reflects the political, financial, and economic history of the period that, in particular, meant the rise of a centralized, authoritarian, and interventionist state that used the institution as a major political instrument. The study of the *Caixa* clearly shows the way those wide objectives were accomplished. António de Oliveira Salazar, the dictator, had a central role, as he rose from finance minister in 1928 to prime minister in 1932, and in the process, he reorganised the fiscal and public account system in Portugal and its colonies. In the midst of the transformative process, in 1929, the government swiftly reformed the *Caixa* with a new statute that consolidated its role as a public investment bank. Importantly, the government gave the reform much publicity, but the changes introduced had little interference in the daily life of the institution. Despite the break in the political status quo, the new and powerful finance minister left in place the chairman appointed by the Republican government (Daniel Rodrigues) and appointed a close political associate as successor (Guilherme Alves Moreira) only in May 1932. The new chair remained in place for more than 25 years, until 1959, and that is again an important sign of how the new regime worked.

In fact, Salazar started his journey to power with a strong reformist impetus that implied overhauling the financial system, with broad institutional, political, economic and social reforms. However, it was a dictatorial regime that stalled politically as many dictatorships do, for lack of capacity to adapt to changes in the social and economic landscape. The 1929 statute was an upgrade on the way the *Caixa* was run, but as the years passed, in a period of rapid transformation, the new set of rules became obsolete. The difficulties brought about by the rigid institutional framework did not overshadow the progress that the

*Caixa* experienced throughout the *Estado Novo* years, in which period it consolidated its position as the leading deposit bank in Portugal and as an investment bank at the service of the state. In 1969, the year after the dictator left power because of ill health and a year prior to his death, the government enacted a new statute that provided the tools to compete in a quite different financial system, where more competitive private banks had consistently increased their market shares. The new statute made by the government of Marcello Caetano, the new dictator, led to a much-needed higher degree of autonomy of the institution, which then became a public company and not any longer a branch of the Ministry of Finance.

During the 'golden years' of growth, from 1950 to 1973, the Portuguese economy delivered rapid industrialisation and growth of exports and overall per capita income. Growth occurred in a context of macroeconomic and financial stability and conservative management of public finances, with moderate inflation and interest rates. Portugal was no exception for the rest of western Europe and the western world. The *Caixa* benefited from this favourable macroeconomic framework with an increase in the deposits and the capacity to contribute to public investment and increasingly to private investment as well, albeit in a context of losing market shares to the more dynamic rest of the banking sector. Yet in the late 1960s, as the demise of the Bretton Woods system approached, the domestic economic situation started turning around due to inflationary pressure and the stress on public accounts balance provoked by the independence wars in colonial Africa. The government somehow managed to conceal the rise of the public deficit from the public, as financial equilibria was a flag of the authoritarian regime, but soon the situation started reflecting financial stability and eventually the pace of change of living standards. The regime imposed by Salazar and his successor became increasingly obsolete and incapable of adapting to the changing domestic and international economic conditions. Largely, the growth that had allowed for a degree of institutional inefficiency and lack of adaptability was no longer there and the regime entered a difficult period, and it would ultimately fall under another military coup on 25 April 1974.

The armed forces, strained by the endless wars in the colonies, triggered the coup and the political opposition fighting the lack of civil liberties, and those affected by the falling economic environment rapidly joined them. Then followed a period of great instability that peaked in another military coup led by the more radical forces on 11 March 1975, which ultimately ended up with the nationalisation of the largest industrial companies, as well as the entire banking system, with the exception of foreign-owned banks. The revolutionary period would last until the inauguration of the first of the constitutional government in April 1976, following constitutional and parliamentary elections. The revolution would ultimately lead to political normalisation, democratic consolidation, and the integration of the country into the European Community. The years until 1976 were thus ones of great uncertainty, but nonetheless the government carried on despite inherent difficulties. Yet the international crisis provoked by the two spikes in oil prices in 1973 and 1979 led to harsh financial disequilibria that would ultimately lead to the intervention of the International Monetary Fund in 1977 and 1983, which somehow ended up contributing to the strengthening of the new regime. These were times when the IMF was for the first time intervening in more developed economies under some degree of political control from the western democracies which were keen on helping the democratisation of Portugal and also Spain. In 1986, both countries joined the European Community and from then on, their financial, banking, and monetary policies became intrinsically connected to the evolution of the European Monetary System and the creation of the euro.

The changes in the national political life ended up strengthening the position of the *Caixa*. This was due to a number of factors, including the fact that the nationalisations did not affect the public bank, either directly or indirectly, as the *Caixa* had no links with the private industrial conglomerates that were also nationalised, or with the colonies that had become independent. Additionally, the bank also benefited from some additional protection from the government that reflected positively on the level of trust it received from depositors. Thus, despite the political turmoil of those years and the many changes in the public policies, the successive governments managed to safeguard the public bank because of the common interests between the state, its bank, and the public. The positive outcome was a question of political self-interest, and it shows how governments may provide positive outcomes even in troubled times. The incentives for growth in the market were not, however, effective in what concerned the needed transformation of the institution, working in a protected environment with reduced competition. Thus, the *Caixa* kept its old traditional practices and failed to change its working methods, which were heavily dependent on manual work, dispersion of tasks, weak chains of command, and few incentives to increase labour productivity. However, the stimuli for the needed change would arrive in short time, with Portugal's accession to the European Community and then to the European Monetary System, the signature of the Maastricht Treaty and the commitment to join the monetary union that ensued.

The period from 1986 to 1992 was again highly transformative in Portuguese domestic politics, as the consolidation of democratisation and the gradual overcoming of the principal undemocratic legacies of the Carnation Revolution mark it. The election of Mário Soares as president of the republic in 1986 marked the return of civil presidents for the first time in decades, a mostly symbolic change, and in 1987, Cavaco Silva, the former technocrat economist with close links to the Bank of Portugal, formed the first full majority government, providing a more stable political environment. Thus commenced a new era in which European integration would stand out as the main political objectives, implying another overhaul of the institutional framework. The *Caixa* was not immune to those changes, and it transformed itself from a public bank working for the domestic market with state protection and reduced levels of competition to a bank that had to face open markets and international competition and a lower level of state protection. In 1993, it became a public company owned by the state functioning under the same legal system as the rest of the banking sector, in Portugal and elsewhere in the Eurozone. The transformation was again successful, albeit with some major caveats, and that was achieved because the state had a direct interest in pushing for the renewal. The reasons were the familiar ones, namely the fact that the state needed the public bank and the public bank could be of service only if it adapted. The changes were also a direct consequence of European integration and a direct response to the creation of the single market and the economic and monetary union.

As the new millennium commenced and the Eurozone entered a period of euphoria and then of troubles and malfunctions, the *Caixa* would go through less positive times, marked by an excess of involvement of successive governments in the business of the institution, which would ultimately end in a number of questionable actions and plain errors. Excessive optimism regarding the achievements of the euro led to a number of decisions that put in peril the Portuguese banking sector, including the *Caixa*, although the public bank was one of the least affected by the wrong decisions. Yet it is still in the process of recovery from those times, and the governments need to recall how the public bank is important to run the country and the economy. That part of the history of the *Caixa* is still in the making and that is the reason we paused the writing of this book in 2010.

★  ★  ★

The history recorded in this book is a long one, but it is worth telling, because it shows how institutions change and governments work under different circumstances and provides tools to test hypotheses about the true sources of those changes and actions. From observing the evolution of public banking in Portugal over almost two centuries, we are able to reach a number of relevant conclusions regarding the reasons behind the choices made by the different political regimes and the many governments that ruled the country. The main conclusions are that governments were able to administer successfully what would become the largest bank in the country because of the coincidence of objectives between the public, the government, and the bank. Thus, in this case, good administration is the outcome of a good set of incentives. Whether this is extensive to other cases is a question that remains unanswered here.

In order to tell the story of public banking in Portugal, we start in Chapter 1 by looking at the formation of a new regime of public finance and of related institutions. Chapter 2 describes the short banking boom that preceded for a few years the foundation of the *Caixa*. These two chapters aim at explaining the creation of the new institution and, just as important, the date of its foundation, which was rather late in the nineteenth century when compared to the rest of western Europe. Chapter 3 shows why the institution took so much time to conquer its space in the financial system, a process that was almost a decade long and extends to the formalisation of a savings bank within it, namely, the *Caixa Económica Portuguesa*, which is studied in Chapter 4. Chapter 5 is mostly about the connections between political change and the history of the public bank, which by then had already gained momentum and entered a phase of no return. The change of the financial regime ended in a financial crisis that had direct consequences on the life of the *Caixa*, and Chapter 6 provides an analysis of such consequences, with lessons for both the institution's life and the nature of the political system. The consequences of the 1890–1892 crisis were more important politically than financially or economically, a conclusion that is well established in the literature and is revisited here in Chapter 7.

Chapter 8 is once more about the financial consequences of another change of political regime, and about how the Republic and the war affected the life of the *Caixa*. The political regime changed again in 1926, and Chapters 9 and 10 study the financial impact of such changes. As the dictatorship consolidated, tellingly under the fascist name of the *Estado Novo*, the role of the *Caixa* as a public policy consolidated in two phases, before and after World War II, which are studied in Chapters 11 and 12. The Portuguese economy followed the rest of western Europe in the golden age of growth, which implied important transformations in the financial sector, which the *Caixa* was unable to cope with, as shown in Chapter 13. History repeated itself after 1974 with another change of political regime to which the *Caixa* responded positively. That favourable response, again, should not be taken for granted, as it was associated with a number of drawbacks that became evident during the period of the institutionalisation of the European Monetary Union, which we analyse in Chapter 15.

The conclusion provides an overview of the links between the chapters and a reflection on questions that this study attempts to raise and that necessarily remain open. The main conclusion here is that the *Caixa* evolved positively because there was a favourable set of incentives that lasted across the period analysed, and thus that the outcome of the performance of governments may depend more on the incentives than on other less tangible factors such as culture or the broader institutional context. Among the questions that remain open, the most important ones are: firstly, whether the Portuguese financial system would have evolved more rapidly and consolidated further without a public bank such as the *Caixa*, and, secondly, whether the set of incentives here identified would have similar results in other national contexts.

# ACKNOWLEDGEMENTS

This volume is the conclusion of a project that started over 20 years ago, when I was invited to write a volume on the History of the *Caixa Geral de Depósitos* covering the first decades of its foundation. As the first volume was completed (and following a long break due to changes in the administration of the bank), I was invited to proceed with two other volumes that would cover the period up to the present times. As I began working on the project, I soon found out that it would not be possible to study the evolution of the most important Portuguese public bank without looking in detail into the political history of the country. That was because of the intricate relationship between public finances and policy, and because the *Caixa* was to fill gaps in the administration of public finances that had to be gradually conquered, taking into account financial and political interests that needed to be identified and explained. From the beginning, one of the aims of the project was to produce a monograph in financial history that would eventually have an English version for a wider audience. The book was then translated and thoroughly revised, in order to take into account the interests of a broader audience. When writing the Portuguese edition, I had the precious help from researchers who wrote research reports for a number of chapters. I would thus like to acknowledge the following chapter authors: Paulo Jorge Fernandes (Chapter 8), Zélia Pereira (Chapters 9 and 10), Rita Almeida de Carvalho (Chapter 11), Marta Santos (Chapter 12), Mónica Fonseca (Chapters 13 and 15), Daniel Marcos and David Castaño (Chapter 14), and Thiago Carvalho (Chapter 15). I would also like to thank Adriana Almeida and Alistair Richardson for the translation, and Christiana Mandizha for editorial assistance, as well as comments from one reviewer. Finally, I would like to thank the publisher for their trust and interest in the theme.

# 1

# THE RISE OF PUBLIC FINANCE, 1820–1870

The creation of a new institutional setting aimed at providing for the increasing needs of public finance marked the rise of the liberal regime in Portugal. This was, however, a long story that evolved from the outbreak of the liberal revolution in 1820 to the varied stages of the consolidation of the new regime. By following the history of banking from its early antecedents to the first official attempt at creating the *Caixa Geral de Depósitos*, this chapter provides a lens to observe the interconnection between state formation and financial development in these early years. A major element that we can draw from this is that reforms took a very long period to materialise, but not for lack of political will or institutional ability. The long transformative process was above all a consequence of the complexity of the problem, imposed by the political backwardness of the country and the large degree of military and political turbulence characterising the first half of the 19th century. It is also possible to argue that the long time it took to reform the country was the result of the low demand for new institutional frameworks, as the emerging liberal order could progress through the traditional methods of conducting the financial business of the state. There were certainly vested interests that had to be overcome, as we shall see, but such factors were less relevant than other elements.

The Bank of Lisbon (*Banco de Lisboa*), founded in 1821 (and the predecessor of the Bank of Portugal, founded in 1846), and the Public Credit Board (*Junta de Crédito Público*), founded in 1837, were the main financial institutions created for the new liberal epoch. They were largely complementary, in terms of both their structures of ownership and administration and their role in the financial markets. The Bank of Lisbon was a privately-owned company with the monopoly of note issuing in Lisbon and carried its business largely by lending to the state and providing other services related to the collection of taxes and payment of public expenditures. The Public Credit Board, on the other hand, was a state institution with an administration mainly composed of private investors and aimed at raising capital from the public also to fund state expenditures. The bank raised capital in order to finance the Portuguese public debt, while the board sought to guarantee an annual income that would allow the state to meet its financial obligations to creditors. The division of roles between the two

1

institutions was not completely defined, especially in the first decades of their existence, but that changed throughout time. In fact, as the liberal state consolidated, the structure of the financial system on which it partially depended became more developed. Notwithstanding, the Bank of Lisbon and the Public Credit Board evolved as complementary institutions because they had different roles in the financial markets. Moreover, the concerns of the public administration and the private financiers to which they were closely connected were generally not divergent, since the principal business of the banks was lending to the state, who depended on them for financing its activity. However, there were moments of significant disruption in the relations between the political and the financial spheres.

In addition to the two main financial institutions mentioned above, the cities of Lisbon and Porto had their own public deposits that collected funds proceeding from contracts between the private sector and the state or resulting from court orders on certain payments, orders that had to be guarded by the state. Outside these main cities, the same functions were carried out by private, uncoordinated entities and with a significant number of flaws and deficiencies in terms of administration and control of accounts. The centralisation and organisation of the public deposit funds were the main justification for the creation of the *Caixa*, which was put under the supervision of the Public Credit Board. For that to happen, however, the state had to gain power and a higher degree of financial autonomy, because it first had to face the opposition of the Bank of Lisbon for many of the new tasks it wanted to supervise.

## The Bank of Lisbon and the Public Credit Board, 1821–1846

The foundation of the Bank of Lisbon in December 1821 was a landmark for the new liberal regime and the financial system that developed in the coming decades.[1] The privileges granted by the state to the new bank included the power to receive deposits, grant loans, discount bills and, above all, the monopoly for issuing banknotes in Lisbon.[2] In exchange, the bank became responsible for the amortisation of the paper currency issued by the state since 1796, which up until then had been guaranteed by the state budget.[3] In its first year of operation, the Bank of Lisbon was to lend 2,000 *contos* to the State, enabling it to redeem the same amount of paper money so that it could be withdrawn from circulation and destroyed.[4] This loan secured a 4% interest to be paid in gold, and it took precedence over all other debts of the state.

State recourse to financing by private entities necessitated a clearer definition of state prerogatives in matters of public accounts. To this end, the 1822 constitution imposed that the state budget had to be approved by the Parliament and that the collection of taxes and other public revenues had to be centralised in the Public Treasury. It also imposed that interest payments accruing from issuing new public debt had to be paid by specific revenues.[5]

The constitution thus gave the state sufficient powers to control the financial companies to which it assigned the administration of public money. The decades that followed the creation of the Bank of Lisbon therefore witnessed a balancing act between the constitutional authority of the state and the financial power of the bank's shareholders. Despite the strength of the private financiers, the fact of the matter was that the state held the upper hand for most of the time. However, the line of separation between the two spheres remained blurred for many years to come. Even though the Bank of Lisbon was not the formal treasurer of the Portuguese state, governments entrusted it with a great diversity of funds. In 1823, it began receiving money from the Public Deposit of Lisbon (*Depósito Público de Lisboa*), next to which its first headquarters were located. In that same year, the bank provided a loan amounting to 800 *contos* to the state, for which the Treasury set up in the Bank an annual deposit, corresponding to 7% of the loan, to cover the payment of interest and amortisation.[6] From 1826, the Bank of Lisbon also received the funds previously administered by a number of public institutions, such as the *Real Junta de Comércio*, the *Casa da Índia*, the *Alfândega das Sete Casas*, and the *Administração de Falidos*, as well as the deposits of the *Alfândega da Mesa dos Vinhos*. These funds were the collateral for the loan of 2,000 *contos* the bank then granted to the government.

The purchase of Bank of Lisbon shares fell short of the 5,000 *contos* fixed in the bank's statute, mostly because of the state of intermittent civil war the country was experiencing. Thus, in 1824, the government allowed the subscription to be closed at 2,400 *contos* and extended the concession term to the bank from 20 to 30 years, ending in 1852. Simultaneously, the government decreed that the Bank of Lisbon was to receive all the funds of the institutions mentioned above. The need for confirmation of previous legislation shows there were some difficulties in the transfer of these funds, but the fact is that no deposits were recorded in the next years until the outbreak of the civil war, in 1832. Two years later, at the end of the war, the new government confirmed the role of the Bank of Lisbon in the redemption of the paper currency. In 1837, the bank also started receiving the funds of the Public Deposit of Porto (*Depósito Público do Porto*), which were sent to the Bank of Lisbon's branch in that city.[7]

In the meantime, in 1832, the Public Credit Board was created, along with a series of financial reforms, including the replacement of the Royal Treasury by the Public Treasury, and the aggregation of financial administration services under the control of the Treasury Department. As in previous instances, the aim was to bring the collection of public revenues under the direct control of the government, at the national and local levels. Additionally, the government passed legislation that imposed that the public accounts should be overseen by the Court of Auditors.[8] The autonomy of the Public Credit Board placed it on a par with the other ministries, with its own budget and funding, to be voted by the Parliament.

From its start, the Public Credit Board was composed of five members, two chosen by the government, one by the Parliament, and two by the larger bondholders; the government appointed the president among the five members.[9] Excluding women and residents outside Lisbon, the number of bondholders with voting rights was a little over a few hundred, and they probably held around 10,000 of the total of 430,000 *contos* of the total Portuguese funded public debt. For comparison, the general assembly of the Bank of Portugal with voting rights was composed by the 120 major shareholders. The main task of the board was to issue public bonds and redeem the payment of interest and amortisations of the debt issued by the Public Credit Board and the Treasury.[10] In 1841, the board also became responsible for the management of the external debt. The board was mostly funded by the Public Treasury, as well as revenues from mail and paper stamps, the sale of national assets, and customs duties. During times of financial difficulties of the State, borrowing money from either the Bank of Lisbon or other financial institutions implied the direct delivery of public income into the board's coffers, without the intervention of the Public Treasury. The Public Credit Board was to receive a number of public funds, but the process was slow, and there were a number of exceptions to the rule. For example, from February to August 1838, the government obtained a loan to the amount of 2,400 *contos* from the Bank of Lisbon, and it gave back as collateral the right to receive the revenues from the customs houses of Lisbon and Porto. The concession was open to tender but only the Bank of Lisbon showed an interest, as it was the only financial institution with the capacity to fund such a large loan.[11] On 25 April 1838, the government also assigned the proceeds of the sale of the national assets to the Bank of Lisbon. Yet, by mid-1845, these contracts had all ended, which implied that, for the first time, the Public Credit Board was the depositor of all of these public funds.

The frequent changes in the overall institutional context ruling public money, as well as the changes in the roles of each of the main institutions, were largely a consequence of the military and political instability of the period. The 1820 liberal revolution, the first Parliament elections, and the 1822 liberal constitution were to be at least partially reverted by an anti-liberal coup in 1823, followed by the re-establishment of an absolutist monarch (D. Miguel), the abolition of the constitution, and civil unrest that lasted for more than a year before the liberal order was restored. In 1822, Brazil became independent, and it was recognised by Portugal in 1825. In 1826, following the death of King João VI, the new King D. Pedro signed a second constitution, less liberal than its predecessor and, in 1828, the absolutist faction staged another coup and gained power, and this ultimately led to a civil war between 1832 and 1834 that the liberals won. Yet disturbances still followed, marked by a radical revolution in 1837, a new constitution the following year, and another coup in 1842. These dates sometimes coincide with changes in the institutional settings or the flow of contracts between the state and the financiers, as the control of public finances was crucial for the consolidation of the conspirators' grip on power. The 1842 coup led to a government that had clear support from the monarch at the time, D. Maria II, but it soon became unpopular in a number of regions of the country. The reasons behind its unpopularity were a succession of tax increases and changes on certain traditions that were imposed on the population, which was largely detached from central power in Lisbon. Consequently, a popular revolt took place in 1846, ultimately leading to another civil war, albeit of short duration due to the help of British and Spanish troops at the request of the government and the monarch.

## The 1846 financial crisis and the foundation of the Bank of Portugal

The *Maria da Fonte* revolt, as it was eventually called, of April 1846 and the ensuing civil war, which lasted over the following year, led to difficulties in raising the funds assigned to the payment of servicing the debt and to high levels of financial instability, which would have a deep impact on the institutional setting. The Public Credit Board ceased to receive funds in its branch in Porto from October 1846 on and, in Lisbon, the problems grew worse as early as April 1847.[12] From the outset, there was a rush on notes at the Bank of Lisbon.[13] Moreover, by the end of September 1845, the government was unable to pay 800 *contos* to the *Companhia Confiança Nacional*, a financial syndicate founded in 1844 to help fund public works. As a way of postponing this payment, the government delivered public debt securities whose maturity was due in the first half of 1846. The *Companhia* accepted the securities, as they were a more certain assurance than that resulting from the contract previously made with the government, and it was paid directly with the proceeds of an income tax (*décima*), as well as the additional taxes created to cover the loan it made to the state. By May 1846, political instability and the government's difficulty in meeting its commitments led the latter to decree the suspension of payment for three months of Bank of Lisbon notes and of promissory notes of the *Companhia de Confiança Nacional*. The suspension would be extended twice. Yielding to such an undesired course of events meant the acknowledgment of the difficulties of both financial institutions, to whom the State owed large sums 'in much larger amounts than that sufficient to pay off all the notes [in circulation]'.[14] By 8 June 1846, the securities issued by the *Companhia* expired and the government asked the Bank of Lisbon and other financial institutions for help to pay what was due.[15] The state was again suffering financial difficulties, and a new period of dependence on additional sources of private funding was about to begin. On August 1846, the government appointed three royal commissioners to the Bank of Lisbon's board, without the right to vote, but with the power of veto over the board's decisions. Aiming to solve the problems of public financing and state debt, the government created a new banking institution by merging the Bank of Lisbon and the *Companhia de Confiança Nacional*, which were closely interconnected, as the bank owned a part of the capital of the company and held two of the seven seats of its board.

The merger brought together two institutions in very different financial conditions. By 1846, the Bank of Lisbon had a reputation for financial solidity, whereas the *Companhia de Confiança Nacional* was on the verge of bankruptcy. It was the bank's main competitor in providing the State with funding, partially redeemable by the revenues of the monopoly of *Companhia do Tabaco, Sabão e Pólvora*. By the time of the merger, the company had a credit account with the state amounting to 6,665 *contos* that added to the 4,852 *contos* the state owed to the Bank of Lisbon, making up about 13% of the total Portuguese public debt. Loans to the Portuguese state amounted to 85% of the capital of *Companhia Confiança Nacional* and 52% of that of the Bank of Lisbon.[16] The creation of the Bank of Portugal would bring changes to the relations between the state and the private financial institutions.[17] As such, the founding statute of 1846 demanded that the cash funds hitherto held in the Public Deposits of Lisbon and Porto be delivered to the new bank in Lisbon. In any other locations where it opened branches, the bank would equally receive the local deposits.[18]

The 1846 contract between the state and the Bank of Portugal was to last thirty years. In exchange for the provision of a large sum of money, the equivalent of 60% of its capital, which surpassed the public revenue for that year, the Bank of Portugal obtained several privileges. The most significant of those was the prerogative of issuing notes and bearer bonds in the administrative district of Lisbon; others included exemption from taxes on profits, protection from pawns on shares, the monopoly over the constitution of new savings banks, and the obligation to the judicial and administrative authorities to deposit with the bank.[19]

The 1846 contract thus restricted the creation of a deposit bank. Adding to the monopoly over note emission, even though confined to Lisbon, the bank kept the prerogative of creating savings banks in Lisbon and Porto. Such privilege went back to a contract of 1844 between the government and the *Companhia de Confiança Nacional*, allowing the latter to open savings banks in any part of the country without the prior consent of the government that was mandatory for any other entity and, in 1850, a new law was implemented that stopped the foundation of new savings banks in Lisbon and Porto.[20]

Many politicians took savings banks as a fundamental tool to educate the population at the lower income levels into thrift habits. The theme was dear to the politicians on the left, such as Silva Carvalho (1782–1856), a prominent political figure of the liberal regime, who wrote about their positive consequences 'on morality and public order', as well as on the well-being of the poor.[21] Hope that such banks would be an aid for the poorest was genuine and corresponded to the desire in Portugal to replicate what was happening in industrialised Europe, such as the UK, France, and Belgium.[22] Yet only the *Caixa* would be able to cater to this population, due to the lack of interest from the Bank of Portugal or, for that matter, from the domestic banking business in general.

Meanwhile, the state had carried on delivering more revenues for deposits in the Bank of Portugal in exchange for loans, exactly as had happened with the

Bank of Lisbon until 1839. The old system had been brought back. The benefits the state bestowed on the bank were not always considered as such by the beneficiary itself, especially when it struggled to collect certain revenues. As early as 1847, for example, after a first refusal, the bank granted the government a small loan totalling 200 *contos*, to which interest it consigned the collection of a number of taxes of the city of Lisbon. However, a few months later, in September 1847, the bank asked for an exemption for collecting these taxes, due to the difficulties in carrying the task out and the low 1% commission it received from the service.[23] The Bank of Portugal's position was further strengthened by the publication of the law of 16 April 1850, which confirmed its privileges until 31 December 1876, despite the reduction of the bank's capital, and the prerogative of note issuance (and creation of savings banks) being restricted to the district of Lisbon.[24] In the same year, the funds from the Public Deposits of Lisbon and Porto were assigned once more to the bank's coffers in addition to administrative and judicial deposits in the locations where it held branches.[25]

In that same year, 1850, a conflict broke out between the government and the Bank of Portugal which was to mark the relations between the two in the years that followed and which would eventually lead to a clarification of the state's power vis-à-vis the Bank. The conflict arose from the government's intent to gain control over an amortisation fund, the *Fundo Especial de Amortização*, created in 1846 to cover the commitments regarding the redemption of the Bank of Lisbon's notes, as well as the debts of the *Companhia de Confiança Nacional*. The operation intended to put an end to the fiduciary circulation and thus allow the return to convertibility of notes. These debts still incurred towards the *Companhia de Obras Públicas de Portugal*, the State pensioners, and *Sociedade Folgosa, Junqueira e Santos*.[26] The revenues of the fund were made up of income from national courts, the sale of national assets, the amortisation of debts of the extinct convents, 120 *contos* delivered by customs, and the redemption of domestic and foreign debt securities.[27] The battle waged over control of income generated by the *Fundo Especial de Amortização* was relatively harsh but of short duration, and it was a firm step towards consolidation of the administrative power of the state.[28]

At the time of its creation, the amortisation fund was administered by a committee made up of three members appointed by the government and three appointed by the Bank of Portugal. With this composition, the government had no direct control over the application of the fund's income and it was therefore considered as an exception to the constitutional rule and should thus pass into the hands of the government.[29] A first attempt of the government to recover the revenues assigned to the same fund happened in 1850, when the new statute of the Bank of Portugal was discussed. The bank resisted, empowered by its capacity to refuse loans to the government, which sorely needed them. Deciding to work closely with the government on the administration of finances and public debt, granting it all the significant loans it requested, the bank was able to keep the Amortisation Fund under its control.

However, in the beginning of September 1850, the then minister of finance, António José de Ávila, opposed what he considered to be the excessive charges demanded by the Bank of Portugal for a loan of 400 *contos*, namely a commission of 2% and the allocation of more state revenues. This loan was finally carried out, with more favourable conditions, by the Public Credit Board. Clearly, the financial conditions in which the state operated had improved. In fact, as early as 1848, the Public Credit Board prided itself of having 'emancipated from the tutelage of banks, companies or any other corporations' in order to effect heir remittances abroad. This ultimately explains the minister's subsequent claims regarding the administration of the amortisation fund.[30] The conflict between the government and the Bank of Portugal resulted from the demand that the latter make a payment to *Companhia de Obras Públicas de Portugal* to help finance the construction of the first section of the railway between Lisbon and Porto. In spite of the noble intention, it was an obvious pretext to withdraw from the bank's grasp an important part of the state's revenues that had been allocated to the payment of a debt that belonged to past times, so as not to bind Ávila's government.[31]

The administrators of the *Fundo Especial de Amortização* appointed by the board of the Bank of Portugal refused to make such a transfer, claiming the fund's income had its own purpose, which was not the one intended by the minister. Following a few incidents, on 5 November 1850, the finance minister dismissed the chair of the fund's board, who had been a governmental appointment. Soon after, the government suspended the fund's board and assigned the functions to the Public Credit Board. Thus, the role of two bodies overlapped, to the point of creating doubts concerning the scope of each other's competence. In a letter addressed to the queen, D. Maria II, on 15 July 1850, the fund's board asserted that there was 'perfect' analogy between the institution they ran and the Public Credit Board, which is why both issued, endorsed, and paid debt securities against the State.[32]

The nationalisation of the Amortisation Fund was not immediately guaranteed since, by December 1850, the minister of finance had only succeeded in diverting the customs revenues from the bank to the Public Credit Board. Full control over the deposits of the Fund and its revenues would come only with the Regeneration and the strong arm of Fontes Pereira de Melo, who finally extinguished the fund in 1851. This was part of the package of measures which revised the terms of payment of the public debt, and which culminated in the forced conversion of public debt securities on 18 December 1852.[33] The Bank of Portugal reacted strongly against such conversion, addressing a complaint to the government, whose text was translated and sent to London, apparently undermining the already fragile reputation as a borrower of the Portuguese state in that market.[34] Such was the importance of the fund, that the bank's chairman made one last attempt to recover it, consenting to grant an 'aid' of

1000 *contos* to the construction of the Northern railway, paid in four annuities, 'provided [the fund's] revenues collection conditions were improved'.[35] The bank ended up backing down.

In the aftermath of the *Regeneração* coup, on 10 May 1851, the Bank of Portugal briefly recovered the fund back from the government a move that was facilitated by the loan the bank conceded to the state through the influence of the minister of finance, Marino Franzini, who was soon to be replaced. The new minister of finance, Fontes Pereira de Melo, oversaw a significant change in the treatment of inherited debts and the relations between the government and the Bank of Portugal were to change for a long period. The outcome of the conflict between the state and the bank reflects the new reach of public administration in matters of state finances.[36]

The role of the Bank of Portugal in public administration was complementary to that of the Public Credit Board, and their respective limits were difficult to define. The overlapping may have been a consequence of the development of the country's financial system being relatively new. During a large part of this period, the state depended on the bank for a significant part of its financing needs. The bank, on the other hand, depended on the state for its business portfolio and for the definition of its legal framework. These relations of mutual dependence, as we have just seen, were not always peaceful, as a consequence of the conflict of interests between private creditors and public debtors, where one party had the power of finance and the other the power to legislate for its own benefit. Notwithstanding, the outcome of these occasional disputes was not predetermined, resulting instead from the balance of power at each moment.

## 1853: the new financial order

The Public Credit Board held an important role in the relations between the state and the private financiers clustered around the Bank of Portugal, since it provided financial intermediation services. When the bank did not follow the government's instructions, and the country enjoyed a better position in the financial markets, those services were transferred from the bank to the government. The latter's functions did not extend further because the bank opted to acquiesce to the government's pressure and comply with its directives. If that had not happened, it is likely the board would have achieved greater prominence, leading to the creation of a deposit bank.

In 1853, an agreement between the government and the Bank of Portugal imposed that the bank would continue collecting a significant part of state revenue, as well as administrative and judicial deposits, because it offered better guarantees in terms of liquidity. The agreement meant the postponement of the creation of a public deposit or savings bank.[37] The Bank of Portugal thus regained the funds of the Public Deposit of Lisbon, the administrative deposits of Lisbon and Porto, and those of the administration of bankruptcies in both cities.[38] In addition to receiving public deposits, the bank kept the monopoly on the creation of new savings banks. However, that was not a privilege the bank's board was greatly interested in, as shown by the fact it had added no new branches to those in Lisbon and Porto which it had inherited from *Companhia de Confiança Nacional* in 1845. Movement in the savings bank in Porto was so slow that, by 1847, the board decided to merge its service into the Bank of Portugal's branch in that city.[39] Still, the bank's prerogative was deemed an important factor for negotiations with the government at certain times. It should be noted, however, that from the time of Fontes Pereira de Melo, the government and the bank's board enjoyed a peaceful period in their relationship.[40]

The Bank's Charter of 6 May 1857 confirmed that the contract with the Portuguese state would last until 1876. The charter also obliged the Bank of Portugal to receive the securities of the funded debt owned by the government, with a set commission of 0.5% over the amounts deposited. These privileges were used as a bargaining chip by the bank's board when the contract with the state was revised in 1876. Above all, the board sought to obtain from the state a status closer to that of an issuing bank.[41] However, as long as the bank held such privileges, whatever the importance given to them, the truth is that the creation of a deposit bank by the Portuguese state would entail negotiating with the bank's board towards the agreement of its managers and shareholders to concede at least the privilege of assignment of public deposits. The end of that prerogative would prove to be important, but on a limited scale, given the field had not prospered under the bank's management and few minds in the world of finance dared foresee a prosperous future in this business. Although their position was not always clear, the bank's board attached little importance to the privileges of public deposits and savings banks simply because their business was slow and showed little potential for development.

The board's greatest concern was the need to broker a new statute for the Bank of Portugal. The bank's action was restrained by the setting of a 5% limit for the interest in its lending operations, which included mainly the discount of bills and other debt and loan bonds on pawns of goods or securities.[42] This maximum interest rate could not be changed without the consent of the government, making it the strongest control mechanism the latter held over its main lender. Understandably, the government was reluctant to let go of such leverage. Still, the board of the bank possibly expected that the government might be willing to relinquish that control in exchange for the savings banks or public deposits prerogatives.

The Bank of Portugal benefited from the public deposit funds, because it was exempt to pay interest on the respective balance, thus saving money. By the end of 1876, public deposits in the bank reached about 1000 *contos*. Assuming the interest payable by the bank would be of 4% at most, the privilege was worth about 40 *contos* per year. Regarding the value of variations in the bank's discount rate, the accounts show that in 1876, discounted bills and loans on pawns amounted to 8470 *contos*.[43] At a 5% interest rate, as defined in the agreement, those loans would yield 424 *contos*, while at a 5.5% interest rate they would yield 466 *contos*—42 *contos* more. In sum, at best, public deposits were worth to the bank as much as a raise by a half percent in the interest rate, and that amount would be only taking into consideration loans to individuals.

In 1857, the creation by the Bank of Portugal of the *Crédito Móvel Português*, a pawn loan bank, was the first sign that it was willing to stand up for its prerogative in the matter of savings banks, considering that both activities were not dissociable. A year later, the government reminded the Bank of Portugal it should go beyond discounting commerce bills, developing its credit portfolio for agriculture, as *Banco Mercantil do Porto* was proposing to do. The latter, just created, had received the privilege of banknote issuance in Porto, but without the mortgage credit prerogative the Bank of Portugal benefited from in Lisbon. However, the savings bank's prerogative was a double-edged sword, for whilst it could be used by the bank as leverage, it could also be made use of by the government who felt entitled to reprimand the bank for not encouraging production through the much-awaited deposits. The bank's board refuted the criticism, arguing credit concession to agriculture depended on the creation of a mortgage law that gave investors sufficient confidence. The argument touched an issue that governments in Portugal were sensitive to, and whose solution was connected to the development of the banking system in the country.

In 1863, the government proposed an end to the Bank of Portugal's prerogative over mortgage credit, and two years later that of the privilege of creating savings banks, on both occasions in exchange for extending permission to the bank to raise its interest rates. Yet the government ended up allowing the rise of rates on both instances without obtaining the termination of the privileges in return, which caused neither concern nor satisfaction in either party. By the end of 1866, the bank's general assembly accepted the end of the savings bank's prerogative as long as they were closed rather than transferred to other financial institutions. But, once again, the government was not particularly concerned, and the savings bank remained open. Later, in 1872, the bank's general assembly, considering the end of the contract in 1876, offered to renounce some of the institution's privileges, including tax exemption, public deposits and savings banks in exchange for the liberty to set its own interest rate. On top of this, it proposed the opening of a credit line of 1,000 *contos* to the government, but that was not a particularly tempting offer since by that time the latter was able to raise credit easily with other investors.[44] In spite of all this, these prerogatives only came to an end with the cessation of the contract between the two parties, in December 1876.

The loss of influence of the bank over the government was made clearer by the end of the 1850s, as the board acquiesced to every loan request by the state without much ado and without demanding some form of counterbalance, as it had in more troubled times. The words of one of the board's members make it clear: the Bank of Portugal ought to loan to the government 'because there was no other business, there was money available', and, of course, 'for patriotic reasons'.[45] Some years later, in 1865, the audit committee of the bank lamented the decrease of state debts, since they offered 'security and ease of cancellation', possibly unlike any others.[46] The matter of the mortgage law raised by the bank was not the only one in line to be sorted by the new post-Regeneration State. On the contrary, it must be considered within the institutional reforms undertaken at that time.

Another significant legal alteration regarding the financial system was the permission given to the board of the Bank of Portugal to decide upon loans to the government without previous consultation of the bank's general assembly, dated of 3 February 1864. To curtail governmental access to credit from the bank, a ceiling was set. Such changes solidified a good relationship between the two entities and paved the way for the creation of a central bank in line with the government's policy. The arguments in favour, as presented by one of the board's members (Arrobas) could hardly have been more forceful: '[...] the government could not subject itself to the delays necessary for a general assembly to take place, nor to then find its request denied.'[47]

One of the highlights of the successive reforms since the Regeneration of 1851 was the effort to set a new consumer tax in 1867. For a number of reasons, the proposal faced unexpected public protest. The following year, the government fell due to a popular revolt known as *Janeirinha*, thus putting an end to almost a decade of relative political stability. During the three years of political instability before the executive lead by Fontes, the country would go through six different governments.[48] Following the revolt, a government presented in Parliament a number of proposals aimed at curtailing the public deficit.[49] Among them were the update of the regulations of the land registry, the raise of personal tax and a tax on some consumer goods, called *real de água*, the imposition of the use of coin to acquire national assets, and the creation of a state savings bank. Commenting on the minister's report, the *Jornal do Comércio* concluded: 'By means of other proposals on industrial contribution, subsidies to inactive classes and creation of savings banks, he expected to achieve the deficit's extinction within two years'.[50] Yet, the proposals did not attract the necessary political engagement. It was still too soon, not least because the Bank of Portugal still held the prerogative over this banking segment in Lisbon and Porto.

In April 1870, Braamcamp, minister of the *Partido Histórico* government, presented to Parliament a set of thirteen draft laws, which showed the will to take a further step in reorganising the country's financial and fiscal systems. There was also a proposal for the creation of a retirement fund for state employees and the last of these measures concerned the creation of the *Caixa*.[51] The position the latter occupied in the list perhaps shows its importance to the minister. It would not succeed, mainly because it collided with certain duties assigned by law to the Bank of Portugal, and which the minister overlooked. The Parliament's reaction was slow, as was often the case. So slow, that the members of Parliament did not have the time to take a stance, since the Parliament was dissolved by another coup just over a month later, on 26 May 1870. On 21 July 1870, one of the first measures of the new government was the end of the Public Deposits of Lisbon and Porto. The same reason that had led to their creation, a century before, that is to secure greater control of public finances, also prompted their extinction, this time in the context of the reorganisation of public finances and, as a first consequence, the boards of the two institutions, who had a certain degree of independence from the government, resigned. The government quickly appointed new boards and ordered the funds held in the public deposits to be transferred to the coffers of the Bank of Portugal.[52] The foundation of the *Caixa* was thus delayed again due to the fall of the government, and it had to wait for more favourable circumstances, which eventually emerged in the aftermath of another Portuguese financial crisis.

Meanwhile, in 1870, the public deposit boards of Lisbon and Porto had already been deprived of most of the powers and functions attributed to them at their creation. Indeed, since 1823, the funds pertaining to both Public Deposits should be entrusted by the respective boards to the custody of the Bank of Lisbon, the predecessor of the Bank of Portugal. The reform of the Public Deposit of Lisbon on 10 September 1868 established that deposits should be delivered directly to the headquarters of the Bank of Portugal in Lisbon, or in its branch in Porto. This meant that by 1870 public deposit boards had merely bureaucratic functions. The decree that determined the extinction of public deposits had as its main goal the simplification of the services linked to public debt, and its preamble gives a good description of how public deposits should be run and it was in fact a complex matter.

To make a deposit with the Lisbon (or Porto) Public Deposit Board, it was necessary to hand in a document emitted by the judicial authority determining the deposit, concerning for instance the payment of the fee to hold the post of public treasurer, or an orphan's inheritance. With that document, the board would issue a new document for the depositor to take to the Bank of Portugal, where the person's identity and the end of the deposit would be confirmed. After all had been duly checked, the bank would keep the second document and write a receipt, which should be handed in to the board, thus confirming the existence of the deposit in cash or valuables, and the process was finished. The only advantage for those who had to go through all these steps was that Lisbon's Public Deposit Board, like the Public Credit Board, ran from the east and central wings of the buildings in Terreiro do Paço, and the Bank of Portugal's headquarters was in Praça do Município, just 200 yards away. In the meantime, for issuing the first document and registering the deposit confirmation, the board charged a 1% commission on the deposit value, whereas the Bank of Portugal did not charge for the service, but neither would it pay interest on the deposits.[53]

Outside Lisbon and Porto, the system remained unchanged, and the mandated deposits were still handed to judicial custodians. The 1870 law determined that such judicial depositors, who were private people or entities, be extinct in districts where there were 'solidly established' banking institutions, and that these should cease to charge any commission for the service (as was already the case with the Bank of Portugal), but should pay interest on coin deposits. At a time when the reform of the contract between the state and the bank was under debate (despite the six years to run on the existing one), the prerogative of custody over public deposit funds was not especially dear to the bank. However, the law of July 1870 was revoked, and Lisbon's Public Deposit Board was reconstituted, replacing the commission created by Saldanha.[54] Political conditions were not optimal for such a reform, nor were the financial circumstances. For the public deposits reform to take place, as well as a series of other important reforms for the entire Portuguese financial system, a significant expansion of financial markets would be necessary, particularly the steep rise of the public debt bonds placed in the country.

## Notes

1  For the financial history of the Portuguese liberal regime, see Esteves (2000), Farinha (1994), Franco (1982), Macedo (1963), Martins (1988), Mata (1986 and 1993), Mata and Valério (1982, 1988, 1991, 1996 and 2001), Pereira (1993), Pereira (ed.) (1989), Pinheiro (1983), Reis (1991, 1994a, 1994b, 1996a, 1996b and 2000), Rocha (1996 and 1998), Silva (1997), Silveira (1987), Valério (1984, 1986 and 1988) and Valério et al (2001).

2  Reis (1996), pp. 78 ff., and Legislação do Banco de Portugal (1946), vol. I, p. 9. For the history of the Bank of Lisbon, see also Peres (1971), Ulrich (1946), Reis (1996) and Lains (2018).

3  Justino (1994).

4  1 conto is the equivalent to 1000$000 (1 million) reis or 222 pound sterling at par value.

5  Martins (1988), pp. 40–41.

6  For what follows, see Legislação do Banco de Portugal (1946), vol. I, pp. 29–32, 55, 85, 90.

7  Reis (1996a), pp. 258–259.

8  Exposição Histórica do Ministério das Finanças (...) (1952), pp. 273–279.

9  In 1870, bondholders had to hold above 5 contos for at least a full year. Members were appointed for three years, but nominations and elections were not carried out with the due regularity. In June 1883, the number of debt security holders was 41,211, of which about 8,000 held a capital above 5 contos.

10  Sousa (1916), pp. 305–306; Martins (1988), p. 78.

11  Legislação do Banco de Portugal (1946), vol. I, pp. 96–97.

12  Relatório da Junta do Crédito Público (1844–1845), pp. 4 and 5. 1846–1847, p. 2, and 1848–1849, p. 4

13  Reis (1996a) and Capela (1997).

14  Legislação do Banco de Portugal (1946), vol. I, pp. 127–137 and 164–167.

15  Reis (1996b), pp. 170 ff.

16  Valério (1984), pp. 74, 86 and 89, and Martins (1988), pp. 86–87.

17  Mata (1993), pp. 193–250.

18  Legislação do Banco de Portugal (1946), vol. II, pp. 29–37.

19  Ulrich (1946), vol. 1, pp. 7, 8, 12, 17; Martins (1988), p. 91 and Reis (1996), p. 99.

20 Legislação do Banco de Portugal (1946), vol. I, pp. 153–154, and vol. II, pp. 7, 213.
21 Diário da Câmara dos Deputados (1845), vol. II, p. 2.
22 Herculano (1983) and Marreca (1983).
23 Ulrich (1946), vol. 1, pp. 26–27.
24 Reis (1996), p. 333.
25 Legislação do Banco de Portugal (1946), vol. II, p. 212.
26 Mata and Valério (1988).
27 Legislação do Banco de Portugal (1946) vol. II, pp. 9–10.
28 Reis (1996), p. 354 ff.
29 Ulrich (1946), vol. 1, p. 152.
30 Legislação do Banco de Portugal (1946), vol. II, p. 225; *Relatório da Junta de Crédito Público*, 1848–1849, p. 10.
31 Legislação do Banco de Portugal (1946), vol. II, pp. 294, 303–305.
32 Ulrich (1946), vol. 1, pp. 182–184, 233.
33 Mata and Valério (1988) and Ulrich (1946), vol. 1, pp. 197–98, 262 e 269.
34 Coelho (1877), p. 117, Carvalho (1887).
35 Ulrich (1946), vol.1, pp. 255–260.
36 Ulrich (1902), p. 189.
37 Ulrich (1946), vol. 2, p. 305.
38 Ulrich (1946), vol. 1, p. 345.
39 Ulrich (1946), vol. 1, pp. 34, 140–141.
40 Legislação do Banco de Portugal (1946), vol. I, pp. 152–155.
41 Carta Orgânica do Banco de Portugal (1857), articles 11, 14, 15 and 20.
42 Legislação do Banco de Portugal (1946), DOR, p. 132.
43 Ulrich (1946), vol. 3, p. 27.
44 Ulrich (1946), vol. 2, p. 493.
45 Quoted in Ulrich (1946), vol. 2, p. 353.
46 Ulrich (1946), vol. 2, p. 427.
47 Quoted by Ulrich (1946), vol. 2, p. 414.
48 Pereira (1959), pp. 36–39.
49 Lobo (1871).
50 Jornal do Comércio, 23 and 30 November 1870.
51 Diário da Câmara dos Deputados (1870), Martins (1988), p. 119n.
52 Jornal do Comércio, 28 July 1870.
53 Jornal do Comércio, 23 July 1870.
54 Jornal do Comércio, 23, 28 and 29 July 1870 and 3 March 1871.

# 2

# FINANCIAL BOOM AND CRISIS, 1870–1876

During the first half of the 1870s, the number of banks and the value of deposits, as well as the public debt, increased considerably. The rapid expansion of the financial sector occurred in a context of incipient institutional development, and it included low levels of regulation. The rise in the issue of public bonds put a great pressure on the services of the Public Credit Board (*Junta de Crédito Público*) and the Treasury and the banking system was hardly able to cope with the pressure on the services they provided. Most of the new banks catered to small cities or urban centres, principally in the north of the country. The financial boom accompanied the growth in economic activity in the agricultural and the industrial sectors, an increase in domestic savings, and, most importantly, a flow of emigrant remittances from Brazil, which was then recovering from the end of the Paraguayan War (1864–1870). The boom made the reform of the financial system, both private and public, ever more urgent. In 1876, a banking crisis put an end to the short period of financial euphoria. The consequences of the banking crisis for the Portuguese domestic economy was not considerable, as banking was still a small share of domestic activity, and because the government had the political power and the financial means to intervene and to protect the domestic bank system. Notwithstanding, the crisis served as a demonstration that public debt bonds provided a better application for domestic savings, opening the doors for the next steps in the reformation of the public financial sector, of which the foundation of the *Caixa Geral de Depósitos* would be a very important part.

## The liquidity boom, 1870–1876

In 1870, there were ten commercial banks operating in Portugal, and five years later the number had risen to 51, while the value of the deposits had increased by a factor of 13.[1] Most of the new banks had their headquarters in the north of the country, where the flow of emigrant remittances from Brazil was higher and remittances were an important source of liquidity. The banks that were created accepted low value deposits and also sold equity with low face value to cater for the small saver, which they did with some success.[2] A fraction of the

16

capital they received came from Spain, where the issuing of lotteries fuelled a speculative market.[3] The Public Credit Board and the Treasury also absorbed part of the liquidity originating in Spain. The risks involved in the rapid expansion of banking quickly raised concerns among the press, but the incoming government took no action in accordance with the liberal spirit that was then rising in the country. One newspaper closely related to the *Partido Regenerador* warned against the perils of the bank rush, pointing to what had happened in other countries, but it added that the government could do little 'in economic matters, errors caused by freedom are less alarming and disastrous than an earnest, suspicious, and repressive prudence by an administration aspiring to omniscience'. From the enactment of the law of the public limited companies in 1867, regulation was mild if not non-existent, as the creation of banks followed the rules of any other commercial venture, not requiring any authorisation from the government. Such legislation was closely associated with the liberal regime at the time, led by a pre-eminent politician, Pereira de Mello, who acted as finance minister, but the system had large support across most of the liberal political spectrum.[4]

The period also saw a rapid expansion of public debt, raised both domestically and internationally by way of Treasury bills issued as floating debt or as perpetuities and managed by the Public Credit Board or the Treasury.[5] In 1875, the total domestic funded debt of 3%, which had been issued in 1852, amounted to 200,000 *contos* in face value and about 100,000 *contos* in market value, as the average share price of those same securities in the same year was 47.6%. In 1873, the Public Treasury issued, for the first time, a redeemable internal loan, for the construction of the Minho and Douro railway. The bonds issued had a very low domination that made them attractive to small investors, at 90$000 bonds and a 6% interest. The demand for bonds exceeded the emission by twentyfold.[6] After that, the Public Treasury undertook five new emissions of bonds, to 1878, then coming to a stop. In 1883, the state paid to bond holders about 15,000 *contos*, 12,000 managed by the Public Credit Board and the remaining by the Treasury.[7]

Between 1870 and 1875, the 3% funded debt, at market prices, rose about twice the value of bank deposits, which had started from a lower base.[8] The 51 banks working in Portugal by 1875 had a total of 25,000 *contos* in deposits with a total capital of about 44,000 *contos*, adding up to 69% of the value of the 3% funded debt securities, which was about 100,000 *contos*. That is to say, in spite of the pronounced growth of banking in Portugal, in the run-up to the 1876 crisis it had absorbed a noticeably smaller amount of savings than that collected by the state through the Public Credit Board alone. After the 1876 financial crisis, a part of the banking system collapsed, whilst the state carried on attracting an ever-growing part of capital in the Portuguese markets.

In Portugal, as in other European countries, individuals and institutions such as charities or savings banks looked to invest in the state. However, unlike in countries with more developed financial markets, there was only a modest presence of intermediate financial institutions providing key services for the placement of securities. As a rule, savings banks played that role, specialising in the collection of small deposits that were then invested in the financial assets of the state. Given the poor development of savings banks, the function was also performed by the Public Credit Board, since it was the platform used by the state to put its debt securities directly at the disposal of the public. The board's role in the investment of private loans and those of some institutions stands out in the historical events leading up to the creation of the *Caixa Geral de Depósitos*, since the success of the public bank resulted precisely from the fact that it took on the functions previously pertaining to the board. In addition to this, the Portuguese public debt was so scattered amongst security holders instead of concentrated in intermediate financial institutions, that some of its features made it unique in Europe. According to one columnist of the *Jornal do Comércio* and a member of the Public Credit Board, until 1881:

> A large part of the [Portuguese domestic] debt represents assets or property which had for centuries been in the hands of corporations and were called *de mão morta*. These, from 1861, were forced to be sold by expropriation laws and its revenues invested in consolidated debt securities or inscriptions of the Public Credit Board. This means that charities, hospitals, workhouses, town councils, parishes, church benefits, brotherhoods, confraternities, convents, shelters guilds, and everything in the kingdom which is inalienable or is under the administration of collective bodies, representatives of public authority or has an independent constitution, *depend* on the interest of the public treasury.
>
> (*Jornal do Comércio*, 31 December 1878)

The list of creditors to the Treasury includes also 'most of the orphans, widows, wards, endowments by spouses of either sex, pensions, warranties, and deposits of different kinds'. And the article concludes that 'from members of the royal family to labourers, household staff, and whoever has managed to save any amount of money, to gather an estate, great or small, for them or for their children, they have done so in the *savings bank* called the Public Credit Board'.[9]

The most important competitor in the market for demand deposits was the bank *Caixa Económica do Montepio Geral*, which paid an interest of 4% on deposits since its foundation in 1844, and 3% from 1853 until 1876. Interest paid by this bank was free from the 10% tax on interests and dividends instituted in May 1872, a law that applied to the Bank of Portugal too, which had been exempt until then.[10] Another bank, the *Companhia do Crédito Predial Português,* was also exempt from that tax. This way, the interest rate of the loans taken out by the State in the domestic market through the Public Credit Board or the Public Treasure, as well as the *Companhia do Crédito Predial*'s and *Montepio*, gained some advantage in face of other financial institutions.[11] The definition of a top limit for deposits made each year and for the total balance of accounts

18

also played an important part in the evolution of deposits. In general, savings banks put a limit on the amount of money an individual could hold in their account, either for operational requirements or from the need to curtail the deposit influx when they were more attractive than other investments. The *Montepio Geral* began with a ceiling of 500$000 for its mutual savings bank, which was altered from 2 *contos* in 1874 to 10 in 1875 and finally extinguished the following year.[12] Until 1875, however, it was merely keeping up with the evolution of the deposits market in Portugal. This is shown by the fact its market share oscillated around 2% and went up to 3% in 1875. From the following year, it experienced an exceptional rise, and by 1880, it held 14% of all demand deposits.

## The 1876 crisis

The banking crisis, which culminated with the moratorium on the payment of notes on 18 August 1876, dealt a severe blow to the Portuguese banking sector, as public debt securities were among the best financial investments on the market. From 10–18 August 1876, three banks in the north of the country, namely in Porto, Viana, and Braga, and one in Lisbon suspended payment of their notes. There followed a rush on the notes of the Bank of Portugal, which was unable to fulfil its obligations regarding the payment of notes in circulation, since it had sent a considerable part of its gold reserves through its branch in Porto to meet the demand by the northern banks. Following a request from the Bank of Portugal, the government established a general moratorium on payments in the whole country, but 'the situation was bad but temporary'.[13] In fact, a few days later, on 28 August, the Bank of Portugal was able to repay its notes at sight, as the government had obtained enough funds abroad in gold to repay its debts to the banks, paying in gold the debts resulting essentially from the contracts of payment to public pensions made in 1872 with a syndicate, and it even advanced other payments.[14] The operation had the support of the Bank of Portugal, which thus acted as the 'bank of banks', a role it would take on more fully later on. The northern banks' problems were resolved relatively quickly owing to the bank's ample gold reserves valued at 14,000 *contos*.[15] Such abundance revealed that the international balance of payments was positioned favourably. This could also be seen in the state of the public accounts, which enjoyed a period of relative comfort, without needing to resort so often to the markets through the floating debt to be able to meet current expenditure.

The number of banks in the country was then reduced from 51 in 1876 to 48 in 1878 and subsequently to 46 in 1883. The dividends paid by commercial banks decreased from 5.3% in 1876 to a stable 4.8% in 1878. Even so, from 1875 to 1879, the value of deposits fell by half and the recovery to previous levels took more than three decades.[16] As evidenced by the Lisbon Stock Exchange, the 1876 banking crisis did not have lasting consequences on the country's financial system. For instance, the average share price of the 1852 3% public-funded debt inscriptions, or of the shares of *Crédito Predial Português*, did not suffer any significant fluctuations in the years following the crisis. The average share price of the Bank of Portugal, also among the main shares traded in the stock market, decreased slightly until 1880, recovering henceforth. However, the shares of *Banco Nacional Ultramarino*, next in line to public securities and the Bank of Portugal's own shares, did drop with the crisis.[17]

Likewise, the crisis did not have a severe impact on the rest of the country's economy, as agriculture, manufacturing, and trade depended little on funding from banks. In fact, according to a learned observer, 'neither politics, nor commerce, nor navigation, nor industry, nor agriculture had suffered [with the crisis] a significant blow', and yet the crisis proved to him that the banking system needed regulation.[18] The most significant consequence of the crisis, however, came to be the decision regarding the role to be assigned to the Bank of Portugal. Mistrust undermined the banks, so those with capital to invest turned to the state. Securities issued directly by the Public Treasury and those sold by the Public Credit Board were probably an unsurpassable option, especially as they were exempt from the tax on interest. The crisis proved that the Portuguese public debt, placed both in the country and abroad, was the best financial investment with the best balance between profitability and safety in the market; possibly the only option with an acceptable degree of risk for those investing a significant part of their income, often given the rather undefined title of 'small savers'.

By the end of 1872, the circulation of bank notes amounted to 3,258 *contos*, and two-thirds of that amount was issued by the Bank of Portugal, which had the monopoly in Lisbon, competing with other banks in the rest of the country, where the city of Porto stood out as the most important market. Bank note circulation had declined from 7,300 *contos* in 1845, before the crisis, and the 1825 level, 4,228 *contos*, still had not been reached. Thus, by 1876, Portugal had one of the lowest capitations of notes in western Europe.[19] The low levels of note circulation were also related to the fact that notes had considerably high denomination and thus were not accessible for transactions for most of the population. Clearly, there was room for more. Given its position as one of the three pillars of the Portuguese financial and banking system, any alteration in the bank's status necessarily implied a change in the status of the remaining financial institutions. Extending the prerogative of note issuance to the whole country, for instance, would have immediate consequences on banks across the country, even though they were attenuated by the small scale of the note business carried out by the banks in Porto. In spite of everything, the new role of the Bank of Portugal faced more opposition there than in Lisbon.[20] Other changes, particularly those concerning the relations between the bank and the state, would have effects on the functions of the Public Credit Board and its general role within the system.

The difficulties faced by the Portuguese banking system in 1876 determined a change in emphasis of the evolution of bank deposits all over the country. Notwithstanding, the savings bank *Montepio Geral* managed to endure these hard times, becoming the number one choice by individuals for deposits in the country. This bank, which was associated to an institution that was essentially a pension fund, consisted of paying higher interest than any other bank, even for very small deposits. The money thus collected was invested mostly in public debt securities and debenture loans, which were becoming much more common, especially from the Public Treasury.[21] The *Montepio Geral's* investment portfolio, composed of loans to individuals and public debt securities, with no investment on any other banks, is the reason the institution withstood the crisis. The bank experienced a run on deposits, but it was brief and easily managed by the board, which obtained credit from the state (as did the other banks) and from banks in London.[22] After the crisis, deposits with the *Montepio Geral* kept on rising and by 1885 they amounted to 4,300 *contos*, that is, 17% of the total deposits in Portugal. However, the difficulty in finding adequate investment for these funds led the bank's board to implement consecutive measures to reduce deposits.[23]

The 1876 crisis clearly showed that the difficulty of the banking business in Portugal lay in the scarcity of possible investments banks had at their disposal and not a potential shortage of capital due to an insufficiency of bank deposits.[24] When banks offered minimum conditions, money would promptly arrive to their counters, principally in Lisbon and Porto. However, banks had little choice for where to place those funds. Those like the *Montepio Geral*, who invested that money with the state, were better protected from potential setbacks in the markets. The challenges the banking system had to face were primarily driven by the absence of a sufficiently developed market where banks could find investments to place their capital and deposits. Since it could rely on investing its deposits in public debt securities and additionally enjoyed tax benefits, the *Caixa* would come to be in an excellent position to capitalise on the development of the Portuguese finance market after the temporary shock of the financial crisis. In a report presented to the Parliament on 14 January 1877, the finance minister, António de Serpa, had found a 'first sign of distrust' regarding the state of the markets in the bankruptcy of the Spanish banking house *Roriz*. The bank had a branch in Porto, where it received funds from Portuguese depositors.[25] According to the minister, the bankruptcy led to the depreciation of the Spanish 3% public debt securities, of which around 70,000 *contos* in nominal value (which had to a market value close to 20,000 *contos*) were held in Portugal. This was a significant amount, corresponding to 20% of the value of the securities the Portuguese state had placed on the national market. The preference for the Spanish securities was because foreign securities traded in Portugal were exempt from paying both the 10% tax established in 1872 and the stamp duty established in 1873.[26] In reaction to these events, the Portuguese banks that had invested the most in Spanish titles revised the value of their assets. The crisis then spread through the banking system, since there was a high degree of interdependency between different portfolios. As such, it was not unusual for banks to be created with the shares of existent banks.[27]

## The Public Credit Board reformed once more

The deep changes in the banking sector provided an opportunity for changes in the Public Credit Board, as it gained importance in the market with an increase in the number of public debt securities and securities holders. According to the statistics on holders of bonds of the Board, the number of securities rose by about 10,000 between the years 1864–1865 and 1869–1870, and by around 14,000 between 1869–1870 and 1880–1881. The dispersion of the securities was already great, since by 1880–1881 a third of the holders had no more than 500$000 *réis* in their securities portfolios. The workload involved in securities issuance, interest payments, and amortisation was too great for the services of the board to handle. The first published statistics on the number of securities traded by the institution shows that by 1865–1866 it moved 187,000 titles dispersed by 14,910 holders, both individuals and institutions.

To receive interest, the holders, also known as *juristas*, had to go to the headquarters of the board or to one of its branches and present not only their coupons but also a record of the registration numbers in the books and the value of the capital of each. In 1863, the government tried to change this procedure without success. Its intention was to ascertain a more accurate overview of the actual value and composition of the public debt. For that purpose, it wanted the Public Credit Board to gather all available information on securities in a 'Great Book of the Public Debt'. This book should formalise securities bookkeeping from legal authorisation to issue securities and its actual issuance to interest payment and amortisation. Such organisation should enable both the board and the government to more easily monitor the whole process. The state was lacking this double-entry book. However, the board warned the government of the difficulty of such an endeavour. Indeed, the register of funded debt securities alone already occupied a total of 167 books each with around a thousand entries; that is, more than 50 metres of books, whose information would have to be transferred by its scant number of employees to this new registration book. As appeared to be the case with many public administration bodies, the board suffered from a chronic lack of staff to carry out its operations. The board knew more about the state of the public debt than the government, hence the latter's intention to change the bookkeeping method. However, the reform was not to be. For the board, paying interest on coupons alone was not a possibility, given the sheer dimension of the accounting work that would represent. Moreover, that had been done and the result had been 'the crowding of a large number of people and the repetition of brawls and unrest inside and outside the office'.[28]

Nonetheless, the Public Credit Board had another plan to improve the organisation of its service. Each holder should have one single account or one security, instead of an average of twelve or more securities per holder. Those corporations called *de mão morta*, such as charities, hospitals, chantries, and other institutions, held literally thousands of small denomination securities which the board thought very convenient to trade for higher value securities. It thus requested from the government, in its 1865–1866 report, the issuance of 5, 10, 15, and 20 *contos* securities that could be exchanged for the smaller ones. On 5 August 1866, the government complied, publishing a decree allowing the issuance of higher value securities. However, the board's goal was not met: the holders did not respond as expected, maybe due to the reduction in liquidity of their capital such change would bring. Indeed, securities with a value above 1,000$000 *réis* seemed to bring no advantage to the holders. That is at least what their relatively low demand suggests. In the ten years following the permission to issue higher value securities, the board had sold only 1,141 securities, with little over 14,000 *contos* of nominal value, while the lower denomination securities added up to 340,000 with the value of about 160,000 *contos*. By 1880–81, this ratio had not been significantly altered: only 11% of the total value of the securities sold through the Public Credit Board had a value of 5 *contos* or more.[29]

Given its thousands of low denomination securities distributed amongst dozens of thousands of individuals, the Public Credit Board was the institution closest to a state financial intermediate. It was in its headquarters in Lisbon's main square, in the Porto branch, or, on a smaller scale, in the local branches around the country that public debt securities were sold, and their interest and amortisation paid. A significant part of those securities was worth 45$000 on the markets, the equivalent to 90 days wage of a 'master builder'.[30] At times, the board's most direct competitor appeared to be the Public Treasury, who directly sold and managed its bonds.

Governments also widened the board's sphere of activity on national territory. Thus, in 1857, it had been permitted to pay holders of credit instruments to the state not only in Lisbon and Porto, but also in the remaining district capitals on the continent. From 1860 it was allowed to pay interest in county seats, in 1865 in the adjacent islands, and in 1866 overseas. Given the growing importance of the Brazilian market for Portuguese securities, from August 1871, the board was able to pay interest also in the general consulates in Brazil. This measure was the culmination of the establishment of the Public Credit Board by the main sources of public funding. There remained only the interest payment of the external debt in London, which was managed by the *Agência Financial de Portugal* (Portuguese Financial Agency) in London under direct supervision of the Public Treasury.[31] However, despite the legal possibility of geographically extending its activity, Lisbon, its headquarters remained the board's main market. In 1880–1881, for instance, 75% of operations took place in Lisbon, while 15% occurred in Porto. The remaining 10% accounted for all remaining branches in the country, overseas and Brazil.[32]

# Notes

1 Pereira (1983), pp. 257–261; Reis (1993). See also Lains (1997). This was a period of low inflation.
2 Jornal do Comércio, 15 January and 27 February 1875.
3 Pereira (1983), pp. 257–260; Lains (1995), pp. 126–127.
4 Jornal do Comércio, 15 May 1875.
5 Sousa (1916), Mata (1993).
6 Bulhões (1884), p. 84; Jornal do Comércio (1877); Castro (1978), p. 14.
7 Bulhões (1884), pp. 84–85.
8 Leite (1926), pp. 23, 24 35.
9 Jornal do Comércio, 31 December 1878.
10 Figueiredo (1873), pp. 144–145; Vieira (1905), p. 326.
11 Oliveira (1866), pp. 11–12; Marques (1989).
12 Nunes et al. (1994), pp. 24–27.
13 Ulrich (1902), pp. 207–210; Santos (1901), p. xii.
14 Jornal do Comércio, 15 January 1877.
15 Jornal do Comércio, 15 January 1877.
16 Cordeiro (1999 [1896]), pp. 71 and 76–78. Lains (1997), p. 7.
17 Justino (1994), pp. 114–116.
18 Martins (1956), p. 50; Castro (1978), pp. 141–142.
19 Jornal do Comércio, 22 and 26 February 1874.
20 Anonymous (1877) and Fortuna (1877).
21 O Montepio Geral no Primeiro Século da Sua Existência (1940), pp. 96–98; Nunes et al. (1994), pp. 9 and 12.
22 Nunes et al. (1994), pp. 27–28.
23 In 1886 interest decreased from 3% to 2% for deposits above 20 contos; the measure was extended to deposits above 5 contos in 1887 and initially, in 1890, to those above $1,000,000, at the same time interest ceased to be paid to deposits above 50 contos (see Nunes et al., 1994, p. 24).
24 Reis (1996), p. 107.
25 Ulrich (1902), pp. 201–211, Cordeiro (1999 [1896]), Castro (1978), pp. 128 ff., and Justino (1994), pp. 112–115.
26 Jornal do Comércio, 15 June 1879; Martins (1956), pp. 48 ff.; Leite (1926), p. 28.
27 Cordeiro (1999 [1896]), p. 69–74].
28 Relatório da Junta do Crédito Público, 1862–1863, pp. 12–13 and 1865–1866, p. 116.
29 Relatório da Junta do Crédito Público, 1880–1881, pp. 276–281. In 1880–1881 there were 342,334 securities between 100,000 and 1,000,000 totalling 158,103 contos, and 1,631 securities between 5 and 20 contos, which made 17,855 contos; in addition, there were 66,143 50$000 securities (certificates with and without coupon) to a total amount of 34,760 contos.
30 The most common public debt securities had a face value of 90$000 and paid a 3% nominal interest. At an average interest rate of 6%, these securities would be exchanged at 45$000.
31 Menezes (1904).
32 Relatório da Junta do Crédito Público, 1880–1881, p. 273.

# 3

# THE ESTABLISHMENT OF THE *CAIXA GERAL DE DEPÓSITOS*, 1876–1880

The legislation concerning the foundation of the *Caixa Geral de Depósitos* was presented to the Parliament by the finance minister with the state budget. It was traditionally a topic that did not provoke many disputes, contrary to what happened with most of the issues regarding financial matters, and some kind of consensus regarding the benefits of having a public deposit that would act as a savings bank was the norm. It was globally taken for granted that the existent system of public deposits was largely obsolete and did not suffice to grant a proper management of the public funds. On the other hand, the Public Credit Board, the institution that would receive the new deposit, had some level of prestige and trustworthiness, at least from the point of view of the deputies of the two main parties. Moreover, it was overburdened with unnecessary work as it received deposits of rather small amounts. It was also determinant that the most powerful financial institutions of the time, the Bank of Portugal and the other banks, had little interest in running the public deposit or developing the business of a savings bank catering for smaller deposits, as the development of that kind of financial business was deemed to be of low potential. However, the creation of a public deposit bank sowed the seeds of a substantial transformation in the Portuguese financial system, although it would be some years before that change materialised.

## The Parliamentary debate

It was in a favourable political and financial context that in the beginning of 1875, the finance minister of the government of the *Partido Regenerador* (António Serpa) presented in Parliament a proposal for the creation of a public deposit bank that should 'receive and manage all deposits in cash or public debt securities that, in accordance with laws and regulations, can be commanded, requested or authorised by any court or State department' (*Diário da Câmara dos Deputados*, 12 January 1875, p. 63). This reproduced a practice already followed outside Portugal: homogenising the system of deposits from the public administration or those resulting from legislation or court orders which were, until then, divided between the Public Deposits of Lisbon and Porto and the legal (or general) depositaries in the counties and other private depositaries scattered around the country. The previous project for creating the bank, from 1870, was integrated into the set of legislative proposals with which finance ministers usually made their presentation in the Parliament. However, this time, the project was given a prominent place, reflecting the greater ambition regarding the role the institution should take. Still, the minister took care to underline that its creation should not collide with the functions of other financial institutions, especially the Bank of Portugal's rights over certain state deposits.[1] The project was approved a year later, in April 1876, since it was necessary to wait for the Bank of Portugal's privileges to cease at the end of that year.

The decree for the creation of the *Caixa* established the possibility for the new institution to receive deposits from the public, making it a true public savings bank, which raised objections given the potential for competition between the public bank and the rest of the country's banks. One deputy (Pereira de Miranda) declared that he feared that the state would have easy access to a large quantity of funds over which it would have to pay interest, thus easily increasing the public deficit. The finance minister replied that private depositors took into account factors other than interest when choosing a bank. Proof for this, he said, was the fact that the Bank of Portugal held deposits, even paying no interest at all. The minister also asserted that the *Caixa*'s coffers would be able to hold only about 1,000 *contos*.[2] One other deputy asked about the tax exemption granted to the interest on public deposits held with the *Caixa*. The minister replied at this instance that the benefit resulting from that tax exemption was the offset of not being allowed to perform some of the operations he believed banks most profited from, namely discounting letters of exchange, foreign exchange operations, and trading in any kind of securities. However, the finance minister, either due to his negotiation skills or because he did not believe in the expansion potential of the *Caixa*, managed to go ahead with his project. The timing was favourable as, in February 1876, the financial markets were flooded with funds available for investment, to which the bank's response was somewhat excessive. A project such as the creation of the deposit bank would also enjoy support from those defending the need to reorganise the Portuguese financial and banking systems after the end of the thirty-year agreement between the state and the Bank of Portugal that was undergoing revision.

Another relevant difference between the two projects regarded the investment of the funds to be received by the *Caixa*. The 1876 proposal did not allow the new public bank to buy public-funded debt securities, but rather Public Treasury loans 'with the same terms and conditions regulating the floating debt of the Treasury'.[3] This was an attempt to reduce the amount of middle and long-term investments with potentially greater risk, which could jeopardise the position of the *Caixa*. Its deposits were expected to be, at least at first sight, deposits, even if bearing interest only at the end of each semester. The *Caixa*'s remaining lending operations, established in the 1876 proposal, included short term loans on securities (up to 80% of its market value) or advance payments of interest up to six months ahead. One last difference to be noted is that, according to the earlier proposal, the Treasury would cover the *Caixa* running expenses, and no ceiling was set on them. The new proposal, on the other hand, established that the cost would be supported by the *Caixa*'s own profit, the Treasury only stepping in if that was not enough, and to the limit of 5 *contos* per year. This turned out to be a pessimistic forecast, as the *Caixa* managed to cover its running costs from the first day, but revealed the idea, generalised in the country, that great undertakings could not be achieved with the funds from public deposits alone.

A further concern expressed in Parliament had to do with the possibility that the new public bank would be a source of unfair competition within the domestic banking system. One deputy argued that the *Caixa* should not be allowed to pay an interest rate on deposits from the public that would divert deposits from the remaining banking system. The statute should thus define a top rate for demand deposits, possibly below the rate paid on public deposits, which was by then 2%. This was a major issue, as the deputy did not want the government to give depositors too many benefits, including government guarantee, that were likely to attract a significant portion of deposits from other banks to the *Caixa*. He feared so many deposits would leave the government unable to handle pressure to raise public expense through requests for road construction, railways, and 'other public improvements'. In his words:

> Governments want to concede such requests and I do not blame them for that. And if they sometimes do not, it is because they have no means to bear the costs such improvements demand, and obtaining credit is not always easy or possible. Well, I fear that when the government has large sums at its disposal it is not able to resist such demands, often unfounded, and undertake improvements of dubious benefit, steering us to an abyss by which we have already stood.[4]

The deputy somehow presaged the functions the *Caixa* would come to take on. The potential competition by a financial institution backed by the state was plainly important. But it was not decisive. The government was not actually interested in creating a very large public bank, as it understood that the funding of the government's accounts could not at that time depend on savings from deposits, even granting a very favourable interest rate. Syndicates had been necessary before to finance the deficit, and that was not going to change now. That was the main reason why the minister of finance accepted the deputy's objection, which he considered a 'secondary point' in his proposal to create the *Caixa*, the main one being the collection of mandatory deposits, the funds of the Lisbon and Porto Public Deposits, and other judicial and official deposits scattered around the country.

The proposal was sent to the Parliament's Financial Committee, which established a ceiling of 2% for deposits from the public and a limit per account of 500$000 *réis*. Such a limit was typical of savings banks, and its existence shows that even before the creation of the *Caixa Económica Portuguesa* (Portuguese Savings Bank) in 1880, the embryo of such measure was already in the charter of the *Caixa*. Anselmo José Braamcamp rose against the interest granted to deposits from the public, proposing instead one of 3.5% a year, which was refused by the Parliament. He was afraid that too low a rate might in fact prevent the constitution of a savings bank within the *Caixa*, since it would not be enough to attract deposits. Indeed, a minimum interest of 3%, as well as a 5% maximum had been established in the charter of the Bank of Portugal's savings banks, dated 25 November 1847, at a time when the bank held that prerogative in Lisbon and Porto.[5] The policy of small steps did not recommend the creation of a savings bank straight away. That way, the central idea in the government's proposal survived nearly unchanged, to give 'unity and uniformity to our system of deposits, both judicial, and official and tax deposits', as well as allowing the state to benefit from managing those funds. In other words, the government wanted to create an institution to replace a number of entities, some of which were still private, that managed the mandatory deposits with varying degrees of competence.[6] An immediate advantage of creating a state deposit bank was the end of the commission's depositaries charged for guarding those sums. These varied between the 0.5% charged by the Bank of Portugal, and 1% and above, probably outside the most important urban centres, and therefore out of reach from any of its branches. Moreover, the *Caixa* started paying a 2% interest on funds placed within its safes.

At its creation, the *Caixa*'s lending operations included loaning against the assignment of interest on domestic or foreign publicly-funded debt securities, or against pawned securities, and also making loans akin to the floating debt to the Treasury.[7] Showing identical care for operations typical of a savings bank, the Parliament rejected the government's initial proposal that allowed the *Caixa* to loan on pawns. The government saw this as a subsidiary operation. Still, it had it included in the project to guard against the disappearance of the floating debt, in which case the *Caixa* would find itself without any opportunity to place its funds. As it will be seen, the minister's estimate regarding the amount mandatory deposits could reach was very low. The integration of the *Caixa* into the Public Credit Board proposed by the government and accepted by the Parliament may have also served to ease its approval, since this way it would not create new administrative burdens with staff, a situation no opposition deputy would hesitate to criticise. Through such integration the *Caixa* could also benefit from the board's network of agents spread throughout the country.

The board sympathised with the government's fears regarding having a public bank with capital in excess of the opportunities offered by the market. There were, however, matters in which the Public Credit Board did not obtain the desired developments, perhaps because they would have required greater investment in the *Caixa* than any finance minister was willing to make. Indeed, fast expansion of the public bank through the rise of deposits could take the state to a situation where it had to handle large sums of money on which it would have to pay interest, and then look for investments offering a higher rate. So, a cautious course was taken and, for years, nothing was done to further develop the *Caixa* towards attracting more deposits. Such an endeavour would have included measures such as opening more branches throughout the country, offering a higher interest than the banks, improving the process of depositing and withdrawing funds, or raising the upper limit of deposit per person. Given the care to avoid too fast an expansion of the *Caixa*'s activity in relation to the state's capacity to absorb its funds, the board's main suggestions were not met by the government.

## The commencement

As the *Caixa*'s administrator, the Public Credit Board published two fairly detailed and informative reports on the establishment and first months of operation of the public deposit bank, released on 30 November 1877 and 16 December 1878. The reports were first presented to the government, who would then take them to the Parliament for approval, as required by law. They should also be released to the press. The report concerning the first few working months of the *Caixa*, from its establishment in January 1877 to August of the same year, essentially describes the process of transferring funds from the different public deposits in the country. According to the report, the new public bank received around 1,000 *contos*, sent by the Public Deposits of Lisbon and Porto and also by the depositaries in the main regional capitals as the result of about a century of balances. Over half of the 514 *contos* that were received came from the Bank of Portugal alone. The funds coming from the public deposits and from the Treasury were put into a single account in the *Caixa*'s liabilities called the Old Account, over which the institution was responsible only up to the amount that had been delivered. This was a way of protecting the *Caixa* from potential demands for amounts higher than those it had received from those accounts. Public deposits likely did not have their accounts in order due to the great instability in the country throughout the first decades of the liberal regime. Statistics published in the first *Caixa* report show that the Public Deposit of Lisbon recorded a balance of 568 *contos* referring to the period of 1870–1876, kept in the Bank of Portugal, which was the result of deposits amounting to 2,070 *contos* and withdrawals totalling 1,837 *contos*. However, among the withdrawals was the refund of deposits made before 1870 adding up to 334 *contos*. This is to say that the Public Deposit of Lisbon was using newly acquired funds to repay old deposits. The *Caixa* inherited this procedure but only took responsibility up to the value of funds received in 1876. In the case of the previous private depositaries, they were responsible by law for any debt they might have incurred. Besides the old funds, the *Caixa* also assumed receipt of public deposits made from the date it started its activity. Soon, this account, called the 'modern account', over which the *Caixa* took full responsibility, amounted to more than 1,200 *contos*. Between January and August 1877, the old and the new accounts added up to a significant amount, as the *Caixa* collected a deposit balance of 2,233 *contos*.

In only eight months of functioning, the amount of deposits had more than doubled the (possibly too cautious) estimate of the finance minister. The deposit balance, exceeding 2,000 *contos*, was by any standard relevant in relation to the public deficit, which in June 1877 (the end of the economic year) amounted to the large sum of 10,132 *contos*. Until June 1880, however, mandatory deposits at the *Caixa*, both in the old and the modern accounts, remained stable. Considering the total deposits of the Portuguese banking system, thus excluding banking houses, for which there are no aggregated statistics, the *Caixa*'s balance represented around 12% of that amount between 1877 and 1880.[8] The description of the *Caixa*'s establishment described in the board's report to the government is especially interesting for portraying the situation of the public deposits transferred to the new institution, and helping identify the alterations the latter introduced to the state's financial administration. Such information could not be gathered from parliamentary debates nor from the legislation, which, given the lack of monographs on the *Caixa*, constitute a major source of information on the institution. The Public Deposits of Lisbon and Porto, the most important depositors, no longer held valuables when the *Caixa* was created, since they had been delivered as deposits to the Bank of Portugal or loaned to the Treasury.

The creation of the *Caixa* changed the organisation of the public deposits' accounts, making a separate account for the old debits so the new institution was responsible only for deposits made after its creation. This was a significant reorganisation, as the Public Deposit of Lisbon alone was owed 2,430 *contos* by the state. This account had collected state debts to the interest board or its successors, from 1776 until 1868, when the deposit underwent the first reform. However, most of that debit referred to the period between the beginning of the French wars at the close of the eighteenth century and the end of the civil war in 1834. The Treasury debit held in public deposit corresponded to the debt owed by the state to citizens who had bought the public debt securities issued by the Public Credit Board. When a separate account was created for that debt in the *Caixa*, with no new deposits coming in, the state stopped directly allocating revenues to repay it, and the citizens could no longer retrieve them. It should be pointed out, however, that this measure faced little objection. It would be hard for any financial institution to emerge unscathed from the tumultuous first half of the nineteenth century, especially one obliged to oversee the consecutive repayment crises of the Portuguese state. The *Caixa* gathered together the deposits of Lisbon and Porto. Here too, advantages were more financial than organisational.

The public bank's functions regarding the rest of the country were more significant because it actually led to the replacement of outdated practices that were ill-suited to the new era of greater political stability and growing weight of the state on the country's economy and finances. In the main two cities, the public deposits already acted as financial intermediaries, but in the rest of the country they merely kept the money received in coffers. Among the latter were the depositaries or treasurers of orphan treasuries. The coffers had three locks, one of whose keys was kept by the depositary himself, another by the county judge, and the third by the warden of the orphans. Coins were kept in such coffers, unlike the equivalent deposits in Lisbon and Porto, where funds were sent to the Bank of Portugal. As such, when the *Caixa* was created, 309 *contos* were moved there from those coffers, of which 82 were from Lisbon and Porto. Overall, these were small sums.

The funds were not necessarily left idle, as the administrators of a number of public deposits in a number of occurrences took 'profit from valuables and money in deposit', rather than just receiving them.[9] However, the fact is that, as with the public deposits accounts in the Bank of Portugal, the transfer of funds from the coffers to the *Caixa* left few records of resistance; on the contrary, there was even some cooperation from the key holders. Indeed, the Public Credit Board showed some surprise at the depositaries' collaboration and at the good order of the inventories of the orphans' assets, which surely resulted from the treasuries being in deficit, as were the public deposits of Lisbon and Porto. Nor did small depositories oppose the creation of the public bank. If they had, things might have gone differently, as in those days, central government would hardly have been able to implement measures that were not fully accepted outside Lisbon. The institutions responsible for the orphan treasuries were so old and had been through such tribulations that there were fears regarding the strength of the accounts of the deposited funds. As the *Caixa's* administrator, the board considered the old debts as falling outside its responsibilities. In the case of the orphan treasuries, only the coffers themselves and the corresponding inventories were moved to the *Caixa* headquarters. The new bank showed no interest in debit and credit balances or in the securities of debt to householders.[10]

The transfer of deposits held by the general legal depositaries of the 142 counties across the reign was not particularly easy, as the *Caixa* was not responsible for paying the deficits of some of these institutions. Indeed, such deposits were registered in a 'New Account', where 'each deposit is responsible for itself and stands for what it received'. The problem with this transition originated in the fact that part of these depositaries used the deposited funds 'as working capital in their trade', making it 'difficult to deliver it promptly'. Since this was the most difficult change, it was also the one the *Caixa's* regulation paid most attention to. Most of the funds were duly delivered by the set date, and by 30 June 1876, the public bank had received 358 *contos* from the counties, with only 95 remaining to be paid. These were small sums. The last phase of transfers to the *Caixa* comprised those from local tax offices and from the districts' central treasuries, which also ran smoothly.

Therefore, except for the amounts in the charge of general and independent depositaries, all the transferred funds were put in the Old Account, which did not guarantee correspondence between deposits and withdrawals. Until the end of the account, any security holder could withdraw its value, but it is not clear what would have happened if withdrawal requests had exceeded the amount deposited. This did not happen for a number of reasons. The New Account was constituted by the deposits made with the public bank, which were the responsibility of the county general depositaries, together with all types of deposits made after the *Caixa*'s creation. This heading was second only to that concerning the funds transferred from the Public Deposit of Lisbon, amounting to 877 *contos* in the period between January and August 1877. The first report on the running of the *Caixa*, regarding its first year (1876–1877), estimated that account could reach 2,000 *contos*. The deposits the *Caixa* received from the Bank of Portugal's board in 1876 amounted to 1,356 *contos* in coin.

The reform of the ailing public deposits was a long-time ambition for successive governments, and it was the *Caixa* that finally managed to achieve that goal and for two main reasons. Firstly, it did not have to cover existing deficits, and secondly it paid a 2% interest. At the end of its first fiscal, the *Caixa* had received a total of 2,813 *contos*.[11] The balance of the New Account, into which were paid the annual mandatory deposits, saw remarkable growth from 568 *contos* to 1,472 between 30 June 1877 and one year later. This was not a natural growth tendency but rather the result of increasing compliance with legal requirements regarding mandatory deposits. In short, mandatory deposits, including those in the *Old* and *New* accounts, rose from 1,295 to 2,103 *contos* between 30 June 1877 and 30 June 1878, but from then on, the growth rate decreased. By 30 June 1879, the balance was 2,456 *contos*, and one year later, 2,572. Besides the slowdown in mandatory deposits, opportunities for capital investment in the state rose, so the amount of cash that was not invested diminished. Indeed, the balance of cash in hand had dropped from 770 to 405 *contos* in the twelve months from June 1877, and the tendency continued for the next two years until it reached 294 *contos* in June 1880.[12]

The changes the Public Credit Board aspired to as administrator of the *Caixa* concerned, initially, the definition of responsibility over Public Treasury debts regarding the old Public Deposits of Lisbon and Porto. In fact, the Public Deposit of Lisbon had left the public bank only enough funds to cover the amount of deposits delivered from 5 June 1872 onwards, and any other deposits were left overdrawn.[13] The ordinance established that it was down to the Treasury to provide the *Caixa* with the remainder after the amount of the 'vacant' deposits (those that had been time-barred and could no longer be claimed) had been ascertained. A debt from the Treasury to the *Caixa* was then created, to the amount of 2,316 *contos*. Between the fiscal years of 1877–78 and 1884–85 the Treasury reduced that debt to 2,071 *contos*, which remained practically unchanged from then on. It was essentially a fictitious heading in the *Caixa*'s balance and came to be eliminated years later.[14] The establishment of the Treasury debt meant the public bank could then publish a smaller balance and a more attractive financial situation. Furthermore, the government became legally responsible for supplying those funds if necessary.

As the public bank was due to pay interest on deposits, its creation was not an obvious advantage to the state. The doubts regarding its actual financial benefits contributed to the successive hesitation regarding creating legislation and other conditions conducive to the growth of the *Caixa*. Frequent references to similar situations abroad suggest that the involved public officials were aware that a deposit bank could weigh on the state budget. However, for the first year of running, the Public Credit Board presented a net income of 25,410$000, corresponding to 1.25% of the balance of the deposits account, or 1.76% of the balance of the account of capital employed.[15]

However, before attracting more deposits from the public with a competitive interest rate or with an arbitrary measure to curtail the interest offered by other institutions, the government and the Public Credit Board had to prove that the public bank was able to invest the deposits it already had so it could pay the 2% annual interest to their holders. The board had an experience of competing with other institutions for the funds it was awarded for the payment of the public debt. The most coveted of such funds, by the government or by the Bank of Portugal, was the income from the Lisbon and Porto's custom houses. As the interest rate to be paid to deposits from the public had been set in the *Caixa*'s charter, the board had limited leeway in this matter. When presenting their draft regulation for the *Caixa*, the board did express the wish that 'the law had been more latitudinal, as it happened in other countries'. Still, the regulation had to conform to the law.

From the time of its first annual report, concerning the period between January 1877 and June 1878, the *Caixa*'s board had some difficulty investing all the capital entrusted to it. The charter of the public bank allowed loans to householders, *misericórdias*, and similar institutions. These investments could take the form of advance payments of interest on any securities of the funded public debt, domestic or external, for up to five years, divided into semesters, and they could also take the form of a pawn on those same debt securities up to 80% of the market value; by law, these loans were revocable.[16] The interest on such loans was payable at the time the contract was signed.[17] These were highly secure investments for the *Caixa*, which appealed to the government since they raised the liquidity of its debt securities. However, the business of lending to householders did not prosper. By 30 November 1877, when the first report was presented, the bank had loaned to householders the very modest sum of 40,856$000.[18] The interest rate for these operations was established neither in the law nor in the provisional regulation, nor is it anywhere stated in the reports.

The alternative was loaning to the state. Between January and October 1877, the *Caixa* managed to employ a total amount of 1,400 *contos* divided into five loans in the form of current account operations to finance the floating debt.

33

This initiative shows a degree of concern by the government regarding the funds accumulating in the coffers of the public bank. In January 1877, the *Caixa* had been able to place 299 *contos* at a 5% annual interest rate. It then had to wait for two months to place another 300 *contos*, albeit at a lower rate. In August, 400 *contos* were again invested, bringing the total amount of loans to the state to 900 *contos*, but with the large amount of 955 *contos* remaining in the coffers. Finally, in September and October, the *Caixa* managed to place 500 *contos* more with the state, this time at an annual rate of 4%, bringing the total of the investments to 1,400 *contos*. Until some projections regarding average annual balances could be made, the *Caixa*'s board was not allowed to make investments for periods longer than six months, although they were renewable. This meant that, at first, the bank could not acquire funded debt securities, Treasury bonds, or the bonds of the *Crédito Predial Português*. On 30 June 1877, the holdings in currency amounted to 770 *contos*, which raised to 1,148 a month later, of which only 500 were employed in direct loans to the state.

However, throughout the bank's first full economic year, from June 1877 to June 1878, the situation changed substantially. Firstly, the balance of the Old Account, registering 727 *contos* on 30 June 1877, gradually decreased to 632 *contos* one year later due to withdrawals. Since this account tended to dwindle, few long-term investments could be made with its funds. By 1880–1881, it contained only around 200 *contos*. The chronology of loans to the state shows a measure of concern by successive governments to guarantee the institution's profitability. In practice, when those balances rose significantly, the government again borrowed from the *Caixa*. Thus, on 31 January 1877, when deposits amounted to 536 *contos*, the government borrowed 200; on 31 March, deposits reached 690 *contos*, and the government took a loan of 300 *contos*. By 31 July, the deposits balance had reached 1,148 *contos*, and between that date and the end of the year the government borrowed another 900 *contos*. In the three lending operations the bank was allowed to engage in, the *Caixa* placed a total amount of 1,441 *contos*, of which only a very small part corresponded to householders' money. When its first report was presented, its vaults held 584 *contos*, corresponding to 28.9% of the balance of its deposit account. This level of voluntary cash reserves was, however, below the average of the remaining banking institutions in the country. Indeed, by the end of 1876, cash reserves in the Portuguese banking system, including the Bank of Portugal, amounted to 41.5% of the sum of total deposits with the issue amount, and to 31.6% if discounting the main issuing bank.

As a display of caution, but also as a consequence of the fact that deposits with the *Caixa* were guaranteed by the Treasury, the first pieces of legislation regulating the *Caixa*'s activity did not demand the constitution of a reserve fund, nor did they assign the distribution of placements on the three possible options, loans or public debt securities. Moreover, the interest of lending operations was also not established by law. As a result, the Public Credit Board, as administrator of the new institution, had considerable freedom in these matters. The outcome of the first months of management was a direct result of the conditions then enjoyed by the Portuguese financial market, where loans to the state were the most profitable and least risky. The administration wanted to constitute a cash reserve, even though it was not demanded by law. However, it seems that was not the goal of the Public Credit Board. In its second annual report, concerning the *Caixa*'s first nine months and presented to the government in November 1877, the board pointed out the difficulties it faced to invest the bank's capital within the State.

To enable themselves to overcome this, the *Caixa*'s executive board wanted the government to consent to the acquisition of debt securities, funded or not, and bonds of the *Companhia do Crédito Predial Português*, which were entirely comparable to debt securities. The board also asked for the alteration of the April 1876 law that prevented the *Caixa* from loaning to municipal and district authorities. In this regard, the case of the French *Caisse de dépôts et consignations* was pointed out. This deposit bank, whose development was then unique in Europe, was the best reference for almost all the managerial ambitions of the board. The operations in question were 'not less secure and were more stable than those already permitted', meaning current account loans to the government and loans on pawned securities, pawned interest, or other assets. By the ordinance of December 1877, the *Caixa*'s new limit for all its operations was two-thirds of the capital 'considered to be of continuing existence', including, of course, the debt assumed by the Treasury mentioned above. By allowing loaning to local authorities, the government showed its will to give the *Caixa* equivalent functions to the most important savings bank in Europe, namely those considered exemplary cases, such as the Italian, German, French, English, or Scottish ones.

Such care, which was reflected in the legislation establishing the *Caixa*, singles it out among banking institutions created with the direct intervention of the Portuguese state, namely the *Crédito Predial Português*, and the *Banco National Ultramarino*, both founded in 1864. Indeed, these institutions were allowed a wide range of financial operations, including bill discounting, buying all kinds of securities on the domestic or foreign markets, and also issuing notes in the case of *Ultramarino*, and bonds and mortgage loans in that of the *Crédito Predial*. However, demanding a broadening of the *Caixa*'s lending operations was not among the Public Credit Board's priorities. It would only become an essential point if the public bank had very significant amounts of unplaced funds in its vaults. Instead, the board's focus lay on defining a staff establishment plan, as well as the appointment of staff and the wages of the executive board members.

## How it worked

In the provisional regulation for the establishment of the *Caixa*, the Public Credit Board asked the government for permission to be granted a relatively wide scope of action in choosing the staff for the new bank, the government establishing only the number of workers and their wages. The board suggested a workforce of 26, which it believed was enough to accommodate potential business expansion.[19] For the management and treasury posts, the board suggested its own personnel double-hat. The remaining employees, that is, the staff exclusive to the *Caixa*, should be placed by contest in the lower levels and by promotion in the higher levels. According to the law establishing the *Caixa*, the board's treasurer should hold the equivalent post in the public bank and be assisted by two treasurers of his choice. In addition, all the *Caixa*'s services should be under the purview of the board's chief accountant.[20] To recompense the additional responsibility, the *Caixa*'s payroll included the expense of a 400$000 bonus for each member of the board's executive board. The board's chief accountant had a bonus of 1,000$000. Finally, the treasurer, who doubled his functions with the *Caixa*, was also rewarded with 400$000. The six board workers who accumulated functions in the *Caixa* were, in practice, a structure simultaneously of management and supervision. They were responsible for presenting the bank's annual reports to the government and to the two chambers of Parliament. These officials took charge of the most important matters of the running of the *Caixa*, including the establishment plan, staff appointment, suggestions on deposits, loan and withdrawal procedures, and the level of interest rates.

The direction of the *Caixa* was handed to a principal clerk and a chief bookkeeper, each heading the respective section: inscription of deposits and bookkeeping. These two full time officials had an annual salary slightly above 1,000$000. There was still an interim deputy chief bookkeeper, earning 900$000 per year. These staff could not accumulate these remunerations with other wages paid by the state, unlike their superiors. As the salaries indicate, these officials in charge of running the *Caixa* were top ranking civil servants.[21] The lower ranks comprised 15 employees, all of them with provisional contracts. A further dozen workers were spread throughout the country, performing the *Caixa*'s functions in the several branches it had in the main district capitals. However, most of the work was done in Lisbon.[22] The April 1876 law established, among its transitory measures, merely that the new institution should take in the former workers of the public deposit boards of Lisbon and Porto, some as permanent workers and others as auxiliaries, without any cuts in their wages.

From an early stage, the Public Credit Board endeavoured to guarantee that it would have effective control over the institution it was to be responsible for. This is a reasonable ambition given the financial responsibility, and quite a significant one. In May 1879, the board's chief bookkeeper and the *Caixa*'s director (Pedro Augusto de Carvalho) was appointed director at the revenue service and replaced the head of the latter (Júlio Ferreira Pinto Basto).[23] The following years saw some regularity in the *Caixa*'s functioning, with the number of employees and their job titles staying the same. In these first years, besides the people inherited from the public deposits, the bank hired temporary workers, thus circumventing the constraints imposed by the establishment plan, even though this strategy had disadvantages inherent to the use of temporaries. The Public Credit Board had the ambition that, in the matter of the establishment plan, the Portuguese government follow the example of its French counterpart, who created the *Caisse de dépôts et consignations* with a high degree of autonomy. The *Caixa*'s 1877 report includes a long description of the way the French government handled its deposit bank. Its interest lies not only in the information it contains on the subject but also in the fact it reveals the board's ambition regarding its own administration of the bank. And the report concludes that 'The authority of the [French] government regarding the [deposit] bank is restricted to performing acts of high political responsibility without any direct action on the direct management of the institution'.[24]

However, the government did not grant it more autonomy and the French model, implicit in the board's suggestions, was patently countered. The first years of consensus on the creation, management, and role of the *Caixa* in the Portuguese financial market were thus followed by a period in which party politics increasingly took over the institution. What is more, the board complained that the increased workload entailed by management of the *Caixa* was not matched by a compensatory raise for the members of its executive board. The 1877 report paints a detailed picture of the problem, even stating that the *Caixa*, the new department of the Public Credit Board, had become the section with the heaviest workload of the entire institution. Besides selling public debt securities and paying its interest and amortisation, its functions now included collecting and accounting deposits made in ten different points around the country and keeping the amounts given in pawn. For all this additional work, the five members of the executive board received no extra pay, and this was their complaint.

Indeed, those officials were paid 600$000 yearly, as established in 1837, which at the time put them at the level of directors-general for public administration. However, these specific salaries had been raised in the two pay reforms, in 1859 and 1867, to 800$000 in the first, and then to 1,300$000 in the second. So, by the time the *Caixa* was created, the Public Credit Board's board members earned little more than a clerk, who took home 500$000 yearly. In 1876, the president of the Parliament earned a subsidy of 600$000 per legislative term, and each deputy a subsidy that could not exceed 300 $000. A government minister earned 3,200$000 yearly, although they could not receive any other payments from the state.[25] The premises where the *Caixa* had to operate were even worse than those of the Public Credit Board.[26] But better days were to come, as the finance minister showed interest on the issue and approved the provisional clauses set by the board, including the possibility of choosing and hiring staff for the new service, and he rose the salary of the board members for running the *Caixa* from 600$000 to 1,000$000.[27] According to António José Seixas, the support from the minister made him one of the 'three statesmen in the Finance Ministry [to whom] the *Caixa* owes its existence'.[28]

# Notes

1 Diário da Câmara dos Deputados, 12 January 1875, p. 63, and 21 April 1870, pp. 132–33.
2 Diário da Câmara dos Deputados, 11 February 1876.
3 Diário da Câmara dos Deputados, 12 April 1875.
4 Diário da Câmara dos Deputados, 11 February 1876, pp. 333–334.
5 Legislação do Banco de Portugal (1946), vol. II, p. 116.
6 Diário da Câmara dos Deputados, 11 February 1876, pp. 330–331.
7 Regulamento Provisório da Caixa Geral de Depósitos, 12 December 1876.
8 Total public debt in June 1877 amounted to the nominal value of 380,000 contos (see Mata, 1993, pp. 175 e 258).
9 Diário da Câmara dos Deputados, 11 February 1876, p. 331.
10 Relatório da Caixa Geral de Depósitos (1876–1877), pp. 16–17, 20.
11 Relatório da Caixa Geral de Depósitos (1877), pp. 26 and 28.
12 Relatório da Caixa Geral de Depósitos (1877–1878), pp. 18–19.
13 Relatório da Caixa Geral de Depósitos (1877), p. 75.
14 The debt was eliminated in 1922–1923 as a mere accounting operation, when it still amounted to 2,028 contos.
15 Relatório da Caixa Geral de Depósitos (1877), p. 39n.
16 Foreign securities were valued at par, that is, at 4$500 for 1 pound (see Fuschini, 1899, pp. 87–89).
17 'Carta de Lei' of 10 April 1876, title III, chapter II, and the provisional regulation of 30 November 1876, article no. 67.
18 For what follows, see Relatório da Caixa Geral de Depósitos (1877), pp. 35–37, 115n.
19 Relatório da Caixa Geral de Depósitos, 1877–1878, pp. 28–29.
20 Regulamento provisório da Caixa Geral de Depósitos of 11 December 1876, title iv, articles 89 to 92, and Relatório da Caixa Geral de Depósitos, 1877–1878, p. 27.
21 Relatório da Caixa Geral de Depósitos, 1877–1878, pp. 28, 72–73, 77; Fernandes (1966), p. 5.
22 Relatório da Caixa Geral de Depósitos, 1877, pp. 43–44, and also 1877–1878, p. 27.
23 Seixas (1882), p. 32.
24 Relatório da Caixa Geral de Depósitos, 1877, pp. 42–43, 48.
25 Vieira (1905), pp. 116–118.
26 *Jornal do Comércio*, 16, 21 and 26 June 1877.
27 Relatório da Caixa Geral de Depósitos, 1877, pp. 75–77.
28 Seixas (1882), p. 31.

# 4

# THE ESTABLISHMENT OF THE *CAIXA ECONÓMICA PORTUGUESA*, 1880–1886

Following the foundation of the *Caixa Geral de Depósitos* by António Serpa, the minister of finance of the *Partido Regenerador*, his successor from the opposing *Partido Progressita* (Barros Gomes), took an interest in the institution's development and presented in Parliament a proposal to found a savings bank within the same institution. The consensus that the public deposit bank had generated was replicated also in this instance, as the two institutions were seen as complementary. However, the fact that the *Caixa* had been created under the administration of the Public Credit Board proved to be a source of problems for the good running and subsequent development of the board and for its relations with the country's governments. In 1881, during a short government of the *Partido Regenerador* (led by Rodrigues Sampaio), a plan for the establishment of the savings bank was presented despite the opposition of the Public Credit Board. There was a limit to governments' interference in the management of the board, as it was imperative for governments that the board's reputation was not affected, since that would jeopardise the public's confidence in the institution. For this reason, the relations between the government and the board would maintain a balance until 1885, when important changes in the permitted operations of the *Caixa* were introduced. The same year saw the creation of a national pensions fund (*Caixa Nacional de Aposentações*), which performed rather poorly in the first years of its existence.

## The debate on the public savings bank

As had happened previously, on 15 January 1880, at the time of the presentation of the state budget in Parliament, Barros Gomes retrieved his predecessor's proposal of the legislation aimed at widening the scope of the *Caixa*'s financial outreach. These proposals were approved and set out in the laws of 1 and 26 April 1880. The first allowed the *Caixa* to buy funded public debt securities and bonds of *Companhia do Crédito Predial Português*, in the amount of up to a third of the total deposits for such investments. The same law allowed loans to local authorities (municipalities and *Juntas Gerais de Distrito*), as well as discounting bills received by the Public Credit Board as payment for the nationalised goods. Finally, the law entrusted the *Caixa* with the custody and management of the municipal road works fund which had been created in 1864. The second piece of legislation, dated 26 April, founded *Caixa Económica Portuguesa*. Both of these were part of a set of twenty draft bills presented by the finance minister to the Parliament.

By this time, the Portuguese public credit was not in a difficult position, as by the end of 1879 the 3% funded debt securities hit a 52% market value in Lisbon and 53% in London. These prices corresponded to real interest of 5.7–5.8%. Similarly, the real interest of the 3% Treasury bonds, first issued on 31 May 1873, decreased from 7.3% to 6.35% on 8 July 1879. The level of interest was as good as the best achieved by the state in the years preceding the 1876 financial and banking crisis. Finally, some floating debt transactions were being carried out also at the relatively low rate of 4.5%.[1] Contrarily, the deficit in state accounts amounted to 2,000 *contos*, and the country carried a large public debt overhang.[2] Still, the relatively unencumbered position of the public credit market allowed the finance minister greater liberty to address the administrative and financial reform of the State. Essentially, the target was to find a new way to finance the state to make budget revenues grow at least as fast as expenses. The draft bill on extending *Caixa* operations to funded debt securities and on entrusting the bank with the municipal road funds was approved without significant dispute on 4 February 1880. However, the same was not true for the creation of *Caixa Económica Portuguesa*, and the Finance Committee sent the draft bill back to the Parliament with a number of changes. Most were minor issues, but the committee decreased the interest to be paid by the new institution from the 4% set out in the ministerial proposal to 3.6%. This change was essentially a precautionary measure regarding the new institution.[3]

After a rather uninteresting debate, *Caixa Económica Portuguesa* (CEP) was created to function through the *Caixa* under the superior administration of the Public Credit Board. The new savings bank should be headquartered in Lisbon and have the counties' tax offices, or their delegations, as branches. Deposits were carried into a specific account, even though they were kept in the custody of the *Caixa* and invested essentially like the latter's funds, with one exception: the savings banks' funds could be invested in debenture loans with district and municipal authorities. Culminating in this second legislative impetus of the *Caixa*'s life, the Public Credit Board also requested the deposit of funds from commercial bankruptcies. At the time, these were assigned to banking institutions under the guardianship of judges, called 'commissioners'. The application was granted in April 1880. For the second time in the *Caixa*'s history, there was a consensus around the idea of creating a state savings bank administered by the Public Credit Board. Banks and banking houses did not seem particularly concerned with the matter, which explains why their voices were not heard in Parliament or newspapers. In addition to the change in the interest rate introduced by the lower chamber's Finance Committee and other minor points, only the Public Credit Board, upon which thus befell the additional responsibility of managing some more deposits and transfers of funds, expressed any opinion on the subject. However, the government was still able to pass the reform in Parliament, but following the government's fall in March 1881 and the popular outburst against the increase in taxes, the replacement government needed to reduce the public deficit and debt.[4]

In December 1880, Joaquim Gonçalves Mamede, the Board's executive member representing the government, died, and the position remained vacant for some time. On 17 March, Barros Gomes appointed to that place Pedro Augusto Franco, future Count of Restelo and an influential member of the *Partido Progressista*. He took office on 24 March, and the government fell the following day. Notwithstanding, Franco was named chairman of the board by the new government of Rodrigues Sampaio on 27 March. With this appointment, the Public Credit Board had a significant political player as chairman for the first time, who was also unique in the fact he had been appointed to the executive board by a progressive minister and chosen as president by a Regenerator minister.

## The plan for the establishment of the
### Caixa Económica Portuguesa

The progressive government was followed by a Regenerator executive led by Rodrigues Sampaio, while Fontes Pereira de Melo remained as head of the party. One of its first measures was to repeal the income tax law inherited from the previous government. Of the whole reform introduced by Barros Gomes, only the 3% tax on the income of civil servants and on the yield of public debt securities remained. To replace the abolished law, an additional 6% on all existing taxes was established.[5] The widening of *Caixa*'s scope of operations carried over from the previous government, as well as a number of other reforms concerning public accounting, the Court of Auditors, customs, and tax enforcement services.[6] In June 1881, the finance minister (Lopo Vaz) implemented a substantial administration reform, centralising public accounting in a single directorate-general and publishing a new Public Accounting Regulation on 31 August. This regulation introduced mechanisms to allow greater control over public expenditure, including the requirement of all ministries to obtain prior permission for spending from the Court of Auditors.[7] Then, on 17 August 1881, ignoring the proposal presented by the Board in July, Lopo Vaz published the first definitive regulation of the public banks. This led to the resignation of one of the members of the board (António José de Seixas). In spite of this, the new chairman remained on the side of the government.

The situation disturbed the harmony in the new institution. The triggering event was the proposal sent by the Public Credit Board to the government, dated 2 July 1881, presenting a plan for the establishment of the new institution. However, this proposal only had the favourable votes of four of the executive board's members, the chairman having voted against it. The fact that the savings bank was about to begin its full operation served as a pretext. Although the savings bank did not represent a significant increase in workload, it created the opportunity to define the staff situation in the *Caixa*, which included only eight permanently employed civil servants out of a total staff of 23.

In the meantime, the board's responsibilities in the *Caixa*'s management had increased owing to the new transactions allowed in the public deposit bank. These transactions represented a significant jump in deposits between the fiscal years of 1879–1880 and 1880–1881, corresponding to the purchase of public debt securities and the increase in direct loans to the state.[8] The Public Credit Board was unlikely to worry too much over being charged with the management of a growing volume of public funds, since this brought it an obvious increase of power in the financial administration of public resources. What did cause concern, however, was the augmented workload it entailed, and the fact it legally constrained the administration of its staff. An institution already moving more than 3,000 *contos* (thanks to the *Caixa*) still depended on the finance minister for permission to contract a handful more employees.

The Public Credit Board wanted clearance from the government to permanently hire the employees working at the *Caixa* from the start, dispensing with recruitment competitions except for the two heads of service. The board's proposal also included some specific objectives regarding a number of workers. Although it had no intention of dismissing or indeed reducing the salary of any of the employees, the board did advise demoting some of them, a suggestion that, for the government, was unthinkable.[9] The board further requested that the *Caixa*'s staff's appointment, promotion, and retirement follow the rules of the Public Credit Board's accounting department, in that they should be independent from the government. Also, it wanted the value of the salaries to be defined, and bonuses of 25% to be added per time of effective service to reward diligence. According to its proponents, this proposal followed the model used in France, although *Caisse de dépôts et consignations* was even more 'independent from the government in the choice and remuneration of its staff'. The scope of these suggestions was clear to those signing the proposal, and expressly stated, revealing a claim that can be described at least as premature.

Seixas opposed and eventually resigned in protest against what he considered to be excessive governmental interference in the administration of the Public Credit Board. He found it unacceptable that the new president had placed himself on the side of the government against the other members of the executive board who 'had been part of the board and running its business, some for twelve, others for fifteen years on successive mandates from its constituents, and managing the *Caixa* for almost five years'.[10] Yet that was not the only problem. To the 26 workers of the *Caixa*, the regulation added seven for the savings bank, which were perfectly dispensable as the savings bank was not yet running. If the Public Credit Board's ambition had been to have as many employees as possible with the best remunerations, it would have been satisfied with the ministry's regulation. Instead of the 26 staff with two salary tiers, the minister offered a plan with 34 posts, divided into three salary tiers, by all accounts a superior solution. And the 25% bonus proposed by the board was also accounted for in the regulation. In this light, the reasons pointed out by António José de Seixas for his resignation do not seem critical. However, one may wonder whether Seixas, with his long experience as a member of the Public Credit Board, had foreseen that the functions of that institution in the administration of public finances were about to undergo great changes. The process of his withdrawal was not a smooth one, given he handed in his notice in January 1882 and it was not accepted until September. His resignation, the death in the previous year of Manuel Alves do Rio (the member elected by the Parliament), and the departure of José Luís Teixeira Mendes (elected by the security holders), resulted in substantial changes to the Public Credit Board. To replace those members, the security holders elected two other members (Sousa Coutinho and Silveira Vieira) and the composition of the board remained stable until 1893.

The episode of Seixas' resignation would eventually lead to a series of publications that revealed important aspects of the functioning of the *Caixa* and the board. In 1882, after making the decision to resign, António José de Seixas published a book explaining the reasons behind his decision. From the moment he had taken on the job, chosen by the security holders in 1867, he had been very attentive to the board's problems, about which he wrote regularly in *Jornal do Comércio*. He could not therefore keep from commenting on a situation he thought was wrong. Symptomatically, when he resigned, he stopped publishing in the Regenerator newspaper. In addition to what the controversy reveals about the struggles surrounding the board responsible for the repayment of the state debt, Seixas' book is also a rare source of information about one of the most important public institutions of the time. Above all, Seixas' prognosis on the future of the savings bank point out the developmental issues of the savings bank, which stemmed primarily from the competition presented by the issuance of public debt securities.

Debt securities issued by the Portuguese state to the domestic market competed with the *Caixa Económica* due to their relatively high yield around a real interest rate of 6%, significantly higher than the 3.6% annual interest rate on deposits at the savings bank. The differential in interest rate was not in itself a problem for the development of the public savings bank. In fact, its survival depended on being able to place its own funds at a rate higher than that at which it paid its deposits, resorting precisely to debt securities. The banks' investments needed to be as secure as possible; thus, the most convenient investments for the savings bank were loans to the current account of the state or local authorities, the purchase of state securities or bonds, and shares guaranteed by the state. The differential between the 6% interest it might receive and the 3.6% it had to give its depositors should have paid for the service the savings bank provided its customers. It was a financial intermediation service, typical of a deposit bank, and consisting of collecting private savings into interest current accounts and applying the funds thus collected in investments.

However, the Public Credit Board itself provided an identical service of financial intermediation, offering conditions that made it the preferred choice for those wanting to save or make investments. The competition was a problem for the first years of operation of the public savings bank. What is more, in the first years, financial investments were made directly through the savings bank, thus duplicating the deposit bank's functions, a procedure that would come to an end in 1885. At the root of the problem were the low value securities the Public Credit Board received from the state. These securities could be directly acquired by individuals with small savings whose amount did not justify going to a specialised institution such as a savings bank. Among the debt securities with 6% nominal interest available through the board were savings certificates with a value per unit of 50$000 and the more common denomination, of 100$000. The service offered by the Public Credit Board itself might be lower quality, but it was also cheaper. Deposits with the savings bank were also subject to competition from Treasury bonds, which had a face value of 90$000, and until 1881, also paid 6%. These bonds successively lowered their nominal interest to 5% in 1882, and to between 4% and 4.5% in 1888. Finally, in this last year Treasury bonds were issued with a face value of 22$500, an amount surely within the reach of any worker, so much so that they became known as 'sopeiras', denoting their success among domestic servants.[11]

Thus, the fundamental point underlying the creation of the *Caixa Económica* was the government's wish to entrust the new institution with a function until then pertaining to the Public Credit Board and to the Public Treasury. This intent resulted from an evaluation of costs and benefits considering both financial and political factors. This system was not very different from one with a savings bank mediating between the public and the public debt. In such a situation, government control over debt issuance would be partially transferred to the savings bank administration. The difficulty would reside mostly in matters of operating costs. That is to say, having savings banks where one could comfortably handle one's accounts and depend on staff to handle individual finances would be a service that individuals with savings to invest were able or willing to dispense with. That way, at least they would not have to face the cost of a financial intermediation service, which was what a savings bank had to offer, that amounted to the difference between interest rates of 3.6% and 6%.

This explains why governments did not invest more in the development of the public savings bank. It would have sufficed, for instance, to withdraw low face value securities from the market, since these were the securities that most directly competed with deposits in the savings bank. The same reading also explains why the savings bank saw some development later, as it points to the existence of a potential market for financial intermediation services. If, in addition, the *Caixa* and the savings bank were deprived of the relative independence from the government the Public Credit Board had always enjoyed, even the board itself would lose interest in the development of a savings bank under its administration. Indeed, it was hard to understand how the board, whose executive board included representatives of its investors, even if in the minority, could approve of the transfer of funds from its own accountancy department, which it ran with some autonomy, to a different accountancy department, that is, the *Caixa* and its savings bank, for which it could not even choose the staff.

With the definitive regulation of 17 August 1881 and the appointment to the savings bank of seven employees whose services were not immediately necessary, the ministry showed its will to establish, within the Public Credit Board, a service more autonomous from the decisions of its executive members. The attentive and experienced António José de Seixas will have noticed the stratagem, which will have motivated his resignation. Moreover, from the point of view of the public savings bank's functioning, the minister's decision was deeply flawed because it put the bank's accounts in deficit. This would have to be paid with the *Caixa*'s profits, therefore by the Public Credit Board, which was the body overseeing the whole public banking structure. In fact, the salary of the seven employees recruited for the savings bank represented an annual expense of 3,900$000. On 30 June 1881, the balance of the deposit account of the savings bank was only 6,568$000. In order to justify that number of employees it would be necessary, as indeed is estimated by the Board in its 1881–1882 report on the *Caixa*, to have an average balance of deposits of at least 300 *contos*; in June 1882 it did not even reach 15 *contos*.[12] Given this situation, every effort to make the savings bank a profitable business would be a futile effort. In 1881, the government placed on the market 10,000 bonds of 5% with the nominal value of 90$000 at the price of 78$875, and the *Caixa* was made to buy them on the same day for 83$000. The dealers profited, to the loss of *Caixa*, 45,944$250 *réis* from this transaction.[13] On 14 November 1881, Fontes Pereira de Melo returned as head of the government and took over the finance ministry himself, replacing Lopo Vaz, who had caused many problems in the relations with the Public Credit Board.[14]

## The wider financial reforms, 1885–1886

In order to correct the actions of the former minister (Lopo Vaz), on 15 December 1882 the Public Credit Board, with the Count of Restelo as president and two new members representing each of the chambers of Parliament, presented a set of proposals for further developing the public savings bank. Heading those proposals was the creation of a popular moveable credit bank operating at the *Caixa* and *Caixa Económica* headquarters and in 'as many branches as needed'. Interest should be set by the administration but could not exceed 8% per year. It was a way of placing the capital deposited with the savings bank or even in the deposit bank itself. This was followed by another proposal with an important scope: to raise the ceiling of deposits with the savings bank. Under the

charter of the *Caixa Económica*, each depositor's annual balance could not surpass 200$000 and the accumulated balance the maximum of 500$000, the new
draft proposed to increase these limits to 500$000 and 1,500$000 respectively.
It was also suggested that interest payments change from annual to half-yearly,
which would marginally increase deposit interest and especially their liquidity.
Regarding asset operations, the Public Credit Board wanted permission from
the government to buy public debt securities, Treasury bonds, and shares and
bonds of any national bank or company on behalf of depositors. A final goal
was to reduce the rigidity of the plan of establishment created by the definitive
regulation of 1881, putting an end to the distinction between employees
working for the *Caixa* and those in the employment of the *Caixa Económica*.[15]
On 30 December 1882, a few days after the presentation of that first list of
proposals, the board also requested that district road funds be entrusted to the
*Caixa*, as had happened to municipal road funds in 1880.

The enlargement of the *Caixa Económica*'s duties and the increase in the
responsibility of the Public Credit Board were well received by the opposition,
even if the board was no longer 'a court with autonomy, as it was before 1834'.
Oliveira Martins, then a major figure of the opposition, supported the increase
in the ceiling on deposits and the constitution of an account for private loans.
Finally, he took issue with the name chosen for the institution to be created
because *caixa* ('bank') was a name of the 'bureaucratic speech', and 'moveable
credit' 'is not understood by the special public for whom the institution is
intended'. He proposed as an alternative the name of *Banco dos Pobres*, or Poor-
man Bank.[16] In this assessment, Oliveira Martins failed to consider the fact that,
in Europe, savings banks did not have a significant proportion of the poor among
their clients, even if the unofficial histories of these institutions still regularly
upheld this distorted image. The attention given by Oliveira Martins to the
board's project for its savings bank appears to show some sympathy for the
institution headed by Pedro Augusto Franco. The Public Credit Board, gen-
uinely concerned with a part of its services that had no movement, did not
seem to be confusing practical issues with matters of principle. The board's
members may have been aware that clients for the savings bank must be
sought among those who had some savings and that were even familiar with
financial intermediation services, especially those offered by the board's general accountancy department.

The report for the reform of *Caixa Económica* presented by the board in
December 1882 was only answered a little over a year later. On 23 February
1884, Hintze Ribeiro presented a draft bill on the *Caixa* in the Parliament
which was included, as some of his predecessors had done, within the set of
bills that had become usual to set forth at the time of discussing the state budget.
The proposal established that the *Caixa* should be given the district road fund, as
well as the funds of the *misericórdias*, hospitals and any other establishments with
state-appointed administrations, among other minor things. Hintze Ribeiro
estimated that entrusting these funds to the public deposit bank would bring an

increase of 40 *contos* to the existing yield of 110. However, this did not come to pass.[17] The minister's proposals generally coincided with those submitted by the Public Credit Board at the end of 1882; however, they failed to meet the board's intention of putting an end to the separation of staff from the savings and deposit banks. The proposal, dated 23 February 1884, was discussed in the editorial of *Jornal do Comércio* on 6 May, in which the 'new conservative party' was accused of 'declaring war on the government's humble and innocent draft for the *Caixa Geral de Depósitos*'. By that time, the *Partido Regenerador* was divided on the constitutional revision, which would put an end to the heredity of peers.[18]

The deputies had more important things to worry about in Hintze Ribeiro's first State Budget. The sixth and final point was a request to the Parliament to give the government permission to issue securities on external debt, perpetual or redeemable, to the amount of 18,000 *contos*. The minister argued this was the amount needed to consolidate the floating debt the state had accumulated in the last years and tackle the extraordinary deficit anticipated for the economic year of 1884–1885. This projection did not include the debt to the *Caixa* the state had accumulated in the meantime, which by June 1883 had reached almost 2,400 *contos*.[19] On 18 March, the finance committee sent to the Parliament their report on the proposals made by the finance minister. The report agreed with the proposals, only making more explicit the possibility of the loan to be placed either in the country or abroad.[20] The committee was quick, not only in drawing up an opinion, but also in turning the minister's proposal into a draft bill. This bill, dated 10 March 1884, was presented to the Parliament some days later, on 19 March. However, the draft was not immediately discussed, and, as had happened before in other circumstances, the matter was forgotten. The debate on the draft about the *Caixa Económica Portuguesa* was postponed, only taking place in May 1885.

To address the problem of state pension payments, that same year Hintze Ribeiro presented draft legislation towards the creation of a National Pensions Fund (*Caixa Nacional de Aposentações*). This fund was also be managed by the Public Credit Board through the *Caixa*, as was the case with the *Caixa Económica*. Probably to gather more support and help have his proposal turned into law, the minister included the board's old claim regarding the change of regime of the establishment plan of the banks already under its administration, seen as immutable. With this measure, the finance minister wanted to extend the utility of the *Caixa* from just financing the floating debt to also cover the payment to state pensioners, which by 1885 represented an annual expense of 350 *contos*. It also aimed to establish a pension system by which civil servants recruited thereafter paid 4% of their salary to the *Caixa*'s coffers, the state matching the total sum of the taxes paid by the workers. Estimates pointed to an expense to the state of 80,000$000 on new employees in 1886, the year following the creation of this public bank. A 4% tax on their salaries towards the pension fund would result in an income of 3,200$000, the state contributing an equivalent sum to the *Caixa Nacional de Aposentações*. The capital thus collected would be handed over to the administration of the *Caixa*, who should manage it in the same way as the remaining funds under its care. This measure had few immediate implications, since it involved only civil servants appointed after the law's approval, as the amounts in question suggest.

Even before the discussion of Hintze Ribeiro's proposals concerning the *Caixa* and the institutions under its custody, the deputy Rocha Cardoso presented a draft bill on the Bank's workforce for a second reading in April 1885. This draft aimed to restructure the organisation of the staff, aligning it with that of the Public Credit Board's accountancy department and to expand it from 32 to 39 employees by offering permanent contracts to seven workers who at the time were working under fixed term contracts.[21] The draft must have been approved, if not actively promoted, by the Public Credit Board, and it complemented the provisions in the package of measures Hintze Ribeiro had presented the previous year and which had not been followed up. There had not been this many proposals in Parliament concerning the *Caixa* since its creation in 1876. The finance minister's goal was to divert more financial resources into the public bank and change its statutory tasks.

The first government proposal to return to the Parliament after going through the finance committee, on 20 May 1885, concerned the delivery of funds from district road funds, *misericórdias*, and other charitable institutions with government-appointed administrations. As to the latter, the finance committee extended the proposal's scope such that virtually every institution under state control would be required to deposit their funds with the *Caixa*. After the proposal was wholly approved on the same day it was presented, debate moved on to the specific issues therein in the following session. Sometimes, generally in the middle of a relatively long period of a single government, as was the case here, the Parliament did indeed work this fast. There seemed to be a consensus about entrusting those institutions' funds to the *Caixa*, due to no one questioning the real issues underlying this kind of measure any longer. The most important of these was, of course, that a central state bank was gradually being established for the safekeeping of capital emanating from the state itself or administered by boards controlled by the state. The funds for the regional road, for example, were kept by district councils. Delivering those funds to the *Caixa* with a deposit interest of 2% implied a reduction of the councils' functions. That same member of Parliament (MP), perhaps with excessive optimism, questioned why general district councils were not allowed to deposit their funds in banks where, according to him, they could earn 4% or 5% interest. These funds left the state coffers to be delivered to the councils; keeping them in the vaults of a public bank seemed reasonable, especially as that would bring them an income they could hardly obtain otherwise.[22]

The draft bill on the transfer of the *misericórdias'* funds was an opportunity to recall in Parliament the difficulties in applying the funds of those institutions and in the development of regional agricultural or industrial credit banks. The deputy from the *Partido Proressista* (José Frederico Laranjo), reminded the Parliament that the *misericórdias* had a fundamental role in granting credit to the communities where they were established from the capital generated by the sale of their assets. *Misericórdias*, hospitals, and other piety or charitable institutions had to sell their property in exchange for public debt securities. In 1867, during his short and troubled passage through a coalition government (led by Joaquim António de Aguiar), Andrade Corvo managed to have a law approved which allowed the *misericórdias* to place the capital obtained from the sale of their property in the creation of credit banks for agriculture. Few *misericórdias* took advantage of this law, with some honourable exceptions, such as *Banco Agrícola de Viseu*. Frederico Laranjo explained this story to Parliament. The deputy was not willing to see this business taken by the state, or rather, by the *Caixa*. Once again, the 'small steps' approach would bear results. As such, the capital of the *misericórdias* had placed with banks should not be delivered to the *Caixa*. The bank should receive only those funds that did not have 'immediate application', as would be specified by the Parliament's high chamber. It would not have been difficult for the minister to give in to this ambition, since the amounts in question were very small. It was above all a matter of principle, and no government would put itself in a position of liability for failing to promote ideas on agricultural banks or other economy-fostering institutions.

The *Caixa* had already proved useful to the financial administration of the state over almost a decade. This was particularly visible in the role it played in placing floating debt at a lower cost than that offered by banks, banking houses, or private financiers. In addition, fears regarding the consequences of a growth of deposits in the *Caixa* had disappeared, as it had become clear there was enough room for manoeuvre whilst placing this increase in floating debt, or possibly funded debt, through the purchase of securities.

In the Parliament, besides those two deputies speaking for the *misericórdias*, no other voice was heard in defence of either the Public Credit Board or the Bank of Portugal, or indeed any of the other banks. Thus, either there was no one in the Parliament who felt the need to defend those institutions, or the new broadening of tasks intended for the *Caixa* was not an actual problem or threat to the established businesses. The only problem the board would experience would be the increase in workload, which should be addressed in a draft bill on the establishment plan awaiting discussion in Parliament. The banks were unlikely to take an interest in the funds of the *misericórdias*, all the more because the main problem the Portuguese banking system faced was not lack of funds, but rather a shortage of alternatives to safely place them. Finally, the Bank of Portugal, who could be divested of the contract for the payment of the retired classes, was not particularly concerned by that loss as long as there were other businesses with the state available, as indeed there were. The bank's executive board was possibly getting ready for more profound reforms that would come to establish a clear distinction between its role in the Portuguese finance and banking system and that of all the other institutions, including, of course, the *Caixa*. Once again, this proposal for keeping funds of the *misericórdias* in the *Caixa* followed the French model, where *Caisse de dépôts et consignations* kept such deposits along with those of the savings banks. The most significant difference was that in Portugal the deposit bank had its own savings bank since, unlike the French case, it had not developed from private initiative.

With remarkable speed, two days later, on 25 May, the Finance Committee returned the draft bill on the reorganisation of the staff of the *Caixa* and the *Caixa Económica* to the Parliament. Few changes had been made to the draft presented on 8 April 1885. The draft included the Public Credit Board's demands, namely, the integration of workers with fixed-term contracts as permanent employees, extending the staff number to 39, and the combination of the two different plans for the establishment of the *Caixa Económica* into one. Mandatory deposits having been broadened, it was thus time to consolidate and reorganise the staff. Everything was heading in the right direction, with no major problems. The next step was having the proposed expansion of the *Caixa Económica*'s operations approved. This debate on the development of the public savings bank revolved around the same arguments already presented in previous discussions in Parliament, in newspapers or in various books, about private savings banks. *Caixa*'s director between 1877 and 1879 (Pedro Augusto de Carvalho) and author of the Parliament's finance committee's draft, argued that savings banks had not developed earlier in Portugal due to 'poor education in the country for a proper understanding of the value and reach of institutions of this nature'.[23] But the fact was that the government, the *Caixa*'s administration and the Public Credit Board were not truly interested in promoting deposits from the public at *Caixa Económica*.

Before seeking to increase that liabilities account, it was convenient for all parties that *Caixa*'s administration make the most of the other liabilities account, namely the mandatory deposits one, for the simple reason that these were paid a 2% interest instead of the 3.6% required by law to mandatory deposits. In addition, it was not yet certain that all mandatory deposits delivered to the *Caixa* would be placed with the state. Between June 1886 and June 1887, the balance of the mandatory deposits account rose from 4,311 to 5,256 *contos* due to the delivery of the funds from the *misericórdias* and public roads construction. The account of deposits from the public rose, albeit to the small value of 188 *contos*. This increase, which amounted to little more than 1,000 *contos*, was matched by a rise of 997 *contos* of the unplaced funds. The Public Credit Board would not be interested in increasing deposits in its new savings bank until the financial balance of the institution was ensured. Otherwise, it would be relatively easy to promote such increase by simply lifting all the legal and logistical constraints that limited the maximum amount for deposits with the bank. In fact, in 1885 the *Caixa Económica* already paid a 3.6% interest, 0.6% more than that paid by its closest competitor, the savings bank of *Montepio Geral*. This difference would increase in 1886, when the general assembly of the *Montepio Geral de Lisboa*, perhaps because of difficulties in placing its deposits, decided to lower the interest rate to 2%.

It is hard to conclude that the impact of the legal limits on deposits with the *Caixa Económica* were the most significant. To begin with, each account could only receive up to 200$000 per year, and any amount above the balance of 500$000 did not earn any interest. These values were, by all accounts, very small; 500$000 corresponded to the value of six public debt securities or, for example, the wage of 90 days' work by a municipal paviour. Another significant impediment from the 1880 law governing the *Caixa Económica* concerned the constitution and handling of deposit accounts. To confirm a deposit made in a branch of the *Caixa Económica* outside Lisbon, a declaration of conformity had to be requested from the administration at the head office and wait for it to be sent to the respective branch, despite there being stamped passbooks held at the agencies when the deposits were made. This process entailed delays arising from bureaucracy and the slowness of transport. In addition, in the first two months of each year, depositors had to send their passbooks to Lisbon to confirm all the movements that had been made in the branches. Any depositor not complying would simply lose their right to all interest in their account. Potential *Caixa Económica* clients living outside Lisbon not only had to deliver their savings to the same place where they paid their taxes, but also had to endure a wait until deposits were confirmed, and they were responsible for periodically sending the respective passbooks to the capital.

To understand these provisions, one must keep in mind that communication was difficult between the main cities in the country. Indeed, the finance committee's draft asserted that the provisions of the law establishing the *Caixa Económica* had been 'almost verbatim transcribed from bills regulating this matter in other countries'. However, as the same deputy subsequently noted, the creation of a central savings bank in England, namely, the Post Office Savings Bank, established in 1861, happened at a time when there were already independent savings banks spread around the country. These served as intermediaries between their clients and the central administration who managed deposits. When the draft for the *Caixa*'s first provisional regulation was presented, the Public Credit Board supported the centralisation of operations in Lisbon. Acknowledging it could be inconvenient, however, the Board endeavoured to highlight its advantages: not only did it harmonise service, but it also facilitated its supervision, all the more because district tax offices were experiencing a shortage of labour. In Lisbon, the situation was not much better. Indeed, the *Caixa Económica*'s headquarters, with its nine employees, was housed in Praça do Comércio on the fourth and highest floor of a building it shared with the Public Credit Board and the *Caixa*. The board's accounting office occupied the ground floor for easy access to the public, given that it was the service responsible for issuing public debt securities and paying its interest and amortisations.[24] Given that this office was physically accessible and offered

51

50$000 and 90$000 securities with an effective interest of 6% or more in a normal situation, few would venture to the fourth floor to hand in their savings, facing practical obstacles and earning a mere 3.6% interest.

## Notes

1 Diário da Câmara dos Deputados, 15 January 1880, pp. 74–75.
2 According to the numbers presented by Barros Gomes to the Parliament, Portugal had a nominal public debt of 3$000 per inhabitant, surpassed only by France (4$426), England (3$746) and Italy (3$590), and higher than those in Hungary (2$088), Austria (1$979), Belgium (1$559), Saxony (1$514), and Prussia ($500) (see Diário da Câmara dos Deputados, 15 January 1880, pp. 75–76).
3 Diário da Câmara dos Deputados, 25 February 1880, p. 599, 1847, 2187.
4 Diário da Câmara dos Deputados, 15 January 1880, pp. 85–86.
5 Vieira (1905), pp. 83–84, 93.
6 Diário da Câmara dos Deputados, 15 January 1880, p. 86.
7 Sousa (1916), pp. 318–319; Martins (1988), p. 126.
8 Consulta da Junta do Crédito Público, 2 July 1881, in Seixas (1882), p. 36.
9 The salary would change from 700$000 yearly to 450$000 with a bonus of 112$500. See Seixas (1882), pp. 40–43.
10 Seixas (1882), pp. 42–47.
11 'Sopeira' was a popular and slightly pejorative designation for female domestic servants. See Sousa (1916), p. 307, Seixas (1882), p. 61, Bulhões (1884), p. 84, Martins (1988), p. 131, and Mata (1993), pp. 220–221.
12 Relatório da Caixa Geral de Depósitos, 1881–1882, p. 13.
13 Carvalho (1889), pp. 45–46.
14 Fuschini (1899), anexos, p. 51.
15 Relatório da Caixa Geral de Depósitos, 1881–1882, pp. 111–118.
16 Martins (1954), p. 7n.
17 Diário da Câmara dos Deputados, 29 February 1884, pp. 401–468 (particularly pp. 465–466).
18 Mónica (1994), pp. 132–134.
19 'Contas da Caixa Geral de Depósitos' and Diário da Câmara dos Deputados, 18 March 1884, p. 734.
20 Diário da Câmara dos Deputados, 18 March 1884, p. 734.
21 Diário da Câmara dos Deputados, 9 April 1885, pp. 1037–1040.
22 Diário da Câmara dos Deputados, 22 May 1885.
23 Diário da Câmara dos Deputados, 22 June 1885.
24 Diário da Câmara dos Deputados, 30 June 1887.

# 5

# THE FINANCIAL REFORMS, 1886–1890

The death of Portugal's most important politician in the third quarter of the nineteenth century and the dissections between his successors paved the way for the end of the *fontismo*: the policy of governing the country with a dangerous mix of taxes and domestic and external public debt. The rise of the opposition party, the *Partido Progressista* (Progressive Party), in 1886 brought important changes to the financial system. After a relatively calm first decade, the *Caixa Geral de Depósitos* received some more attention from the government. The new government negotiated a contract with the Bank of Portugal, according to which the bank would take charge of some of the responsibilities of managing public funds until then held by the Public Credit Board. By this agreement, the board was practically emptied of its functions. However, since the board formally maintained the supervision of state payments, it could not simply be dissolved. Likewise, the board was still the administrator of the *Caixa*. The ambitions of the Progressive government stemmed from the desire to reorganise the financial system. This included the concession of the monopoly of issuing banknotes to the Bank of Portugal, as well as a larger role as treasurer of the state, which necessitated that the responsibility of the Public Credit Board had to be reduced. These goals were achieved without demurral from the Regeneration opposition. The lack of opposition can be ascribed to the momentary weakening of the party, as its president, Fontes Pereira de Melo, died in early 1887, but it was also due to many members being favourable to the strengthening of the Bank of Portugal's role as central bank. However, the Progressive government met resistance when it tried to subject the *Caixa*'s administration to its own control. This failure was facilitated by the government's loss of political weight, as its reformist policy became more extreme, and as the *Partido Regenerador* (Regeneration Party) regained strength under the new leadership of Hintze Ribeiro. These years between 1886 and 1889 crucially show that there were in fact two different currents regarding the financial administration of the state. Once more, the history of the *Caixa* provides an excellent lens through which to look at these issues.

53

## The Progressive financial revolution

In February 1886, the newly elected head of the *Partido Progressista* (José Luciano de Castro), formed a government. It was the second time the party came to power, but it now showed more vitality than in its previous period of government, from June 1879 until May 1881. In addition, there were signs of erosion in the sphere of the *Partido Regenerador*, and some desire for change. That is suggested by the fact that Fontes Pereira de Melo himself, two days before leaving the government, proposed the appointment of his opponent, Luciano de Castro, to the Council of State, which was in all respects a clear sign of willingness to rotate power.

The Progressive government emerged strongly, benefitting from the presence of important figures within its political spectrum, such as Emídio Navarro, who took over the Ministry of Public Works and, above all, Mariano de Carvalho, who headed the Finance Ministry. Only Oliveira Martins had been left out, due to objection from Mariano de Carvalho himself. This new government would last five years. The common practice was that the monarch would appoint the new head of government, the Parliament would dissolve, and elections would be called which confirmed the ruling party.[1] On this occasion, Progressives indeed called elections, but Parliament did not immediately reconvene, and, as such, they ruled for about a year as a 'dictatorship'. During this period, they implemented a number of reforms, the list of which has been compiled in a collection of laws.[2] Parliament was due to reconvene in January 1887 for the statutory three-month session, but that only happened in April. This adjournment was caused by the creation of state monopoly on tobacco, that is, the *régie*, by the law of 27 January 1887; it was to become one of the most controversial measures of the government of Luciano de Castro. Mariano de Carvalho was a well-known figure of the financial and political spheres, and his joining the government pleased many. Referring to his 'particular friend', João Franco, perhaps with some irony, commented in Parliament shortly after its opening that 'Mr. Mariano de Carvalho becoming Finance Minister brought hope to many of seeing the State finances balanced once and for all'. This hope could be bolstered by the fact that the new government had plans for reorganising the administration of public finances, having as pillars the Public Credit Board, the *Caixa*, the Bank of Portugal, and the remaining banks and banking houses of the country.[3] The distinguishing character of the new minister's ideas became evident in the reforms he strived to introduce.

The contrast between Regeneration and Progressive financial policy should not be overstated, for in many instances it was more a case of differences between individuals than between parties or ideologies. The reforms initiated by Mariano de Carvalho sought to confer on the Bank of Portugal a role closer to that of a central bank, which implied granting it the monopoly of money issuance for the whole country and the reduction of its purely commercial functions. The same João Franco, who took it upon himself to assess the new minister in Parliament on the opposition's behalf, concluded that 'in my view […] it has never been easier to delimit the divergent theories and doctrines of both parties on the matter of finance as at present'.[4]

After elections had taken place and Parliament had again started work, on 16 April 1887, Mariano de Carvalho presented one of the longest state budgets the Parliament had ever analysed.[5] Its central point was, once again, 'to reduce the nominal value of the Portuguese public debt'. The minister was in a singularly favourable position to carry out his proposals, since the financial markets at home and abroad were in a particularly advantageous situation for the placement of public debt securities. Apparently, remittances from Portuguese emigrants in Brazil had been increasing since 1886, while wine exports to France had risen to unusual levels, which meant that Portugal was relatively well stocked with gold and foreign currency. The relatively good state of the country's balance of payments situation was reflected in the quotation of securities of the funded public debt. Thus, the price of the 3% consolidated debt rose from 47.2% on 1 July 1885 to 49.5% one year later and 55.3% and two years later. This meant a gradual lowering of the effective interest rate of those same securities from 6.36% in 1885 to 5.42% in 1887.[6]

The fall of the floating debt interest rate was even more pronounced. In fact, between August 1886 and sometime in early 1887, the government sold, on three different occasions, Treasury bills through a call for tenders from the Treasury Directorate-General (*Direcção Geral de Tesouraria*). Between these security issuances, interest fell from 4.3% to 4%. By this time, interest in London was between 3.5% and 4%, in Paris, 3%, and in the Bank of Portugal, the discount rate stood at 5%. The total value of these three issues of floating debt securities amounted to about 13,000 *contos* and their subscription had more than doubled, standing at 28,318 *contos*. It was a truly comfortable situation for the state to issue debt, reversing the tendency for rising interest rates that the minister had inherited. When Mariano de Carvalho had taken over in February 1886, interest on domestic floating debt stood at 6.5% and external floating debt at 7.07%.[7]

The death of Fontes Pereira de Melo on 22 January 1887 and the subsequent division of the *Partido Regenerador* he had led paved the way for the reforming impetus of the Progressive minister.[8] However, for the first time in a long while, the state budget presented to Parliament proposed no reforms regarding the *Caixa*, as the Government aimed at a full reshaping of the country's financial structure. Among the first and most important measures of Mariano de Carvalho in public finances was the use of public calls for tenders for the issuance of floating debt, the free export of gold, selling public debt securities in Paris, and introducing them in the German markets. The reforms would relieve the Public Credit Board of part of its functions, and it would no longer receive state revenues allocated to paying the public debt. The Bank of Portugal would be granted the exclusive right to issue banknotes with legal tender, and the role of banker of the Treasury. Finally, the administration of state finances would be centralised in the Public Treasury through a new directorate general of public accounting.[9]

The conversion of the public debt carried out by Mariano de Carvalho to reduce its nominal value would involve, for the first time, the placement of the *Caixa*'s profits. The profit that the bank had begun to bear, though still insignificant in the vast sea of Portuguese public finances, drew the minister's attention. The accumulated value of the issuance of the 3% consolidated public debt had risen, between March 1873 and March 1884, to the astronomical sum of 152,570 *contos*. In 1886, total public debt with the public, that is, not including the titles kept in the state coffers, amounted to 494,000 *contos*, which corresponded to 81% of the Portuguese national product.[10] Such high nominal values of debt were reached in part because they were generally issued as 3% fixed-income securities at a time when interest was around 6%. The increase in consolidated interest from 3% to 5%, for example, would reduce the nominal value of public debt, if no other change occurred, from about 153,000 *contos* to 92,000 *contos*.[11] The conversion would enable the amortisation of the external public debt within 75 years.

The minister highlighted that between 1878–1879 and 1884–1885 the *Caixa* had already given the state a profit of 481 *contos*. He anticipated an average annual profit of 100 *contos* for the next few years, which he believed would be enough to amortise the foreign debt. The reckoning was simple because, if the Public Credit Board succeeded in acquiring on the market the 80% Treasury securities, the placement of the 100 *contos* annual profit over 75 years, as foreseen in the minister's plan, would allow the repayment of 199,790 *contos* of the debt. It really was an extraordinary, inexpensive, and indeed miraculous operation, and it was approved the day following its discussion. Whatever the reasoning behind Mariano de Carvalho's financial operation, the fact is that it entailed changing the law ruling the placement of the *Caixa*'s profits and would change the rules of the game of the financial system in Portugal for years to come, and not necessarily for the better.

## A new statute for the Bank of Portugal

The financial reform by Mariano de Carvalho also entailed a new contract between the state and the Bank of Portugal with a view to entrusting the monopoly of note issuance for the whole country. The bank already had that prerogative for the region of Lisbon, and other banks had fiduciary issuing competence in Porto. As noted in the opinion of the Parliament's finance committee, the minister's proposal was not original, since it revived an initiative made in 1877 by António de Serpa, then minister of finance, following the banking crisis of 1876.[12] In exchange for the monopoly on money circulation, the Bank of Portugal undertook to pay the pensions owed to public servants. At the time, the total pensions to be paid added up to 1,800 *contos* per year, which was by all accounts a significant sum. By the terms of the contract, the government was responsible for paying only 800 *contos* of that amount, in addition, of course, to the interest and repayment of the proposed 1,000 *contos* loan. To that end, it should have constituted a national pension fund linked to the *Caixa*. The amortisation cost of the 1,000 *contos* loan accompanying the contract was 1% of the capital value. The interest had been calculated considering the quotation of the 3% consolidated securities, which, at 54%, would be 5.5%, fluctuating in line with the prices of those securities in London. This way, the government charged the Bank of Portugal with the payment of old pensions while at the same time promoting the establishment of the National Pensions Fund, the civil servants pension fund. This dual role, which happened in other fields, is another sign of the existence of a common business area between that bank and the *Caixa*. The contract had resulted from a call for tender launched by the law of 29 July 1887, to which only the Bank of Portugal responded. The Bank of Portugal also formally became the treasurer general of the state. This meant that from then on it would receive the funds deposited in the coffers of the different public revenue offices, to which it would pay 3% interest. Finally, the central bank would open a current account for supplies to the government, that is, for its floating debt, up to 2,000 *contos*, charging 4% interest. In the meantime, on 28 October 1887, just before the new contract came into force, Mariano de Carvalho appointed Pereira de Miranda, an influential member of the *Partido Progressista*, to replace the similarly aligned Barros Gomes as head of the bank.

Oliveira Martins, the historian-cum-politician who closely surveyed the financial operations of the state, and then a member of the Parliament's finance committee, supported the project, arguing that floating debt was being placed on the markets at rates of 8%. According to him, the working balances of the central administration would amount, in December 1886, to 1,800 *contos* in cash and 6,553 *contos* in advance payments and other funds, totalling 8,353 *contos*. These figures were beyond the *Caixa*'s capacity, both administratively and financially. It should be recalled that the Bank of Portugal had undertaken to pay a 3% interest on such deposits, therefore higher than the 2% interest the *Caixa* paid to mandatory deposits, and that represented a burden to the Bank of around 250 *contos* per year. According to Oliveira Martins, another important clause in the agreement between the state and bank was the new freedom given to the latter to change its discount rate, without prior authorisation from the government, to anything up to a maximum of 7%. Thus, by entrusting the funds in the public revenue offices to the Bank of Portugal and opening a current account between that bank and the government, Mariano de Carvalho showed a clear preference for that bank, to the disadvantage of the *Caixa* and its administrator, the Public Credit Board. The *Caixa* received the public revenue funds of the municipal and district authorities, including road funds, the *misericórdias*, and deposits resulting from the action of the courts, that is, publicly contracted collateral from jobs with financial responsibility. Beyond the *Caixa*'s reach remained only the role of treasurer of the central government.

However, the contract the government and the bank signed on 10 December 1887 granted that financial institution another business, one which could be of interest to the *Caixa*, namely a current account open to the state to the limit of 2,000 *contos* with interest of 4% to debit and 3% to credit.[13] By 1886, the government had already determined that the *Caixa*'s coin reserves should be paid into the Bank of Portugal as the general public bank. The Public Credit Board made no protest against this measure, which the government had carried out driven by lack of money, 'without the consent of Parliament and by means of a simple regulatory provision of the issuing bank'.[14] The *Caixa* struggled to find placement for the funds it received in deposit. Loans to the state were one of the best investments for banks, as shown, for example, by the unfortunate experience of the banking upsurge that ended in the systemic crisis of 1876. In the 1881–1882 financial year, the *Caixa* held 1,554 *contos* in current account loans to the state, and 1,361 *contos* in public debt securities. In 1885–1886, current account loans fell sharply to 103 *contos*, securities raising only to 1,836 *contos*. In counterbalance, the balance of the cash-in-hand account increased from 360 *contos* in 1881–1882, to 644 *contos* in 1885–1886, continuing to rise significantly in the subsequent years.

Mariano de Carvalho's decision to hand over the public revenue funds to the Bank of Portugal and to open a current account between that bank and the state could have had other, less obvious reasons, but the fact that the conditions offered by the Bank were better than those the *Caixa* could ever grant was justification enough. The Bank of Portugal's asset and liability interest margin was only 1%. In *Caixa Económica Portuguesa* (CEP), for example, the margin between what was paid to depositors and the average interest rate of its investments was somewhat higher, since it paid 3.6% to deposits and received 5% from the *Caixa*. The *Caixa* paid 2% to mandatory deposits, and, therefore, the 4% interest the state would pay the bank would be sufficient to balance the *Caixa*'s accounts.

In addition to a low financial margin, the Bank of Portugal also had to account for the burden of the salaries of the accounting officers, who were now under its responsibility, as well as the cost of transfers between the various points in the country where taxes and other revenues of the state were collected. The 1887 agreement led the bank to assume functions that would fit within the *Caixa*'s responsibilities. The government showed manifest inclination to entrust these charges to the largest bank in the country, possibly for purely financial reasons. If assigned to the *Caixa*, the amounts involved more than 3,000 *contos* given the conditions at the time would have to be used in credits to the government or to municipal authorities. In the bank's custody, these amounts could either be used in loans to the state through its current account, which could go up to 2,000 *contos*, or invested in other ways.

The fact the Bank of Portugal and the *Caixa* could offer the state the same type of service had already been noted on previous occasions, namely regarding savings banks, the management of the public deposit funds, and current account loans. At the time, these coincidences of interest did not provoke any kind of conflict. Neither the bank's executive board nor any deputy or journalist in its defence opposed the creation of the *Caixa* or any of the legislative measures adopted to foster its growth. By the time of the 1887 contract, some opposition might have been expected from the Public Credit Board, but it did not come to pass. Indeed, the care to avoid further favouring the Bank of Portugal regarding, for instance, loans on pawned public debt securities to individuals, a form of business the bank continued to engage in, shows that the government did not want to jeopardise some of the operations the *Caixa* also engaged in. In fact, the *Caixa* could lend on pawned securities up to a maximum of 80% of their market value. The 1887 contract gave the Bank of Portugal the possibility of doing the same, but up to 90% of the value of those securities in the national or foreign markets. Two deputies from the two main political parties, the *Regenerador* and the *Progressista*, proposed that the *Caixa* was allowed to lend up to 90%, which was approved.[15]

The law authorising the government to consign the monopoly of issuing banknotes with legal tender in exchange for services to the state was approved on 29 July 1887. On 10 December, the contract with the Bank of Portugal was signed. Five days later, with Parliament now closed, the government published a decree with the contract's regulation. On the same day, another decree created the Directorate-General of Public Debt (*Direcção-Geral da Dívida Pública*) and remodelled the Public Credit Board.[16] Although it did not put an end to the Board, it did divest the institution of its remaining responsibilities. From that moment, it was reduced to a relatively irrelevant advisory role, limited, as the board came to acknowledge after its restoration in 1893, almost to giving an opinion on matters of public debt the government deemed pertinent to consult it on. And as the government never thought it necessary to hear this corporation, it can be said of the Public Credit Board that it only existed in name.[17] The responsibility of the Public Credit Board in the administration of the public debt faded with the new statutes of the Bank of Portugal in force since 1 January 1888. However, the board would not remain for long divested of its powers: the approaching financial crisis would impose its renewal with a view to recovering the confidence of creditors in the Portuguese state's commitment to fulfil its financial obligations. Moreover, the board also kept its functions as administrator of the *Caixa*, as well as the other financial institutions connected to it, namely the savings bank and the retirement fund.

## Government control

Once the role of the Public Credit Board had been reduced, Mariano de Carvalho turned his attention to reforming the *Caixa*'s administration. Thus, when presenting the state budget at the beginning of 1888, the minister at last included the *Caixa* in the set of public administration reform proposals for that year. The plan was intended to change the way the deposit bank was managed, as well as the type of operations it was allowed to perform. According to the minister, the purpose was to meet the changes brought by the decree of 15 December 1887, which had created the Directorate-General of Public Debt. The *Caixa*'s administration was to be given more executive powers, thus 'further concentrating the duties and responsibilities, and creating by the side of the administrative corporation [the Public Credit Board] another one with fiscal duties'.[18] The minister wanted the *Caixa* to have an executive board, a role that would be fulfilled by the Public Credit Board, now with more powers, and a fiscal council. The executive board would comprise a governor, a position assigned *ex officio* to the chairman of the Public Credit Board, a deputy governor, elected by the Parliament, and a third member, chosen by the Chamber of Peers. An important detail of this proposal was that the governor was appointed for life, as was the rule with the directors-general of the state. The fiscal council, for its part, would be composed of the four remaining members of the Public Credit Board's executive board, being chaired by the respective dean. Instead of receiving a fixed annual stipend as until then, both boards would be paid a percentage of the *Caixa*'s profits, namely 2.5% to the executive board and 1.5% to the fiscal board. Finally, the minister's proposal also determined that the executive board meet every week, and the fiscal council every month. Mariano de Carvalho also wanted to grant the *Caixa* permission to acquire public debt securities and shares or bonds of the Bank of Portugal and the *Companhia do Crédito Predial Português* on behalf of depositors who so requested. Furthermore, he wanted the *Caixa* to start managing the collection of interest on state securities in the hands of the *misericórdias* and similar institutions. Both types of operations already pertained to the *Caixa Económica*. However, since the savings bank only had facilities in Lisbon, the minister wanted to use the branches of the *Caixa* to extend those operations to the rest of the country.

This proposal resulted in the election of two new board members and the separation of administrative and fiscal functions. The Public Credit Board was segmented: its chairman took the role of governor, or administrator, and the remaining members constituted the fiscal council. The Parliament, whose majority was held by the *Partido Progressista*, would choose the deputy governor. If the proposal was successful, Mariano de Carvalho would have a supportive majority in the *Caixa*'s administration, provided the board's chairman, the count of Restelo, who had already been reappointed in office by a Regeneration majority, maintained his allegiance to the party. The finance committee's opinion endorsed the minister's justification of the administrative reform he proposed for the deposit bank. Since the Public Credit Board's accountancy department had been deprived of its functions, it busied itself with the administration and supervision of the *Caixa*. However, when, on 31 December 1887, the finance committee presented in Parliament a draft law which, among other things, created the post of governor of the *Caixa*, conferred *ex officio* and for life on the Public Credit Board's chairman, and the opposition reacted vehemently. In effect, this was installing the Count of Restelo indefinitely as governor of a public institution. *Jornal do Comércio* immediately contested the government's project, even before it was released by the finance committee on 16 January 1888. At that point, the newspaper was still run by António de Serpa, Fontes's successor as head of the *Partido Regenerador*, and according to a Progressive MP, he had written the article himself.[19] The commentary was much harsher than the paper's customary pieces. In the years to come, *Jornal do Comércio* would harden its tone even more under the direction of Eduardo Burnay, but already the Regeneration ranks showed unusual concern about this Progressive government over which the party leader, Luciano de Castro, seemed to have little control.

The newspaper's criticism of the *Caixa*'s new administration and supervisory organs may have had little difficulty finding approval among its readers. The author made an analysis of the project's writing, noting two different styles: in one of them he believed to have found the hand of the finance minister himself. It is not possible today to judge the accuracy of this deduction, but the differences in style it pointed out are plain to see. Indeed, the part concerning the assignment of new operations to the *Caixa* is explained in the same vein as equivalent legislation produced in previous years. Conversely, everything regarding the new form its management should take and the earnings of the board members is conveyed in a confusing way. Putting aside the picturesque aspects of poor drafting, opposed by *Jornal do Comércio*, the project is worthy of careful analysis.

The creation of the position of governor of the *Caixa* with 'the status and other benefits enjoyed by the Ministry of Finance's directors general', as well as life appointment, created some problems. In fact, the *Caixa*'s governor was, by inherence, the chairman of the Public Credit Board, who was appointed by the government for a period of three years. This led *Jornal do Comércio* to conclude with some humour: 'If the chairman of the Public Credit Board is the Governor of both public banks, since the first is elected for a fixed term, as are all board members, and the second chosen for life, after a few years we will have as many governors of the *Caixa* as there are stars in the sky'. The article carried on its criticism, showing how the new proposed structure was difficult to achieve. As the article explained, all members of the Public Credit Board, barring the chairman, would form the *Caixa*'s fiscal council, due to supervise the deposit bank's administration, whose board was headed by a governor. The governor was simultaneously the chairman of the Public Credit Board, and as such also presided over the members of the fiscal council. As explained:

> On the first floor of the building, the governor of the two banks has leverage and a casting vote in the fiscal council; on the second floor, the governor is, at least twice a month, judged by the first floor neighbours, who will step above him in supervision and judgement duties. Who has ever seen such mess?[20]

The newspaper does not offer any alternative to this proposal, which shows there were points whose solution was not necessarily simple. Indeed, it made sense, as was argued in the Parliament when discussing the project of the finance committee, that the *Caixa* should have a governor able to deal directly with the minister of finance. The directors-general who dealt directly with ministers were indeed appointed for life. Since its establishment in 1837, the Public Credit Board, made up of five members, had under its responsibility an accountancy office that administered the service of the public debt. In January 1877 the department for the administration of the *Caixa* was added, created by law the previous year. Immediately below the board's members, there were two management positions, one per department: the general accountant of the board, who was also accountant of the *Caixa*, and the latter's director. After having had the management of the public debt taken from its control, the Public Credit Board became responsible only for the administration of the *Caixa Geral de Depósitos*. However, the board was still formally an advisory body for the government on matters of public debt and for that reason could not be merely converted into the deposit bank's administrator.[21] This solution, however, was not brilliant. It was indeed a clumsy political move by the minister, who could surely expect the opposition to object to the creation of two more member places in the *Caixa*'s administration, and to increasing the salary of all the members.

The changes introduced by the draft law of the finance committee included a new composition for the fiscal council: it was to be chaired by the director-general of Public Accounting, with two other executives, places to be filled by the members of the Public Credit Board chosen by the security holders. The board's chairman and the two members elected by the two chambers of Parliament would be in charge of running the *Caixa*. This was clearly a much simpler project: the deposit bank's administration was entrusted to a body emanating from the government and Parliament, while its oversight was carried out by an appropriate directorate-general and by the security holders. The chairmanship in both organs became perpetual and, of course, were assigned by this Progressive government. The changes introduced by the finance committee—whose composition nearly always reflected the majority of the Parliament and therefore the government—did not obtain the approval of the opposition. The Regeneration deputy Ferreira de Almeida was the first in the Parliament to comment on the draft law. He was not a common deputy: he had been arrested by the Progressive government at the time of the Porto riots following the reestablishment of the tobacco monopoly in 1888.[22]

Feelings were running especially high in Portuguese politics that year. Mariano de Carvalho could not really expect the opposition to be restful, especially in face of a project intended to install a man of the minister's confidence in perpetuity at the head of the *Caixa*, now that the institution was starting to show its importance in financing the floating debt. The criticisms in the Parliament added nothing substantial to those published by *Jornal do Comércio*, except referring to the Count of Restelo by name. In face of this, the rapporteur of the finance committee's opinion, a deputy whose name did not appear frequently, recalled with some pertinence that the Count of Restelo had been appointed as a member of the Public Credit Board, in a first instance by the *Partido Progressista*, and a second time by the *Partido Regenerador*. It should be recalled that the Count of Restelo had been appointed on 17 March 1881, a week before the fall of the Progressive government of Braamcamp, and again, for no apparent reason, since the post had a three-year term, on 12 June 1882, by the government led by Fontes Pereira de Melo, after the interregnum of the equally Regeneration-led government of Rodrigues Sampaio. The problem seemed to lie not between the two parties but somewhere else: 'Therefore, both of the branches the *Partido Regenerador* is split into nowadays, I repeat, cannot but accept as a good thing [the permanence in office of the Count of Restelo] [...] since both claim to be heirs to the legacy of Fontes'. The draft bill was still discussed in the following session but did not reach the vote in the Parliament.

In January 1889, Mariano de Carvalho punctually submitted his second state budget to Parliament. In the proposals preceding it he had not insisted on the reform of the *Caixa*'s administration. Among other protectionist measures, he proposed amendments to the legislation on cereals, aiming to put an end to the almost free entry of wheat into the country by increasing import tariffs. He also proposed the creation of a loan for the construction of roads, to the amount of 3,200 *contos*, represented by bonds of 22$500. This was a rather low face value, well below the more common 90$000, but not unprecedented in his time in office. Finally, the minister predicted that in the following two years the country would enjoy the financial prosperity resulting from the public deficit and the floating debt having reached stable levels. At the same time, said the minister, the market value of the consolidated debt securities had been rising since the end of 1886. The floating debt was placed on the markets with an annual interest of 3.63%, while in September 1886 the interest was 4.31%. According to the Minister, these rates were lower than the rates charged by the Bank of Portugal, in January 1889, or in London and Paris, which were between 4.5% and 5%. Once again, Mariano de Carvalho proved to be right. In fact, between the years 1886–1887 and 1887–1888 the actual deficit had fallen for the second year running, thanks to the unusual increase of about 20% in revenue collection by the state. In addition, the market price of the consolidated amount had risen in the four years leading up to July 1889, from 49.5% to 64.1%.[23] The merit he claimed was, however, not unanimously accepted. Even his fellow party member Barros Gomes, who would come to replace him temporarily as finance minister in February 1889, argued by the time the rectified budget was being discussed: 'If my colleague had had to contend with a disadvantageous exchange rate from Brazil and penalising conditions in the European markets, in spite of all the skill he may have, he would not have been able to achieve such a result.'[24]

In the meantime, Mariano de Carvalho had to leave the government as a consequence of one of his major financial moves. Perhaps to make amends to the issuing banks of Porto regarding the Bank of Portugal having been given the monopoly of fiduciary issuance for the whole country since 1888, the minister had promised to compensate them for losses they had incurred through their investments in the 'Salamanca syndicate'. The so-called 'Salamanca syndicate' had been constituted by a group of banks from Porto in 1881, during the Regeneration government of Rodrigues Sampaio, to invest in the construction of the Douro and Minho railways and in the connection to the Spanish trade network by extending the Barca de Alva line up to the Spanish city of Salamanca. The financier Henry Burnay was part of the group and had even obtained the works contract. In the meantime, Mariano de Carvalho had managed to raise Portuguese capital to take control of the national railway company, the *Companhia Real dos Caminhos de Ferro*. He would become director of the company in September 1884.

Thus, Mariano de Carvalho wanted the state to embark on investments in Spanish territory, taking the contract for building and running that country's western line. These decisions, which turned out to be financially ruinous, were grounded in a certain strategy. The intention was to break the *cinta de hierro* ('iron belt') formed by the design of the Spanish railway network, which channelled traffic headed for the peninsula's coast to Vigo or Cadiz instead of Porto or Lisbon.[25] Despite including the 'Regeneration Count' (Burnay), this syndicate was from a city that had long been 'an invincible stronghold of the *Partido Progressista*'.[26] The benefit materialised in the concession of running the harbour of Leixões to a company the syndicate would form. The extraordinary thing about this final move was the fact that Mariano de Carvalho committed the government without previously consulting the president of the council, Luciano de Castro, or even the foreign affairs minister, Barros Gomes, who should also have been involved given the investment was in Spain. The reputation this whole affair brought him severely cut back the minister's leeway for action, especially since, at this time, the *Partido Regenerador* was regaining strength under the new leadership of Hintze Ribeiro.

On 9 November 1889, the director of the mint (*Casa da Moeda*), Augusto José da Cunha, took office as finance minister. However, his time in office would end in just two months, since the Progressive government would fall four days after the British ultimatum to the pretensions of Barros Gomes in the Portuguese colonies of Africa. The ensuing Regeneration government, headed by António de Serpa, tried to heal diplomatic relations with London. However, Hintze Ribeiro, the foreign affairs minister, was humiliated in the Parliament by a motion to support the achievements of the *Partido Progressista* at the time of the presentation of the so-called rose-coloured map. The motion obtained the votes of some deputies from the *Partido Regenerador* close to the minister of justice, Lopo Vaz, a close associate of the former prime minister, Pereira de Melo.[27] Neither Hintze Ribeiro nor António de Serpa were likely willing to endure such affront in Parliament, all the more because a political solution was being drawn that would drive the Ministry of Finance back into the hands of the *Partido Progressista*, to whom many perhaps ascribed a pivotal role in the origin of the financial problems of the country. These were becoming ever more conspicuous, influenced by the public deficit and the reduction in the imports of capital and remittances of emigrants. The governments that followed sought to bring together the forces of the two main parties, but the Ministry of Finance remained in the hands of members of the *Partido Progressista* or men close to it. The following years would see profound changes regarding party politics, public administration, banks and finance, and the monetary system. In this veritable revolution, the *Caixa* briefly disappeared from the political radar, only to re-emerge later to end up benefiting from the changes in the political and financial situation.

# Notes

1 Almeida (1991) and Mónica (1996 and 1999).
2 Colecção de Leis, Decretos e Regulamentos da Ditadura (1887)
3 Pina (1893).
4 Diário da Câmara dos Deputados, 10 June 1887.
5 Diário da Câmara dos Deputados, 16 April 1887.
6 Sousa (1916), p. 420.
7 Diário da Câmara dos Deputados, 16 April 1887, p. 89.
8 Carvalho (1887).
9 Santos (1901), pp. 24 ff.; Mata and Valério (1982).
10 Mata (1993), p. 255.
11 Diário da Câmara dos Deputados, 3 June 1887.
12 Diário da Câmara dos Deputados, 7 June 1877. See also Reis (1994).
13 Mata and Valério (1982), p. 54.
14 Jornal do Comércio, 28 March 1893.
15 Diário da Câmara dos Deputados, 3, 10 and 14 June 1887, pp. 981, 1195, and 1244.
16 Diário do Governo, no. 290, 24 December 1887.
17 Relatório da Junta do Crédito Público, 1893–1894; Sousa (1916), pp. 378–379.
18 Diário da Câmara dos Deputados, 16 January 1888.
19 Diário da Câmara dos Deputados, 23 April 1888, pp. 1192, 1202.
20 Jornal do Comércio, 27 January 1888.
21 Diário da Câmara dos Deputados, 24 April 1888, pp. 1201–1202, 1213–1214.
22 Diário da Câmara dos Deputados, 10 June 1887, p. 1165, 23 April 1888, p. 1195, 1201–1202.
23 Mata (1993), p. 189; Sousa (1916), p. 420.
24 Diário da Câmara dos Deputados, 22 and 24 May 1889.
25 Pinheiro (1987), pp. 56–57, 68–71; Alegria (1990), p. 293.
26 Cordeiro (1999 [1896]), esp. pp. 95–97].
27 Ramos (1994), pp. 185–186.

# 6

# THE FINANCIAL CRISIS, 1890–1892

In the early 1890s, Portugal's public finances were in distress due to the accumulation of high levels of debt principally raised in the Paris and London markets and which had to be redeemed in gold or foreign exchange, which was obtained either by revenues from exports, remittances of Portuguese emigrants in Brazil, or capital imports. This fragile balance was shaken by a fall in Portugal's main export item, wine, by the contraction in remittances due to the financial crisis provoked by the Republican revolution in Brazil. In 1890, a number of crises in other Latin American countries shook the international financial markets strongly affecting Baring Brothers, the main financial intermediary of the Portuguese state. However, the domestic financial crisis was also a consequence of the policies followed by the finance minister Mariano de Carvalho and the government of the *Partido Progressista* that aimed at revolutionising the way public finances were conducted in the country. In fact, by the end of his first year as finance minister (1887), he had curtailed the influence of the Public Credit Board (*Junta de Crédito Público*), an institution that had earned some power in public debt securities markets, while giving greater control to the Bank of Portugal, at whose helm he came to place men of his trust. A year later, the minister struck a blow to the other pillar of the *Partido Regenerador*'s finance structure, the financier Count of Burnay, through the nationalisation of the tobacco trade. With this step, he threw the state into unreasonable amounts of debt. At the time he took these measures, however, optimism prevailed in the markets, which translated into good creditworthiness of the state and reasonable pricing of its funds.

For some years after the departure of Mariano de Carvalho, the Ministry of Finance was to remain in the sphere of influence of the *Partido Progressista* with just a short interregnum, during which João Franco of the *Partido Regenerador* ran the ministry. During Franco's government, the arch political enemy of the *Progressitas*, the Count of Burnay, regained control over the tobacco business with a loan he obtained in Paris, to which he was able to consign the income of tobacco imports. After two further minsters of finance, in May 1891, the office came back to the command of Mariano de Carvalho, who would soon decree the inconvertibility of the notes of the Bank of Portugal and raised the limit of borrowing from the state to the bank. Such measures were not sufficient to stop the crisis, as the currency continued to devalue and the minister resigned to give place to Oliveira Martins. The highly regarded historian-cum-politician was politically unaligned and praised by both the right and the left of the political spectrum, albeit famously closer to the ideas of the *Partido Progressista*, at least in financial matters. In fact, in his writings, Martins had been for some decades a sharp critic of the *Regenerador* or *fontista* system, to the extent that he dared to go through uncharted waters regarding the management of the public debt and the relation between the state and the Portuguese, and more importantly, foreign bondholders.

## How it started

The *Partido Progressista*'s financial policy did not end with Mariano de Carvalho and Augusto José da Cunha, however. The Regeneration government that followed, led by Serpa Pimentel, did not last long. It was doomed from the start, since it included among its ministers the three de facto candidates to succeed Fontes as party leader: Lopo Vaz, João Franco as finance minister, and Hintze Ribeiro in foreign affairs. In the Parliament, Hintze Ribeiro would face a motion of support to the *Partido Progressista* and the publication by Barros Gomes of a famous rose-coloured Map, in a motion that had the votes of some deputies from the *Regenerador Party* who were close to Lopo Vaz. As a result, the government fell.[1] In October 1890, Serpa was replaced as president of the council by the 80-year-old General João Crisóstomo, a military man with a progressive background who had been minister of public works of Loulé in 1864 and 1865, and minister of war in Braamcamp's government between 1879 and 1881. After a brief period with Melo Gouveia as finance minister, the office was again handed over to Augusto José da Cunha.[2] In the meantime, the situation inherited by Cunha was not at all easy, as he later confessed in the Parliament:

> When on 24 November of last year [1890] I took over the affairs of finance, I realised that the imperative, pressing need to supply the Portuguese markets with gold, which had been completely shaken by the political events of the previous September, and the run against Montepio Geral had forced my worthy predecessors to exhaust the Treasury credits in London or Paris. Thus, not only were there no funds in the account of the floating debt, which then amounted to about 33,800 *contos*, ready for paying the bills approaching maturity, but also it was inevitable and urgent, in any transaction that was made, to insure the necessary means to pay the external coupon due on January 1st.[3]

The *Montepio Geral* was still the largest savings and deposit bank in the country, and it was apparently not in a very good position, principally because it invested a large part of its capital in public debt.[4] In spite of the withdrawal of large sums of money, the *Montepio Geral* intended to redeem a loan of 1,000 *contos* from the Bank of Portugal out of 5,500 *contos* invested on floating debt securities. To prevent greater withdrawal of deposits, in 1890, *Montepio's* board reinstated the ceiling from 1 to 5 *contos*, for 3% interest, and to end the 50 *contos* ceiling above which it paid no interest. Total deposits in the mutual savings bank fell even further between 1890 and 1891 (but returned thereafter to an upswing phase until reaching a level close to 15,000 *contos* between 1905 and 1910).[5] Still, the crisis at *Montepio Geral* was not at the top of the long list of problems that the banking and financial sectors faced.

In fact, according to one account, in 1890, the Bank of Portugal could no longer provide the foreign currency the market requested. Down to the end of April of the same year, the bank was only able to increase its reserves by £1,564,384 [that is, 7,040 *contos*], whereas it had sold £2,664,114 [11,989 *contos*]. In addition, the supplies it obtained abroad were reduced by 2,000 *contos*.[6] In other words, there was an excess of demand of foreign currency totalling 6,949 *contos*. According to the same source, this included the 2,000 *contos* reduction of the bank's credit ceiling and 4,949 *contos* resulting from the difference between the value of the foreign currency with which the bank had supplied the market and the value of those it was able to buy back. In order to settle the external accounts, in the absence of other means of payments to the foreign market, it was necessary to resort to exporting gold. In 1891, Portugal, which had traditionally been an importer of gold, had to export 21,535 *contos* of bullion. This was a considerable part of the money in circulation in the country.[7]

In November 1890, the Minister of Finance Augusto José da Cunha attempted to raise a loan in London to pay for the coupon in debt, but he did not succeed, partially because of what had happened to the state's main broker in that market, Baring Brothers. Sensing an opportunity, Count of Burnay proposed to the Portuguese government to negotiate with the French bank *Comptoir d'éscompte* a loan amounting to as much as 13,500 *contos*, which would have had as collateral the tobacco revenues, which was a state monopoly since 1888. Burnay thus had to go back to Mariano de Carvalhoas much as who had instituted the monopoly.[8] What Burnay proposed was already implicit in the 1888 law. Indeed, one of the purposes of the tobacco monopoly was precisely to potentially serve as guarantee for loans to the state. As the minister Augusto José da Cunha himself declared in the Parliament, Burnay's proposal enabled the payment of the foreign debt interest before 1 April 1891. The highly complex financial operation did not involve 'fresh money', as the newspapers reported; it consisted of transferring the credits Burnay had with the Portuguese state to the *Comptoir d'éscompte* with the additional guarantee of the consignment of the income from the tobacco monopoly, which was due to the state. In order to have access to the tobacco monopoly revenue, Burnay offered an annual payment to the state of 4,250 *contos*, to be risen to 4,500 *contos*, in 35 years. In addition, the contractors would lend the state up to 36,000 *contos* in nominal terms. This was a crucial lifeline for the minister who had a limited number of options at hand.[9] The proposal was highly complex, with plenty of caveats and numerous details, and involved a financier, the state, a public monopoly, and a foreign bank, precisely the kind of potentially perilous connections the *Partido Progressista* had planned to put an end to.

The minister and Burnay signed the deal in February 1891, but they did so without the guarantee that the two political parties supporting the government would approve. The deal was highly controversial, not only because it implied the return to the old financial order, which the public associated with the country's financial distress, further aggravated by the fact that the board of the proposed tobacco monopoly company had a majority of foreign members, an unprecedented feature in Portugal's public financial matters.[10] To make matters worse, the Parliament had to extend its session at the request of the contracting company, so that the agreement could be turned into law. In March 1891, the Finance Committee, who had already examined the tobacco monopoly proposal submitted by the government, presented a draft bill identical to the proposal, warning that the government made its wording 'a matter of ministerial pride'. In other words, the government would resign if the wording of the proposal was substantially changed. The deal was approved by law on 23 March 1891.

Burnay's deal faced the reaction in the Parliament of two future finance ministers. The first, Augusto Fuschini, from the *Partido Regenerador*, presented a rather mild objection, criticising the negotiation of the loans contracted by the state abroad being placed in the hands of a single banker, seeing this as a sign of Cunha's lack of expertise in financial matters. Years later, he would describe the operation orchestrated by the 'incapable hands' of João Franco, who had actually charged Burnay with negotiating the deal, as 'one of the biggest mistakes made during our constitutional administration'.[11] Fuschini also praised Mariano de Carvalho, who, in his view, had done a good job with public finance, even succeeding in dividing the 'interests of the bankers'.[12] The second deputy, José Dias Ferreira, accused Cunha of wanting to benefit Burnay at a time when the state had alternatives to the contract. Politically, what happened in Parliament was a union between leaders of the two parties and the opposition of an independent deputy, who was more to the left.

According to Dias Ferreira, the public debt funds at 3% were quoted in the markets at 58%, which meant an effective interest rate of 5.17%, so 'nothing suggested serious disruption in the credit, [and therefore] it was difficult to understand that a loan should be taken at 8%'. In his reply, the minister reminded Dias Ferreira that the government had to face a floating debt whose amount had not been addressed since 1846. He further recalled that he had inherited negotiations with Burnay from his predecessors in the ministry, namely João Franco and Melo Gouveia. He concluded: 'These are the means of borrowing I know: national subscription, tenders for bankers, and the direct collaboration between the government and a syndicate,' adding that, 'unless the illustrious deputy wants the minister to descend to the condition of broker and go knocking door to door'. Dias Ferreira bluntly replied: 'may the two major parties reserve for themselves the glory of the responsibility of approving this measure and leave to independent [members of Parliament] the right of free examination and freedom of vote'.

Crisóstomo's government was able to pay the interest of the external debt in 1891, albeit with some difficulty.[13] However, the agreement left unchanged the amount of the public debt and the interest to be paid. In the 1891–1892 financial year, the revenue for the state from the new tobacco deal amounted to 5,011 *contos*, a substantial rise compared to 2,829 *contos* in the last year of the free trade period when it was levied at the customs. However, the total income of the state did not increase, as the remaining import taxes suffered a sharp decline.[14] Consequently, in May 1891, the government decided to suspend the conversion of the Bank of Portugal's notes for sixty days. This was the last act of the minister before the return of Mariano de Carvalho.

Carvalho's comeback happened at the end of that month, still under the leadership of João Crisóstomo. In this national unity government, the *Partido Progressista* was represented by a man not entirely aligned with the party leader, whereas the *Partido Regenerador* had its main factions represented by the names of Júlio de Vilhena, João Franco, and Lopo Vaz. Lopo Vaz appeared to be on good terms with Mariano de Carvalho, from whom he expected new ideas to straighten out the situation of the Treasury without resorting to extreme measures such as declaring bankruptcy or sweeping cuts in public accounts. This coalition government between the progressive minister and the *Partido Regenerador* would last for about eight months.[15] Carvalho did not disappoint those who admired his ability in the financial administration of the state, as he quickly draw a new plan of reforms, included in the *Lei de Meios* ('Law of Means') presented to the Parliament in June 1891. The plan was given careful attention by the deputies. One of them, the experienced José Frederico Laranjo, displayed his pleasure at the plan's requirements for clarity in the accounts of the state, oversight of accounts and simplification of departments. However, the plan seemed to him to be far too ambitious, since the minister was asking Parliament to be allowed to 'reform freely almost all the public economy, currency, banks, taxes, the payments of public works, the fishing industry, emigration, etc.'. In addition, Mariano de Carvalho wanted to revise the contract with the Bank of Portugal, introduce silver currency, and restore the monopoly on alcohol.[16] In the face of all this ambition, Laranjo declared that he would join the negative vote of all the members of the *Partido Progressista* to that of the leader of the Parliament, Veiga Beirão.

In spite of the opposition in Parliament, Mariano de Carvalho began immediately to take measures to change the country's financial system. On 9 July 1891, he signed the decree indefinitely extending the suspension of exchange of Bank of Portugal notes for gold and silver, something that had been temporarily granted on 10 May of that year. The same decree confirmed the

Bank of Portugal's monopoly of banknote issuance for the whole country, since the 1887 decree had not come to completion. The bank was also provided with the conditions to withdraw the banknotes of some Porto banks still in circulation.[17] The departure of Portugal from the gold standard system opened the possibility for the state to finance itself through the issuance of banknotes by the Bank of Portugal. This was clearly one of the measures with the least domestic and external implications available to the minister to resolve the crisis. The aim of the legal tender was, above all, to counter the depletion of the Bank of Portugal's gold reserves, which was well underway. In December 1891, a new law allowed the bank to extend the limit of fiduciary circulation to 38,000 *contos*, which could eventually be raised by increasing the bank's capital. The law also increased the credit limit of the government's current account with that bank from 2,000 to 6,000 *contos*.[18] However, Carvalho's days in the government were numbered, as he was removed soon after a serious miscalculation, namely not having asked for the necessary government or parliamentary permission to grant loans to the *Banco Lusitano* and the *Companhia Real dos Caminhos de Ferro*, which competed with Burnay in different markets and were closer to the minister of finance (Marquis of Foz and the Count of Moser). Be it either a pretext or the truth, this episode closely resembled Carvalho's previous departure from the ministry in 1889.[19]

## The radical solution

One of the candidates for leadership of the *Regeneradores*, Lopo Vaz, shifted alliances and joined forces with Oliveira Martins, until then in the opposition, with the explicit backing of King D. Carlos, pushed for a cross party government led by José Dias Ferreira with Oliveira Martins as finance minister. The events throughout the year 1892 would be, above all, the result of policies deliberately chosen by the new finance minister. He would have to face renewed difficult times for the service of the public debt, at home and abroad, but the solution he pursued was obviously not the only one, nor perhaps even the best. Oliveira Martins had spent many years contesting what he called *política fontista*, which for him consisted in maintaining imbalances in public accounts financed by resorting to public debt. According to the new finance minister, this strategy had not created the necessary wealth for the country, having instead served to enrich some bankers and politicians. In addition, according to his reasoning, it was becoming clear that the difficult period the country was going through since January 1890 was the result of that policy. Oliveira Martins saw his heading the finance portfolio as an opportunity to put an end to this vicious circle. He was not the first in his position to set such a goal, and the formula he proposed had long been known: raise taxes for paying off the public debt instead of resorting to issuing yet more debt. And at the beginning of 1892, he did precisely that, resorting to the only source of taxes that was immediately accessible and guaranteed profit: the yield of public debt securities. This was a highly unpopular manoeuvre that no one from the *Partido Progressista* or the *Partido Regenerador* had dared pursue. With this measure, Oliveira Martins struck a heavy blow to the Portuguese financial system, changing overnight the rules of a game that had been ongoing for at least forty years. The measure harmed the state's creditworthiness both domestically and abroad, cash circulation, the banking system, as well as thousands of people who had gathered their savings in public debt securities acquired at the Public Credit Board's counters and in Treasury bonds purchased in the Lisbon Stock Exchange.

Whilst the government's leeway abroad was not great, it had not completely disappeared. Tobacco revenue had already been granted to a monopoly, but the state still had secure revenues that could be pawned as collateral for other loans. A clear example was that of the revenues from import taxes. In 1902, Hintze Ribeiro's government would assign them in order to restore the financial order in the country. In 1892, Portugal's situation was still far from one, such as had happened in other countries, like Greece or Egypt, where external creditors obliged national governments to appoint their own representatives to supervisory bodies of public revenue and expenditure. This was, in other words, the situation Augusto Fuschini was already worrying might happen to Portugal when the discussion on the tobacco loan took place in December 1890.[20]

Shortly after taking office in January 1892, by the time the report and draft bills that accompanied the budget were submitted, Oliveira Martins presented an assessment of the situation, which he would use to justify his drastic measures. The minister started by reminding his audience that the economic year 1890–1891 had closed with a deficit of 11,550 *contos* in the public accounts, which corresponded to 29% of total budget revenue. He predicted that in the twelve months leading to June 1892, deficit would reach a minimum of 10,000 *contos*. Concerning the Treasury accounts, the minister presented an estimate for the floating debt amounting to 23,011 *contos*, of which 16,929 were placed in the country and 6,983 *contos* abroad. According to him, the state had no funds to pay the coupons on its debt. Oliveira Martins also recalled that the State was still owed large sums from credits it had given to banks and other companies to help them through critical moments they had faced.

In the case of the Salamanca Syndicate alone, the state was creditor of 5,350 *contos*. The Marquis of Foz, the Count of Moser and *Banco Lusitano* owed the state 500 *contos*. The *Companhia Real dos Caminhos de Ferro* (the Royal Railway Company) owed the sum of 4,390 *contos*. The Bank of Portugal had also received guarantees from the state to the amount of 1,044 *contos* to secure loans to other banks. Finally, the debt of the *Companhia da Mala Real Portuguesa* (the Royal Mail Company) was 910 *contos*. On the whole, the Treasury was a creditor of 11,210 *contos* and had given guarantees in the amount of 1,796 *contos*, totalling 13,006 *contos*. The minister concluded: '[This is] a very large sum of Treasury credits, which would on its own reduce the floating debt by half; however, it is unattainable in a timely manner'.[21] According to Silva Cordeiro, by choosing not to pressure companies to pay their debts, Oliveira Martins repeated what had been done in the first phase of the 1876 crisis. Then the government had sought to 'save the three or four large companies of the country compromised by the fall of exchange rates and hampered from liquidating unavoidable [financial] commitments abroad'. However, contrary to what happened in 1876, in 1891 the state had to resort to the Bank of Portugal's aid, paying with legal tender and by increasing fiduciary circulation.[22]

Making matters worse, the loan of 36,000 *contos* provided in the tobacco deal with Henry Burnay floundered. The minister explained:

> Given there was no solidarity between the groups who had contracted that loan and the stakeholders of the 1890 4% loan, and because the part of this efferent to the Portuguese group was not placed, this group pulled back on the state, meaning the Treasury failed to receive 26,000,000 francs. And since out of the 150,000 bonds of the tobacco loan, the government considered it necessary to retake 90,000, selling 78,000, of which 30,000 underwritten and 48,000 as an option to the Ephrusi group and delivering 12,000 to the Crédit Lyonnais in Paris, the Treasury also failed to collect the corresponding differences.[23]

In other words, two attempts by the state to place loans, in 1890 and 1891, had been unsuccessful. Markets were no longer interested in lending to the Portuguese State under the conditions it had to offer. The situation as described by Oliveira Martins demanded a change in strategy. Unable to recover its credits and guarantees or to use the markets, the minister had no alternative but to increase the revenue of the state. To this end, he resorted to the 1880 law of Barros Gomes and proposed a raise from 3% to 10% of the income tax for civil servants, including employees of corporations and pious institutions, subsidised or not by the state. In addition, he proposed increasing the income tax levied on the interest of domestic public debt securities from 3% to 30%, extending it to every other credit paper. Finally, he proposed to seal an agreement with the foreign creditors.[24] Oliveira Martins concluded the presentation of his package of measures stating:

> The government estimates that the sacrifice imposed on creditors, civil servants, and taxpayers will produce a sum above 8,500 *contos*; and that the administrative savings, whose value can never be very high for fear of causing anarchy in the services, added to the income from taxes on the production of alcohol, matches, and oils will reach 1,500 *contos*.[25]

With one single blow, the 10,000 *contos* deficit would be settled.

In Parliament, the financier Augusto Fuschini proposed that interest on foreign debt be left untouched and that on domestic debt pay no more than

10% tax. According to him, this would be possible by 'adequately setting the deficit and looking for fairer rates of broader incidence'. For Fuschini, the settlement of the public deficit was not an absolute priority; he felt that it was more important to fairly distribute the sacrifices imposed on the population in order to counter the state's financial crisis. According to him, taxing the interest on foreign debt, as proposed by Oliveira Martins, would also jeopardise the placement of new loans abroad. Other deputies came to champion this idea, which was eventually enshrined by the Finance Committee. Fuschini raised yet another concern regarding the minister's draft bill: domestic debt was the main 'means for the placement of national savings', even though, 'for the past twenty years some development of the country's vital economy [had] provided other means of placement'. 'On the other hand,' he continued, 'the expropriation laws forced a large number of pious institutions and charities to turn their real estate into bonds'. He concluded: 'By setting a 30% [tax] on internal debt, the project under discussion will therefore harm the poor classes'.[26]

The Public Credit Board had not published statistics on the distribution of the various types of securities and the number of holders since its 1882–1883 report. According to that data, as the deputy Augusto Fuschini recalled, in 1882–1883 there were 41,211 holders of Portuguese funded debt, of which 13,532 had a nominal capital of between 50$000 to 500$000, 10,093 between 550$000 and 1,500$000, 6,048 between 1,550$000 and 3,000$000, and 2,532 between 3,050$000 and 5,000$000. Fuschini concluded that small holders, since those possessing 5 *contos de reis* could not be called large, represented more than 80% of the total number! And the holders of up to 10 *contos de reis*, that is, earning 300$000 *réis* per year, about 90% of the same total.

He added that the same should be true for coupons or bearer bonds, which, in his view, were better suited for transactions than for capitalisation.[27]

In 1892, the *Caixa Económica Portuguesa* had a deposit ceiling of 1,500$000, meaning it did not pay interest to any amount above that value. Considering a 50% average market price, this amount corresponded to securities of up to 3,000$000. It can therefore be inferred that the 29,673 securities holders with less than 3 *contos* in nominal value—that is, 72% of all security holders—could be depositors in the state's savings bank if it paid interest able to compete with Public Treasury issues. Oliveira Martins was certainly aware that most securities were scattered among thousands of small holders, and that, in spite of the setback it had suffered in 1887 under Mariano de Carvalho, the Public Credit Board was still a real savings bank, as António José de Seixas had described it in 1881. Indeed, that is surely why his proposal included an article providing a sum of up to 250 *contos* in the state budget to cover deficits in the accounts of guilds (*montepios*), pension funds, and other pious corporations arising from the tax rise on the interest of the securities they held, provided that revenue did not exceed 300$000 per year. The provision was therefore meant to help pious institutions with few resources.

Augusto Fuschini's long speech ended with the example of France, who he said had succeeded in restoring its finances after the heavy indemnity it had paid Prussia as a result of having lost the 1870–1871 war. In France, different taxes had been raised such as stamp duty, and he suggested the same could be done in Portugal. The comparison with the French case did not convince Oliveira Martins. He had a point: not only was France a richer country, it was also a major exporter of capital, part of which had been repatriated via the rise of domestic interest rates, thus compensating for the outflow of capital caused by war reparations. The minister preferred comparisons with other cases, notably that of Italy, who in 1863 had brought down the interest rate on its internal public debt by 8.8% and in 1866 by 13.2%. Austria had undergone a similar process in 1867, reducing the interest of its debt by 16%; even more notably Spain reduced its own by two-thirds in 1876. It should be noted, however, that all the examples the Minister provided, with the exception of Spain, showed less drastic reductions than the one he proposed for Portugal.

Oliveira Martins further argued that the distribution of securities was not as widespread as asserted by Fuschini, grounding his position on the statistics of the distribution of the 3% consolidated amount published in the last General State Account. According to that, of the 260,000 *contos* of the internal debt 100,000 were registered in immovable assets, 30,000 belonged to pious establishments, pension funds, and guilds, 12,000 to dowries, and 15,000 to minors, totalling 157,000 *contos* (nominal value). Thus, only 60% of the public debt belonged to the poorer classes and to pious corporations, not 80% as Fuschini argued. The budget was approved in the Parliament on 13 February 1892, and then rose to the Finance Committee, which had a Regeneration majority and was headed by João Franco. It returned to the Parliament two days later as a draft bill. The committee had limited the 30% income tax to the interest of domestic public debt, exempting interest on foreign debt, and a 10% tax on all other national securities.

The bill was eventually approved by the deputies of the two major parties on 26 February 1892, with only three votes against from deputies of the *Partido Republicano*.[28] Later, a friend of Hintze Ribeiro's wrote:

> The political men of all the parties, in close harmony with the opinion of the whole country, have acknowledged that the administrative regime of large deficits, given it implies recourse to credit, has been the main cause of [recent] financial and economic disasters.[29]

The measures Oliveira Martins was barred from establishing, however, were taken on by José Dias Ferreira four months later, when he became finance minister. On 13 June 1892, Ferreira signed the decree reducing interest on foreign debt to one third, paid in gold, the rest paid in notes of the Bank of Portugal, minus the 30% tax which, since February 1892, was also levied on interest paid within the country, thus reducing its nominal interest from 3% to

1%.[30] Unlike Oliveira Martins, now his political enemy, Ferreira did not provide for the rights of external creditors, with whom Oliveira Martins had tried to sign an agreement regarding the share of their interest that would start to be paid in Portuguese currency. In Paris this was met with a negative reaction, not least because the measure formally harmed external creditors (who had their interest reduced by 66%) more than domestic creditors (whose interest was reduced by 30%), even though the first were paid in gold.[31]

The financial impact of Ferreira's measures on the Portuguese public debt paid abroad was not as great as the wave of political reaction suggested. Until 1891, external debt securities yielded between 4.5% and 6%. While the suspension of payment of two-thirds of interest lasted between 1892 and 1902, the yield on those same securities fell only to between 3.3% and 5%. Once the agreement was made in 1902, Portuguese securities rose to between 4.4% to 5.1%. Thus, since throughout this whole period English securities stayed below 3%, the yield on Portuguese securities remained attractive. These numbers illustrate that the confidence in the solvency of the state was impacted neither by Dias Ferreira's partial suspension of payments nor by the 1902 agreement and resulting conversion.[32]

Hintze Ribeiro clearly affirmed that the measures taken since 1891, when the impossibility of paying the interest on the foreign debt was announced, resolved the crisis of Portuguese public finance in the best possible way. He observed that an analysis of the accounts of the Treasury with the Bank of Portugal from 31 December 1890 clearly showed the difficulties the Treasury went through between 1890 and 1892; the veritable deliverance to the economy provided by the fiduciary issue; the depression the bank's metal reserves went through; how much the contracts and measures taken by the government helped the Treasury during the worst of the crisis; and, mainly as a result of this, the rapid improvement seen in the financial state of the country and Treasury from 1893. Lastly, the said accounts showed how opportune the contract of 9 February 1894 had been: it did not affect the stability or security of the bank, nor did it reduce its liquidity, its credit resources, or the scope of its operations, whilst being very profitable to the state.[33]

Despite having the support of both major parties, the measures introduced by Oliveira Martins were closer to the policies followed by the *Partido Progressista* than to those of the governments of Fontes Pereira de Melo and, later, António de Serpa. Instead of enlisting the good offices of bankers, such as Burnay, to raise loans abroad and, if necessary, offer income guarantees, Oliveira Martins opted to strive for more independent conditions for the finances of the State. It was a sound principle, but since the Bank of Portugal had already given as much as it could, to the point of exhausting its reserves of gold and pounds sterling. The alternative to tax earnings was not at the reach of the government, as the salaries of the civil servants had just been cut.[34] It was therefore necessary to tax the interest on the domestic public debt, whose securities, as seen, were scattered among tens of thousands of people. All this effort was aimed at achieving in a single year, and in especially difficult conditions, what no government had managed to do since at least 1852, namely to balance the public deficit.

## The progressives once more

Towards the end of a legislative consent period granted by the Parliament, José Dias Ferreira, perhaps anticipating the return to power of the *Partido Regenerador*, decided to finish the revolution in public financial administration started by Mariano de Carvalho, striking the final blow on the Public Credit Board. On 30 December 1892, Ferreira published a decree removing the administration of the *Caixa* from under the board's control. This left the board no function other than that of consultant on public debt matters, which no government ever used. Dias Ferreira's government would leave the finance portfolio less than a month later. His decree determined that the *Caixa* should have a director, a role which was handed to the head of the accounting department, Júlio Ferreira Pinto Basto, who was already informally performing that role. The decree also created a supervisory board for the *Caixa*, composed of the directors of public accounting and of the Treasury, and by a third member appointed by the government, the old count of Restelo (Pedro Augusto Franco).

The minister aimed at a 'reorganisation plan for the departments of the *Caixa Económica Portuguesa*', which was part of a broader plan to restructure the services within his ministry. The proclaimed goals were to follow the law of 26 February 1892, which ordered expenses to be cut in all ministries. The restructuring of the Treasury Directorate-General (*Direção Geral da Tesouraria*) had allowed a saving of 56,462$000 thanks to the reform of 28 April 1892, and the minister now intended to save an additional 11,740$000, sums that were small by any standard.[35] The *Caixa* would thus acquire new powers that were by then under the *Direcção-Geral da Dívida Pública*, that is, the government department for the running of the public debt. The public bank also received authorisation to receive demands deposits directly and not only through the *Caixa Económica*, and to buy, on behalf of depositors, public debt securities, shares and bonds of the Bank of Portugal and *Companhia Geral do Crédito Predial*, and shares in any other companies that had yielded at least 5% of dividends in the prior year. But the most important measure included in the plan concerned the increase of the ceiling for deposits in the *Caixa Económica* from 500$000 to 1,000$000 per year, and the total balance per depositor (above which the bank would not pay interest) from 1,500$000 to 3,000$000. It was a copy of Mariano de Carvalho's draft bill of 31 December 1887, except that there was now no place for the four members of the Public Credit Board, who in the previous law should form an executive board.[36]

The reforms enacted by the *progressista* finance minister (Mariano de Carvalho), soon after he came to power in 1886, were now being continued by Dias

Ferreira, his successor, with the 1892 decree. The Parliament was not called for the discussion of the legislative act, and thus we need to follow the discussion concerning it by looking at the main financial newspaper, the *Jornal do Comércio*, which was aligned with the *Partido Regenerador*.[37] The newspaper strongly criticised the changes in the structure of the Public Credit Board, as it transformed the board as 'a bureaucratic committee entirely dependent on the government', as it refused to obey the orders of the government concerning a number of financial transactions. It also defended that the *Caixa* should be put again under the control of the board.[38] The government had withdrawn from the Public Credit Board the management of the *Caixa*, which was given to its director and created a supervisory board constituted by the old count of Restelo and two other members, who were ex officio the directors-general of accounting and of the Treasury (António Maria Pereira Carrilho and Luís Augusto Perestrelo de Vasconcelos). Yet, the long-time serving director of the *Caixa* (Júlio Ferreira Pinto Basto), who was at the institution since its foundation and its director since 1879, died soon after the decree was published. His role in the institution certainly weighed on Minister Ferreira's decision to increase his managerial powers, although their familial ties (they were brothers-in-law) probably had some influence as well. The chief accountant stepped into his place.[39] In addition to losing its director in the beginning of 1893, *Caixa* also had to deal with the new law of 30 December 1892, which, according to the same *Jornal do Comércio*, was anything but clear. Firstly, the law did not define properly the functions of the supervisory board, leaving it open to future regulation. According to the same newspaper, Ferreira made changes to *Caixa*'s management because the outgoing administration had refused to carry out a number of financial operations for the government. *Caixa*'s life had definitely become more difficult after 1891.

The consequence of ending the Public Credit Board's control over the *Caixa* was the interruption of the publication of the annual reports of the board, the *Caixa*, and the *Caixa Económica*, which were usually handed to Parliament together. Indeed, the same was true for the last 'Report and documents of the acts of the Ministry of Finance' (*Relatório e documentos dos actos do Ministério da Fazenda*) of 15 July 1899.[40] For some years, the reports of the banks managed by the board had contained only the accounts of each institution, with still a few scant comments. Moreover, as the lengthy and clarifying article in the *Jornal do Comércio* explains, the life of the *Caixa Geral de Depósitos* was in a twilight zone. The reasons for this prolonged state of gloom were simple.

The decree of 13 February 1892, which set an increase from 3% to 30% in the tax on the interest of public debt securities and which, in turn, implied a nominal interest reduction of 2.9% to 2.3%, resulted in a fall in the market price of those securities at least equivalent to the reduction of their interest. A security yielding 2.9%, with the average market interest rate at 6%, would be quoted at 48.5%. If its interest fell to 2.3%, its price would also have to drop, if everything else remained constant, to 38.3%. Following the contract between the state and the Bank of Portugal carried out by Mariano de Carvalho in December 1887 and in force since the following January, the *Caixa* made cash loans backed by debt securities valued at 90% of market value. Until 1888, the *Caixa* accepted securities as pawn but only up to 80% of its value. The new 30% tax on securities' interest lowered their market value to 85% of what it was before. Thus, all those who had traded securities for loans with the *Caixa* would benefit if they failed to pay the interest on these loans, delivering instead what they had left as collateral: now devalued securities. As a result, the *Caixa* found itself with coffers full of public debt securities worth less than the loans it had granted against its collateral, leading to evident losses. The long interruption in the publication of the *Caixa*'s reports was certainly related to this. As its administration later explained, the bills continued to be presented to the government, but ceased to be shown to the public.[41]

## Notes

1 Ramos (1994), pp. 185–186.
2 Fuschini (1899), p. 108.
3 Diário da Câmara dos Deputados, 6 Mach 1891, p. 6.
4 Cordeiro (1999 [1896]), pp. 73–74].
5 Nunes et al. (1994), pp. 24, 29, 118.
6 Ulrich (1946), vol.1 (?), p. 227.
7 Reis (1991); Lains (1995), p. 236.
8 Mónica (1992), pp. 24 and 27; Santos (1974).
9 Diário da Câmara dos Deputados, 6 March 1891.
10 Ulrich (1902), pp. 217–218.
11 Fuschini (1899), pp. 99, 101.
12 Diário da Câmara dos Deputados, 12 March 1891.
13 Salazar (1997), p. 173.
14 Mata (1993), p. 136.
15 Ramos (1994), p. 203.
16 Diário da Câmara dos Deputados, 25 June 1891.
17 Reis (1994).
18 Legislação do Banco de Portugal (1946).
19 Ramos (1994), pp. 202–203.
20 Diário da Câmara dos Deputados, 13 March 1891.
21 Diário da Câmara dos Deputados, 30 January 1892. See also Cordeiro (1999 [1896]). Fuschini (1899), pp. 32–44, publishes detailed information on the 'subsidies and aids' granted to banks and companies that the Treasury department had sent him at his request while he was finance minister. According to that list, on 24 February 1893, the debt alone (so, not counting guarantees) amounted to 12,275 *contos*.
22 Cordeiro (1999 [1896]), pp. 34–35; also Castro (1978), pp. 128 ff.
23 Diário da Câmara dos Deputados, 30 January 1892 and 13 February 1892.
24 It is difficult to follow the changes undergone by Oliveira Martins' project, with the exception of those introduced by the Finance Committee. According to Anselmo Vieira (1905), pp. 10 and 115–116, taxes rose to 30% on the domestic public debt (and later also on the external debt), and to 12.5% on the income of civil servants and public corporations. At the same time, the government created top-up for 15%

to the property, industrial, and luxury taxes, and one of 12.6% for the taxes on house rents. The latter would be suspended by decree on 31 December 1892. For the successive salary cutbacks for civil servants, see also Mata (1993), p. 31.

25  Diário da Câmara dos Deputados, 30 January 1892 and 13 February 1892.
26  Ramos (1994), p. 171.
27  See for what follows, Diário da Câmara dos Deputados, 11 and 15 February 1892.
28  Fuschini (1899), annexes, p. 56.
29  Vieira (1905), p. 11.
30  Holders of these securities were allowed to convert them into securities of the 3% domestic debt, whose yield had already been subjected to the new 30% tax of 26 February 1892.
31  Burnay (1897), p. 6. Cordeiro (1999 [1896]), pp. 156–157.
32  Valério (1986), pp. 3–5.
33  Diário da Câmara dos Deputados, 16 March 1896.
34  Vieira (1905), pp. 115–116; Mata (1993), p. 31.
35  Diário do Governo, no. 1, 2 January 1893, p. 6.
36  Diário da Câmara dos Deputados, 23 April 1888.
37  Jornal do Comércio, 27 January 1888.
38  Jornal do Comércio, 28 March 1893.
39  Jornal do Comércio, 28 February 1893.
40  Laranjo (1903), p. 59.
41  No general accounts of the financial administration of the State were published between 1896–1897 and 1906–1907. The provisional account, however, carried on being published every month in the Diário do Governo (see Mata, 1993, p. 29).

# 7

# BACK TO THE OLD ORDER, 1892–1910

Following the October 1892 Parliament election, on 23 February 1893, the *Partido Regenerador* returned to power. As its leader, António de Serpa, was ill, the government was handed to Hintze Ribeiro. King Carlos, who was increasingly intervening in politics, and his close friend Oliveira Martins, were happy to see Dias Ferreira removed from office.[1] Hintze was young and conservative, but he was also able to ally with João Franco who, alongside Augusto Fuschini, were members of the faction in the party called *Liga Liberal* (Liberal League), and was entrusted with the Ministry of Finance. This was clearly a return to the pre-1886 political order, when Fontes Pereira de Melo reigned.[2] It is important to spell out the names of the leaders, because Portugal was indeed run by a bipartisan system and the differences in policies were important and much dependent on who was leading the government. And the role of the monarch was increasingly important, a fact that would appear even more evident in the following years. We need to recall here that the king had the constitutional power to close the Parliament and appoint the prime minister who would organise the subsequent election, and whose party would expectedly win the vote.

The new liberal finance minister wanted upfront to appease the foreign creditors, but the domestic political ambience was not favourable to extreme measures, which were deemed to go against national pride. The collective memory of every politician, and the people on the streets, was still fresh with the crisis, and for some, the humiliation of the 1890 British ultimatum on the presence of the Portuguese military in the zone defined by the then infamous rose-coloured map. It was thus politically inviable for the minister to offer a guarantee of payment to foreign bondholders of the revenues of colonial customs or reexports of colonial goods, which were by then increasing at a rapid pace. As such, Fuschini could only reiterate what his political opponent, Dias Ferreira, had ruled in June 1892, namely the payment of 1/3 of the interest on bonds in gold. However, in May 1893, the new minister added the guarantee of one half of the income of domestic customs exceeding 11,400 *contos,* leaving aside the revenue from imports of tobacco and cereals, and also guaranteeing that the government would cover the losses if the gold premium fell below 22%.[3] Until 1897, gold remained above this value whilst customs revenues increased, which meant external creditors earned 2,446 *contos*.[4] The law of 20 May also authorised the government to reconstitute the Public Credit Board, determining, however, that all five members must be Portuguese.[5] Only the three Republican deputies and one *Regenerador* deputy (Rodrigues dos Santos), ally of the leader of the former government, voted against the law.[6]

## The return of the *regeneradores*

The new government of the *Partido Regenerador*, led by Hintze Ribeiro, would last for a full term of four years, something that had not happened since Pereira de Melo left seven years prior. Ribeiro had by then a strong grasp in power, which was reinforced a year later when he also assumed the role of Minister of Finance. The return of the *regeneradores* was an opportunity to regain control of the main financial institutions and the running of financial policy, and the story of the recovery can be followed closely through the *Jornal do Comércio*, which was the paper closest to the party. In an article published in March 1893, the newspaper made a full report about the sentiment on what to change in the administration and the business of the public bank.[7] Firstly, the reestablishment of the new order imposed that the Public Credit Board should administer the *Caixa* as before, as that was the best way for it to regain its independence from the government. Secondly, the lending to the state, either directly or through the deposits that the *Caixa* was compelled to make in the Bank of Portugal, should be better controlled and substantially reduced. Finally, and most importantly, the government should compensate for the securities it withdrew from *Caixa* and which were placed in the market. It was also asked in the newspaper that the members of the Public Credit Board should be paid for their work as administrators and supervisors of the public bank because, as stated, 'it is preferable that the government use these strategies and really reduce the savings bank's interest rate to 3% than establish free services by the administration which, for that same reason, inspire no confidence' (*Jornal do Comércio*, 28 March 1893). Finally, the *Jornal do Comércio* addressed the problem of *Caixa*'s premises, recalling their poor conditions:

> It runs in a large building, on the fifth floor, where employees work with the roof over their heads, without air or light and packed like sardines in a bowl. A pitiful place, which the health council would not allow to function, were it to inspect it as it does schools and other establishments where it is convenient to keep hygienic standards.

These were the facilities of the *Caixa Económica Portuguesa*, which were still on the top floor of the building at Praça do Comércio, above the premises of the Public Credit Board. In the meantime, the building the *Caixa* had acquired with some of its profits had burned down in 1886 and awaited restoration by the government, which also wanted to establish some departments of the Ministry of Public Works on site.[8]

The newspaper's long piece suggests the bank had suffered a serious setback in its development as a self-governing financial institution, as early as the beginning of 1888, when Mariano de Carvalho's measures entered into force. Since then, the *Caixa* had lost its profits to the repayment of public debt. Instead of constituting a reserve fund; it lost its cash reserves to the Bank of Portugal; it paid 3.5% to mandatory deposits, with no compensation; it loaned to the state under less favourable conditions than those stipulated in 1881; it did not have a fully functioning administration or even management; and finally it continued to operate in inadequate premises.

On 14 August 1893, Augusto Fuschini signed the decree to reconstitute the Public Credit Board, from which date the institution was again entrusted with the repayment of the internal consolidated public debt service and also became responsible for the external public debt service, except for the tobacco loan of 26 February 1891.[9] The services of the public debt had been assigned, by a law of 15 December 1887, to the directorate-general for the public debt, created for the purpose and where the service of the funded debt was centralised. However, there were still the directorates-general for accounting and for the Treasury, both of which played a part in the payment of interest on domestic debt. At the time there were also financial agencies in London and in Rio de Janeiro, under control of the Ministry of Finance, responsible for servicing the external debt. These agencies were, however, extinguished on 28 April 1892, following a decree of 26 February by Dias Ferreira.[10]

As before, the Public Credit Board consisted of two members elected by each of the chambers of Parliament, two members elected by the holders, and a fifth element appointed by the government. The article establishing the composition of the board also determined that all the members should be Portuguese. The Public Credit Board found the service of the public debt in great disorganisation. In fact, the securities of 1888, which had been converted in 1891, were still to be burned, some located in the directorate-general for the public debt, which had just been closed, and others in the directorate-general for the Treasury. All these securities were to be destroyed, together with others resulting from the conversion made in 1892–1893. As for external funds, the report said that 'the service had not been done regularly for a long time. The board found crates and boxes of coupons received from abroad intact, not even having been opened to see if their content was indeed paid coupons'. In the 1898–1899 report, at the end of the second triennium since its reconstitution, the Public Credit Board announced with 'pleasure and pride' that the services were again up to date.[11]

On the same day the decree restoring the Public Credit Board was signed, the finance minister appointed a new representative of the government on the board, replacing the Count of Restelo, who had held the position since his first nomination in 1881, in one of the last acts of the progressive government of Anselmo Braamcamp. Fuschini chose Manuel Pinheiro Chagas, a successful writer and historian, peer of the realm and a member of Dias Ferreira's *Partido*

*Constituinte* for the position.[12] In the meantime, at the end of the legislative session on 13 July 1893, the Parliament had elected Joaquim Pedro de Oliveira Martins as its representative in the board.[13] The Chamber of Peers elected Alberto António Morais de Carvalho, a member of the *Partido Regenerador*. Only the security holders had yet to choose their representatives, as ordered by decree of 14 August 1893. On 18 August, Morais de Carvalho took office as chairman of the restored Public Credit Board.[14] The day after the publication of both decrees, as was to be expected, the ever-watchful *Jornal do Comércio* (now headed by Eduardo Burnay, brother of the tobacco financier) praised the measures, which it ascribed to the president of the council, Hintze Ribeiro, and not to the minister of finance. Among other things, the newspaper commended the reconstitution of the Public Credit Board as 'a shield to the idea of the so-called foreign control' over the Portuguese public debt service. The comments on the process or selection of the board's members, all of which were new to their posts, are innocuous, yet revealing. For the newspaper, José Augusto da Gama, effectively being the representative of the Chamber of Peers since 1869 and the representative of the Parliament, António Caetano do Carmo Noronha (although the paper did not name him directly), elected in 1891 as substitute on the death of the member Joaquim Alves Chaves, had been replaced 'by pressure of the government'. The upper chamber elected a Regeneration peer and the lower house a deputy from the *Partido Progressista*. *Jornal do Comércio* also praised the element selected by the government, who became chairman of the Public Credit Board, Manuel Pinheiro Chagas.

From the moment the Public Credit Board lost control over the *Caixa* in 1893, since the bank no longer had its annual reports, it is not certain if the accounts of the new administration were as detailed as those made by the Board. Later, in 1909, the then appointed administration was able to publish a summary of retrospective accounts. In the meantime, some information on the accounts of the *Caixa Económica*, though not the *Caixa*, can be found in articles of the *Jornal do Comércio*, as well as in reports of the finance ministers. Indeed, between 1894 and 1895, the newspaper published four articles on savings banks that looked for the reasons behind the limited growth of the public savings bank.

In December, Hintze Ribeiro, leader of the *Partido Regenerador* and president of the council, replaced Fuschini as finance minister, and on 16 March 1896 presented his first report and draft bills to the Parliament. The last three of a list of fifteen draft bills concerned the *Caixa*, and would start a new period for the institution. He proposed creating a pension fund for employees, founding a guild (*montepio*), and finally reorganising the *Caixa* itself, who was to manage the two institutions thus created. It would change its name to the *Caixa e Instituições de Previdência*.

The proposed pension scheme was but an extension of the National Pension Fund, created in 1885 by the same Hintze Ribeiro, then finance minister. The difference was that the first had been intended only for civil servants recruited after its creation, while the new institution covered all employed workers. In addition, the minister wanted to guarantee that his institution was now effectively established, which had not been achieved by his first creation. The national guild (*Montepio Nacional*), which the minister wanted to create simultaneously, was intended to widen the business of loaning on pawns as an investment strategy of the *Caixa*, since the contributions to the pension fund would increase the bank's available reserves.[15]

The return of Hintze Ribeiro to the Finance Ministry was accompanied by a new series of reform proposals for the *Caixa*, for the first time since 1885. And once again, the Minister of Finance attended to the *Caixa* because the state's financial situation showed some improvement. The best sign of this improvement was the evolution of the market value of the 3% consolidated bonds. As a consequence, the difficulties of financing the public deficit, after 1889, and secondly of the 1892 tax on interest yield, the price of the consolidated account dropped from 64.1% in 1889 to a minimum of 28.4% in 1893, with a slight increase to 36.1% in 1896, falling again until 1898.[16]

Hintze Ribeiro defended that the different measures taken since 1891, when the interest on the foreign debt was declared impossible to pay due to lack of gold or pounds sterling in the coffers of the Bank of Portugal, solved the crisis of the Portuguese public finances in the best possible way. The minister observed that an analysis of the accounts of the Treasury with the Bank of Portugal from 31 December 1890 showed clearly and undeniably the hardships faced by the Treasury between 1890 and 1892; the truly saving role to the country's economy of the timely fiduciary issue; the depression the bank's metallic reserve went through; the succour delivered to the institution, in the hardest period of the crisis, by the contracts and the measures of the government; and especially, since 1893, the rapid improvement of the financial conditions of the Treasury and country. Finally, it showed how convenient was the contract of 9 February 1894; despite being very profitable for the state, it did not affect the stability and security of the bank, nor did it restrict the conditions of its movement, the resources of its credit, or the scope of its operations.[17]

## The 1896 reform

In May 1896, the *Caixa*'s statute was reformed again, leading to a restructuration and extension of its services and a more independent Board. The public bank was divided into five departments: Accounting, the *Caixa Geral de Depósitos*, the *Caixa Económica Portuguesa*, the *Caixa de Aposentações* ('Pension Fund') and *Monte de Piedade* (pawn credit). The departments were to be supervised by a chief executive, who presided over the executive board, the first to actually hold that name in the *Caixa*'s history. The chief executive could contact the government directly for proposals and consultations. He was appointed by the government and could only be exonerated or dismissed under the same terms applied to the members of the Court of Auditors. This was common practice in certain echelons of civil service. However, this could raise suspicion that the government's intention was to put someone of the same political leanings at the head of the deposit bank and make their removal difficult for subsequent governments, who would need to change the legal framework to do so. The *Caixa*'s new administrative structure further included a supervisory board, headed ex officio by the chairman of the Public Credit Board. Its other members were the directors-general for accounting, for the Treasury and for general statistics and trade, and the chairman of the Chamber of Commerce and Industry of Lisbon (*Câmara de Comércio e Indústria de Lisboa*). The latter was the only member not in the civil service. Under the 1896 law, the supervisory board should meet at the *Caixa*'s headquarters, unlike its predecessor, created in 1892, whose meetings happened in the premises of the Public Credit Board. Although practically this change meant moving the meeting place only a few meters within Terreiro do Paço, in fact this represented relieving some of the *Caixa*'s dependence on the Public Credit Board, within which it had been created.

However, the new law presented some problems. One of the undefined elements it introduced was immediately apparent when the supervisory board was installed. It stipulated that the chairman of the Public Credit Board would only assume the leadership of the new *Caixa* after the end of the term of the chairman of the previous supervisory board, who had been appointed in 1892. This meant having the man who had headed the Board until 1894, the Count of Restelo, stay as chairman of the *Caixa*'s supervisory board. The operation of the board was further hampered by the president of the Lisbon Chamber of Commerce, Júlio Pinto Basto, refusing to take part until the consequences of the rise of the income tax on interest paid by the bonds, and until the administration restarted publishing their annual reports. His position was justified, since it was the responsibility of the supervisory board to give the opinion on the report and accounts of the *Caixa*, and these had not been provided since 1892. The 1896 law also determined the creation of a branch in Porto. This had to be run by a head of service, placing it at the level of the other four departments of the *Caixa*. In the remaining district capitals and counties, coffers or offices of the Treasury continued to serve as branches of the *Caixa*. The 1896 law brought another change to the *Caixa*: the monopoly on deposit accounts opened solely for the acquisition of public debt securities. Interest on retail deposits remained unchanged at 3.6%, but the law allowed the administration, with government consent, to vary interest rates between 2% and 4%, instead of 3% and 4% as before. The deposit limits stayed the same: 1,000$000 per deposit and 3,000$000 as the ceiling above which the *Caixa* ceased to pay interest. Moreover, the *Caixa Geral de Depósitos* and the *Caixa Económica Portuguesa* were merged into the same institution. It should be recalled that the legislators had established them as separate entities, the deposit bank being the destination of the savings bank's investments, for which it had to pay an annual interest of 5%. The fusion of the two meant, above all, that the savings bank no longer had a guaranteed 5% lending interest rate. However, this amendment in fact ratified the already established practice, which did not permit the separation of the accounts of the two banks; it also put an end to the project of creating a savings bank autonomous from the deposit bank.

The *Caixa* continued to pay 2% annually on mandatory deposits and maintained all other provisions, namely that interest was accrued daily but paid only after 60 days of deposit. The state guarantees for all deposits remained, which was probably the main advantage of both the *Caixa* and the *Caixa Económica* regarding the mutual savings bank of *Montepio Geral*, their main competitor in the deposit banking business. As for investments permitted by the new law, the main change concerned the possibility of granting loans to administrative corporations, namely town councils and other national or municipal public services. Finally, the law also determined the creation of a pension fund for workers not entitled to state pensions. However, this fund saw little development, since the financial allocations it received were too small. Participants had to accumulate a monthly quota of $250 for thirty-five years and be over the age of 55. The law of May 1896 regarding the *Caixa* was followed in October by that reforming the Public Credit Board. This reform put an end to the board's role of supervising the servicing of the Portuguese public debt.

The *Jornal do Comércio*, the financial newspaper that followed more closely the life of the public bank, was quick to react to the changes of the board, which it argued increased the dependence on the government. The new supervisory board, still led by Restelo, was now composed of four instead of two members, namely the Treasury director-general (Luís Augusto Perestrelo de Vasconcelos), the director-general of statistics (António Eduardo Vilaça), the director-general of accounting (André Severiano Roman Navarro), and the president of the Chamber of Commerce and Industry (Eduardo Ferreira Pinto Basto). For the supervisory board meetings, the bank's chief executive, Tomás Pizarro de Melo Sampaio, also joined them. However, this new supervisory board also had operating difficulties. Indeed, the board had its first meeting as soon as 9 June 1896, but the only member not belonging to the financial administration of the state, Eduardo Pinto Basto, failed to attend. In addition, the other ex officio members sent surrogates in their stead, which can be seen as a deliberate devaluation of the supervisory board.

The council reconvened twice in a row over a year later, first on 30 November and then on 2 December 1897, but Pinto Basto was again absent. In the meantime, on 7 February 1897 the government had changed and was now in the hands of the *Partido Progressista*, headed by José Luciano de Castro. Finally, on 14 June 1898, the president of the Lisbon Chamber of Commerce appeared for the first time at the *Caixa* headquarters to explain his absence from the supervisory board meetings. His attention was immediately directed to the bank's accounts, requesting explanations for a loss of 40 *contos* that, according to the minutes, the supervisory board had approved in the previous session. In fact, the *Caixa*'s accounts for the fiscal year 1896–1897 budgeted revenues at 479 *contos* and expenses at 295 *contos*. However, the revenues included the state's debt of 224 *contos* to the *Caixa* from the annual interest of the Treasury bonds the government had withdrawn from the bank's coffers some years before. In light of this situation, the supervisory board concluded that 'The absence of recovery can, as in previous years, lead to a deficit of 40 *contos*.'[18]

Melo Sampaio, the *Caixa*'s chief executive, recalled the conditions under which the state's debt to the *Caixa* had been contracted, explaining that the problem was being addressed since the May 1896 law allowed the government to issue the securities necessary to pay the debt. He recalled equally that the *Caixa*'s difficulties had also resulted from the 1892 emergency measure of raising the debt securities income tax from 3% to 30%. That rise had led to a marked devaluation of those securities, which were the *Caixa*'s main asset.

The reform of 1896 had placed the administration of the public deposit bank under the control of the government. Yet, in the meantime (June 1898), the government of Luciano de Castro, sworn in February 1897, had put an end to the *Caixa*'s board of directors, its duties passing on to the supervisory board. The new decree also extinguished the post of head of service in the Porto branch, thus terminating another unachieved good intention of the 1896 legislator. The continual absence of Pinto Basto in the meetings probably voided them of purpose. The supervisory board would meet only ten times in the eleven years that followed, until the next reform of the *Caixa*, in 1909.

Questions regarding the return of the debt securities that the government had secured from the *Caixa* dominated the meetings of the supervisory board, as minutes show. This was the least visible aspect of a situation that everyone with an interest in the field might have suspected, regarding the fact that the *Caixa* had been virtually paralysed for more than a decade by an arbitrary government decision of 1890, justified only by the distress the public debt service was then undergoing. Under these circumstances, the remaining provisions of the 1896 reform, which purported to constitute new services within the *Caixa*, could not be developed. The issue of the return of the bonds entrusted to the government and the payment of the respective interest was surpassed in 1908. Until then, the bank's administration did not publish the reports and accounts it was due to submit to Parliament every year, and the supervisory board—who was supposed to monitor the accounts—did not comment on the matter. The reduction of the role of the Public Credit Board and the *Caixa*'s greater dependence on the Treasury and the Ministry of Finance were key components in this happening.

Several reasons may justify this pact of silence. First of all, it could be simply an extension of the agreement between the two major political parties that seemed to exist around issues related to the *Caixa* administration. This was reflected above all in the continuity of the bank's directors and executives, even whilst the parties rotated in government. The pact would eventually be respected within the financial sector, which would not want to jeopardise the welfare of the *Caixa*, as it already had an important place in the banking business. The position of the rest of the sector regarding the *Caixa* not publishing its accounts could be understood as a natural reaction to the public bank being an overly open financial institution. In fact, no other financial institution had to display its accounts publicly as was legally required of the *Caixa*. Private banks were not required to publish their accounts and commercial banks only had to present their accounts at shareholder meetings, which were not necessarily open to the press.

Independently of the reasons behind the apparent silence and the seeming lack of protest regarding the unpublished *Caixa* accounts, the public's confidence was not affected. In fact, the value of the balances of deposits from the public with the *Caixa*, after a peak in the year 1889–1890 and having regressed the following year, began to recover as soon as 1891–1892. In 1895–1896, the value of that balance had already recovered to the level of the peak before the financial and payment crisis of 1890–1892. Judging from the continued rise in the balance of those deposits, whose value would double until 1901–1902 until stabilising thereafter, the subsequent reform of 1896 and the end of the Public Credit Board's role in the management of the *Caixa* also did not affect the public's confidence in the institution. Interest on deposits remained at a rate of 3.6% per annum, higher than that offered to private deposits by any other bank. The remaining deposit conditions were left unchanged.

The growth in deposits from the public led to an increase in the *Caixa*'s investment in public bonds, which rose from about 200 *contos* in 1891–1892 to around 3,000 *contos* in 1908–1909. Twenty years after its creation, the *Caixa* finally replaced the Public Credit Board in collecting deposits for the acquisition of public debt securities. The growth in deposits was above all due to a favourable situation for the institution and not so much to the plans of the government or the administration. Paradoxically, its development happened at a time when the value of its main assets was severely affected by a change in the taxes on the interest, both country and state were undergoing a significant financial crisis, and the *Caixa* was not publishing its accounts.

Despite the signs of instability and excessive government intervention, the *Caixa*'s administration once again remained stable. The man who was its director from 1894 until 1896 became chief executive, holding this post between 1896 and 1907 despite successive government changes. It is possible that the Portuguese financial system as a whole suffered with the excessive development of the public deposit bank; if so, this may have been the main negative consequence of *Caixa*'s predominance in the financial markets. In the meantime, the country's financial situation had improved. As such, the Portuguese government signed an agreement with the external creditors in 1902 that allowed access once again to contracting loans abroad. The situation of the public credit improved considerably during the 1900s, resulting in a rise of public debt securities' market price. For the *Caixa*, the improvement of the financial position of the state directly translated into an increase in the value of its financial assets, which allowed the institution to regain its financial rebalance. The first effect of this new balance was the return of the annual reports and renewed government attention, which necessarily resulted in a new reform that occurred, in 1909, on the eve of the fall of the monarchy, with effects during the highly politically and financially unstable period that followed.

## Notes

1 Cordeiro (1999 [1896]), p. 316.
2 Fuschini (1896), pp. 135 ff.
3 Report of the Corporate Chamber n. 14/V, in Diário das Sessões n. 81, 9 March 1951, p. 540.
4 Burnay (1897), pp. 6–8.
5 Menezes (1904), p. 288.
6 Ribeiro (1896), pp. 77–80.
7 Jornal do Comércio, 28 March 1893. The description of the premises is particularly relevant and unique in the sources.
8 Jornal do Comércio, 28 March 1893. The building bought in 1886 was the Palácio Sobral, in Calhariz; *Caixa* would move there in 1897.
9 Diário do Governo, no. 182, 16 August 1893, pp. 2131–2133.
10 Exposição Histórica do Ministério das Finanças (...) (1952), pp. 282–285; Relatório da Junta do Crédito Público, 1892–1893.
11 Relatório da Junta do Crédito Público, 1895–1896, p. 2, and 1898–1899, p. 7.
12 Mónica (1994), p. 130.
13 Diário da Câmara dos Deputados, 13 July 1893, p. 17.
14 *Exposição Histórica do Ministério das Finanças (...)* (1952), p. 316; *Diário do Governo*, No. 182, 16 August 1893, p. 2133.
15 Diário da Câmara dos Deputados, session 45, 16 March 1896; Ribeiro (1896).
16 Sousa (1916), p. 420.
17 Diário da Câmara dos Deputados, session 45, 16 March 1896, p. 615.
18 Livro de actas do conselho fiscal, minute No. 3, of 2 December 1897.

# 8

# THE REPUBLIC, 1910–1926

In October 1910, the monarchy fell by another military coup, which led to the instauration of a Republican regime. By that time, the *Caixa Geral de Depósitos* had achieved a prominent position as the deposit bank and a major financial instrument of the Portuguese state. The path had been long and fraught with difficulties, but the outcome was beyond even the most optimistic projections of the institution's creators more than half a century before. Consensus between the main political forces of liberalism regarding the advantages of a public bank had allowed the *Caixa* to develop. To the depositor, the bank offered guarantees of financial stability and competitive interest rates and handling fees. Thus, it became the largest Portuguese bank, holding around a third of all deposits in the country, and having a fundamental role in raising funds to finance the state in its increasing roles in the economy. The reform of the *Caixa*'s statute of September 1909, the last of the monarchy, had paved the way for greater administrative autonomy, but also for a closer relationship with governments and an increase of the state's prerogatives with the institution. That reform had created the post of chairman, who was appointed by the government, and an Executive Board with deliberative and audit duties, constituted by the director-general of the Treasury and four members elected, respectively, by the Chamber of Peers, the Parliament, the Supreme Administrative Court and the Public Credit Board, who elected the chairman and Vice-chairman.

The regime change brought on by the military coup of 5 October 1910 naturally left a mark on the history of the *Caixa*. In the past, the institution had felt the effects of changes of government, but this coup brought much more radical changes. The governments of the Republican revolution intervened in the *Caixa*'s business in a more radical and less prudent way than their predecessors, leading to a number of problems, which nonetheless did not hinder the institution's overall performance. That was so because even the most committed Republican partisans, once in the administration, would change tack to protect the institution. When another coup d'état took place, in 1926, the institution was relatively successful in attracting deposits. The Republicans' greatest impact was the increase of the number of agencies, in an effort to bring the bank closer to the people. Ideologically, it was an understandable strategy, but it had high financial costs.

## The new political regime

The Republican coup d'état in 1910 was a direct consequence of the failure of the monarchy to deal with the political transformations in the country, stemming from about half a century of industrialisation and overall economic development, which increased the standard of living but also increased the number of people disenfranchised with the ruling political system. An authoritarian government imposed by King Carlos in 1907, the assassination of the King in 1908, and a succession of political disturbances preceded the Republican coup. Contemporaries pointed to the incapacity of the parties of the monarchy to run the country, particularly its finances, which were in many instances unbalanced. Yet, by 1910, the financial situation of the country was on balance and the economy had clearly improved in comparison to the situation half a century or so before. The dissatisfaction was mostly political. The Republicans promised changes, such as increasing the number of people with access to vote, improving the quality of life of the poorer strata of the society, including agricultural and industrial workers, but many of the promises were not kept, because the problems were of a deep structural nature, rather than an outcome of the type of political regime. Paradoxically, in comparison to what would happen in the Republican regime, during the monarchy public finances were actually one of the few areas of consensus in the financial and political setting.

Whatever the background, the fact of the matter was that the new regime soon showed the will to overhaul the financial establishment. The choice of the finance minister was crucial, and it was not immediate. According to his own testimony, one of the most important leaders of the Republican coup and a pre-eminent voice in economic and financial matters refused the nomination because the political instability that followed the coup had made very difficult the implementation of a balanced fiscal policy.[1] Facing this most relevant refusal, the leaders of the coup (Afonso Costa and Bernardino Machado) extended the invitation to lead the Finance Ministry to another important Republican leader who took office on 12 October, and soon after dismissed the secretary-general of the old regime and appointed another important element of the revolution.[2] On 21 October 1910, the new minster removed the governor of the Bank of Portugal (José Adolfo de Mello e Sousa), who had been appointed by the 1907 dictatorial government supported by the monarch (João Franco's Liberal *Partido Regenerador*), who was replaced by deputy Governor Augusto José da Cunha). In March 1911, Inocêncio Camacho was designated governor of the central bank. In March 1911, the government of the Bank of Portugal would be handed over to Inocêncio Joaquim Camacho Rodrigues.[3] The purge of the old figures of the state financial elite of the Monarchy was extended to the High Court of Tax Litigation (Tribunal Superior do Contencioso Fiscal), led by the same João Franco (October 1910), to the customs (António Teixeira de Sousa) and the chief administrator of the royal household (Eduardo Serpa Pimentel). All of them were associated with the monarchy. In the many previous revolutions and coup d'états that had occurred in the country, it was uncommon to have such an important number of replacements in the high spheres of power. *Caixa* would of course follow suit and in due time, as demanded by its relative importance in the financial structure of the regime.

Yet changes in the administrative structure of the *Caixa* was a more complex process, for a number of reasons but mostly because the health of the institution depended on the evaluation the depositors made on its integrity and independence from political intervention. As such, the government started by appointing a Commission of Inquiry, allegedly by request of a member of the board charged with investigating the institution's accounts. This movement was unprecedented in the life of the *Caixa* and clearly stemmed from clear political motivations, revealing the destabilising atmosphere at the time. The *Caixa* was not the only financial institution to be instigated by the new government, as similar commissions were designated to look into the mint (*Casa da Moeda*), headed by a royalist who was declared a political enemy of the republic and who would take his own life in difficult to understand circumstances.[4] The government also had to deal with the fate of other documents related to the state's financial activity.[5] He ordered that the archive of the tax office (*Próprios Nacionais, Contribuições Directas e Tesouraria*) be sealed, and threatened to apply the same procedure on the *Caixa* and the Public Credit Board, arguing that that would safeguard the documents pertaining to the administration of public accounts, making it possible to control all the debits to the public purse.[6]

In the meantime, a member of the *Partido Republicano* (Estêvão de Vasconcelos) was appointed as interim chairman on 21 October 1910, and shortly after his nomination, on the afternoon of 28 October, the minister of finance (José Relvas) paid a rare visit to the bank's facilities, as a sign of the relevance of the *Caixa* to the new executive.[7] Despite the ongoing investigation into the *Caixa*'s accounts, the new chairman vouched the accounts for the previous year.[8] Before the publication of the outcome of the Commission of Inquiry, and in an apparent change of tack, in March 1911, the government reinstated the *Caixa*'s board, albeit with important modifications. The minister of finance appointed directly a member of the leading *Partido Republicano* (Estêvão de Vasconcelos) as chairman, as well as an official accountant with no voting rights and whose duties a subsequent law would regulate.[9]

In the midst of these events, the finance minister was striving to convey an optimistic message. When questioned by a journalist about the real financial situation of the country, he replied that it was 'comfortable', adding further that the new Republican regime was accepted by the 'whole world with clear displays of trust', as shown, according to him, by the positive evolution of the exchange rate.[10] In fact, the financial situation of the country in the first years of the new regime continued to improve, as had occurred in the last years of the monarchy. The financial problems only started following the outbreak of World War I, which Portugal joined on the Allied side by the end of 1916, and the worsening of the international economic and financial situation.[11]

Nevertheless, the *Caixa* was left without a permanent board still for some time, to the disaffection of the interim chairman. It was only after the new

Republican constitution was passed on 21 August 1911, and a new legislature commenced that the Parliament elected the two members (one permanent and a substitute) to the *Caixa*'s board. But instability proceeded for some time, as the interim chairman, Vasconcelos, left the *Caixa* for a short period of time as he was appointed Minister of Public Works, remaining in office until 16 June of 1912, then agin returning to lead the *Caixa*.[12] A new statute was approved on 14 December 1912, slightly increasing its powers in terms of the power to sign contracts with the state and private individuals, setting the interest rates of the various banking operations, stipulating the conditions and limits for opening current accounts, giving opinions on government proposals, solving contentious matters, making propositions to the government on the enlargement of the work force, and setting the annual budget. The choice of the chairman, however, remained a prerogative of the government.[13]

## The impact on the *Caixa*

In June 1911, the *Caixa*'s annual report for the last financial year under the Monarchy (1909–1910) was published. In it, breaking with a long tradition, the new president of the board did not assume the responsibility for the acts of the previous administrations and 'limited himself to drawing from the figures the conclusions they permit', expressing some pessimism on the outcomes of the past administrations.[14] This critical tone was due to emphasise the rupture the republic intended to bring to financial policies and, in particular, to the way the *Caixa* had been run up to until then. The problems were relevant, as in previous instances, running from deficient administration of the public pension fund to the slow growth in profits. There were also problems concerning the rapid expansion the previous boards had pushed, which opened delegations in all the 21 regions of the country, some with very low movements. In a number of parts of the country, the delegations of the *Caixa Económica* simply had no deposits from the public. In others, the amounts deposited were far from sufficient to cover running expenses, such as was the case of Évora, which had a turnover of only about 295$000 *réis*, which was rather small in comparison to the second largest city in the Alentejo, Beja, which managed to attract 121 *contos*. To make up for the inefficient distribution of the *Caixa Económica*'s delegations, the board proposed to create branches in Lisbon's working neighbourhoods (Alcântara, Belém, and Xabregas) and in dozens of other counties around the country. In total, the interim government planned to open 85 new delegations to add to the existing 48. The idea would prove to be unfounded from the point of view of the financial administration of the state, but it reflected the dominant spirit in the press and in many political circles in the country. Optimistic thinking considered that the development of savings by the general public was crucial for improving living conditions of the poorest, and thus for the country's economic prosperity. The *Caixa* should play a key role in that field by providing banking services to low income workers, particularly to industrial workers, thus allowing for the growth of savings. This would be achieved by opening branches in working-class neighbourhoods. However, what the new Republican administration failed to realise on due time was that this had not been done earlier, not for lack of will, but because the financial assessments showed that an expansion of the branch network was not necessarily cost-effective.

At the closure of accounts for 1910–1911, the *Caixa Económica* had a negative balance of 1,094 *contos*. However, the poor results were ascribed by the executive board 'to the revolutionary events that led to the advent of the Republic'. And for the supervisory board, the negative balance resulted from the 'natural contraction produced by the political events that occurred in the first period of management'. There could hardly be greater consensus on the causes of a less successful result.[15] The same report states that the political situation had normalised, and the exploitation of these new branches was producing positive results, even though *Caixa*'s net profits in 1911–1912 had decreased slightly compared to the previous year. The finance minister and head of government, Afonso Costa, had a more optimistic but perhaps unfounded perspective. Costa declared in Parliament that the *Caixa* boasted strong financial health, which he saw as a reflection of the country's prosperity. Despite the rebellion on the streets, the Portuguese people 'did not stop delivering their money to the state every day, either depositing it with *Caixa Geral de Depósitos*, or acquiring Treasury bills'.[16] The minister's intention was to reassure the public. Costa acknowledged that the executive 'needed to implement substantial developmental measures', but to achieve them he could not aggravate the living conditions of the working classes. Furthermore, he argued that the loans granted by the *Caixa* were essential for the accomplishment of works that would boost the economy.[17]

Despite the new delegations' negative balance, the *Caixa* decided to carry on its expansionist policy. According to the Annual Report for 1911–1912, 151 delegations had been created since October 1910, 78 new branches were planned for the mainland, a subsidiary was opened in Coimbra, and the one in Porto was renovated. Not all members of the executive board agreed on the rapid expansion of *Caixa* agencies; a controversial case was that of the subsidiary in Coimbra, given the small transactions anticipated.[18] In addition, the *Caixa* was also preparing the decentralisation of interest payment services, a notoriously deficient department that undermined the institution's popularity with depositors.

The administration prepared a set of measures to send to the finance minister.[19] The minister defended the measures, which were justified by the increase in the bank's movement. This implied improving the departments that in Lisbon were autonomous, but in the rest of the country depended on tax offices.[20] Subsidiaries had recently been opened in Belém, Benfica, Alcântara, and Xabregas (all around Lisbon) precisely in the industrial and working-class areas where Republicans felt most supported. But in the rest of the country, delegations were directly dependent on tax offices. It was therefore necessary to give full operational autonomy to the *Caixa Económica Portuguesa*, separating it from *Caixa Geral de Depósitos*. In the press, the newspaper *Jornal do Comércio e das Colónias* acknowledged that '*Caixa Económica Portuguesa*, with its subsidiaries scattered throughout the country, is a magnificent instrument for collecting capital for such a wonderful way of developing our economy'.[21] But the newspaper likewise highlighted that the multiplication of subsidiaries and delegations was mainly a political operation, raising questions as to how the government would use the *Caixa*'s available funds given that the floating debt absorbed a significant part of the capital the bank held. However, it was the government's decision, and the expansion plan was duly carried out. In September 1913, Estêvão de Vasconcelos was able to proudly pay a visit to the premises in Coimbra and Porto.[22]

The following years proved to be positive for *Caixa*, which showed 'rather large cash flows due to the increasing influx of depositors at headquarters, subsidiaries, and delegations'.[23] To explain the development of business, the administration emphasised state corporations' compliance with the obligation to deposit their cash holdings with the *Caixa*. The savings bank, the *Caixa Económica Portuguesa*, had also achieved its best result since its establishment, with 9,628 new passbooks being issued in just one year, which resulted in the balance of its deposits increasing by 35% compared to that of 30 June 1913.[24] The number of *Caixa Económica*'s depositors in Porto increased from about 19,000 in January 1914 to approximately 26,000 in October of the following year. In the same period, in Lisbon, the number rose from 17,000 to 24,000. Simultaneously, there was an increase in discounts of industrial warrants, cash transfers through the *Caixa Económica*, and loans to the state and municipal councils.

The expansion of the *Caixa*'s activity led to increasing difficulties of management and of relations with depositors, as the number of employees remained virtually unchanged. Hiring staff was dependent on authorisation from the Finance Ministry, which was hard to get.[25] Insufficient staff and the progressive expansion of services provided were pointed out as the cause of the delay in collecting the elements necessary for producing the 1915–1916 Annual Report. The report was usually presented in January, but in 1917 it came out at the end of February. Around that time, another issue highlighted the need to urgently resolve those points: the discovery of an operation of falsification of documents in the *Caixa Económica*'s Porto branch, which was attributed to 'insufficient staff for the good execution of the service'. In April 1917 seven employees of the Lisbon headquarters were sent to Porto to verify the records of the *Caixa Económica* subsidiary. However, the departure of these employees, in addition to those who had been mobilised for the Great War, further impaired the regularisation of the *Caixa*'s departments in Lisbon.[26]

The institution that the new regime found was solid, with a diversity of investments in national and local entities, including the *Imprensa Nacional* (National

Press), the *Arsenal do Exército* (Army Arsenal), and a number of local authorities.[27] The new regime continued to demand funds from the bank for its undertakings. In March 1917, the Ministry of Public Works requested a new loan up to the amount of 5,000 *contos* for constructing and repairing roads. The bank refused the loan on the grounds that the funds to service the loan were not included in the public budget.[28]

## The second Republican reform

In March 1917, Estêvão de Vasconcelos suspended his activity in the bank due to illness, subsequently dying on 17 May. As the government did not immediately address the matter of his succession, Raul Carmo e Cunha of the board became interim chief executive. On 15 October, Daniel José Rodrigues, a member of the supervisory board until that date, took office as chief executive. Rodrigues had graduated with a law degree from the University of Coimbra, had been a consultant judge for the Public Credit Board, and was part of the ranks of the *Partido Republicano*. However, he would have no chance of furthering his work. On 5 December 1917, with the bulk of the army still fighting in Flanders and in Africa, and the head of government, Afonso Costa, on a mission outside of the country, some military units in Lisbon revolted under the leadership of Sidónio Pais. The rebellion, carried out with the political support of the *Partido Unionista*, of which Sidónio was a member, wished for Portugal to withdraw from the Great War and to put an end to the 'dictatorship' of the *Partido Democrático*.

The ministry, temporarily headed by General Norton de Matos, resigned, while the President of the Republic, Bernardino Machado, received a summons to leave the country, subsequently taking refuge in Spain and France. Afonso Costa was arrested when he returned to Portugal. Sidónio Pais then established a military dictatorship. He concentrated power in his hands, dissolved Congress, introduced a presidential regime, and was elected president of the Republic by direct elections and universal suffrage in April 1918. Unionists, however, disgruntled with the dictatorial facet of the so-called 'New Republic', soon withdrew from the government and moved to the opposition. The three major political parties refused to run in the legislative elections of April 1918, and Congress was largely filled by the newly formed *Partido Nacional Republicano* and a Catholic, monarchical minority. Since he was a partisan of the *Partido Democrático*, Daniel Rodrigues was temporarily removed from the post of chief executive in February 1918, and replaced by Eurico Máximo Cameira Coelho de Sousa, a captain of the Army, considered to be one of Sidónio Pais' most faithful collaborators. Cameira, who was also Minister of Labour, was appointed by decree of 2 February 1918, taking office on 5 March.

The reform of *Caixa*'s organisation would take place in the middle of the Sidonist period, by means of Decree 4,670 of 14 July 1918. The *Caixa* remained obliged to contract with the government to place securities or any legally issued loan or other funds held by the state; the bank equally retained the capacity to manage deposits made through the *Caixa Económica Portuguesa*. The *Caixa* was authorised to buy and sell securities in its own name and to loan any amounts against pawned securities, the executive's sanction not being necessary. The state was responsible for ensuring the restitution of all deposits, as well as providing a guarantee to the operations carried out by the *Caixa Económica*. Some important changes were introduced in the composition and duties of the executive board. The chief executive was joined by six executive members, to be appointed by the government for a term of five years, which could then be renewed. Under extant legislation, the government could freely appoint the members of the board, who could only be dismissed or discharged from office on the same terms and manner as other civil servants. The *Caixa*'s management became formally autonomous and independent from the government, even though the latter maintained supervisory powers over accounting procedures and the movement of funds, making board members accountable to the courts for any abuse or misconduct.

The 1918 law also addressed old claims, especially since it gave the executive board the power to establish subsidiaries, branches, delegations, or agencies with their own staff where it deemed necessary. In addition, it could fix the establishment plan and hire the staff it considered convenient for the headquarters, subsidiaries, delegations or agencies. The list of operations allowed to the *Caixa* was also extended. Among the most significant were: granting loans to the Treasury under the Treasury's floating debt regular conditions, giving it preference over any other clients; buying public debt securities; discounting letters of expropriation operations; financially assisting in the construction of affordable housing for the less affluent classes; engaging in agricultural or mortgage credit deals; renting safes for the custody of private objects or valuables; and carrying out rediscount operations. In this way, credit to such important sectors as agriculture and construction was guaranteed. The interest rate on deposits from the public could be changed by the *Caixa*'s management, after hearing the supervisory board and publishing a notice in the government gazette ten days in advance.[29] During the short period of Sidonism, the *Caixa*'s everyday routine hardly changed. In the meantime, the assassination of President Sidónio Pais had direct consequences for the administrative structure of the *Caixa*, since the end of the regime determined the return of Daniel Rodrigues to the post of chief executive in March 1919.

The internal situation of the *Caixa* at the beginning of the post-war period was encouraging. The 1917–1918 Annual Report would only be published in early January 1920, since their conclusion was dependent on elements provided by delegations under charge of finance personnel not directly subordinate to the *Caixa*'s administration. Service was 'extraordinarily delayed' due to the events that disturbed the 'administrative life of the country'.[30] Notwithstanding, profits continued to rise, a clear sign of public confidence in the institution and its creditability, despite the setbacks generated by the political conjunctures. In the economic year of 1917–1918, 34,383 passbooks had been issued, whereas the previous year had seen only 20,418. The number of deposits made had also risen. According to Alberto Xavier, the new chairman of the supervisory board, the bank's capital placement was governed by a 'patriotic' policy of supporting all that contributed to the development of national industries, the protection of agriculture and the promotion of local development.

The *Caixa*'s delegations that were run by personnel of the Treasury had only belatedly sent the data required to make the activity reports, thus delaying the clearance of accounts. Besides, an enormous amount of work remained concerning the payment of interest to deposits at the *Caixa Económica*, in addition to civil servants strikes and a stoppage of the services of the national press. Still, indicators of public confidence remained high. Even though the number of passbooks issued fell to 32,002, the number of deposits on account increased from 98,929 in the previous year to 117,548. The expansion of the *Caixa*'s services continued, this time through the creation of the *Casa de Crédito Popular*, a body designed to help the disadvantaged by providing loans on pawns, thus seeking to provide a benefit to the poorest groups of the population. In the early 1920s, the *Caixa* was committed to solving one of its main operating problems, namely understaffing. The admission of employees indispensable to the development of departments rose in 1919–1920, accompanied by the increase of salaries. And although the number of passbooks issued continued to decrease slowly (31,226), the number of deposits reached 133,954. On the other hand, 15 new agencies of the *Casa de Crédito Popular* were added to the 13 established at its creation. Concurrently, the *Caixa* opened four of its own subsidiaries and six agencies.

The years since the end of World War I witnessed major banking turmoil, marked by the closure of some banks and banking houses and the opening of new financial institutions.[31] The *Caixa* weathered the instability but was much less affected than most by the crisis, mostly due to its position as state bank and thus its ability to offer guarantees to depositors. The banking turmoil was mainly due to the monetary and financial instability the country was experiencing, reflecting the successive imbalances in public accounts and the difficulties in economic and financial relations with the rest of the world. It was also a consequence of ill-adjusted banking laws, particularly as regarded capital requirements. Instability showed the urgent need to revise the laws governing the financial market, in particular rules on minimum requirements for capital and reserves of the banking system. Inflation and currency depreciation would decline in Portugal from 1924. This was closely connected to the improvement of conditions of the international financial and monetary markets following the Dawes Plan of 1924 and also to a series of reforms carried out by the Portuguese government. 1925 saw a new banking law, redefining the role of the Bank of Portugal as central bank, obliging banks and banking houses to increase their capital and reinforcing the role of the Finance Ministry in supervising the banking system. The new law also gave the State greater control over foreign exchange reserves, in which the *Caixa* played an important role since it was entrusted with managing the Financial Agency of Rio de Janeiro. This agency was an important tool for channelling the remittances of Portuguese emigrants in Brazil. The *Caixa* was also given a seat at the then-created Banking Council (*Conselho Bancário*), together with the Bank of Portugal, *Banco Nacional Ultramarino*, and other representatives of the state and the banks. However, these changes took time to produce results.[32] In order to understand these moments of recovery at the end of the Republican period, it should be noted that these years of the 1920s saw some economic recovery in Portugal and in other European countries, such as France and Great Britain. These positive trends help explain the relatively favourable development of *Caixa* throughout the Republican period.

The Republican regime did not hold for long due to government instability, popular dissatisfaction with the political situation, and permanent civil unrest. The motives behind the fall of the regime were mostly political, as the Republican political parties were not able to fulfil the promised new economic and social order, and the regime evolved to a *de facto* monopoly of power of the dominant *Partido Democrático*, which won all but one of the elections to the Parliament in the period. On top of the political instability, the Republican regime also had to face severe financial distresses mostly resulting from the negative international context caused by World War I, but also because of mismanagement of the successive governments. Financial distress was however over by 1924, as the rest of Western Europe briefly recovered from high inflation and international imbalances. Despite the political and financial difficulties, the economy managed to expand at unprecedented growth rates, due to rapid industrialisation under tariff and state protection, as well as the expansion of agriculture and the service sector. The end of the regime has thus to be explained mostly by political factors and the opposition of the traditional forces that had been put aside, mostly the royalists and the conservative Catholics. The Republic ended with another military coup, in 28 May 1926, with the aim of imposing order in the streets and restoring the power to the conservative forces put aside. The political transition was difficult, occurred within a context of high political instability, and the increased financial disequilibria became controlled only after 1928, when the head of the military dictatorship appointed Salazar—the future dictator—minister of finance.

## Notes

1  Teles (1912).
2  Relvas (1977–1978), vol. I.
3  Diário Popular, 16 October 1910; Jornal do Comércio, 22 October 1910; Diário Popular, 22 October 1910.
4  Diário do Governo, 28 October, 4 November and 3 December 1910, pp. 198, 285 and 630.
5  José Relvas (1977–1978), vol. I, pp. 170–177.
6  Jornal do Comércio, 15 October 1910.
7  Jornal do Comércio, 29 October 1910.

8 Diário do Governo, 28 October, 4 November and 3 December 1910, pp. 198, 285 and 630.
9 Livro de Actas do Conselho de Administração, no. 1, session of 19 June 1912. Diário Popular, 26 October 1910.
10 O Imparcial, 19 October 1910.
11 Lains (2003), chapter 5; Valério (1994), Ramos (1994) and Lains and Silva (eds.) (2005), vol. 3.
12 Diário do Senado, 1 September 1911, pp. 1–4, 29 December 1911, pp. 21–23.
13 Diário do Governo, 19 December 1912, p. 4502.
14 Relatório e Contas, 1909–1910.
15 Relatório e Contas, 1910–1911, p. 4.
16 Diário da Câmara dos Deputados, 1 May 1913, p. 6.
17 Diário da Câmara dos Deputados, 8 May 1913, p. 34.
18 Livro de Actas do Conselho de Administração, no. 1, session of 20 May 1913.
19 Livro de Actas do Conselho de Administração, session of 8 June 1913.
20 Diário da Câmara dos Deputados, 20 May 1913, p. 9.
21 Jornal do Comércio e das Colónias, 23 May, 2 November 1912.
22 Livro de Actas do Conselho de Administração, no. 1, session of 23 December 1913.
23 Livro de Actas do Conselho de Administração, 8 April 1914.
24 Relatório e Contas, 1912–1913, 1913–1914.
25 Livro de Actas do Conselho de Administração, 3 August 1914, 5 June 1916. Livro de Actas do Conselho Fiscal, 26 November 1916.
26 Livro de Actas do Conselho Fiscal, 28 February 1917.
27 Livro de Actas do Conselho de Administração, 26 July 1912; Relatório e Contas, 1910–1911, pp. 3–4.
28 Decreto-Lei no. 3216, of 28 June 1917, established the conditions under which loans could be granted to administrative bodies for that purpose.
29 Lei Orgânica (anotada): Decreto com Força de Lei no. 4,670, 14 July 1918.
30 Relatório e Contas, 1917–1918.
31 Reis (1995a); Valério (ed.) (2006–2010).
32 Reforma Bancária... (1925). See also Simões (1930) and Pereira (1956).

# 9

# THE NEW ORDER, 1926–1929

By 1926, the *Caixa Geral de Depósitos* enjoyed a significant degree of administrative autonomy, although it was governed by high ranking political figures of the Republican regime. It also had a comfortable financial strength, still taking a large share of the market for deposits, as interest rates offered by its subsidiary, the *Caixa Económica Portuguesa*, remained attractive for small and medium depositors and for the rest of the banking sector. The investment portfolio included public debt securities, loans to central and municipal government bodies, as well as loans to the industrial and agricultural sectors, to construction, and to other banks. In addition, the *Caixa* provided currency exchange services, particularly in the Brazilian trade, and ran funds of a number of public institutions, particularly government expenditures in public works. It was by then a well-established publicly-owned bank, but one which became too connected with the republic that was overthrown by another military coup, this time backed by authoritarian political forces, which ultimately evolved into a fascist dictatorship that lasted for decades. The new regime was soon to be led by Salazar, who acted with some care, preserving an appearance of legal and ultimately constitutional rule. The way the new regime took hold of the *Caixa*'s administration and business is quite paradigmatic and its study provides, again, an excellent perspective on how politics and finance were interconnected.

## Before Salazar

Even though the 1918 and 1922 statutes imposed a board composed of six members who were appointed for life, at the time of the coup the *Caixa* was run by only four administrators, including the chairman, a preeminent member of the ruling *Partido Democrático* (Daniel Rodrigues), as well as two military members and one civilian (Carmo e Cunha) closely connected to the deposed regime. Despite its allegiance, the board did not express much concern with the coup, but that proved an error of judgement as the political status would soon change. Although throughout the institution's history, we observed that the administrators quickly became more interested in the life of the place they were running than on following strictly any political loyalties, the new regime

102

at this time did not acknowledge any fidelity with the institution. In fact, the 1926 coup was more severe than most previous ones, at least since the mid-19th century, a fact in line with the increasingly tumultuous politics in Europe, with the rise of fascist autocratic regimes such as the one that was going to rule Portugal for decades to come.

In the immediate aftermath of the coup, the new political state of affairs was quite unstable, and it took a number of years before civil order was truly re-established. That meant a quick succession of prime ministers and finance ministers and thus little time for the government to deal with day-to-day policies, and the *Caixa* was certainly not at the top of policy priorities. Yet, the circumstances would soon change rapidly with the appointment of one of the top five military of the coup as finance minister (General Sinel de Cordes) in July 1926. Soon after, in August, the new minister appointed a fifth member to the board and subsequently, in October, ended the statute's provision concerning the duration of the mandates, restricting to five years in the case of the president of the board and three years for the remaining members. Moreover, the renewal of the appointments became a prerogative of the government, thus putting an end to the independence of the bank's board.[1] Portugal's finances were highly unbalanced as an immediate consequence of the coup, and the finance minister had to resort to all sources in order to redress the state and the external financial imbalances. In 1927, the finance minister, General Sinel de Cordes, signed a deal with the League of Nations for a conditional loan. Salazar, the man that would succeed him as an even more powerful minister, firmly contested the deal, in a move that served to strengthen his political power, which he would fully use when taking charge of Portuguese finances in 1928.

But the general had also to deal with the *Caixa* in order to stop the drain of gold and foreign exchange reserves, directly interfering with the powers of the board. The *Caixa* had assumed a role in the foreign exchange markets since 1924, when it constituted a foreign exchange service. The following year, the institution took over the administration of the *Agência Financial de Portugal* in Rio de Janeiro, which, in addition to providing various services to the Portuguese community in Brazil, also carried out operations of foreign currency acquisition.[2] The *Caixa* had formal autonomy to set the exchange rate level and at the end of October 1926, following the *escudo*'s devaluation in the markets, the board devalued the *escudo*–sterling exchange by just 0.2% (from 94$75 to 95$).[3] This was done without reporting to the Ministry of Finance who publicly opposed it, and the board officially contested arguing that the keeping of the exchange rate would negatively affect the *Caixa*'s balances. On December 1926, the minister produced a decree (No. 12,794) with a number of provisions regarding the exchange market and without previously consulting the board, moved out the *Caixa*'s foreign exchange service and placed it under the responsibility of the directorate-general for the Treasury and ordered the immediate cessation of all foreign exchange operations carried out by the *Caixa*, which led to problems in the administration of the institution. The most important was the fact that the accounts on foreign exchange which the *Caixa* could no longer run amounted to 2,400 *contos* at the end of the 1926–1927 financial year, and it took several years before those accounts were finally closed.[4] However, that was not all. On 18 January 1928, the finance minister published a decree (No. 14,908) that moved the deposit of the funds from all public institutions and services to the Treasury account with the Bank of Portugal out from the *Caixa*, and those funds amounted to a few thousand *contos*.[5] In February, a new incident revealed how the government intended to act, with repercussions on the *Caixa*'s activity, irrespective the opinion of the members of its administration. This time the board's criticism was directed at a draft decree on cheap housing by which the *Caixa* was required to grant loans at randomly reduced interest rates, as shall be seen below.

## Salazar as finance minister

The replacement of Sincl de Cordes with Oliveira Salazar did not immediately bring about changes in the relationship between the *Caixa* and the government. However, soon divergent views on Salazar's governance arose among the board's members. The board was, however, crucially divided, as two of its members, Raul Carmo e Cunha and Gabriel Pinto, aligned with the new regime, whereas two other members, Manuel Maria Coelho and Daniel Rodrigues, opposed it. The discussion in the board concerning the government's request for the conversion of public loans exemplifies how the administration was divided. In July 1928, Carmo e Cunha was entrusted by the finance minister with clarifying to the board the purpose of assembling the various loans of the state into a single contract, with a 25-year term and at a 7% interest rate. Salazar had explained his thoughts about this operation to Carmo e Cunha, particularly stressing the Treasury's interest in it, and had asked for the 'greatest haste' in the resolution, since he was counting on it to finalise the state budget.[6] The operation itself resulted in the immediate saving of 2,000 *contos* for the state, with a clear loss to the *Caixa* due to the extension of the loan term to 25 years and the generalised reduction of the interest rate to 7% per annum. This allowed a positive projection in the state accounts in the short, medium, and long term, creating an image of immediate benefit in the budget.

The discussion was heated in the executive board, and the gulf between the positions widened. Carmo e Cunha accepted Salazar's proposal, adhering to its perspective of benefit for the state. Gabriel Pinto acknowledged the loss to the *Caixa*, but accepted the proposal nonetheless. Daniel Rodrigues declared he had analysed the government's request, considering the minister's public assertions that the operation would be undertaken without loss to either party, and had decided to offer a counter-proposal. This had already been conveyed to the ministry 'using the powers pertaining to the executive board', who exercised 'management with administrative and financial autonomy and concomitant responsibility'. In its view, Salazar deciding the operation's interest himself and refusing to accept any other meant the end of the *Caixa*'s 'administrative freedom', in addition to the fiscal loss it would sustain. Accordingly, given Salazar was assuming 'full power, overriding the legislation in force and even contractual freedom', Rodrigues declared he would refrain from intervening in the matter, abnegating any responsibility that might lie with him as member of the executive board. On 30 July 1928, Decree No. 15,086 determined the conversion of most of the loans contracted by the state, and the contract was signed a few days later. The operation resulted in the unification of 95 contracts, representing a capital of 76.7 thousand *contos*.

In early October 1928, Carmo e Cunha again voiced the finance minister's ideas at an executive board meeting. This time, the minister asked the institution to study the potential alteration of interest rates applied to deposits, as well as credit operations for capital employment and also the current account in the Bank of Portugal, warranted by the Treasury. According to Carmo e Cunha, Salazar wanted the administration to analyse the issue, taking into account the market situation with regard to interest on both borrowed capital and cash deposits, in view of the Bank of Portugal's discount rate, and interest on Treasury bills. Carmo e Cunha was charged with studying the interest rate issue and, at the end of October, presented a report with several suggestions to change the rates on credit operations and deposits. In the case of loans, he recommended reducing the various interest rates and extending amortisation periods. Loans for the construction of buildings as well as agricultural and industrial credit would have the same interest rate and respective premium (8.5% and 0.25% per semester). Amortisation for land and agricultural credit would be extended to seven years, with a current account for the first two. Regarding deposits, Carmo e Cunha suggested a unification of the different rates applied to term deposits into a singular rate of 6% and some reductions in the value of the rates applied by the *Caixa Económica*, in accordance with the deposit amounts. Essentially, the proposal intended to progressively lower interest rates on the savings bank deposits as the deposit amounts grew. This meant that the higher the deposit, the lower the interest rate it yielded, thus promoting deposits typical of savings banks, that is, those from clients with small to medium holdings.[7]

This was an attempt to discourage banking institutions from making deposits with the *Caixa Económica Portuguesa*, where they enjoyed the highest interest rate in the banking system. One of the consequences of those large deposits, which amounted to tens of thousands of *contos*, was that their movement produced fluctuations in the *Caixa*'s current account with the Bank of Portugal. Gabriel Pinto and Carmo e Cunha had already presented proposals to the executive board to restrict these deposits. In April 1928, Pinto had drawn attention to the speculation undertaken by the banks. They benefited from the interest rate offered by the *Caixa Económica Portuguesa*, using it to cover the interest they gave small deposits of their own clientele at a lower rate. He also believed this was detrimental to the national economy, as it diverted large amounts of capital, not only from the necessities of the operation of trading markets, but also from investments of public interest. At the time, Pinto proposed limiting deposits from banks to 500 *contos* or not paying interest to any amount above that limit, but he failed to obtain the approval of the board. His proposal was rejected, garnering only one other favourable vote in addition to the proposer, that of Raul Carmo e Cunha.[8]

A few months later, Carmo e Cunha himself raised the issue, taking advantage of the discussion of a proposal by Daniel Rodrigues to raise the limit of small deposits in the *Caixa Económica Portuguesa* and to reduce the interest rate on deposits above 100 *contos* to 3%. Carmo e Cunha highlighted the disadvantages large deposits brought to the *Caixa*, in particular the speculative behaviour of other banks, proposing a rate as low as 2% on deposits above 100 *contos*. However, with the exception of Pinto, the remaining members of the board were not receptive to major changes in interest rates. Instead, Rodrigues' proposal was approved, although the limit above which a 3% rate would be applied was raised to 200 *contos*, postponing any change regarding small deposits. Despite Salazar's measures envisaging a period of currency stabilisation with a possible downward trend in interest rates, some of the board's members were still cautious, maybe even distrustful, of the measures' potential results of this financial policy. A new interest reference table for the *Caixa Económica Portuguesa* was only established through the direct intervention of the minister, who, as noted above, had asked the executive board to study the matter. It came into force in February 1929 and clearly favoured small deposits. The rate of 5% previously applied to deposits of up to 5 *contos* was extended to those of up to 10 *contos*, which previously yielded 4%. On the other hand, the rate of 4%, previously applied to deposits of up to 200 *contos*, became applicable to those between 10 and 100 *contos*. From 100 to 200 the value fell to 3%, and for amounts above that limit, the applicable rate was only 2% instead of the previous 3%. It was also determined to lower the interest rate for term deposits made by banks and banking houses from 6% to 5%.

## Beyond public bonds

The largest portion of the loans granted by the *Caixa* went to the public sector, encompassing the central government, the local government, and other public entities. However, although it represented a smaller amount of capital, a special role was played by a number of other different operations, valued and encouraged by the *Caixa*'s board as a means to diversify the bank's investment. These included lending to agriculture, manufacturing, and construction based on mortgage loans, as well as keeping investment in state bonds and securities and the discount of Treasury bills. In the particular case of industrial credit, the *Caixa* provided loans backed by mortgages on factories and other immovable property and the commercial pawn of machinery. It also loaned through the warrant system, the pawn of raw materials, or manufactured products deposited in the state's industrial warehouses and which the

*Caixa* accepted to discount. Due to fluctuations in the direction of the country's industrial development, the *Caixa* did not follow a defined criterion in their financing of companies, using only its own means of information to assess the activities to be financed.

Shortly after the 1926 military coup, the government asked the *Caixa*'s board for suggestions regarding the reorganisation of industrial credit. It promptly complied, soon discussing and approving groundwork to present to the minister.[9] The administration proposed an industrial credit council be set up to study the conditions of the industries able to contribute to the national economy; credit proposals would be submitted to this council and, if approved, directed to the *Caixa* for financing. The council should also administer a special industrial credit fund to cover possible losses from the operations carried out, and which would be funded by the profit from a risk premium to be charged with the loans made. In addition to this special fund, the administration also proposed that the state be responsible for the repayment of the credits granted. In order to prevent the industrial credit board from centralising the power to grant loans, potentially undermining the *Caixa*'s tradition of autonomy and independence in managing its funds, the board reserved the right to refuse lending and to request further information whenever it felt the candidates had not provided sufficient guarantees.

The finance minister showed no interest in immediately reorganising industrial credit, in contrast with the bank board's concern with the investment in several firms. These were times of strong market fluctuations that affected the performance of some industrial companies, particularly those more dependent on exports, such as cork and canned fish. The same report insisted on the need to reorganise the industrial credit, making public the project the administration had presented to the Ministry of Finance.[10] At the end of 1926, the *Caixa* suspended discount operations of warrants guaranteed by raw materials. In addition, the canning industries wanting to renew their loans were now required to redeem at least half of the loaned capital and replace the collateral in raw materials for manufactured preserves.[11] The industrialists were not pleased with these measures, and some appealed to the intervention of the minister of commerce. In July 1927, the *Caixa*'s board suspended all new industrial credit operations, during an unstable economic and financial environment. The decision was revoked soon after, in October 1927, probably under the government's pressure. In order to lower risk, the new loans had to be backed by the official *Comissão Administrativa dos Armazéns Industriais* (Industrial Warehouses Administrative Committee), and the capital for such credits was capped at 25% of the value of the property and machinery given as collateral, which were evaluated by the bank. A decrease in the number of industrial credit operations followed.[12] But the level of risk remained high according to the board's evaluation, and it called for the intervention of the government in order to increase the level of state guarantee to the loans conceded to the industries. The response of the government came later and in a structured way through the creation of the *Caixa Nacional de Crédito* (National Credit Fund) within the *Caixa*'s own structure.[13] The board proposed to the government a similar institutional setting for agricultural credit, arguing for the specific conditions in the sector, but it did not develop. Nevertheless, in 1928, the agricultural credit conditions were somehow alleviated, as the interest rate was slightly reduced from 9% to 8.5%, the total loan as a percentage of the valuation of the collateral was increased from 30% to 50%, and the maximum duration of the contracts was extended from seven to ten years.

Yet a more extensive reform of the whole institution was still to come, in the aftermath of Salazar's nomination for minister of finance in 1928. This reform involved a larger overhaul of Portugal's banking and financial sectors which to a great extent was but a continuation of what had been started in 1924 and 1925 under the Republican regime. The dictatorship, just as the regimes before it, needed justification for keeping power, and institutional reform was certainly one such justification. But Salazar was a sharp politician and moved slowly, albeit with tenacity, taking advantage of the parts of the deposed regime that he liked, and fostering reforms based on the existing reality; that is one of the mains reasons for the duration of the regime. The way he moved is quite clear, once more, when we observe closely how the government changed its public bank from within, in order to be able to use it as an economic policy tool.

## The 1929 reform

On 2 February 1929, Salazar, recently appointed as finance minister, was interviewed by a leading daily newspaper, the *Diário de Notícias*, which he used to publicise the institutional and political reforms he wanted to carry on, under the general concept that new life had arrived to the Portuguese economy, led by a strong government. The sectors he chose to mention were road and rail transportation, seaports, dams for irrigation and electricity, particularly in the north of the country (the Douro and Zêzere rivers), and, lastly, the need to 'restore the credit for economic activities'.[14] Shortly afterwards, on 20 February, the minister sent two copies of a draft for a new statute for the *Caixa*, asking the board to give its appreciation and provide feedback. The draft of the decree had a long introduction in which the ultimate purposes of the reform were explained. The draft contained four decrees. The first concerned the overall organisation of the *Caixa Geral de Depósitos, Crédito e Previdência*, the second and the third focused on the new services—the National Credit Fund and the Social Security Fund (*Caixa Nacional de Previdência*)—and a fourth was on the establishment plan for the *Caixa*'s retired staff. Another document was sent which established some grounds concerning the organisation of the National Pension Fund (*Caixa Geral de Aposentações e Reformas*). A letter that accompanied the documents asked precise questions to the board, mostly related to the structure of the administration of the new *Caixa* with its extended services.[15] The questions were clearly on minor issues considering the breadth of the reforms proposed. Less than a week later, the Ministry of Finance sent the same projects again, this time in the form of typographical proofs ready to be sent to the national publisher office. The government was in a haste and gave little or no time at all for the board to react, but the formality of consulting with it was thus fulfilled.[16] The memorandum which the government sent to the board was later reproduced in the preamble of the 27 March 1929 decree. It began by stressing the fundamental goals of the 'national transformation' program the government intended to carry out, which was a reform of the administrative services of the state, taking advantage of existing bodies, the increase of economic activity without provoking imbalances in the budget, and the reorganisation of the credit system.

It was necessary for the *Caixa* to assist in pursuing had necessarily to fit into these goals and help with the financing of the reforms in an important way. It was justified by the government's long-lasting desire to improve its conditions, but mainly with the intention of reinforcing its activity and taking advantage of its experience and extensive network for other major special purposes: developing credit operations and establishing a social security institution that could unify the various existing welfare agencies for civil servants.

The *Caixa Nacional de Crédito* was conceived to address the issue of credit and 'rebuild the country'. The private sector did not have enough strength to achieve that goal, so the state had to step in. In addition, the intervention of the government would also help to reorganise the banking and financial sector, as the credit with state support was carried on by different and competing bodies, such as the *Caixa* and the Bank of Portugal, as well as small mutual agricultural credit banks and the Ministry of Agriculture. In contrast, industrial credit had no dedicated institutions besides the service provided by the *Caixa* itself. According to the same preamble, the amount of capital invested in loans to industry was extremely small. Thus, state intervention was deemed highly necessary. Besides, the text asserted that the state had also granted large sums of money, in the hundreds of thousands of *contos*, to banks and companies with an interest in industry in addition to the guarantees given to loans granted through the *Caixa*.

The decree was discussed in the board's sessions following its reception, with the members presenting various suggestions. However, the minutes remain silent on the content of the discussion.[17] Yet, one of the members (Daniel Rodrigues) sent a memorandum to the Ministry of Finance in response to the request.[18] The text raised three main questions. Firstly, the board contested the government's wish to reduce the number of the *Caixa*'s branches across the country. Secondly, the board did not appreciate the creation of *Caixa Nacional de Crédito* and *Caixa Nacional de Previdência*. Thirdly, the board was not happy about the lack of change in the statute of its staff, which remained too much under the rule of the ministry.

The memorandum expressed that the board was not in favour of the creation of a separate credit department in the institution and preferred to run all the services in a coordinated way, with the administration controlling all the operations. The typographic proofs sent to the board have notes by Rodrigues which suggest he considered the *Caixa* ready to develop the credit system without need for a specific institution for the purpose; the state would only have to endorse the evaluation of agricultural and industrial goods so that operations could be carried out with 'all ease'. Both the text of the memorandum and the handwritten text indicate that the board preferred the loans be the direct responsibility of the Ministry of Finance, choosing not to bear the administrative burden of the projected department. However, the aim of the government was precisely to assign this responsibility to the *Caixa*, in order to have all operations centralised in one institution, albeit under different administration, pointing to the preference for a clear transfer of responsibility from the Ministry of Finance to *Caixa Geral de Depósitos*.

Given that credit to agriculture and industry was a fundamental part of the government's economic policy, the increase in the role of the *Caixa* went along with the need for the government to increase its control over the board's decisions, thus curtailing the partial autonomy the institution had gained in the 1918 statute. This was perhaps the board's greatest fear. As the number of board members was not complete, the government could legally appoint loyal members and thus change the composition of the board with little opposition. This was important not only because the new regime wanted to appear as fulfilling the legal and constitutional order, but also because government interference had to be silent in order not to scare the depositors on which the *Caixa*'s business was naturally highly dependent.

Whilst differences between the board and the finance minister regarding the creation of the *Caixa Nacional de Crédito* were essentially focused on details and the manner of reorganising the credit system, the *Caixa* openly opposed the *Caixa Nacional de Previdência*'s integration into the bank's departments. Given its functions were mainly of a social nature, the board suggested as an alternative the creation of an independent body, such as a social security institute. The administration highlighted the disparity between the welfare-driven purpose of the *Caixa Nacional de Previdência* and the necessarily profit-focused practice of any banking business, such as the *Caixa*. The very problematic history of the pensions system in Portugal explains the fears of the executive board. The institution of the *Caixa Nacional de Crédito* and the *Caixa Nacional de Previdência* also raised concerns within the board regarding the functioning of an administration common to the whole institution. Finally, there were also matters related to the statute of staff. On this point, the report made an appraisal of the *Caixa*'s performance and Daniel Rodrigues's notes sometimes show indignation at the considerations made therein. It was said, for instance, that the *Caixa* was sound and deserved 'absolute confidence of the depositing public', in addition to offering conditions to be 'extensively used in the endeavour of lifting Portugal'. But it also referred the 'need for internal reform' to obviate 'certain woes', an assertion that deserved the question mark placed by Rodrigues in the margin of the text. However, the contradiction was evident, and it was political rhetoric with well-defined purposes. The bank's efficiency and financial soundness was acknowledged so as to legitimise its use to support the policies designed to 'lift the nation'. Nevertheless, the organisation of the *Caixa* was painted negatively, in order to justify a re-modelling of its structure and personnel that would allow the full control of the institution by the political sectors linked to Salazar, whilst presenting it as a 'rationalisation' of resources. Also at stake was the wide financial and administrative autonomy granted to the *Caixa* by the law of 14 July 1918, which had given the bank freedom to hire staff without requiring ministerial authorisation.

*Caixa* was further accused of having its profits rise after the extension of autonomy, not because of the development of its operations but instead at the expense of the Treasury. The report analysed the net profits obtained by the *Caixa* and the interest paid to it by the Treasury before and after the 1918 legislation, with the clear purpose of proving that the *Caixa*'s autonomy had harmed the state and should thus be withdrawn. In the margins, alongside the remarks, Rodrigues wrote question marks and a rather sarcastic question: 'But what link can there be between the interest the state pays as debtor and that it receives, without any exertion on its part, from the *Caixa*'s management?' In the memorandum sent to the Ministry of Finance, the administration refuted the claims that the *Caixa* had 'prospered' at the expense of the Treasury. The interest the state paid to the public bank concerned loans it had requested. Moreover, by sharing in the *Caixa*'s profits, the state was receiving proceeds from an activity in which it did not invest capital, 'merely providing guarantees to the *Caixa*'s operations, ensuring solvency'. It was also recalled that the *Caixa* provided services to the state that brought it losses, such as those of the *Agência Financial de Portugal* in Rio de Janeiro, which represented an encumbrance to its budget.

The memorandum also criticised the number of subsidiaries and agencies, as well as the increase in the number of employees. It asserted that the new branches had been created 'with no economic grounds, their costs exceeding their gross profit', and that the number of employees had 'grown excessively', above that considered appropriate for the natural expansion of the *Caixa*. All in all, the aim was to prove that the public bank had been poorly managed, due to excessive administrative autonomy. However, these charges were not entirely well founded. In their reply to the accusation of opening an excessive number of subsidiaries and agencies, the administration noted that in none of them did expenses exceed income. Indeed, this was one of the few points to be changed in the final wording of the preamble. Where it previously said that the new branches had been created 'with no economic grounds, their costs exceeding their gross profit', it now read 'we hope that all have been [created] for real economic reasons and may none of them see their expenses exceed profit'. The government entrusted a top political figure, José Araujo Correia, with drafting the plan for a new structure for the *Caixa*, thus side-lining the board, as Daniel Rodrigues, the more vocal anti-government member who had briefly been under political arrest, complained.[19] In the meantime, the relations between the government and the board worsened, as Araújo Correia accused the latter of fraudulent practices and called for the intervention of the police, which the board did nothing to stop.[20]

## The politics of regime change at the *Caixa*

The 1929 statute reorganised the institution's structure, creating areas and dynamics that allowed the placement of key personnel close to Salazar in effective control of the renewed institution. Nonetheless, the change in the executive board had begun immediately after the new finance minister's appointment, in April 1928. From the outset, some elements of the *Caixa*'s own administration were amenable to the propaganda developed around Salazar. This was especially true for Raul do Carmo e Cunha, who from the first moment gave way to the minister's intentions regarding the conversion of the state's debts to the *Caixa*. In October 1928, Salazar terminated the commission of Captain Morais Rosa under the decree issued by Sinel de Cordes two years earlier. At the same time, he reappointed Carmo e Cunha, who at the next board session promptly assumed the role of spokesperson for different demands regarding interest rates.[21] In the meantime, the finance minister showed little inclination to appoint a substitute for Morais Rosa, most likely because he was already planning the reform—which he would use to place elements of his trust at the head of the *Caixa*.

The implementation of the *Caixa*'s reform began precisely when Rodrigues, who was one of the leaders of the Portuguese *Partido Republicano*, was imprisoned. The chief executive was detained, without charge, from 20 April to 16 May 1929.[22] The first of these dates coincided with the inauguration of three new board members appointed by the minister of finance: José de Araújo Correia, Carlos Bessa Tavares, and Paulo de Morais. The executive board was thus complete with the seven members stipulated by Decree no. 16,665. The president of the board was not immediately appointed as the incumbent was 27 years old, and, instead, the government published a law making compulsory public servants' retirement at the age of 70, thus leaving the way for the appointment of the new president.[23] Thus on 18 July 1929, the minister of finance appointed his long-time associate Guilherme Alves Moreira as president, and now the board had a majority closely connected with the minister of finance. Daniel Rodrigues, the only remaining opponent in the board, had been arrested early in the year but, on his return, he fought tenaciously against the measures proposed by the new administrators.

As soon as he took office, the new board member, Alves Moreira, presented a set of proposals aimed at implementing the *Caixa* reform to the extent that, in his view, the March 1929 decrees had established, reorienting the administration policy. Many of the proposals he presented to the board in the years that followed came from the finance minister himself, and Rodrigues often voted against them, accentuating his opposition to Salazar's strategies regarding the *Caixa*'s involvement in the country's economic life and in the bank's internal management. Moreira also displayed authoritarian behaviour towards employees who showed any disagreement with the policies followed. On the other hand, he sought to promote the idea of maximum economic profitability with the lowest possible expenditure. One of the proposals most criticised by Rodrigues was the closure of some of the agencies, justified by their activity being allegedly slow and by the need of allocating personnel for more important departments.[24]

On 7 April 1930, Daniel Rodrigues was again arrested by the Information Police (*Polícia de Informações*) for 'political reasons'. Nine days later, he was ordered to set up residence in his homeland in the north of the country (Famalicão) for ninety days.[25]

The 1929 reform of the *Caixa Geral de Depósitos* should be considered in the context of the reforms carried out by the military dictatorship, which became the hallmark of Salazar's arrival in power and the birth of the *Estado Novo*. The *Caixa* was becoming a leading institution in the financial administration of the state, and, therefore, its good functioning was fundamental in the conduct of the government's policy. The changes brought by the 1929 reform were a continuation of previous revisions and took advantage of a period of growth in the *Caixa*'s business. In a period of great financial instability, as Portugal and the rest of the world had been facing for a number of years, the *Caixa*'s great financial capacity, the confidence it inspired with its strong connection to the interests of the state, and its history of some independence and more-or-less reliable management, increasingly made it an exception within the country's banking and financial system. The *Caixa* was not always able to sustain this image, but the occasions of greater governmental intervention were frequently associated with poor conduct of ministers, rather than possible managerial issues, which resulted in a positive image for the *Caixa*. Blame did not necessarily lie only with governments, since the *Caixa*'s heavy dependence on the state made it convenient for the institution to also exploit the benefits that link carried. The 1929 reform was therefore generally welcomed in the institution.

## Notes

1 Rosas (1994); Lains and Silva (eds.) (2005). See also Reis (1995a).
2 Belo (1952).
3 See for what follows Livro de Actas do Conselho de Administração, 26, 27 October, 3 November 1922, 3 November, 8 December 1926.
4 Relatório e Contas, 1925–1926, p. 10 and 1926–1927, p. 6. Livro de Actas do Conselho de Administração, 15 March 1927.
5 Relatório e Contas, 1927–1928, p. 6.
6 For the following see Livro de Actas do Conselho de Administração, 24, 25, 27 July 1928, 9; 31 October 1928.

7  Livro de Actas do Conselho de Administração, 2 and 16 January 1929.
8  Livro de Actas do Conselho de Administração, 10 April 1928, 12 June 1928 and 25 January 1929.
9  Livro de Actas do Conselho de Administração, 5 and 6 July 1926.
10 Relatório e Contas, 1925–1926, pp. 8–10.
11 For what follows, see Livro de Actas do Conselho de Administração, 6 December 1926, 21 April 16 May 1927, 4 July 1927, 14 and 25 October 1927.
12 Relatório e Contas, 1926–1927, p. 7, and 1927–1928, p. 7.
13 Livro de Actas do Conselho de Administração, 5 August 1926, 25 October 1927, 15 October 1928.
14 Brito (1989), p. 52.
15 Letter from the head of office of the Ministry of Finance to the chief executive of Caixa, dated 10 February 1929, in Originais de Decretos Publicados pela Caixa–Caixa Nacional de Crédito, 1918–1936, folder titled 'Projecto de modificação dos serviços da Caixa Geral de Depósitos' (AHCaixa).
16 Card from the head of office of the Ministry of Finance, dated 26 February 1929 and proof copy with typographical proofs titled 'Projectos para a reforma da Caixa', in Originais de Decretos Publicados pela Caixa-Caixa Nacional de Crédito, 1918–1936, folder titled 'Projecto de modificação dos serviços da Caixa Geral de Depósitos' (AHCaixa).
17 Livro de Actas do Conselho de Administração, 2 March 1929.
18 Letter from Daniel Rodrigues to the head of office of the Ministry of Finance, dated 4 March 1929, in originais de Decretos Publicados pela Caixa-Caixa Nacional de Crédito, 1918–1936, folder titled 'Projecto de modificação dos serviços da Caixa Geral de Depósitos' (AHCaixa).
19 Livro de Actas do Conselho de Administração, 12 July 1929.
20 Livro de Actas do Conselho de Administração, 27 June 1929, 26 July 1929.
21 Livro de Actas do Conselho de Administração, 9 October 1928.
22 Daniel Rodrigues' personal file: no. 467 (AHCaixa).
23 Decreto no. 16,563, of 2 March 1929, article 1.
24 Livro de Actas do Conselho de Administração, 4 December 1929.
25 Livro de Actas do Conselho de Administração, 9 October 1931.

# 10

# THE PATH CONSOLIDATION OF THE ESTADO NOVO, 1929–1935

The reforms imposed and undertaken by Oliveira Salazar from the moment he became finance minister changed the state's capacity to intervene in the economy substantially. The sustained fiscal consolidation, which was mainly the outcome of tax increases, and an improved balance of payments, paved the way for greater state intervention in the economy. This was undertaken through strengthening investment in public works and greater intervention in the granting of credits to commerce, industry, and agriculture, an area in which the reformed *Caixa* would play a crucial role. The *Estado Novo* economic and financial policy closely followed what was being done elsewhere in Western Europe, and not only in similarly fascist regimes, such as in Italy. The intervention of the state stepped up from the late 1930s onwards, and particularly so after World War II. Even so, this aim was already clearly incipient by this time, when government policy was aimed at the restoration of monetary and financial balance and relaunching the state's instruments of financial intervention, of which the *Caixa* would be a major player.[1]

## Financial stability

The 1930s started well for the *Caixa* accounts, both in terms of deposits and the evolution of their financial investments. One of the attractions for private savings was the interest raise in the *Caixa Económica Portuguesa* in 1929. It was also decided to change the organisation of term deposits, which, since 1924, relied on the issuance of mortgage notes, a kind of bearer promissory notes. With the creation of the National Credit Fund, which had the power to issue notes and bonds as a form of finance for agriculture and industry, there was no need for the private departments of the *Caixa* to carry on issuing mortgage notes. Their issuance officially ceased on 1 January 1930, at which point the *Caixa Económica* started issuing 'economy notes' (*cédulas de economia*) as proof of the amounts it received in deposit and which it would henceforth manage. The minimum term for these deposits was one year, with 5.5% annual interest of up to 100 contos and 5% for higher amounts.[2] Holders of mortgage notes issued and withdrawn before the end of 1929 were allowed to convert into term deposits with the *Caixa Económica* or request a reimbursement. Nevertheless, several mortgage bonds still subsisted in 1932, showing that take-up of the new modality was not immediate, not least because depositors continued to be paid interest by the previous scheme. It was therefore necessary to 'invite' note bearers to request reimbursement or replacement and it was decided that interest payments would cease from 1 July 1932 as a way of encouraging the streamlining of the situation.[3]

On 7 March 1932, a government decree imposed limits on the interest rates on discounts and loans made by banks and other public or private credit institutions. This had special significance for the *Caixa*, which was forced to change the interest rates and to review the conditions on which credit and discount operations were based. Among the law's provisions was the end of certain taxes, premiums and other banking fees, and the establishment of new rules for the collection of default on interest payments. One of the first consequences of the new law, that mainly had an impact on the rules for granting loans, was a reduction in profits, which was reflected in the rules for lending. Its provisions, together with the reduction of the interest rate, affected not only the field of credit but also the relations between the *Caixa*'s private departments and the *Caixa Nacional de Crédito* due to the latter's current account and likewise in relation to the *Caixa Económica* deposits.

The downward trend in interest rates continued in subsequent years as directed by the government, namely on loans to municipalities for public works and those granted to economic corporations.[4] However, the board continued to pay special attention to deposits with the *Caixa Económica*, particularly the deposits from the public. The *Caixa Económica Portuguesa* was seen as symbolising the progressive rise of the movement of deposits freely made by individuals and the 'small savings'. Even though global balances had increased, and most depositors were low-volume customers with deposits below 100 *contos*, this did not necessarily mean a trend towards the creation of 'habits of economy', as annual reports since 1929 claimed. The *Caixa Económica* deposits continued to increase, so much so that in 1932 they accounted for about 50% of all bank deposits in the country.[5] It was also this mass of capital that the government sought to channel to the various forms of credit with a view to the financing of its development projects.

## Credit to the economy

The *Caixa*'s credit activity in the early 1930s would be marked by significant investment in the country's productive output, particularly in agriculture, the most defining example of which was the financing of the Wheat Campaign. In May 1929, even before the launch of the official wheat program, which would take place in August, one administrator (Carlos Tavares) presented the executive board a draft decree previously approved by the finance minister, designed to assist farmers with wheat production that year. The decree was meant to enable the *Caixa* to lend directly to farmers, taking the crops as pawn, at 8% interest, paid in advance. All members of the board approved the project, with the exception of the chief executive Daniel Rodrigues, who had been trying to maintain his opposition to the Salazar-driven dynamic within the *Caixa*. Rodrigues criticised the project, which he believed was only presented to the board for 'mere deference'. He thought it did not sufficiently guarantee the solvency of the debtors, and that it represented a limitation on the free operation of the board. However, the chief executive had long been in the minority and the project was published less than a week later.[6]

On 21 August 1929, Decree No. 17,252 was published, setting the framework for the organisation of the Wheat Campaign for the year 1929–1930. Among the means of action were: advertising, technical and financial assistance, aid in agricultural equipment, acquisition means, choice of fertilisers and seeds, and crop subsidies, all of which required funds from the *Caixa*. Under this law, a number of loans were granted with immediate effect from the institution's available funds, which promptly generated some concern within the board, not only about the amounts involved, but mainly about the guarantees for the amortisation of those credits.[7] In view of the increase of farmers' debts, and despite the 30,000 *contos* limit on the credit available for the 1930–1931 Wheat Campaign, the board sought to set stricter rules to limit bad loans. Faced with the reality of the situation, and considering that many of the applications for farm funding were, to some extent, sponsored by the Ministry of Agriculture, which forwarded many of the requests it received to the *Caixa*, the board decided to present the problem to the finance minister.[8] In fact, after two years of existence, the *Caixa Nacional de Crédito* was faced with farmers' debts. These debts were made possible because of the combination of the mismanagement of capital lent to individuals—some acting on bad judgment, others even abusing the credit system, using the money for activities other than farming—and the deficient level of subsequent supervision.

In June 1931, the government allowed a few months' suspension pending court proceedings for wheat and fallow campaign loans.[9] By the same time, the *Caixa Nacional de Crédito*'s budget was increased by 15,000 *contos*, so that it could secure more financing and thus counter speculation on the prices of produce. The government did not appear particularly concerned about the situation it was creating for the *Caixa*, specifically the financial effort it was imposing on the bank in order to expand credit. That is exemplified by the fact that the decree approving the framework for the 1931–1932 agricultural campaign was not submitted to the *Caixa* before the decision to publish it in the official publication (*Diário do Governo*). As had happened before with other administrators, it was now the time for Araújo Correia to address the government and complain about the fact that the new legislation was not sent to the board before its publication.[10] Whilst that initiative brought no change to the aforementioned decree, Salazar agreed to have the board study a new way of financing the Wheat Campaign. In addition to a credit expansion, wheat farming had enjoyed additional benefits between 1929 and 1931, including price guarantees, provision of seeds and fertilisers, and special concessions for the transport of equipment, thus reducing operating costs. In addition, the measures taken to regularise the exchange rate and the implementation of a protectionist agenda had succeeded in making the problem of wheat imports less pressing, relieving its weight on the balance of payments. Nevertheless, the government was still interested in providing a special credit scheme for wheat production, so lending methods needed to be changed.[11] At the end of October 1931 a decree was published containing several provisions regarding the form of financial support for the 1931–1932 Wheat Campaign.[12] Part of the previous framework was amended, and the principles and rules adopted in previous years were revised in order to change the conditions for granting loans, their terms, and the responsibilities of borrowers, as well as to ensure the fulfilment of commitments made to the *Caixa*. The decree called on municipalities to provide aid in the process of crop financing, establishing the cooperation of the technical teams of the agricultural production campaign, and leaving the responsibility for setting the interest rates for the *Caixa*.

In the meantime, thanks to the experience acquired in organising and financing agricultural production, the main lines for what would become the *Federação Nacional dos Produtores de Trigo* (FNPT, National Federation of Wheat Producers) began to be outlined. It also opened the door for the establishment of a new arrangement for cereals, which regulated trade of domestic and exotic wheat, distribution and prices, also covering the milling industry and bread making. FNPT was given the monopoly of wheat storage and marketing, thus countering the drawbacks already emerging from overproduction, which were creating conflicts between farmers and industrial millers. After having been created (by the decree of 24 July 1933), an appeal was made to the *Caixa* for finance through its private departments. However, the sum requested was high: 150,000 *contos*, above even the balance of the *Caixa*'s own account with the Bank of Portugal. It raised concerns in the executive board due to the risks involved in blocking such an amount, even if for a short period. The government's endorsement of the operation instilled some peace of mind. Yet, as a precaution, the board decided to secure the express agreement of the finance minister after presenting him their thoughts on the measure's impact on the *Caixa*'s financial welfare.[13] At the end of 1934, the Ministry of Agriculture considered it unnecessary to continue granting credit for the development of wheat production, given that enough had been produced for the year 1934–1935.

The great emphasis on agricultural activities in the first half of the 1930s pushed credit to the industrial sector into the background. In 1930, for example, industrial credit accounted for only about a third of the volume of loans granted by the *Caixa Nacional de Crédito*. The largest share, in capital terms, of industrial credits granted in the first half of the 1930s went to industries in some way related to agricultural activities, such as milling, textiles (linen, wool, colonial cotton), metallurgy (agricultural machinery), and chemicals (fertilisers). Concurrently, financing was also given to activities which ultimately benefited the development of the internal market, such as transport. When closing the accounts for 1932–1933, the executive board acknowledged that industry in Portugal was at a disadvantage regarding agricultural activity. They listed a number of reasons for this, including poor organisation of the sector, the impact of the global financial crisis on companies with inadequate capital, technical lag, and even the lack of raw materials. Perhaps due to the uncertainty surrounding the future of industrial credit, the moulds of its operation until 1929 were not significantly changed with the establishment of the *Caixa Nacional de Crédito*. Warrant discount operations continued to be carried out, with minimum adjustments regarding contract terms and interest rates on amounts paid against commodities kept in industrial general warehouses.[14]

## Social housing and urban improvements

Financing construction, mostly public, was the business of the *Caixa* for a long time. During the Republican period, the bank financed a number of government initiatives on low-rent housing, either directly through its capital, or as an intermediary for government funds.[15] However, despite the abundance of legislation on the matter, only a few estates were started. Political instability, financial difficulties, the internal and external context, all prevented the creation of favourable conditions for works of this nature, abetted by the lack of experience and organisation of urbanisation processes under the state's responsibility.

In October 1926, taking advantage of the discussion of a draft decree to finance the completion of residential buildings in Lisbon, one administrator (Carmo e Cunha) suggested the *Caixa* should intervene directly in the construction of low-rent housing as a form of investment. He proposed that a portion of the bank's reserve funds be allocated annually, suggesting the board immediately assign 5,000 *contos* for that purpose, and instruct its Works and Buildings Section (*Secção de Obras e Edifícios*) to further its studies on the subject. The executive board discussed the matter extensively but eventually rejected the proposal, all members voting against it with the exception of one (Gabriel Pinto).[16] In March 1929, the Annual Report for 1927–1928 stated that the *Caixa*'s action could be more extensive in the area of construction credit, although that action did not depend entirely on the bank. The report referred a number of attempts to facilitate the *Caixa*'s assistance in this matter but denounced the fact that these measures did not meet the efficiency that was generally proclaimed. However, the *Caixa* was believed to be the financial institution best equipped to help solve the housing problem, both through loans and by direct intervention in construction, so the matter required urgent analysis.

Without prejudice to these or other measures, Gabriel Pinto believed the time was ripe for the *Caixa*'s direct intervention due to the available financial resources, the shortage and deficiency of decent housing for civil servants, and the need for social order, which required that the housing crisis be thwarted. According to Pinto, this intervention could also help solve the unemployment crisis, especially in the construction industry, creating jobs for many of its workers for several months. The board members thus renewed a previously presented proposal for the application of up to 20,000 *contos* in acquiring land and building housing for civil servants, with preferential conditions to be determined for the less affluent classes. He also proposed that payment of the houses be made through monthly instalments, whose value could not exceed the average rent of the time deducted from the salaries of the buyers. Mortgages taken out by the owners would serve as guarantee of payment.

Araújo Correia, who voted favourably on the proposal, said that he had already drafted and presented a project with the study of three estates in Lisbon to the minister, budgeted around 15,000 *contos*. According to him, his project would also include construction of housing in Porto, Braga, and Coimbra, totalling another 5,000 *contos*. Those projects would require the support of the *Caixa*, as established in the 1928 decree. Guilherme Moreira said that, in principle, the proposal's purpose of helping the less affluent was deserving of his sympathy. He, however, preferred that no definitive resolution be taken without prior agreement from the finance minister, to ensure that the action of both the government and the *Caixa* follow 'an overall plan and a harmonious and convenient direction'. The council approved the proposal in principle, leaving the final resolution dependent on prior agreement of the government.

In December 1932, the *Caixa* decided to reduce various interest rates, including those applying to operations carried out by municipalities. The work order disclosing the decision internally included a specific reference to 'the desire to enable municipalities to carry out the operations they need'.[17] Henceforth the necessary conditions were created for the pursuit of government policies for urban development, with future effects on the programmes for the construction of economic housing and the development of urbanisation plans, as well as on the system of land expropriation for these purposes. In fact, the government had created a powerful weapon to force municipalities to work closely with the policies defined at government level. Direct state contributions, through the Unemployment Commissioner (*Comissariado do Desemprego*), varied between the allocation of non-repayable grants and loans with varying but always very favourable conditions. The terms of the loans granted by the *Caixa* for the remaining 50% ranged from twenty to twenty-five years, with interest rates varying between 3% and 5%.

The economic housing programme (launched by Decree No. 23,052, of 23 September 1933) was the first major direct intervention of the *Estado Novo* in housing, combining the regimes tested during the military dictatorship and the related theories in vogue in Europe since the beginning of the century. This programme was the first in which the criteria for the *Caixa*'s relationship with the state and municipalities on matters of urbanisation were systematically applied in practice. The same system was used in all subsequent programmes relating to social housing. Even though the state assumed the job of building the houses, involving the *Caixa* in the management of the respective funds and in granting financial advantages, occasionally the board tried to intervene in the construction itself, when it perceived difficulties in the municipalities' abilities to ensure the enterprise. This was the case, for example, with the estate in Setúbal. The board proposed to the minister that the *Caixa* be directly granted the role that the Municipal Council of Setúbal would have otherwise taken in the construction of that estate.[18]

## *Caixa* and the Empire

The economic model of the empire which developed from the last years of the constitutional monarchy and reinforced during the republic, particularly in the period immediately following the Great War, had mainly focused on exporting colonial products and investing in communication infrastructures, roads, and railways that would allow the rapid distribution of these products. At the political level, endeavours were being made to achieve administrative autonomy and fight against forced labour in order to bring the colonies into the world economic system. The choices of the constitutional monarchy and the republic had produced positive results until 1923, mainly in Angola, where exports grew, their values increasing up to ten times in a few years. In order to finance major infrastructure projects, the high commissioner for Angola, Norton de Matos, resorted to external credit, which led to the rise of the external debt and also to credit with the *Banco Nacional Ultramarino* (BNU), increasing fiduciary circulation several times in a few months.[19]

In 1923 there began what was to be a long period of price deflation of some colonial products. The 'great works' either were not finished or did not yield as much as expected. To make things worse, there was recurrent international criticism of the colonial administration because of the difficulties in changing the forced labour regime. Foreign loans began to run out, and those of the BNU became unrecoverable. The bank began a process of creating difficulties for transfers, and eventually, virtually paralysed them, causing a serious crisis in the relations with the metropolis. Importers who wanted to buy colonial products in Lisbon could not afford them. The same was happening in Mozambique, albeit on a much smaller scale.

During the military dictatorship, with Sinel de Cordes heading the Ministry of Finance and João Belo the Colonies Ministries, an issuing bank was created for Angola, replacing the *Banco de Angola e Metrópole* after it had been involved in a note counterfeiting scandal, which had further discredited the financial standing of the colony.[20] The capital of the new bank belonged to the state and to the BNU in an attempt to remedy its critical situation. Concurrently, the import of products from the colonies for national consumption was promoted, and relatively moderate credits were made available for the empire at the expense of the liquid assets in the metropolis. It was within this context that the *Caixa* was called upon to cooperate, continuing the state's tradition of resorting to the *Caixa*'s funds whenever there was need for funding carrying political and economic importance reflecting governmental prestige.

In 1927, the *Caixa* was compelled to open several lines of credit to Angola. Two credits are worth mentioning: first, the loan of 19,350 contos to the Companhia de Caminhos de Ferro do Aboim (Aboim Railway Company); second, the loan of 10,000 contos requested in April by the colony's high commissioner to be used for agricultural credit and the public.[21] The *Caixa*'s board had some reservations regarding the latter. It agreed to carry out the operation on the proviso that the interest rate would be 9% per year and that repayment should be made by the Angolan Public Credit Board (*Junta do Crédito Público de Angola*) with the monthly income of the Customs of Luanda.[22] The conditions were laid down for consideration by the colonies minister, who urged that the interest rate be reduced, albeit accepting that the revenues of Angola guaranteed the contract, underwritten by the government of the metropolis. As early as June 1927, the executive board decided to authorise the credit with an interest of 7%. This gave rise to a protest from the chief executive, who was absent from the meeting where the remaining members voted on the loan. Daniel Rodrigues argued that the transaction should not have been carried out for less than 9%—that was the general rate established for all public loans, and granting this concession meant creating a precedent that could later be invoked by other official bodies.[23] However, even though Gabriel Pinto tried to reconcile the different views by proposing a consultation with the fiscal council, the loan was eventually carried out at 7% interest, to the clear benefit of the government.

The creation of the *Caixa Nacional de Crédito* allowed greater control by the state over the Bank of Angola (*Banco de Angola*), since the share of the capital belonging to the *Banco Nacional Ultramarino* passed to the *Caixa Nacional de Crédito*, who thus became one of the main shareholders of the Angolan issuing bank.[24] The following year, Cunha Leal, governor of the Bank of Angola, would be removed from office after vociferously criticising Salazar's financial policy. In 1929–1930 there were slight improvements in the situation in Mozambique, but it was far from being resolved in Angola. As an indication of the scale of the Angolan crisis, it should be noted for instance that of the debt the colonies owed the metropolis by June 1930, estimated in 765,000 *contos*, as much as 612,000 pertained to Angola.[25] From 1929, financial difficulties were associated with the repercussions of the international crisis, which accelerated the fall in prices of colonial products. Colonists were increasingly desperately seeking financial help from the metropolis.[26] Many colonial societies turned to the *Caixa* for financial aid. As it was not especially geared for colonial credit, the administration requested the advice of Salazar, who suggested the *Caixa* grant only the most urgent subsidies.

A new relationship between the empire and the metropolis was being forged. In the view of the men designing it, the viability of the previous model of colonial development was compromised by the international crisis. As this was expected to last, the goal was to adopt substantive measures that would enable survival to the depressed climate. It was therefore necessary to curb short-term solutions that addressed financial difficulties as temporary problems. Nevertheless, the urgency of solving the crisis of the colonial companies, indebted to foreigners, was indeed the immediate need to avoid letting them fall into the hands of those creditors. Among the companies most affected by the economic crisis were the *Companhia Agrícola do Ganda*, the *Companhia Agrícola do Cassequel*, the *Companhia do Aboim*, and the *Companhia Colonial de Navegação*. To attend to the troubles of these companies, in April 1930, the *Banco do Comércio e Ultramar* (Bank of Commerce and Overseas) asked the *Caixa* for a 10,000 *contos* loan. Although, following Salazar's advice, the *Caixa* had shown availability to assist the Angolan economy, on this occasion it refused the loan, suggesting alternatively the intervention of a 'first-tier' bank or direct financing by the *Caixa Nacional de Crédito*.

Plans already existed for a colonial development bank, but until that was created, intervention was needed to quickly respond to the survival needs of commercial enterprises. For this purpose, the government created a committee for financial assistance to the colonies and authorised the *Caixa Nacional de Crédito* to carry out credit operations with those companies until the formal creation of a dedicated bank. The *Caixa Nacional de Crédito* was thus called upon to intervene directly, and urgently, in the colonial economy. Despite acknowledging the need to address overseas economic problems, particularly from a political point of view, the *Caixa*'s board was not very enthusiastic about the role it was asked to play. One of the concerns was that, at a distance, the bank had no means to verify the viability of the loans requested. It had to rely solely on information provided by the interested parties, even if only those approved by the financial assistance committee. The bank had no possibility of ascertaining the suitability of the applicants, could not verify the value of the guarantees offered, and even less could it supervise on site if the amounts loaned were being correctly applied.

In the financial year of 1929–1930, tens of thousands of *contos* were channelled to Angola, in funding both to colonial enterprises and directly to the state. One of the loans to the state was directed at works in the harbour of Lobito, having been especially requested by the colonies minister in September 1929. Another loan would be added, of 30,000 *contos*, for various development works in Angola.[27] These were added to other amounts previously borrowed by the state for use in that colony: two loans made in 1922 and 1923, represented by the discount of general bonds of the Public Credit Board, and the loan taken in 1927. Angolan companies were granted loans amounting to 20,000 *contos*, secured by pawned shares of the *Companhia Agrícola de Angola*, mortgages of property, and pawned commodities of some of the companies and also on the guarantee of some of its managers.[28] Such was the scale of the *Caixa Nacional de Crédito*'s financing for colonial operations, that the amounts involved at this time exceeded those granted, for example, to the Wheat Campaign. It was therefore necessary to regulate this type of financing and to fulfil the plan of creating a bank dedicated to colonial credit. Thus appeared the

*Banco de Fomento Colonial* (BFC, Colonial Development Bank) created by a decree of 8 July 1930, on the same date the Colonial Act (*Acto Colonial*) was published. However, the bank's creation was ineffective, since it did not have a body of private shareholders, elective bodies, or its own fiscal council. Araújo Correia was appointed the *Caixa*'s representative on the BFC's executive board, given the *Caixa Nacional de Crédito* held a significant share in its capital. A current account was created for the new bank in the *Caixa Nacional de Crédito*, who was charged with granting the loans on behalf of the BFC until the new bank was fully established.

The Colonial Act and the measures of exchange control with the colonies defined the government's plan for the empire. Economic and administrative centralism was instituted on an unprecedented scale. The colony's financial autonomy collapsed. Budget balance was imposed at the expense of tightening of credit and large investments. In order to counter the effects of the international crisis, the link between the empire and the metropolis was strengthened by the reinforcement of mutual trade, industrial conditioning, and exchange control. Colonial enterprises were made to produce for the metropolitan market, supplying raw materials to the national industry, who, in turn, fed its products to the colonial markets.

The fears some of the *Caixa*'s administrators showed regarding the viability of colonial operations were soon confirmed. By early 1931 two of the loans to Angolan companies were already overdue, totaling 47,000 *contos*. Term extensions and payment facilities were granted, but such measures had no practical effect. The *Caixa*'s executive board made repeated requests to the Angolan companies to liquidate their debts to the *Caixa Nacional de Crédito*, but the firms kept postponing repayments incurred under the pretext of awaiting ministerial approval for a restructuring project. In April 1931, after further postponement in the payment of interest due, the board decided Araújo Correia should collaborate closely with the finance minister to merge some of the debtor companies.[29] That work resulted in the layout of the so-called *Companhia Geral de Angola*, with a renewed administration. The new company would have capital injected through the issuance of mortgage bonds, which would be acquired from the various companies in the group that had been granted loans. The aim of the bond issuance was to try to obtain the settlement of outstanding loans with its product.

At the same time, this provided the state with another means of controlling the economic activity of the colony. The reorganisation of the *Companhia Geral de Angola* was, however, complex, especially due to the debts to foreign banks. The possibility of having to deliver the companies to foreign creditors led Salazar to allow the *Caixa Nacional de Crédito* to continue to provide financial support for the survival of the Angolan firms, albeit a precarious one. In April 1932, in the face of new pressures from creditors, the *Companhia Geral de Angola* asked the government to endorse the acquisition of second bonds by the *Caixa Nacional de Crédito* the company intended to issue, totalling 15,000 *contos*.

The request caused a dilemma in the executive board. On the one hand, there was the desire of supporting the government, which had claimed public interest in its effort to regularize the financial situation in Angola. On the other, such acquisition would aggravate the situation of debt to the Caixa which already had the responsibility for a large number of first bonds.[30]

A long discussion in the executive board on the concession of this new loan left opinions divided. Some argued a special authorisation was necessary for the *Caixa Nacional de Crédito* to carry out the operation, while others believed the most appropriate course of action would be to issue legislation to acquire the new bonds on behalf of the BFC, as had happened before. The option to deny credit was discussed but immediately put aside, given that the consequence could be the collapse of the company and its liquidation. Such possibility jeopardised the payment of the accumulated debts to the *Caixa Nacional de Crédito* through the BFC and, indirectly, the large share capital the *Caixa Nacional de Crédito* had in the Bank of Angola, within which the company had high liabilities. A compulsory liquidation implied loss to the Bank of Angola and, ultimately, to the *Caixa Nacional de Crédito* and to the state. In the end, the acquisition of the second bonds of the *Companhia Geral de Angola* was made on behalf of the BFC, for a total amount of 13.500 *contos*.[31]

Indebtedness to the *Caixa Nacional de Crédito* due to colonial transactions was growing rapidly. In addition to the large volume of capital already invested in Angola, at the end of 1932 funding to the amount of 40,000 *contos* was directed to the colony of Mozambique, at the request of the Colonies Ministry, to constitute a fund for the mobilisation of foreign exchange. This raised concerns within the board, particularly because the minister requested the credit be granted from the current account and because the guarantee of the government had not been secured. Despite Salazar sanctioning the transaction, thus supporting the Colonies Minister, the board insisted that the contract include a clause determining that, in case of non-payment of any of the instalments, the *Caixa* would retain the equivalent amount from the state share in the profits.[32]

Whilst colonial transactions with the state always had the possibility of receiving sufficient guarantees for the restitution of the capital employed, the same did not happen with direct funding to companies. All capital injections and successive steps to facilitate amortisation and interest payment were proven useless in view of the increase of overdue instalments and the considerable debt accrued. Even though the board tried to limit funding to colonial companies to the operation of the *Banco de Fomento Colonial*, this line of action was broken in 1933, with the granting of a loan to the *Companhia Agrícola de Angola* made directly by the *Caixa Nacional de Crédito* together with the Bank of Angola. This exception, especially sponsored by the Colonies Ministry, was then justified by its urgency, since it was intended to guarantee the production of coffee that year.[33] Guilherme Moreira was particularly concerned with the fact that the loan being granted directly rather than through the *Banco de Fomento* meant widening the *Caixa*'s field of action, especially into an area for which the credit structure was not designed nor prepared. Carmo e Cunha manifested his opposition, equally pointing out that the *Caixa* was not sufficiently equipped to extend its action to the colonies. He also doubted the value of the guarantees supplied and feared the consequences of the technical information usually required in transactions carried out by the *Caixa Nacional de Crédito* having been dispensed with. Both agreed that the interest expressed by the colonies minister was not enough to justify the loan and promoted the idea of asking Salazar his view on what the *Caixa*'s strategy on colonial and economic matters should be.

At the end of 1933, a loan granted to the *Companhia Colonial de Navegação* matured. The board, who had expressed doubts about the guarantees supplied, believed there was no room for renewal and presented its reservations to Salazar, seeking further guidance.[34] However, the minister advised against cancelling the contract and to instead wait for the presentation of a report requested to the administrative committee of the company, who were to also submit a proposal for the reorganisation of the services of the Portuguese merchant navy.[35] Once again, the board agreed to grant a moratorium—and the same happened in similar situations with other companies. A year later, the situation was on the verge of becoming unbearable. At the end of 1934, the *Companhia Geral de Angola* requested a new moratorium to settle its debts, justifying the need with a new reorganisation project for the company. Guilherme Moreira, speaking within the board, argued that granting further credit to this company was unfeasible, ideas he had already presented both to the finance minister and to some of the representatives of the company's bondholders. The *Companhia Geral de Angola* had an elevated financial liability, there was no prospect of ensuring amortisation and the proposed reorganisation plan itself entailed high burdens. The decision on the moratorium was delayed, ostensibly because of having to analyse the application and consult the *Comissão Financeira para as Colónias* (Financial Committee for the Colonies). However, the committee was in favour of aiding the company to guarantee its survival, given its importance in the colonial economy.

The case of the *Companhia Geral de Angola* was the subject of successive debates in the executive board, who concurrently also faced the worsening situation of the *Sociedade Agrícola do Cassequel* (Cassequel Agricultural Society), which had run out of funds to meet its most urgent commitments.[36] Once again, the 'superior interest of the nation' eventually overrode the risks resulting from the difficulties in obtaining reimbursement of the capital invested through the virtually fictitious the *Banco de Fomento Colonial*. In 1935, after many mishaps around the reorganisation of the *Companhia Geral de Angola*, which had not garnered the *Caixa*'s approval, Salazar finally showed support to the public bank. He at last concurred with the executive board's resistance in granting new facilities, such as the reduction of the interest rate or even its temporary suspension for a few years, as proposed by the administrative committee of the *Companhia Geral de Angola*.[37] Accordingly, the board decided to demand payment of the outstanding amounts, threatening to declare the credits matured and to proceed to the execution of the company. The threat had some effect, since a new reorganisation project would be approved by mid-1935, at which point new directions were outlined for future funding to the colonies. It should be noted that there was probably no intention to actually execute the *Companhia Geral de Angola*, but only to bring about a solution more adequate to the company's financial situation and to the economic environment in Angola.

# Notes

1 For this period, see Correia (1938), Amaral (1992), Nunes and Brito (1992), Rosas (1994), Valério (1994), Reis (1995b), Mateus (2013), Lains (2003) and Lains and Silva (eds.) (2005), vol. 3.
2 Livro de Actas do Conselho de Administração, 5 October 1929, 18 and 23 December 1929; see also *Ordem de Serviço*, No. 3,189, 24 December 1929.
3 Livro de Actas do Conselho de Administração, 8 March 1932.
4 *Ordem de Serviço*, no. 3689, 19 December 1934, in Ordens de Serviço, Livro 15.
5 Ibid., 1932–1933, p. 12.
6 Livro de Actas do Conselho de Administração, 21 May 1929; see also Decreto No. 16,890, 27 May 1929.
7 Livro de Actas do Conselho de Administração, 15 October 1930.
8 Livro de Actas do Conselho de Administração, 19 May 1931.
9 Decreto No. 19,877, 12 June 1931.
10 Livro de Actas do Conselho de Administração, 28 July 1931.
11 Livro de Actas do Conselho de Administração, 9 October 1931.
12 Decreto No. 20,451, of 31 October 1931.
13 Livro de Actas do Conselho de Administração, 3 August 1933.
14 Decreto No. 19,354, 14 February 1931 and No. 19,409, of 4 March 1931.
15 Decreto No. 4,670, of 14 July 1918, No. 13, article 1, base 2.
16 Livro de Actas do Conselho de Administração, 28 October 1926, 30 November 1926.
17 *Ordem de Serviço* No. 3,673, 12 December 1932, in Ordens de Serviço, Livro15 (AHCaixa).
18 Livro de Actas do Conselho de Administração, 16 November 1934.
19 Telo (1994a), p. 235.
20 Decreto No. 12,131, 17 August 1926.
21 Decreto13,068, 24 January 1927.
22 Livro de Actas do Conselho de Administração, 13 April 1927.
23 Livro de Actas do Conselho de Administração, 2 and 17 June 1927.
24 Decreto No. 17,177, 27 July 1929.
25 Decreto No. 18,460, 14 June 1930.
26 Telo (1994a), p. 238.
27 Decreto No. 18,525, 27 June 1930.
28 Livro de Actas do Conselho de Administração, 24 June 1930.
29 Livro de Actas do Conselho de Administração, 17 August 1931.
30 Livro de Actas do Conselho de Administração, 18 April 1932.
31 Decreto No. 21,376, 20 June 1932.

32 Livro de Actas do Conselho de Administração, 27 September, 21 October and 1 and 4 November 1932.
33 Livro de Actas do Conselho de Administração, 12 March 1933.
34 Livro de Actas do Conselho de Administração, 24 November 1933.
35 Livro de Actas do Conselho de Administração, 19 December 1933.
36 Livro de Actas do Conselho de Administração, 6 and 9 November 1934.
37 Livro de Actas do Conselho de Administração, 22 March 1935.

# 11

# PUBLIC INVESTMENT, 1935–1950

The balance of public accounts achieved by Oliveira Salazar was of great importance and proved crucial to the survival of the regime, contributing to the restoration of government authority and effective state control over the country. Yet for the regime to survive, it needed more goals than simply balancing the public accounts. It needed to show concern for the improvement of people's living conditions and for economic growth. In fact, Salazar had succeeded in balancing public accounts thanks to the gradual improvement in the international financial situation, but also by reducing public expenditure and raising taxes by means of a tax reform. The circulation of money was put under control through the reform of the banking system. These policies had been in development for some time, as far back as the late years of the republic. They had many supporters, not only among those who backed the dictator, but also among disaffected Republicans and influential bankers and financiers, as well as large segments of the population affected by the high levels of inflation.

However, the balancing of public accounts by reducing expenditure and increasing taxes had a negative effect on the pace of economic growth. It was difficult for a government to follow this path for a long period time, even under a dictatorship. Besides, this was the time when Keynesian-type policies were at the top of the agenda of any government that was facing economic depression. Salazar showed he had a plan. The first step was to balance the accounts, putting an end to inflation, and thereby to win support from those it affected. The level of state intervention would then need to be increased to help the national economy grow. Greater intervention by the state was a traditional goal underpinning the action of many governments in Portugal since the time of the monarchy, but Salazar was able to gather unique conditions. For the first time, and in a consistent manner, the state ceased to be dependent on external financing to intervene in the economy.

From the point of view of domestic funding, this was made easier by the increasing levels of savings in the banking and financial systems, including growing deposits made by small and medium-sized savers with the *Caixa Geral de Depósitos*. The higher interest rates and the confidence imparted in the institution through direct state association made the *Caixa* one of the most important banks in the country. For this reason, it became an element in decision making on public investment and economic support for the governments succeeding Salazar. None of this was new, given that the *Caixa* already had some history of supporting public investment. Still, soon its part in the economic policy of the country would grow and become more consistent.

## The new state and the economy

The first sign that the concerns of the *Estado Novo* went beyond the country's economy and finances was the inclusion in 1932, in Salazar's first government, of a Ministry for Public Works, absent for many years from the executive, which was handed over to Duarte Pacheco. This was followed by a series of legislative measures framing the state's support to the economy and the respective funding. The 1930s saw a number of investments in construction of primary schools, modernisation of the road network, construction of economic housing, and construction and repair of public buildings, amongst others. These were funded largely with money borrowed from the *Caixa*, with reduced interest rates and long amortisation periods.

As stated in the report of the *Repartição de Operações Financeiras e Bancárias* (Financial and Banking Operations Office) for 1934–1935, 'the state recognises the private sector as the most fruitful instrument of progress and of the national economy and therefore the government cannot aspire to transform the state into the nation's only banker'. However, 'the progressive interventionism of the state' would repair the 'excesses of liberal capitalism' and would allow the 'improvement of credit in order to control and direct it or for urgent reasons of unforeseeable origin' implied that a 'long period of state capitalism will become necessary'.[1]

In 1935, the Economic Reconstitution Law (*Lei de Reconstituição Económica*) was enacted. This was a public investment plan for the period from 1935 to 1950. It identified priority areas for investment: roads, ports, the telegraph and telephone network, the national grid, agricultural hydraulics linked to irrigation and settlement, schools and state department buildings, repair of national monuments, urbanisation of Lisbon and Porto, colonial credit, and, crucially, army and defence.[2] The law's preamble declared that the balance achieved in the state's accounts enabled 'a large accumulated sum' to be put in the service of the country, together with 'a potential of moral and material resources for larger and wider applications than those made until this day'. The state was no longer 'oppressed by its debt' and was able to resort to credit.[3] Deposits with the recently reformed *Caixa* would be one of the funding sources for this ambitious program.

During the discussion of the economic reconstitution draft bill in the National Assembly (*Assembleia Nacional*), Araújo Correia, who was both a deputy and a member of the *Caixa*'s board, wholeheartedly praised the consolidation of public accounts, which he ascribed to Salazar's leadership. He also applauded the goal of implementing policies of state stimulus to the economy: 'in a country of constant deficits, of almost always disordered accounts, where interest rates on public loans frequently reached rates much higher than 10%', it was now possible to, 'after only a few years of work, in a time of world crisis, make predictions for fifteen years; with the possibility at the same time of borrowing at rates of 4%, almost the same as those granted to states with decades of financial stability'.

By this time, governmental policies were still the subject of some debate, albeit timid and cautious, and limited to a restricted circle of men relatively close to the regime. Araújo Correia objected to the law in Parliament, claiming its duration was too long and funding insufficient was therefore not a shock. He suggested economic policy be subject to five-year plans, to be examined every three years by a central economic board. Such body should be set up with the purpose of 'drawing up the plans', 'obtaining and coordinating the necessary elements', 'preparing the necessary bodies' and 'overseeing all matters relating to the solutions' to the stated problems. Araújo Correia also wished the National Assembly had a larger role in the elaboration of the plan and that it was not simply the result of governmental decree.[4]

The report of the Corporate Chamber (*Câmara Corporativa*) on the draft bill, written by Fernando Enes Ulrich, also advised some caution. It argued that making fifteen-year predictions of the income of public monopolies was risky, since they depended on 'the terms established in the agreements between the government and the interested parties'. Also, savings achieved by the reform of public administration departments were expected to be lower than anticipated, since 'the preservation and renewal of the improved war material to be purchased or already acquired' would necessarily increase expenses considerably.[5] In addition, the listing of investment areas was criticised for not conveying a 'gradation of preference', and it was suggested that an order of priority for development was defined in the wording. During the discussion, a proposal was made to also include investments in railways and airports, both of which would eventually be incorporated into the definitive text of the law.

The Economic Reconstitution Law was indeed instituted for fifteen years and neither was the National Assembly given more power, nor any control body created. The programmes explicitly included were agricultural hydraulics, ports, river regularisation, hydroelectric plants, navy installations, urbanisation works, school buildings, Lisbon stadium, economic housing, national monuments, public buildings, rural development, prison establishments, the National Road Authority (*Junta Autónoma de Estradas*), the secondary road networks in Madeira and the Azores, hydroelectric plants in Madeira, airports and aerodromes, a subsidy for the establishment of airlines, a national telegraph and telephone network, a Special Fund for railways (*Fundo Especial de Caminhos de Ferro*), and a National Broadcasting Plan (*Plano de Radiodifusão Nacional*). The funds required to implement these guidelines would come, not only from ordinary revenues, but also from the positive balances of the Treasury General Accounts and from an increase in public income through the revision of revenues on some of the monopolies granted by the state, namely those of tobacco and matches.

It was estimated that, throughout the fifteen-year period, a total of 350,000 to 400,000 *contos* per year would be spent. The state would contribute 3,750,000 *contos*, 2 million would be borrowed, and 700,000 *contos* would come from the existing balance in the state's coffers. In total, about 6.5 million *contos* would be employed over those fifteen years.[6]

The plan required the definition of priorities, which had to be considered by the *Caixa*'s administrations when deciding on the allocation of loans. The government and the bank were not always in agreement on when an assessment of the financial capacity of the credit applicant was necessary, nor on the amounts involved and the interest rates to be applied. During this period, the role of the *Caixa* was most noticeable in public works carried out by local authorities, but also in funding some of the government plans, most notably railways, the state radio (*Emissora Nacional*), school buildings, courts, and jails. From 1935 and 1939, the *Caixa* showed signs of stability and growth, and the stocks of loans to the administrative bodies rose significantly. The following years would see new legislation published with the same purpose of boosting this type of investment.

## World War II

By the end of 1939, however, the cash reserves at the *Caixa* were relatively low, as a result of the expansion of funding to the state, namely to corporate and economic coordination bodies. Another reason was the decline in the credit situation by the *Caixa* of several banks, which fell from 94,000 *contos* in August to 53,000 at the end of October. In addition, new funding for the public sector was anticipated and therefore some disturbance in the normal conditions of income and outflows was to be expected.[7] According to the Annual Report, in 1939 the Treasury account with the *Caixa* had suffered a significant decrease, having fallen to 22% of the total value of demand deposits. However, the reduction in loans to the Treasury had freed up funds to be applied in loans to the economy, including industry, agriculture, and, of course, public works. The report, in a clear sign of praise and identification with the government's intentions, declared that 'the development of the country, recently intensified as a result of financial reconstruction, currency stability, and the "normalisation" of public order, requires significant capital. And, following tradition, only the *Caixa*, with its vast assets, can supply it in good conditions of price and repayment'. It was further pointed out that a large number of the significant improvements undertaken were due to the *Caixa*'s contribution.[8]

The fluctuation in the *Caixa*'s available funds led to occasional doubts being raised regarding some loans for the financial effort they entailed. At the end of 1939, the Lisbon City Council requested a loan of 162,000 *contos*, asking that the repayment period be stretched from fifteen to twenty-five years and the interest rate reduced to 4.5%. In a letter to Salazar, now president of the council as well as minister of finance, the chief executive, Guilherme Moreira, tried to show how detrimental it would be to the *Caixa* to increase the repayment term and charge an interest rate below 5%, the limit hitherto applicable to loans to administrative bodies, with the exception of economic housing construction.[9] He also noted that the reduction in interest rates on loans had not been 'sufficiently compensated by the decline in interest rates on deposits', thus a sharp fall in the *Caixa*'s profit and loss accounts and in the amounts of participation of the state should be avoided, all the more so because 'the conditions of the moment, as a result of the present war situation, are not favourable'. The amounts involved could jeopardise the provision of extraordinary aid justified by the state of war, since the *Caixa*'s board believed the political and economic environment of the time demanded 'special safeguards due to the fluctuation [...] of deposits and the uncertainty of loan repayments'. Deposits from the public were already showing a trend towards stabilisation and 'only through the capitalisation of interest have the respective balances not been reduced'. Thus, everything pointed to the coming of a trend of deterioration of the *Caixa*'s cash footing.

In his reply, Salazar noted 'with pleasure' that the institution continued 'to employ intelligent and careful efforts to bring together the satisfaction of the greatest needs of the state and the national economy with the security of the institution and loyalty to the good principles of a prudent administration'. Since the resources of the institution were 'smaller than the amounts public and private bodies sometimes demanded from it', each operation should be weighed against its interest to the 'national community'. It should also be taken into account that 'a period is approaching when there will be great interest within the national economy in credit operations that perhaps only the *Caixa* can carry out'. Salazar believed that the recent withdrawals in private deposits might prove to be unrelated to 'any fears of the war' and, if they were, that would be shown by the data referring to the months following its outbreak. Otherwise, he said, 'we have before us the natural effects of the price rise and the consequent stockpiling that may, unsurprisingly, bring a period of inflation'.[10] In view of these considerations, Salazar was favourable to the 100,000 *contos* loan to the Lisbon City Council for a term of twenty-five years, although he agreed with the rejection of the interest rate decrease and made no comments on the conversion of old loans.[11]

In May 1940, the *Caixa*'s balances showed no 'symptoms of improvement' and the board again expressed its misgivings to the minister about 'voting for new and long-term loans, particularly in the presence of a state of war, by virtue of its natural consequences'. On 30 September 1939, the liabilities of the *Caixa* and the National Credit Fund were 493,000 *contos*; on 24 May 1940, they had risen to 547,000 *contos*. In these conditions, it would be unwise to authorise a new loan. According to one account, 'at a time of such uncertainty, knowing that little can be done to significantly increase the *Caixa*'s resources, it would be unacceptable that 'by its action and under its sole responsibility, without depending on the government's solidarity, the board added new, large sums to the liabilities and extant commitments'.[12]

The prudence expressed in the board's communication with the official bodies had no correspondence in the 1940 Annual Report. The report stated that the *Caixa* accounts 'give evidence, every year, of the economic situation of the country', and in that year in particular they already showed 'influences of the conflict', even though they were presented as tenuous and not 'seriously damag[ing] the normal activity of this public institution'. There were no signs of 'distrust' or 'anxiety' yet. 'Instead, the conviction remained that, now as in the past, the country will emerge with honour and dignity from the convulsion that shakes the foundations of civilisation today'. The explanation given was that 'the faith of a people in its destiny' had resulted during 'the hectic year of 1940' in the continuation of 'normal activity in the business sphere, which, as far as the *Caixa Geral de Depósitos* is concerned, means the rhythmic increase in deposits and in the regular progress of transactions', so that the variations registered did not deviate from the averages of other administrations.[13] The *Caixa* continued to participate in the share capital of companies of public interest, such as hydroelectric firms, through loans, flotation, and bond subscription. Bond issuance was also used as a way of financing some of the state's own bodies. Finally, the 1940 Annual Report warned of a likely increase in price indices: 'If the war continues for a long time, if conditions of transport and other supply difficulties remain, and crops do not compensate for the excess cost resulting from higher burdens with fertilisers, treatments, and mechanical equipment, it is natural, and to be expected, that the price index deteriorates'.[14] By 1941, despite this being the year in which the *Caixa*'s profits reached their maximum value, recourse to credit had begun to decline, a situation that would intensify in the following two years, together with the trend to reduce interest rates.[15] That year, the lower demand for funds, which did not include loans to the state and to administrative bodies, whose balance increased slightly, was offset by the increase in the income of securities owned by the *Caixa* and by the development of the *Caixa Nacional de Crédito*.

The 1941 report predicted the trend of the following years would be 'towards less transactions and lower yields'.[16] In addition, between 1942 and 1944, the current account balance with the *Caixa Nacional de Crédito* decreased in value. In 1942, asset growth culminated in an increase of 1,500,000 *contos*, a trend that would last until 1945, although not as rapidly. The change stemmed from the growth of short- and long-term deposits. According to the board, the fall was the outcome of the fall of foreign reserves, due to the fall of imports, by the 'reduction of business in certain areas of economic life'[17] and by rising export prices, thus forming, as stated in the 1945 report, a 'plethora of capitals in the market that had no employment' and could only be absorbed by the economy when the war was over.[18] There was also a significant increase in mandatory deposits due to new legislation on social security institutions.[19]

The balance of loans to administrative bodies showed a moderate increase in 1942, declining in the following two years, to rise again slightly in 1945. The amount allocated to corporate bodies grew between 1942 and 1945, with a sharp rise in the latter year due to funding to imports of products, such as coal and metals. From 1943 to 1945, the balance of assets related to loans to the state decreased.[20] Despite abundant funds and low interest rates, mortgage credit suffered a slight decline of 10,000 *contos* in 1942, both because of 'construction costs' and because of 'scarcity of materials'.[21] In addition to the decrease in loan capital and the rise in expenditure (subsidies to civil service and multiplication of departments caused by the transfer to the *Caixa* of non-profitable operations), the lowering of interest rates, which by mid-1944 was 4%, contributed to the drop in the *Caixa*'s profits from 1942 onwards, and the consequent reduction of the state's share in the results.[22] In his opinion on the 1943 Treasury General Accounts, Araújo Correia blamed the drop on the 'abundance of money in the market and in the Treasury, [which] weakened the recourse to credit in spite of lower rates, reaching a level never seen in the Portuguese financial environment'.[23] The analysis of the Treasury General Accounts of the following year noted that the government was making an effort to avoid loans leading to the increase of money supply and, consequently, of purchasing power, 'with its terrible repercussions in markets insufficiently supplied with consumables'.

## After the war

In 1946, the balance of the *Caixa* continued to rise, albeit more slowly, due to the successive decrease in credit and the increase in deposits, which that year reached the maximum value of 170,000 *contos*.[24] There was also an improvement in the current account balance of the National Credit Fund, with the development of mortgage credit. These increases counterbalanced the sharp decline in credit to corporate bodies and a decrease in lending to the state, despite considerable loans being granted to the public radio, and to prisons and courts. As the decline in loans was offset by the improvement in income from operations with households and by the current account with the *Caixa Nacional de Crédito*, it seemed to point towards a greater demand for capital and thus a rise of profit in the following years. In the view of the fiscal council, this scenario reflected 'the reaction of the country's internal economy after the long, laborious, and difficult period of the war'. In 1947, the *Caixa*'s accounts suffered an asset decrease of approximately 130,000 *contos* (minus 1.5%) as a result of the liquidation of liabilities encumbering the liabilities of 1946 (financial operations). There was also an increase in the headings 'Current accounts' and 'Loans and other transactions',[25] which had begun recovering slowly in 1945. This progress was related to the growth of the current account balance with the *Caixa Nacional de Crédito*, which had reached a peak in 1940, subsequently decreasing until the end of 1944, and rising again until, in 1947, it reached its highest value to date, 178,000 *contos* greater than in 1946. Loans to the state also grew that year due to credit given to prisons and courts, after a survey of the capital still available turned out a total of 38,000 *contos*. Lending to administrative bodies increased considerably, from 343,000 to 418,000 *contos*. A substantial part of the loans granted by the *Caixa* to local authorities was directed to Lisbon and Porto. Credit to corporate and economic coordination bodies also experienced growth. Similarly, mortgage loans, which had already increased in 1946, strengthened the trend, their balance going from 405,000 to 893,000 *contos*, due to the development of civil construction in and around Lisbon. Only loans to the colonies decreased, due to amortisations or liquidations, and although a new, 150,000-*contos* loan was granted to the colony of Angola for development works and purchase of materials (allowed by Decree No. 35,669 of 28 May 1946), by the end of 1947 the money had not yet been used.

The increase in loan capital due to the rise in the demand for cash was not matched by the progress of compulsory deposits. Total demand deposits, which had already fallen in 1946, suffered a decline of 13,000 *contos* in 1947. This was not a concern, since retail deposits, excluding inter-bank accounts, increased by 43,000 *contos*, a sign that the *Caixa* continued to attract private savings, as was the main desire of both the board and the government. Following the trend since 1945, term deposits declined, probably facilitated by the limits on the amounts that could be invested in this kind of deposit and the reduction of applied interest. Mandatory deposits rose mainly due to funds coming from social security. The poor performance of deposits would lead to a reduction of 1,400,000 *contos* in liquid assets. Nevertheless, since assets increased the most in the years that deposits grew the most, it was anticipated that a slowdown in the evolution of deposits would have repercussions 'in the upward march of the assets value, delaying its pace', as came to happen in 1948 and 1949.[26] The reduction of assets was evident, in spite of a 110,000 *contos* increase in the heading of securities held by the *Caixa*. This partnership often took the form of subscription of securities and bonds from various companies, as a way to favour initiatives deemed of economic importance, such as hydroelectric plants, which were also financed through the *Caixa Nacional de Crédito*.[27]

A decree from December 1944 established that the state could participate in the capital of firms that followed the electrification plan. Three months later, another decree (*Lei da Reorganização Industrial*) explicitly provisioned that the state should participate in the capital of new companies, directly or through its credit institutions. Daniel Barbosa, the economy minister since early 1947, deemed the *Caixa*'s holdings in the capital of public-interest companies insufficient. In a letter to the president of the council (dated 1 October 1948), he accused the chairman of the *Caixa Nacional de Crédito*, Araújo Correia, of impeding his action. He believed Correia had a decisive voice within the *Caixa*'s executive board regarding financing of industry and electrification. Paradoxically, even though Correia maintained that those sectors were pivotal in combating the imbalance in the balance of payments, when the Economy Ministry intended to 'equip the country with new industry, and help by promoting or keeping from falling existing ones relevant [to the national economy], when it wants to facilitate the path for our electrification, it finds a major obstacle in the action of Mr. Araújo Correia within the *Caixa Geral dos Depósitos*'. Barbosa believed that for the bank to fulfil its duty to assist the government, a reform of the *Caixa Geral de Depósitos* and the *Crédito e Previdência* was necessary, 'so the government can, with certainty and balance, make use of the necessary tools to carry out its industrial upgrade programme'. But more than a reform of the *Caixa*, what the minister wanted was the immediate 'exit of Mr. Araújo Correia as member of the *Caixa*'s board and the entry to his post of a person of known repute who the Economy Ministry can trust to study matters quickly and, for each matter, consider solely the national interest and not the satisfaction of his personal vanity, or dislike for the person who had them designed and presented them to the country'.[28]

However, Salazar did not accept Barbosa's proposal; he resigned on 16 October, while Araújo Correia remained in the *Caixa*'s board and at the head of the *Caixa Nacional de Crédito* until 1964, meanwhile financing industrial companies of marked public interest, such as the cases of the *Empresa Hidroeléctrica da Serra da Estrela* and the *Companhias Reunidas Gás e Electricidade* between 1949 and 1950. The *Caixa Nacional de Crédito* also took shares and bonds on behalf of other companies, such as the *Hidroeléctrica do Zêzere* and the *Companhia Nacional de Electricidade*.[29]

In a statement made by the government in November 1948, at the close of an exhibition celebrating fifteen years of the Ministry of Public Works, Salazar presented that ministry's activity as 'a varied, multiform body of work, of majestic buildings and small graceful dwellings, wide roads and rustic tracks, factories and churches, harbours and dams, schools and hospitals, castles and barracks'; it was 'modest without misery, progressive without leaving behind the past of which it is proud'.[30] It seemed the country was again tidy and shining on all fronts, perhaps as never before in its history.

In short, 4,000,000 *contos* were invested under the Economic Reconstitution Law, at constant prices, a little below the anticipated 6,500,000.[31] About half of this was spent on defence. The necessary loans were almost entirely contracted in the domestic market, and therefore did not affect the foreign debt or interest of the country. In a final assessment report on the law, Salazar emphasised that the works had been essentially carried out by private companies, the state merely providing technical and financial aid. However, the state promoted the creation of mixed capital companies which contributed greatly to the realisation of investments. These were the cases of the *Companhia Portuguesa dos Caminho de Ferro*, the hydroelectric plants of Zêzere and Cávado, the *Companhia Portuguesa de Petróleos*, the *Companhia Portuguesa de Celulose*, and the *Companhia Nacional de Electricidade*. According to the same report, the implementation of this law forced public administration to subordinate its activity to previously established plans. Unemployment was reduced by the absorption of the available labour force and, despite the period of application of the law having been traversed by war and bad harvests, 'the life of the country underwent great transformation in the last years' for the better.[32]

The balance for 1948 meant a sharp increase of the *Caixa*'s profits, which would continue to grow in the following years.[33] There was a significant increase in the balance of the current account with the *Caixa Nacional de Crédito*, especially in relation to industrial credit, due to the investments made in the electricity and chemical industries, a trend that would persist. There was also a substantial increase in colonial loans due to the opening of credits to Angola (150,000 *contos*) and Cape Verde (40,000).[34] The balances of loans to administrative corporations and bodies rose from 492,000 *contos* in 1947 to 636,000 in 1948. There was also a rise in the value of loans to corporate bodies and bodies of economic coordination due to the need, 'acknowledged by the government', of aiding the production and food policies then required by the country by granting new and important credits in the short-term. Mortgage credit also underwent significant expansion, mainly influenced by two factors: 'greater demand for this kind of credit at a time of bank credit contraction due to early signs of deflation, and the great growth of civil construction, mainly in the districts of Lisbon and Porto'. It was believed that by allowing this credit modality to develop, even within limits, the *Caixa* had contributed to 'delay the pace of the ongoing deflationary process, thus allowing time for the national economy to make smoother preparations for a readjustment of income to the surrounding environment, and give the government a longer period for studying the means of intervening for when time was ripe'. On the other hand, by allowing greater scope to civil construction, 'the state contributed significantly [...] to solve the pressing housing problem, especially in the districts of Lisbon and Porto'.[35]

There were no profound changes in the outline of the *Caixa*'s funds and in the development of its operations in 1949. Although the trends of the previous year remained, capital investment grew, especially in industrial credit for energy production (whose balance amounted almost to one million *contos*) and loans to administrative bodies (211,000 *contos* more than in the previous year), including a loan to Porto City Council for the redemption of the public transport licence. However, by then the rise in municipal loans began to worry the *Caixa* administration.[36]

The post-war period saw an expansion of the credits awarded by the *Caixa*. The reasons behind this trend were likely not the same as that which led to an identical movement in commercial banks (import of consumer goods, production goods, and vehicles with no counterpart in exports, hampered by international political conditions), but 'above all the investment in enterprises of proven importance for the life of the nation, such as farming and civil construction',[37] thus also seeking to delay deflation. In 1949 there were already signs of a new phase for the Portuguese economy. The deflationary trend that had begun in 1946 seemed to be 'on the verge of ending: in the first half of the year, the rate of deflation eased; in the second, almost suddenly, there were signs typical of a stable situation'.[38]

Throughout this period, the *Caixa Geral de Depósitos* contributed decisively to the funding of many sectors of public works that can be considered to have been covered by the Economic Reconstitution Law. Firstly, credit was granted for water supply works, which the government promoted through loans with favourable rates and repayment conditions, and 'by awarding large contributions'. By mid-1952, the *Caixa* informed Salazar that the loans used to supply water to the population amounted to 208,000 *contos*, far exceeding the budget provided for in Decree No. 33,853 of 1944, which was 150,000. It should be added the loans granted to the *Companhia de Águas de Lisboa*. Incentives for the construction of economic housing were budgeted at 85,000 *contos* in 1948, decreasing to 31,500 in 1953.[39]

Years later, the Law of Economic Reconstitution would be seen as the first state plan, providing a basis for the development plans that would follow after 1953.[40] The law established standards and criteria for selecting the priority investments to be supported by the state, as well as the respective budget allocations and the availability of resources. However, the nature of the Economic Reconstitution Law differs significantly from the development plans. Firstly, it lasted for fifteen years, a manifestly long period for the feasibility of a governmental plan, as many then critically pointed out. Secondly, that law served, above all, to condition investment decisions and keep them within the budget available, thus preventing public investment from leading to state deficits. This basic principle would be followed by the development plans, especially before the end of the 1960s. But these plans were more elaborate documents, with more detailed analyses of the state of the economy, investment needs and the country's financial resources, and more precise guidelines on investment decisions.

## Notes

1 Relatório da Repartição de Operações Financeiras e Bancárias, 1934–1935 (AHCaixa).
2 Lei No. 1914 of 24 May 1935; Nunes and Valério (1983), Rosas (1994) and Lains (2003).
3 Diário da Assembleia Nacional, 23 January 1935, p. 72.
4 Diário da Assembleia Nacional, 27 February 1935, p. 393–397.
5 Diário da Câmara Corporativa, 12 February 1935, p. 251.
6 Nunes and Valério (1983), pp. 338–339.
7 Relatório e Contas, 1939, p. 23.
8 Relatório e Contas, 1939, pp. 9, 19.
9 Letter from Guilherme Moreira to the President of the Council and Finance Minister, dated 31 October 1939, in Oficios do Conselho de Administração, vol. 3 (AHCaixa).
10 Letter from António de Oliveira Salazar to Guilherme Moreira, dated 5 November 1939, in Oficios do Conselhode Administração, vol. 3 (AHCaixa).

11  Letter from Guilherme Moreira to the Mayor of Lisbon, dated 21 November 1939, in Ofícios do Conselho de Administração, vol. 3 (AHCaixa).
12  Letter of 24 May 1940, in Ofícios do Conselho de Administração, vol. 4 (AHCaixa).
13  Relatório e Contas, 1940, pp. 5–6.
14  Relatório e Contas, 1940, p. 8.
15  Relatório e Contas, 1947, p. 8.
16  Relatório e Contas, 1941, p. 19.
17  Relatório e Contas, 1942, pp. 7–8, 17; 1943, p. 21, 1944, p. 23.
18  Relatório e Contas, 1945, p. 8.
19  Relatório e Contas, 1943, pp. 5 and 8, 1943, p. 10, 1944, p. 10.
20  Relatório da Repartição de Operações Financeiras e Bancárias, 1941 (AHCaixa); Relatório e Contas, 1945, p. 18.
21  Relatório e Contas, 1942, p. 19.
22  Ofícios do Conselho de Administração, vol. 6 (AHCaixa); Parecer sobre as Contas Gerais do Estado, 1946, p. 47.
23  Parecer sobre as Contas Gerais do Estado, 1943, p. 63.
24  Pare4er sobre as Contas Gerais do Estado, 1944, p. 43.
25  Parecer sobre as Contas Gerais do Estado, 1947, pp. 7–8.
26  Relatório e Contas, 1947, pp. 6–9, 36.
27  Relatório e Contas, 1948, p. 9.
28  Rosas et al. (2002), pp. 137–138.
29  AOS/CO/FI-5C, PT. 7 (IAN/TT); see also Guilherme Moreira's letter to the administrators of Hidroeléctrica do Zêzere, dated 12 April 1950, and Ofícios do Conselho de Administração, vol. 8 (AHCaixa).
30  Salazar (1937–1961), vol. 3, pp. 342–343.
31  Nunes and Valério (1983), pp. 331–359.
32  Relatório da Execução da Lei de Reconstituição Económica, pp. 6–7.
33  Relatório e Contas, 1948, p. 34.
34  Decreto-Lei No. 35,669, 28 May 1946; Decreto No. 36,780, 6 March 1948.
35  Relatório e Contas, 1948, pp. 11–14.
36  *Ofícios do Conselho de Administração*, Livro 10 (AHCaixa).
37  Relatório e Contas, 1950, pp. 10–11.
38  Relatório e Contas, 1949, p. 5.
39  Amaral Neto, session of 19 March 1953, *Diário da Assembleia Nacional*, 20 March 1953.
40  (III) Plano de Fomento (…) (1967), vol. 1, p. 25.

# 12

# BETWEEN THE STATE AND THE MARKET, 1950–1968

The economic policy of the Portuguese government after World War II had two fundamental aspects. The first was the continuation of public investment in infrastructure and support for the development of certain industrial sectors, most within the domestic market, but also some export oriented. The second was the follow-up of the process of tariff reductions among western European countries, which would culminate in Portugal's accession to the European Free Trade Association (EFTA) in 1959. The *Caixa Geral de Depósitos* was one of the government's most important tools for the pursuit of these goals, particularly concerning financing the policy of public works and supporting industrial and agricultural investment. The *Caixa*'s contribution was increasingly significant since the institution held a dominant position as the main deposit bank in the country, and the funds deposited therein became decisive for the conduct of public investment policies. The *Caixa*'s role in the internationalisation of the national economy was less relevant, since Portugal, like most other European countries, followed a policy of exchange control, which implied greater direct intervention by the Finance Ministry and the Bank of Portugal. The internationalisation of the national banking system would include receiving emigrants' deposits; this became an important source of foreign currency for private banks, but the *Caixa* kept only a small part in this business.

Soon, the *Caixa* would face the competition of private banks, who were about to experience great development.[1] This posed new challenges to the *Caixa*, as it implied a substantial improvement in the quality of services, particularly to depositors. Such improvement entailed considerable operational reforms, hampered by the straitjacket imposed by the institution's statute, which dated from 1929, in spite of the many revisions it suffered. The statute was updated to suit modern times in 1969, following Salazar's departure in 1968 for health reasons (he died in 1970). Before that, the main institutional change within the *Caixa* in the 1950s, as far as legislation is concerned, was the reorganisation of its departments in 1955. Alves Moreira continued as chief executive until 1959, when he was replaced by Ulisses Cortês, until then minister of economy. Cortês remained in the *Caixa* until June 1965, at which point he returned to the government as finance minister. Despite these changes in the

*Caixa*'s administration and in the stewardship of the finance and economy portfolios, this was a relatively stable period for the institution.

## Financial concerns

The years following the end of World War II were marked by an atmosphere of great uncertainty throughout Europe. Portugal was an exception as until 1947 prospects were good. During the war, large trade surpluses had accumulated from the growth in exports of some raw materials and processed food products. There were many who felt that the country could go through the coming years immune to the problems of war-torn Europe. However, as early as 1948, Portugal's optimism darkened, again in a counter-cyclical trend, since by then Europe was beginning to take decisive steps towards economic reconstruction. The reserves of the trade surplus were rapidly dwindling due to severe shortages in the supply of food to the population. As an additional source of concern, the inflationary pressure that had followed the 'war economy' in Portugal still lingered.[2] Gradually, however, national pessimism would subside as the country became involved in the economic and political integration process that was gaining strength in Europe.

Portugal's accession to the European integration movement was milder than that of most western European countries, with the exception of Spain. It was, however, achieved to the extent of the possibilities, and perhaps the needs, of the small peripheral economy. The government's decision to eventually accept aid from the Special Mission of the United States Economic Cooperation Authority (Marshall Plan), following the initial rebuttal for political reasons, and thereby participate fully in the Organisation for European Economic Cooperation (OEEC) and the liberalisation of tariffs, was fundamental to improving the sentiment about the future of the national economy. Another crucial element of economic policy would soon be created: the First Development Plan. It came into force in 1953, replacing the Economic Reconstitution Law (1935–1950), with a much better structured form. In the years that followed, European participation and the framework for public investment provided by the development plan were crucial for the national economy and for the main economic and financial agents of the country, including the *Caixa Geral de Depósitos*.

Post-war European recovery was largely due to the political and economic cooperation movement that took place shortly after the end of the conflict. The Marshall Plan and the OEEC, created in its wake the following year, were the initial foundations of European economic integration.[3] This was to gain momentum with the creation of the European Coal and Steel Community (ECSC) in 1951, the European Economic Communities (EEC) in 1956, and EFTA in 1959. Portugal was able to follow the European path of recovery mainly because Salazar's government closely followed the institutional transformations that led to the reduction of barriers to international trade and the process of economic and political integration in western Europe.[4]

The *Caixa* administration showed concern on several occasions about the problems the Portuguese economy was going through. They were well justi-fied, since the *Caixa*, by virtue of its size, was increasingly dependent on the national macroeconomic development and on the financial situation of the state. The central place the bank held in the country's economic and financial life in the beginning of the 1950s is well represented by the fact that one of its administrators, the economist José Araújo Correia, was also a long-standing member of the National Assembly and rapporteur of the opinions on the Treasury General Accounts. In his report on the 1950 accounts, he forewarned precisely of the problems of inflationary pressure because of the state's 'exces-sive expenditure', which he thought should be avoided in order to prevent public deficit and 'currency depreciation, with serious repercussions on social life'.[5] The *Caixa*'s board was naturally concerned about the inflationary spiral, since inflation would necessitate the rise of the interest rates on the loans granted, which depended on government decisions that might not come in time. But the *Caixa* was proud to have applied some parsimony in granting credit during the war. A letter by Guilherme Moreira to the finance minister dated 20 January 1951 explained: 'By keeping large sums inactive during the time of war and accumulating them, albeit with self-sacrifice, the *Caixa* was doubtless coop-erating with the policy then required. It not only failed to support, but even countered the euphoria in, life and business that was the cause of the greatest difficulties emerging after the war. The *Caixa* is certain to have, later, with new circumstances, contributed to greater security of the national banking system'.[6]

The *Caixa*'s credit awarding activity rose some concerns to the board, as it had not always been grounded on the best financial decisions. Sometimes the board was forced to lend to public bodies on the basis of political criteria. Given the *Caixa* was a public bank, such decisions were inevitable. Further-more, the board had limited autonomy, with low decision-making ability on loan conditions, values and interest rates, as well as personnel management. The burden of these limits grew as the bank increased the volume of its financial investments. This dependence on public administration marked the running of the *Caixa* over the years addressed in this chapter. Yet, the main concern was to make sure that politically motivated credit and the remaining financial activity of the bank were well thought out. In the 1950 Annual Report, after recal-ling how 'very high [was] the sum of authorised investments, which sup-ported undertakings of public interest, particularly those arising from the initiative of administrative bodies', the board argued for the need to reduce the amounts loaned to state bodies.[7]

Among the public bodies financed by the *Caixa*, the board was most con-cerned about municipal councils, whose funding was the subject of a varied exchange of correspondence between the *Caixa* and the government. At the end of 1949, the long-term loans granted to administrative bodies by the *Caixa*'s private services alone accounted for 36% of all loans and employed 27% of total deposits.[8] Given this, in November 1950, the chief executive told the finance minister that any vote on new aid for administrative bodies had to be an exception.[9]

The *Caixa*'s efforts to reduce capital employed in administrative loans some-times ran up against other governmental interests. Despite asserting that the conditions of the capital market and of the institution itself advised against new credit, the administration was faced with the need to approve funding deemed important by the government. One example of this involved the municipal council of São Vicente, Madeira in late 1950, shortly after the chief-executive had told the minister that new loans should only be considered exceptionally. Likewise, in 1951, the executive board approved of the financing for water supply and electrification works proposed by the government, leading the minister of public works, José Frederico Ulrich, to praise the *Caixa* for its 'collaborative spirit that has done so much to facilitate the great work of material reconstruction of the country carried out in the last decades'.

This 'collaborative spirit' was reaffirmed by the board to Ulrich when, in July 1951, the board informed Ulrich that the amount authorised for new loans to administrative bodies had been raised from 35,000 to 42,000 *contos*, and that the liabilities open to them had been raised to 130,000 *contos*. Nevertheless, some apprehension was shown for the money involved already amounting to one million *contos*.[10] A letter from the chief-executive to the minister dated 6 August, agreeing to analyse loan applications from some municipalities for water supply works, pointed to even higher amounts: 'The funds authorised by my board since 1 January 1951 to administrative bodies already surpass 45,000 *contos*, which includes 31,000 *contos* of the loan scheme for the current year designed in your ministry'. Notwithstanding, Moreira emphasized that 'the resolution adopted will once again give [...] absolute certainty of our continual desire to cooperate, and our regard for public interests that merit your protection'. The minister appre-ciated the decision, underlining that the *Caixa* once again contributed 'to make possible the accomplishment of some enterprises of the highest interest'.[11]

The regular granting of long-term credit imposed by the government raised significant problems for the *Caixa*'s executive board, recurrently referred to in the correspondence between the bank and the government, as well as in internal work orders of the *Caixa* and minutes of the executive and supervisory boards. Thus, at the end of 1951, the administration had to analyse a request for a 15,000 *contos* loan to the General District Council of Angra do Heroísmo for a hydro-electric plant on the island of Terceira, commissioned in a draft bill sent by the minister of finance. The analysis concluded the interest rate should be 4.5% rather than the 4% the Minister wanted. The board argued this was 'fully justified by the development seen in the internal market in interest rates on long-term loans'. The official reply to the minister was accompanied by a separate note from Guilherme Moreira, in which he mentioned his concern about the incon-venience of legislative bills regulating the conditions for loans to administrative bodies.[12] On 19 December 1951, Moreira reported to the minister that loan authorisations to administrative bodies since the beginning of the year amounted to 67,000 *contos*, the available balance of loans already granted was 60,000, and the total value of authorised loans dependent on contract amounted to 33,000 *contos*. Consequently, he defended that new loans to be authorised in 1952 should not exceed 45,000 *contos*—35,000 for a commitment already made on 14 June 1951 and 10,000 for a new loan to Lisbon City Council.

The 1951 Annual Report reaffirmed the board's position: the growth in money supply begun in 1950 and further developed in 1951, owing to the increase in overseas exports, demanded 'parsimony in granting credit, as confirmed by experience, in order to prevent the expansion of credit from dangerously accelerating the pace of monetary expansion'. Credit policy was thus based on the attempt to 'prevent the damaging effects that credit, randomly going up and down, may have on the national economy'.

However, in spite of attempts to reduce credit to administrative bodies, the overall balance of the various loan headings still held significant amounts. The current account with National Credit Fund increased by 105,000 *contos* in 1951, industrial credit seeing the most significant rise: electrical industries (310,000 *contos*), chemical industries (158,000), ceramic and building material industries (120,000). This was pointed out in the Annual Report as evidence that the *Caixa* had not 'put an end to financial support to enterprises relevant to the country's economy, within the framework of the economic development policy'. Loans to administrative bodies, in turn, exceeded those of the previous year by 29,000 *contos*. The increase of these loans in the previous five years amounted to 543,000 *contos*, which was given as example of the 'financial support provided by the institution to works of public interest undertaken by administrative bodies, in particular those concerning collection and distribution of water and electrification within the councils'.[13]

The endeavour to contain the growth in the value of loans to administrative bodies continued in 1952. Yet, the *Caixa*'s prudence bothered the Ministry of Public Works, who, in a memorandum of 24 April 1952, accused it of making loans granted to water supply works dependent on the limits established in the Administrative Code that stated that the debt burden of an administrative body could not exceed one-fifth of the ordinary revenue collected in the previous economic year. Under these conditions, many municipalities would not be able to resort to credit, a situation for which the minister saw no justification, since the loans would be guaranteed by the sale of water and therefore did not affect the councils' ability to dispose of their revenue to carry out financial operations for other improvements. The minister also criticised the increase in interest rates (4%, instead of the initial 3.5%), as well as the reduction in the loans' use and amortisation terms (respectively, from three years to one, and from twenty to fifteen years).[14]

The arguments of the Ministry of Public Works were assessed by the board, who then presented its defence to the minister of finance. Guilherme Moreira argued that the minister of public works seemed to want to turn town councils into mere intermediaries in the water supply works in municipalities, making the *Caixa* the entity that was actually responsible for its implementation, whilst it was not covered by the state's subsidy and by the expected water yield. It was also denied that the board was following limits established in the Administrative Code, since loans for works subject to municipalisation were covered by an exception provided for in the code itself. On the other hand, in view of the evolution of the capital market and interest rates, the extension of the *Caixa*'s long-term operations was no longer advisable. As an example, Moreira provided figures showing the considerable rise of loans to administrative bodies since the enactment of Decree-Law No. 33,863 (15 August 1944), authorising municipal councils to contract loans in the *Caixa* for water works: 'from 31 August 1944 to 31 May 1952, the outstanding balance of the loans rose from 371,000 to 973,000 *contos*'.[15] And if the reduction of the repayment term could 'temporarily represent a burden for councils that which, moreover, is entirely recoverable', it in turn created 'more favourable prospects to those and other councils, by accelerating the course of loans'.

Regarding the interest rate, Moreira noted it was 'patently low', and that the increase of 0.5% represented a 'small contribution by the councils' to the works, when the revenue from the sale of water was not enough. Finally, he reaffirmed the position of the *Caixa*'s board against loan conditions being established in the decree, justifying that these should be 'analysed during the negotiations between the administrative bodies and the *Caixa* or, at the very least, between the *Caixa* and the Ministry of Finance'. In this instance, the board had greater leverage over government decisions, as compared to previous episodes of conflict of interests with the government.

By mid-1952, loans authorised to administrative bodies for that year had reached 61,000 *contos*, thus denoting a 'continued aggravation' of the situation, as Moreira pointed out. Their debit balances had increased from 948,000 on 31 December 1951 to 978,000 *contos* on 30 June 1952. To these were added 39,000 in loans already contracted and 52,000 in loans with pending contracts, which, all in all, amounted to around 1,000,000 *contos*. Debit balances therefore accounted for about one-third of all loans through the *Caixa*'s private departments, making the bank reluctant to assume new liabilities in long-term operations.

In the following months, the administrative bodies' debt continued to grow, particularly from loans granted to city councils. Other contracts involving significant amounts include that with the *Companhia das Águas de Lisboa*, which, up to the end of 1952, benefited from loans in excess of 173,000 *contos*. By the end of the year, a further 20,000 *contos* were destined for the Domestic Settlement Board. Circumstances of falling retail deposits, the main source of capital for investment, then aggravated the *Caixa*'s board's concerns about the total amount committed to credit operations with administrative bodies. The 1952 Annual Report stated that the *Caixa*'s existing financial resources remained unchanged.[16] This explained the board's insistent appeal to the Finance Ministry for prudence in this type of loan to administrative bodies, whose debit balance exceeded 1,000,000 *contos*, and whose excessively long repayment terms compromised the *Caixa*'s results and future financial abilities.[17]

## The development plans

The government's objective of involving the *Caixa* in the funding of the First Development Plan (1953–1958) was also considered advantageous by the bank's board. It was, after all, materialising the decisions on the bank's financial investments, and the state was the best customer for the *Caixa* to invest the large sums it had accumulated over the years from deposit growth. The plan established the priorities for public investments and dictated they be carried out once their financial sustainability was guaranteed, thus becoming a fundamental instrument in the definition of medium-term public policies. This framework was already partly provided for by the government, but the development plan made it more consistent and predictable.

The analysis of the scarce extant correspondence between the *Caixa*'s board and the government shows that the bank preferred this model, which provided more clarity and definition of public policies, even though this still implied that many management decisions had to comply with the stipulations of the government. In short-term financial management, the *Caixa* was bound to impose the discipline that came with the knowledge that its existing funds ultimately depended on the public, since the overwhelming majority of its assets lay in deposits made by individuals. The *Caixa*'s history is marked by this dichotomy: an endeavour to share in the interests of the state, balanced by caution regarding the profitability of the loans granted.

The *Caixa*'s participation in the financial execution of the First Development Plan was initially set at 420,000 *contos* (Law No. 2,058), of which 120,000 were intended for small rural and urban electricity distribution (loans to administrative bodies) and the remaining 300,000 to the *Correios Telégrafos e Telefones* (CTT, the Postal, Telegraph and Telephone Company). Although the full amount originally anticipated for direct financing was not fulfilled, the total sum of the *Caixa*'s planned contribution was largely exceeded due to the subscription of shares and bonds of many companies covered by the scheme. The unforeseen participation increase was determined by political and economic convenience of the state. In conclusion, distinguishing between independent sources of the state and sources directly or indirectly dependent on the state, the participation of the public authorities reached as much as 67% of total funding. However, within the dependent sources of the state, the total amount of the *Caixa*'s participation in the financing of projects under the First Development Plan reached 568,000 *contos*, corresponding to only 6% of total funding. It is not easy to accurately quantify the financial participation of the *Caixa* in the First Development Plan, since funding sources were not always sufficiently broken down in the plan's annual results presentation. The *Caixa* was sometimes included in the generic designation 'saving banks', even though almost the entirety of the funding under this heading came from its coffers.[18] This is similarly shown by the final clearance of the first plan's results, confirming that expenditure far exceeded the initial forecast.[19] For a long time, the *Caixa* had been showing general concern over the financing of administrative bodies, whose outstanding balances had grown substantially. In the previous years, the institution had raised difficulties regarding borrowing, leading to long delays. Furthermore, given the precariousness of their financial life, municipal councils were practically unable to borrow from private banks, as the Administrative Code (Article 763) determined town councils could not borrow at a rate higher than that of the *Caixa*, then 4.5%.[20]

Although the plan especially favoured sectors such as electricity, transport, and communications, the government showed interest in using the scheme to invest in other areas, such as the wine sector, agriculture, and the hotel industry. That interest was reflected in the *Caixa*'s credit activity. In the case of wine production and trade, bodies such as the National Board for Wine (*Junta Nacional do Vinho*) had significant outstanding balances with the *Caixa*. In February 1954, the bank highlighted the problems of granting new credits, when it solely shouldered the high risk involved in the implementation of the wine policy. The bank should bear only the normal risk inherent to its function of providing credit, a function which remained unchanged even when financial aid was intended to benefit large sectors of the national economy through corporate bodies. Therefore, the *Caixa*'s collaboration should be seen as conditional to the provision of guarantees by the state, and the government should create the appropriate means to secure this.[21]

In 1955, the finance minister requested the *Caixa* effectively participate in the funding to farmers for the construction of dams and irrigation works. He explained that farmers preferred to borrow from this institution, even though the Domestic Settlement Board had been created to carry out the technical and financial assistance policies provided for in the Agricultural Development Bill. The Settlement Board had the necessary powers to grant loans up to thirty years at a 2% interest rate, thus more favourable conditions than those offered by the *Caixa*'s long-term loans. The government acknowledged the inconvenience of this development policy to *Caixa*; to help transfer financing, the state would assume payment of the difference between the interest rate of both institutions, subject to agreement. Despite agreeing to grant the loans, relying on the state's commitment, the board noted that the law in force at the time already allowed the institution to carry out such funding. The *Caixa* could, in line with the government, set an interest rate and period considered adequate, although it refused repayment periods above twenty years. The administration also had some difficulty making decisions on loans due to the shortage of specialised personnel for the appraisal of investment projects and the supervision of works in progress.[22]

## Housing

In the postwar period, construction of social housing had to change due to the increase of civil construction costs, leaving councils and *misericórdias*, the main proponents of this type of work, in financial imbalance, which affected loan conditions. In turn, housing cooperatives faced many difficulties in Portugal, both obtaining financing and purchasing land at reasonable prices. Despite the facilities set forth in Law No. 2,007 (7 May 1945) for low rent houses, cooperatives lacked credit. These companies essentially lived off borrowed capital and that law provided they could borrow from the *Caixa* at interest rates of no more than 4%, at up to twenty-five-year terms.

However, as deputy Amaral Neto explained at the National Assembly in 1953, the *Caixa* had not considered investment in these cooperatives advisable since they were facing major difficulties. In other banking institutions credit had higher interest rates (at least 5.5%) and shorter repayment terms. The difficulty in recourse to credit through the *Caixa* was strongly criticised by Neto, who accused the institution of showing 'disinterest in long-term applications with low interest', even considering it 'imprudent' to rely on it for this type of financing.[23] In the National Assembly, there were voices calling for a revision of Decree-Law No. 34,486 (dated April 1945), which had set forth the forms of financing construction of houses for low-income families. The goal was to increase the established non-refundable subsidy and facilitate recourse to private banking, allowing the same guarantees given to the *Caixa* to be offered to those banks.[24] Despite these instances, during the period that coincided with the execution of the First Development Plan, there was no significant increase, within the framework of the *Caixa*'s credit, in investment in social housing compared to previous years.

In December 1957, the decree authorising the revenues and expenditures for 1958 was presented to the National Assembly. It established that the government should promote the necessary studies to ensure civil servants of the state and administrative bodies had access to housing with rents appropriate to their income. The government was further authorised to establish the conditions under which the *Caixa* could invest its capital allocated to the permanent fund for the acquisition and construction of property for civil servants as rented or conditional property.[25] This problem far exceeded the narrow scope of the First Development Plan, which was nearing its term. Following the adoption of the Means Law, the discussion on the role of welfare institutions in the construction of economic housing was once again brought to Parliament. The experience of the 1945 legislation was a failure, for in twelve years no *casa do povo* had been able to make use of the possibility of borrowing from the *Caixa*. Deputy Agostinho Gomes suggested direct loans be granted to workers. He believed this was more feasible, as it would avoid dispersion of welfare institutions' loans through cooperative bodies, given their economic and financial constraints and the advisability of ensuring adequate supervision.[26] On the other hand, Henrique Tenreiro, who pointed out that the *Caixa* had shown 'all the readiness and understanding' in providing the necessary credit to the construction of numerous estates for the fishing sector, suggested cooperatives be given more support and protection, offset by effective supervision of their activity.[27]

Some of the claims presented at the National Assembly would only receive a reply in 1960, with the publication of Decree-Law No. 42,951 (27 April). This allowed the application of the amounts assigned to the permanent fund of the *Caixa Geral de Aposentações* (CGA), which then exceeded 343,000 *contos*, in the acquisition and construction of housing for employees of the state and administrative bodies as rented or conditional property. The *Caixa* thus became more involved in the field of housing for civil servants. The following year, the first property acquisitions took place, fulfilling individually submitted applications. And once the appropriate legal and technical instruments had been created, the *Caixa* directly assumed construction competence through the creation of a technical office, which undertook several projects, namely in Lisbon (Olivais), Porto, Coimbra, Castelo Branco, Vila Real, and Ponta Delgada. Over time, the *Caixa* started preferentially directing available funds as loans for civil servants to purchase their own houses.[28]

## The new banking framework

Legislation regulating the Portuguese banking and financial system was beginning to show its age, still a consequence of the 1925 reform, in a context of inflation and turbulence in both the national and international financial markets. There had been an attempt to reform it in 1935, when the Economic Reconstitution Law was enacted, but it did not come into force for lack of regulation. The creation of National Credit Fund in 1929 and the new agreement between the state and the Bank of Portugal in 1931 had helped to better define the functioning of the credit market in Portugal. In the meantime, however, profound changes in the international finance system and the development of the Portuguese economy with the greater financing needs it implied meant the 1925 law was no longer adequate. In 1948, Portugal joined the Marshall Plan and the Organisation for European Economic Cooperation and in 1950, the European Payments Union. The need to channel the US financial aid into the national economy highlighted how the Portuguese banking and financial systems were lagging behind. In addition, the government was preparing the accession to the Bretton Woods institutions. Portugal was not a founding member of the World Bank nor of the International Monetary Fund but would join both in 1961; the following year it joined GATT, the General Agreement on Tariffs and Trade.

The economist Henry C. Wallich, a future member of the US Federal Reserve, visited Portugal as part of the Marshall Plan to assess the functioning of the financial system and propose reforms, resulting in an important report published in 1951. The mission included interviews with government officials, bankers, and other economic agents. Wallich was particularly concerned about limitations in the money supply resulting from the conservative management of the banking system and the Treasury. This conservative management made the supply of credit fall short of the 'needs of the various sectors of the economy'.[29] Wallich thought the conservative nature of the Portuguese financial system stemmed from concerns about the stability of the domestic currency (the *escudo*) and the budgetary balance that characterised national monetary policy since at least the 1930s. Among the main problems were the limitations to the Bank of Portugal's operations in capital markets (the 'open market' operations), implying restrictions on money supply. According to the report, the Portuguese financial system was still based on four pillars, namely the Treasury, the Bank of Portugal, the *Caixa Geral de Depósitos*, and the commercial banks. Savings flowed to the Treasury, that is, the Public Credit Board, who sold state bonds to the *Caixa*, which was deemed as inadequate as a credit bank. It would be up to the banks to attract more savings and increase their credit portfolios.

Among the main recommendations of the 1951 report was, firstly, allowing the Bank of Portugal to conduct open market operations. The *Caixa*, as the main lending bank for economic activity, should increase its medium and long-term credit supply, with interest rates adaptable to market conditions. Portugal was also recommended to join the IMF, so the country could benefit from credits from foreign banks associated to the fund's drawing rights. As the following years would show, Wallich's recommendations were in tune with the response capacity of the national financial institutions. In addition, macro-economic conditions were favourable to further expansion of credit, as the Bank of Portugal's gold and foreign exchange reserves could cover the increase in money supply and flows of funding to economic activity.

The appointment of Pinto Barbosa to the finance portfolio in 1955 brought a new line of thought on the development of the national economy. The aim was to avoid undermining the financial health of the state, which was still a relatively important issue in the Keynesian environment dominant in Europe and, increasingly, in Portugal. All the more so because above all these winds of change hung the figure of Oliveira Salazar, whose endorsement was indispensable for any real change, and who showed no inclination to give up on his principles of careful handling of the state's accounts, and controlling the public deficit, external deficit, and inflation. In 1956, when the budget was discussed, the new finance minister showed agreement with at least part of Wallich's recommendations and argued for the need to adjust the evolution of money supply to the growth rate of economic activity.[30] The urgent need for a revision of the financial sector's framework was also voiced at the Corporate Chamber (*Câmara Corporativa*) at the end of 1957, where it was argued that the country needed an 'organic and institutional review of the [financial] markets that allowed the indispensable articulation' between savings and investment.[31]

The new banking organisation gained shape in November 1957 with Decree-Law No. 41,403, regulated in November 1959 by Decree-Law no. 42,641.

Above all, this reform aimed at increasing the flexibility of the financial market. It endeavoured not to jeopardise the system's security, took measures to reduce banking risk, created a mechanism for regulating the functioning of the credit apparatus, and sought to increase the degree of market transparency. From the institutional point of view, the most important change was the creation of the *Conselho Nacional de Crédito* (National Credit Council), chaired by the finance minister. The *Caixa* was represented by its chief-executive, who held responsibilities for coordination of, and in consulting upon, the financial system.

The 1957 law stipulated that the Bank of Portugal and the *Caixa* should coordinate their action with the ministry of finance. The *Caixa*'s reserves represented more than 45% of the total reserves in all the credit institutions.[32] In spite of this, the *Caixa* ran liquidity risks in the case of massive withdrawals by its depositors. Eventually, it was authorised to borrow from the Bank de Portugal (Article 35), but the need would never arise. The law also provided for the creation of investment banks to address the lack of private institutions dedicated to medium- and long-term credit. However, the new demands economic activity had been imposing on the credit system called for the creation of investment banks.

After the reorganisation of the banking system and the establishment of rules for the creation of investment banks in 1957, the grounds for the establishment of a public investment bank, the *Banco de Fomento Nacional*, were defined (1958).[33] According to one deputy, 'if the establishment of the *Banco de Fomento* represents the culmination of a process, the response of Salazar's government to a need for our economic development, it is also a victory of the finance ministry as evidence of fidelity to noble traditions'.[34] Another pointed out that the establishment of the *Banco de Fomento* arose at a time when 'Portugal, under the impulse of various world events, such as the constitution of the European Economic Community, [...] the new political and economic structuring of much of Africa, and the colossal expansion of the Soviet Union and China, could by no means persist in dangerous economic inaction'.[35]

The new public bank was the successor of the National Development Fund (*Fundo de Fomento Nacional*), created in 1949, whose purpose was to handle subsidies granted by the state to large development projects, repayable in a relatively short term. This way, centralised development operations, such as the development of the merchant navy or investments in hydroelectric plants, were financed through the sale of public debt securities.[36] For Daniel Barbosa, who in 1965 would be appointed governor, it was incumbent upon BFN to 'attract a large part of national savings' to channel into 'truly productive investments, while guaranteeing those who saved and deposited the money the financial protection that prompted them to make the deposit.[37] Opening its doors in January 1960, the *Banco de Fomento Nacional* incorporated the assets and liabilities of the *Fundo de Fomento Nacional* and the Development Department (*Departamento de Fomento*) of the Bank of Angola. Its area of activity encompassed the metropolis and the colonies, and its main objective was to provide medium and long-term credit to the private sector for economic development. However, it was also entrusted with the task of guiding investment and setting in motion economic development programmes through technical and economic analyses. It was also responsible for supporting private enterprise under the development plans. The reorganisation of the financial and banking system implemented by the 1957 and 1959 laws and the creation of the *Banco de Fomento Nacional* had laid new foundations for private banking, but also for a stronger intervention from the state in the economy.

As previously, the private sector was only referred to in rules concerning the intervention of the state with measures of constraint, tax protection, capital holdings, credit granting, or any other form of stimulus, guidance, aid, and control, although they were rather meant as initiatives. A total investment of 31,000,000 *contos* was predicted, of which 22,000,000 were to be applied in the metropolis, the rest overseas. However, over the execution period, the annual programmes carried out totalled 38,000,000 *contos*, mainly due to a rise in metropolitan investments. The participation of the *Caixa* in the funding of the Second Plan far exceeded the foreseen annual amounts. In fact, the forecast of the *Caixa* financing within the various programmes totalled 1,700,000 *contos*, fourfold the forecasts of the previous plan. However, loans made directly or through bond subscription during the period of the plan amounted to 3,800,000 *contos*. Even though this sum includes transactions that were already settled, it does not diminish the importance of the bank's cooperation.[38] The *Caixa* strongly supported the funding of several economic sectors, such as production and distribution of electricity, transport and communications, and some basic industries. In addition, aid to electrification became a decisive factor for the transformations the country underwent in the 1950s and 1960s. Some of the financed projects had great impact on the economic life of the country, such as nitrogen fertiliser industries, steel, hydroelectric plants, the Lisbon underground railways (*Metropolitano de Lisboa*) and equipment and modernisation of ports, railways, and the national telephone network.

Administrative bodies continued to be called upon to participate in the country's economic development by investing in key areas such as electrification and water supply. However, in view of the poor financial situation of the overwhelming majority of municipal councils and the *Caixa*'s standing policy as their main funding body, to obstruct an accelerated expansion of credit, it was difficult for councils to match the plan's aims. In December 1959, when the National Assembly discussed a bill establishing several conditions councils would have to fulfil in order to borrow from the *Caixa*, deputy Augusto Simões took the opportunity to criticise the bank's action towards administrative bodies. He argued for the increase of the interest rates, which had been in force for more than 20 years, as well as loan repayment terms, maintaining that the institution was an organ of the state with large annual profits, and that reducing the burden of councils would increase local development. He pointed out that the *Caixa*'s risk in lending to municipalities was nil, since it was assigned the 'top-up tax' to the direct contributions of the state as guarantee. He also noted that the *Caixa* justifying the rates with the loans' long terms had no grounds, given the compulsory requirement for administrative bodies to make their deposits to the *Caixa* itself. Augusto Simões accused the *Caixa* of practicing compound interest by not paying, on average, much more than 2% on capital deposited there, and in contrast, charging councils 4% to 4.5% for credit to works of development, which would benefit the state.

From the 1957 and 1959 laws and the creation of the Banco de Fomento Nacional up to 1965, there was steady growth in the activity of the *Caixa Geral de Depósitos*, with a sharp increase in demand and term deposits, as well as in credit provision to economic activity. In addition, there were important changes in the institution's public image, with the inauguration of the new headquarters in Lisbon, on Rua do Ouro, in 1963. However, the growth of commercial banking was even faster and the *Caixa* continued to lose market share of deposits, particularly term deposits. Concurrently, the *Caixa* started to lose workers, attracted by better salaries and careers in the private sector, not only in banks but also in wider activities. This mostly affected the senior staff, who had been trained at the institution, making the losses all the more important. The situation of the *Caixa*'s employees was slightly improved in 1965, with the restructuring of the establishment plan (Decree-Law No. 46,305), which somewhat staunched the departure of senior staff. In 1965, 264 workers, out of a total of 1,937, left voluntarily. The following year, the number of employees rose to 2,120, and departures dropped to 197. In 1967, leavers fell again to 151.[39] In view of the increasing competition in the market, the protection the state provided the *Caixa* in the deposit and credit business was no longer enough to offset the running costs, too constrained by public administration legislation. This situation had been long known, but it took yet longer for the government to acknowledge the urgency of reforming the *Caixa*. In fact, that would only be achieved after Oliveira Salazar left the power.

## Notes

1 Sérgio (1995); Silva (1966).
2 Lains (2007).
3 Rollo (2007).
4 Leitão (2007).
5 Parecer sobre as Contas Gerais do Estado, 1950, p. 107.
6 Ofícios do Conselho de Administração, vol. 12 (AHCaixa).
7 Relatório e Contas, 1950, pp. 9–11.
8 Letter of chief executive Guilherme Moreira to the finance minister, dated 8 November 1950, in AOS/CO/UL–8E, pt. 7 (IAN/TT).
9 Ofícios do Conselho de Administração, vol. 11 (AHCaixa).
10 Letter of 28 July 1951, in Ofícios do Conselho de Administração, vol. 12 (AHCaixa).
11 Ofícios do Conselho de Administração, letters of 6 and 7 August 1951.

12 Ofícios do Conselho de Administração, letters of 6 and 7 August 1951.
13 Relatório e Contas, 1951, pp. 9–10, 12–15.
14 Ofícios do Conselho de Administração, vol. 13 (AHCaixa).
15 Minute No. 5230 of the executive board, dated 20 June 1952, in Livro de Actas do Conselho da Administração, no. 95 (AHCaixa).
16 Relatório e Contas, 1952.
17 Letter of 20 May 1953 in Ofícios do Conselho de Administração, vol. 14 (AHCaixa).
18 Pereira (2007), p. 302.
19 Relatório e Contas, 1959, p. 20.
20 Diário da Assembleia Nacional, 14 and 15 April 1955.
21 Order of the executive board of Caixa Geral de Depósitos, Crédito e Previdência, letter of 2 February 1954, in Ofícios do Conselho de Administração, vol. 14 (AHCaixa). Correspondence between the Finance Ministry, minister's office, and Caixa Geral de Depósitos, Crédito e Previdência, letter dated 15 February 1954, in Ofícios do Conselho de Administração, vol. 14 (AHCaixa).
22 Correspondence between the *Caixa* and the Finance Ministry, minister's office, letter of 23 June 1955, in Ofícios do Conselho de Administração, vol. 15.
23 Diário da Assembleia Nacional, 20 March 1953.
24 Diário da Assembleia Nacional, 21 March 1953.
25 Diário da Assembleia Nacional, 18 December 1957.
26 Diário da Assembleia Nacional, 30 January 1958.
27 Diário da Assembleia Nacional, 7 and 8 February 1958.
28 Diário da Assembleia Nacional, 29 November 1961.
29 Wallich (1951), pp. 7–8.
30 Diário da Assembleia Nacional, 11 December 1956.
31 Actas da Câmara Corporativa, 26 September 1957.
32 Actas da Câmara Corporativa, 26 September 1957.
33 Decreto-Lei No. 41,957, 13 November 1958.
34 Diário da Assembleia Nacional, 18 October 1958.
35 Sousa (1960), p. 23.
36 Decreto-Lei No. 37,354, 26 March 1949.
37 Rosas et al. (2002), p. 387. See also Barbosa (1972), p. 7. See also Barbosa (1959).
38 Relatório e Contas, 1964, pp. 31–32.
39 Relatório da Secretaria da Administração, 1966, p. 4, 1967, p. 4.

# 13

# STAYING BEHIND, 1968–1974

The nature of the *Estado Novo* regime changed throughout its duration, and that was particularly so in the period covered by this chapter as the regime's dictator, António de Oliveira Salazar, fell severely ill in 1968 and was replaced by a former student with whom he had not always been in tune. The change of leadership did not lead to a full opening of the regime and of course not to a democratic form of government, but it led to a number of important changes in terms of economic and financial policies. In his last years as dictator, Salazar's advanced age was notoriously associated with a decline in the capacity to make decisions and reform what needed to be reformed, even within the logic of the regime. The regime was clearly falling into sclerosis, and the consequences were probably less serious because a number of technocrats managed to keep the state running in terms of economic policy and to bypass established policies, mostly in manufacturing, banking, and foreign economic relations. Thus, in many instances, industrialists were able to overcome the formally strict policy of industrial licensing. Foreign exchange controls loosened for lack of bureaucratic capacity, and foreign investment and trade with the European partners increased, despite the imperialistic rhetoric of the dictator. Regarding the concerns of the *Caixa*, the 1929 statute was still in effect, but the administration and the clerks of the bank made all efforts to adapt it to modern times, however difficult that was. In any case, the assumption of government by the new dictator, Marcelo Caetano, led to the release of the pressure and allowed a few institutional changes to happen. Salazar was directly involved in the writing of the *Caixa*'s 1929 statute, which made it harder to revise during his consulate. Not surprisingly, it was one of the first institutional changes, which occurred with a new statute in 1969. The analysis of the institution's history shows the effects of the aging of the regime.

The relevance of the *Planos de Fomento* was both economic and ideological, and provides important insights into how the state conducted public policy in the country, in the context of the absence of free press and free discussion of matters. There are other important sources of information, such as a number of books written by economists that managed to pass censorship under the label of technocratic publications, the OECD annual country reports, or even some of the reports of the Corporate Chamber, which also presented valuable and, to a certain extent, independent analysis. More than a decade of economic growth naturally had an impact on the society and the regime was under pressure for change, which was coming first and foremost from those concerned with the economy, particularly with public investment where the *Caixa* had a relevant role. Despite the new technocratic rhetoric, the new dictator Caetano failed to change the political essence of the regime. As in previous moments, the history of the *Caixa* provides a window to look at the essence of the evolution of domestic politics. For the study of the public bank, two documents are of high relevance: the new statute of 1969 and what went behind it, and a report on the institution produced by OECD consultants, in 1971.

## The technocratic dictator

The appointment of Marcelo Caetano to the presidency of the Council of Ministers in 1968 improved the capacity of the government to carry out simple reforms, without putting into question the fundamentals of the regime in terms of the nature of the regime. The new government had a developmental and technocratic stance, contrarily to its predecessor, and geared towards increasing Portugal's economic position in the European and Atlantic economies. Yet Caetano soon found out that radical adventures were not allowed and faced the opposition of the more conservative alleys of the regime, particularly the political and military establishment involved in the repression of the opposition and the wars in Africa. The apex of the changes consisted mainly in reforms of social security, the banking system—including the *Caixa*—and the industrial and commercial policy. In 1972, following a similar agreement made by Francisco Franco's government in 1970, the Portuguese government signed a trade agreement with the EEC, which increased the degree of openness of the national borders to the import of industrial products.[1] The history of the *Caixa* plainly reflects the changes in the political situation and provides a clear method of understanding them. The 1969 statue turned the *Caixa* from a branch of the ministry of finance into a state-owned public company with a considerably higher degree of administrative autonomy. The new statute also reorganised the services and allowed the *Caixa* greater participation in the banking market.

The changes that occurred in 1968 were not officially recognised by those in power, who preferred to guarantee that the regime was not changing.[2] Dictatorships need to cement their legitimacy, and thus it was important to draw on the continuity of the regime from its origins. Moreover, it was necessary to maintain a difficult balance between the old guard and the new. The fact that the constitutional duty to appoint the president of the council pertained to the president of the republic, kept the power with old regime supporters to which the president pertained. One current of historical interpretation prefers to see the last decade of the regime as a failed transition period and, therefore, one of institutional and political stagnation. This interpretation shows the importance of the perpetuation of the dictatorial regime, of the absence of political freedoms and concomitant repression, and, perhaps most of all, of the political effects of the wars in Africa. However, it cannot conceal the changes that actually occurred.

At the start of the period here analysed, most perspectives on Portugal's economy were optimistic, as the economy was following closely the western European golden age of growth. The sources of the optimism were several, including an increase in the living conditions of large stretches of the population, despite the fact many remained poor and isolated from the modern sectors of the society. The performance of the economy was not as clearly anticipated as may be gauged from the fact that all the main macroeconomic goals of the government's plans were largely surpassed. Moreover, the economy had grown at 6.4% a year since 1959, and in 1965 national per capita income was slightly above the level registered in the Second Development Plan for 1959–1964, which was one of the main instruments of the government's propaganda on the economy.[3] As such, it looked as though the government could proceed on the same path for years to come. Yet that was not the case, as the international economic context, particularly within western Europe and the European communities, was changing rapidly. In addition, because of the single largest and most stressing problem of Portuguese society at the time—the increasingly violent independence wars in Africa—likewise prohibited the government from continuing along the same path.[4]

The Portuguese economy was thriving in response to the rapid process of economic integration in the EFTA and the European Communities, the continuation of public investment policies, and the growth of private consumption, savings, and investment. Economic expansion went along with significant structural change, as the share of the agricultural sector shrank and that of manufacturing and services increased, with high productivity gains, particularly in manufacturing. These positive signs went along with less favourable social and economic realities related to the poor conditions in which many people still lived, especially in the regions furthest from the main cities, and in urban centres that could not adequately absorb the influx of people arriving in search of work. The increase in emigration to Europe was also a sign of the lack of jobs and opportunities for small entrepreneurs, although the poorest were not necessarily those who left, as was the rise in inequality.

Increasingly, the five-year development plans were the most visible side of the economic and financial policy of the *Estado Novo*. It was where the Portuguese government established the priorities for public and private investment and provided the legal framework for the policy decisions. In addition, the plans also began to announce general concerns about problems in the functioning of Portuguese society, including issues of social and regional development. According to the strategy defined there, the state should provide guidance on investment priorities and correction of deficiencies in the economic structure. The plans also focused on methods of financing investment, paying particular attention to the operation of financial markets, the channelling of private savings, the use of resources available to the state, and the raising of foreign capital. Standing out amongst the national resources available to the state were the *Caixa* funds, financing both public and private projects.[5]

The development plans were a most relevant source of information on government policy guidelines for those who played prominent roles in the conduct of government policies, including senior officials of the state, such as the *Caixa*'s administrators and directors, and the heads of private companies. It is worth focusing on the development plans, as they contain analyses of exceptional quality on the situation of the Portuguese economy and options of economic policy. The Third Development Plan (1968–1973) was particularly well developed. The Interim Plan (1963–1965) and the draft of the Fourth Plan (1974–1979) also provide an interesting reading, albeit of a more limited scope: the first, because it had a smaller range; the second, because the government chose to become more opaque in the discussion of national economic problems.

In the period this chapter focuses on, the first plan is the Interim Development Plan for the period 1965–1967. It was considered a provisional plan, since the government did not want to jump too quickly into a more profound document, as happened with the following plan. The Interim Plan, however, brought some changes regarding the extent of the state's intervention in the economy. The document defined a strategy intended to be global, albeit limited by 'uncertainty arising from the difficulty in anticipating the financial burden of the nation's defence', as well as 'the complexity of the process of progressive unification of national markets and [...] Europe's indecision regarding its own economic integration'. The plan determined the state should prioritise investment in sectors with 'higher, more direct, and immediate economic profitability', 'production activities of goods and services capable of satisfying demand in foreign markets or of replacing importation of other goods', and the infrastructures which most directly contributed to 'the improvement and expansion of the population's productive potential'.[6] Nevertheless, the priority was to stimulate the growth of domestic product. To this end, the Interim Plan identified the need to increase agricultural and industrial production, providing investments in infrastructure, support for improvements in operating conditions, and some legislative amendments. These investments would enable the strengthening of the 'incipient Portuguese industrial structure' and provide the country with an industrial environment that allowed it to '[compete] in European markets as well as in the domestic market'.[7] The plan also set out goals of a social nature, explicitly advocating the 'acceleration of the pace of accrual of national product, accompanied by a more balanced distribution of the incomes obtained'. Concurrently, it anticipated investment in social housing to solve the shortages in accommodation caused by the internal migrations to the cities. Finally, as a novelty, it showed concern for correcting regional imbalances.

On the financial front, the most important issue was the need for the state to compensate for the 'misalignment of a cyclical nature' hitting the markets, where insufficient funds were being channelled into public investment, despite the high level of savings the country had already achieved. Thus, the Interim Plan maintained that the government could contribute to the best 'use of the available financial capacity and the attainment of adequate investment'. The state would be responsible for those undertakings that, by their importance or low economic profitability, were not attractive to private investors. However, that was not enough. The state should also 'guide, coordinate, and encourage private investment and ensure, as far as possible, its financing'. Thus, the execution of the plan's goals required fiscal incentives and orienting the financial market towards channelling private capital into economic development, while discouraging unproductive investment. For this end, the need to reform the administration and the banking system was acknowledged, as well as the granting of various tax incentives, including the reduction of capital duties.[8] These goals had been achieved some time before by keeping a tight monetary policy, which was in turn possible due to the smaller size of the task. In fact, given the expansion of the Portuguese economy since the end of World War II, the need for investment in infrastructure and economic modernisation was increasingly high and more complex, requiring more funds to be raised and further easing of financial and monetary markets. Thus, changing the conditions of economic development of the country required a change in monetary policy, for which it was necessary to progress the modernisation of the financial and banking sector, following the path initiated with the banking reform of the late 1950s.

The OECD annual report on Portugal for 1966 pointed precisely in that way. In particular, it advised a revision of the fiscal policy to prevent it having a deflationary impact, and measures promoting the expansion of credit granted to the economy by the banking system. This goal required a revision of the banking legislation to change deposit reserve requirements and reference interest rates. However, this implied a substantial change in the conduct of macroeconomic policy, which did not take place immediately. The Keynesian atmosphere prevalent at the time among economists in Portugal was similar to that experienced in the rest of western Europe and reached the main members of government with economic and financial responsibilities. However, the atmosphere was changing, and that change would strengthen the role of the *Caixa Geral de Depósitos*.[9]

The participation of the *Caixa* in the funding carried out under the Interim Plan largely exceeded previsions. Of the 34.8 million *contos* of total investment planned, the *Caixa* was expected to supply 1.2 million, but this value rose to 3 million. The difference was due almost exclusively to the plan not providing for the *Caixa*'s participation in the funding of the industrial sector, which totalled 1.9 million *contos*. The *Caixa* was able to up its contribution thanks to the large growth of deposits resulting from the growth of savings in the country. With regard to public investments, the administration's autonomy was restricted by the *Caixa*'s status as a state bank; naturally, it followed the government's guidelines set out in the development plans as to how their assets were invested. The *Caixa* faced growing competition in this role from other financial institutions, particularly private commercial banking, then experiencing a period of noticeable modernisation and growth. The *Caixa*'s other rival, namely, the recently created *Banco de Fomento Nacional*, had never gained prominence. Despite the competition, the public bank was able to maintain a predominant role, aided by the protection afforded by the state. This protection arose from the mandatory deposits by public entities and because, unlike the rest of the banking system, the interest the *Caixa* paid on deposits was not subject to tax. But the *Caixa* had advantages over private banks also because it was closer to the public, especially lower-income depositors.

The Third Development Plan (1968–1973) was a more elaborate document which included an excellent analysis of Portuguese economic problems. It was based on the same structure and concerns as its forerunner, where the possibilities for economic development were conditioned by the financial effort of the wars in Africa and by the need to keep internal financial stability and the external solvency of the currency. To these concerns was added another goal, stated explicitly in the plan. It concerned the need for the government to prepare the economy for its gradual integration into wider economic areas. According to António da Motta Veiga, then minister and future president of the *Caixa*, the European economic integration movement was 'an imperative need of our times' and the 'modernisation of the productive structures' was paramount, 'not only because of the desired acceleration of the growth rate of the national product', but also due to the urgency of guaranteeing those structures' 'conditions for competing in international markets and in European markets in particular'. These were new words to the official lexicon of the government, and still very rare to find, especially in documents with as much exposure as this plan would have.

The reformist element of the Third Development Plan also pointed to the need for changes in public administration. The various problems highlighted included poor professional qualification of civil servants and low salaries compared to the private sector. Running and management problems were also identified with high levels of bureaucracy, centralisation, and hierarchy. This was aggravated by the complexity of the legislation governing public administration, the deficiency of public facilities and buildings, and the lack of equipment. With regard to the state's business activity, the need was felt to define business types and schemes that would adapt to the respective functions. The ambition of the third plan was also seen in the proposed investments and the corresponding financial effort. Indeed, those investments implied a 75% increase over the previous plan and would represent about two thirds of total national investment over the six years of the plan's duration.[10] To realise this huge effort, the government had to rely on national savings, both from the state and private sources, as well as on capital imports, albeit in a much smaller share. It was therefore necessary to boost savings and develop financial institutions to channel investment. This was a major problem, as the text of the plan itself recognised, devoting the largest of its six chapters to it.

The national financial and banking system had undergone a major reform, embodied in the banking laws of 1957 and 1959, which brought some added flexibility, as addressed in the previous chapter. However, the problems related to attracting savings and granting credit remained. The main issue was not the savings offer, but their convenient conversion into bank deposits, since interest rates remained low and unattractive, and the banking network's expansion was relatively limited. Regarding credit, the problems stemmed not from the levels of investment demand, by all means high, but from the fact that the credit granted was mainly short-term and based on mortgage guarantees, making it difficult for some entrepreneurs to access bank financing. The plan was more concerned with the response of public institutions to the growing need for funding than with that of private banks. The truth is that public institutions were less flexible and less prepared to keep pace with the development of the domestic financial market, while private banks had already undergone major changes throughout the 1950s and the 1960s.[11]

Once more, the *Caixa* took on a significant share of the funding of the Third Development Plan, which would again surpass forecasts, this time by an even greater margin. The plan anticipated the *Caixa*'s participation to amount to 3,900,000 *contos*, out of a total of 168,000,000. The *Caixa*'s planned share implied a reduction in the annual participation compared to the previous plan, although a substantial increase in overall investment was expected. However, the *Caixa*'s share amounted in fact to 18,500,000 *contos*. The difference was due to the estimates made of the investments the institution supported in the energy sector (in the total amount of 5,000,000 *contos*) and in transport and communications (where it employed 8.1 million) when previous forecasts had pointed to insignificant values for both sectors.[12] This prominent role contrasted with the problems the *Caixa* continued to experience in an increasingly dynamic banking market, which made the reform of the institution ever more urgent. Time was ripe for reforms.

In 1968, the *Caixa* was still the largest bank in the country, although without the projection it had acquired in the 1950s. It held 23.5% of total demand deposits, including interbank deposits and deposits in the Bank of Portugal, or 19.4%, if Bank of Portugal's deposits were excluded. However, the share in term deposits was substantially lower, with the *Caixa* holding only 7.7%. The development of private banks had led to the growth of term deposits, which went from 31.5% to 45.8% of total bank deposits in the country between 1965 and 1971.[13] Part of this growth resulted from changes in legislation regarding maximum interest rates for term deposit and minimum bank reserves. These changes led commercial banks to attract funds previously deposited with the *Caixa Geral de Depósitos*. Concurrently, private banking was undergoing a move towards concentration, with the top five private banks accounting for 69% of deposits in 1974, and the largest seven, 84% of total deposits.[14]

The deposit structure compelled the *Caixa* to make a greater effort in reserves. Thus, while reserves on demand deposits were 32.1% in *Caixa* and 31.4% in commercial banks, their respective shares were 26.9% and 18.4% when considering the demand and term deposits together. As to the proportion of credit granted in relation to total deposits, both the *Caixa* and commercial banks had ratios of around 75%. Credit to the private sector accounted for 54.8% of total loans granted by the public bank, a proportion on the rise, particularly in industrial credit. The *Caixa* also relied heavily on mandatory deposits, which represented 43.5% of total deposits, while voluntary demand deposits amounted to 40.3% and term deposits to 16.1%. This structure was undergoing significant change, since voluntary and term deposits were the fastest growing items.[15]

The *Caixa*'s weight was greater in the channelling of funds for investment, accounting for more than half of such funds. In 1966, financial institutions contributed 28.1% to gross capital formation, the remainder being provided by the public sector (22.8%), individuals and non-financial corporations (21.1%), and external financing (28%). Of the financial institutions share, 15.1% were provided by the *Caixa*, followed by the *Banco de Fomento Nacional* (2.2%), and the remaining 10.8% by the rest of the banking system. The *Caixa*'s relative contribution, however, had increased considerably from the corresponding value in 1960, which was only 6%.[16]

With the help of the *Caixa* and the rest of the banking system, the forecasts for savings growth were largely surpassed. The text of the fourth plan's project, published in 1973, concluded that the Portuguese financial system had 'in general responded satisfactorily to the economy's financing needs, and there [were] therefore no limitations to the process of expansion' of the economy. It added that credit to the economy had developed rapidly, both in short-term and long-term lending. The *Caixa*'s role in long-term credit—and *Banco de Fomento Nacional*—was highlighted, albeit the latter had a smaller role given its limited network of agencies, with acknowledgment of the limited intervention of commercial banks in this type of credit. The document still suggested the *Caixa* should improve the 'financial coordination with the Bank of Portugal, with a view to the broader, and regular, use of institution's medium- and long-term credit potential, including based on an adequate "transformation" of resources'.[17]

## The public company

Since its early years, the *Caixa*, like other services, had been part of the public administration with little or no administrative autonomy, and that was a problem with increasing negative consequences. The *Caixa*'s employees were civil servants with the respective rules concerning promotion and salaries, and many of these left the institution, with their experience and learned expertise, in favour of employment at the private banks, which were gaining market shares and hiring. The anachronism of the legal framework had been evident for some time; however Salazar's government stalled all reforms for different reasons, but mostly because in his last years the dictator was simply unable to let even his closer technocrats do their job. As such, Salazar's replacement by the younger and apparently more dynamic and pro-reform Marcelo Caetano provided room for some kind of reform. Their employees were formally public servants with the same wage scale, and any promotions and hiring needed authorisation by the central administrative bureaucracy. The list of public services transformed in public companies, apart from the *Caixa*, included the alcohol monopoly (*Administração Geral do Álcool*) in 1966, the telephone company (*Telefones de Lisboa e Porto*) in 1967, postal services (*Correios e Telecomunicações de Portugal*), social housing (*Empresa Pública de Urbanização de Lisboa*) both in 1971, and the national printing office (*Imprensa Nacional - Casa da Moeda*) in 1972. The list was planned to include other public and military services, including military factories, the administrations of the harbours of Lisbon, Douro, and Leixões, as well as the Lisbon airport. The statutes of these companies remained different with regard to the status of their workers, accounting and the exercise of supervision by the state, but the change was nevertheless significant.[18]

The text of the *Caixa*'s 1969 charter was based on a project that António da Motta Veiga presented as a member of the *Caixa*'s executive board on 25 November 1968.[19] After several meetings, the project was approved by the administration on 4 March 1969, with the corresponding decree-law (No. 48,953) being published on 5 April. This procedure, which involved the participation of the *Caixa* in drafting the laws governing it, was common and the urgent need of the reform is suggested by the rapidity with which it proceeded. However, unlike the Telefones de Lisboa e Porto (TLP) and the Correios de Portugal (CTT), the *Caixa*'s charter maintained the civil service regime and the supervision of the minister of finance, and, besides, it required budgetary writing in addition to business writing, which was included in the state budget and subject to the supervision of the Court of Auditors. Despite the lower level of autonomy, the fact is that the chief executive and the executive board acquired greater decision-making power over current management issues related to staff or credit conditions.

The number of laws this reform repealed shows how sorely it was needed. In fact, that number was 38, in addition to various articles of other laws. More than half of the repealed laws dated back to the 1930s, followed by four decrees published in the 1940s; only one decree dated from the 1950s and five from the 1960s.[20] Knowing the operation of the *Caixa* was not perfect, one can see there was resistance to changing an inheritance closely associated with the conduct of the financial policy by Salazar. This is another instance in which the *Caixa*'s history helps understand the nature and institutional evolution of the *Estado Novo*, showing reorganisation in the 1930s, followed by years of atavism that would only come to be partially broken during the governments of Marcelo Caetano.

According to the preamble of the 1969 decree, the fact the *Caixa* was a public service and subject to the same rules that governed the bureaucratic administration of the state brought certain drawbacks for the institution, the main one which concerned the rigidity of its structure and functioning, particularly with regard to the organisation of services and the recruitment of staff. Qualified personnel were easily attracted by the private sector, where they could earn higher salaries. The new law therefore intended to give the *Caixa* greater flexibility and dynamism, increasing its autonomy and thus its productivity and guaranteeing it had employees able to perform all kinds of functions.[21] From 1969, the employees of the *Caixa* had a special regime of ranks and salaries, even though they remained in the civil service.

This meant its employees would benefit from salaries equivalent to those of the rest of the banking system, in order to prevent qualified staff from preferring the private sector to working at the *Caixa*. However, in matters of welfare and pensions they would remain associated with the civil service. Aiming at administrative flexibility, there would no longer be a rigid establishment plan, allowing the staff to adapt to the needs of the institution. The goal was to offer 'banking and financial services in conditions of relative competition with the other institutions in the system', while obtaining enough resources for the running of the services, as well as profits for the state. On 11 April 1969, when the new charter came into force, the executive board attended to the definition of the new professional ranks the law required, as well as salaries, even though nothing was then defined.[22]

In the department reorganisation, the National Credit Fund, the branch responsible for some of the agricultural and industrial credit operations, became an integral part of the *Caixa*, which led to the elimination of double-entry bookkeeping. The *Caixa* was now allowed to set the conditions for granting credit, namely the terms and guarantees. It would also have the capacity to oversee the actual application of funds to the purposes for which they were granted. The autonomy and independence of the *Caixa*'s management were therefore reinforced by this new charter. The 1969 reform aimed at applying a business-type structuring to the bank's financial management, independent from the strict public account norms and regulations. On the other hand, the new situation of the institution's employees, with the revision of ranks and salaries provided for in the new charter, would lead to a sharp increase in personnel costs in 1969, with a rise of around 32,000 *contos* between 1968 and 1969. The 1969 law raised some problems with the public. This is shown by the account of an incident at a *Caixa* branch in Lisbon, where the manager had to reassure clients who feared the bank becoming a public company implied its operations losing state guarantees. The minute concerning this meeting also referred that the administration had already taken appropriate action to tackle this problem, which shows it had happened before.[23]

## Hard times

The *Caixa*'s activity experienced significant growth throughout the decade covered in this chapter, shown by a substantial rise in retail and public deposits and in the increase of loans granted. This strong growth, however, was not accompanied by the necessary updating of the institution's operation, which would increasingly be felt as a problem to address. The new charter contributed to some changes, but the regime came to an end before the *Caixa*'s departments were properly transformed. According to an assessment, operational problems were more relevant and persistent in the treatment of credit granting procedures and internal management of deposits than in the relationship with the public. This meant that the reforms were not yet urgent, since operating deficiencies did not critically affect the *Caixa*'s position in the national banking market. The fact that the *Caixa* remained largely a public bank dampened the impact of the growing competition from the rest of the banking system.

The *Caixa* collected deposits in its own agencies making up the most important part of the funds received, as well as at tax offices and post offices. It received voluntary deposits from private depositors, and mandatory deposits from state departments, municipal councils, economic coordination bodies, and social security. Total deposits in the *Caixa* trebled between 1965 and 1973, with mandatory deposits growing 2.1 times and voluntary deposits, 3.2. In 1965, mandatory deposits accounted for about 30% of total deposits received. The ratio fell slowly, reaching 25% in 1970 and 22.5% in 1971. The greatest transformation the structure of deposits with the *Caixa* underwent resulted from the large growth of demand deposits by individuals, which rose more than 28 times in the same period. In relative terms, term deposits were only 4% of total retail deposits in 1965, rising to 16% in 1968 and to 42% in 1973.[24] This increase was partly due to the rise of interest rates in 1967, from 3.5% to 4%.[25]

The *Caixa* credit operations, given through the accounts covering loans to the state and to other sectors of the national economy, reached about 16 million *contos*, by the end of 1965, of which a little more than half corresponded to credit to the private sector. In 1965, of the approximately 8 million *contos* granted to the private sector, 3.4 were allocated to industrial credit, followed by agricultural credit and credit to urban construction, with about 1.2 million *contos* each. Mortgage credit was given about one million *contos*. Public sector loans were very diverse, including loans to Ministry of the Army factories and to municipal councils. Less significant public loans include those for water supply and electrification, mostly for rural populations and small urban centres. Similarly, credit distribution did not change substantially, and, in 1973, loans to the private sector were still 60% of the total credit granted by the *Caixa*, with the remainder being given to the public and corporate sectors.

Loans to the private sector were allocated to industrial, agricultural, and construction credit, continuing this now increasingly traditional practice. This was mainly short-term credit, although renewable and under guarantees of both property and securities. Approximately 95% of the loans to the private sector were aimed at the direct fostering of economic activity, a practice valued by the administration, declaring it 'the *Caixa*'s clear preference for the promotion' of productive activities.[26] In the meantime, credit for acquisition and construction of houses grew sharply, reaching 41.5 million in 1970. Perhaps noting the trend and predicting this would become a preferential area of business for the *Caixa*, the newly appointed chief executive, António da Motta Veiga, defended the need for the bank to promote housing credit and the opening of accounts for this purpose. He deemed it necessary to gather 'a sufficient volume of capital to invest in existing enterprises, and in new initiatives, both by companies and by the state and public bodies' every year. This capital consisted of the savings of 'private individuals, corporations and the public sector itself'.[27]

In the late 1970s, house purchase savings accounts were created. These deposits were associated with the granting of loans under special conditions for the acquisition, construction, or repair of owned dwellings. This was aimed at contributing to the solution of the housing problem, simultaneously emphasising that 'the increase of the "thrift spirit" is closely linked to the process of economic development'. Despite being such an important form of deposit and having received 'generally very favourable' public acceptance, there is no reference to its development in the reports of subsequent years. The only information available is the quantity of the loans intended for the purchase or construction of homes, referred in the 1974 report of the executive board. According to this, between 1972 and 1974, the *Caixa* loaned about 4.4 million *contos*, corresponding to the purchase or construction of about 18 thousand homes. Of these, about 76% were houses of relatively low value, not exceeding 500 *contos*, which indicated that the *Caixa* remained in the low-to-middle income market, as was its tradition.[28]

The steep growth of retail deposits and the growing desire to extend credit in other modalities entailed a considerable escalation of work, since the number of operations increased exponentially. In addition, the public sector made an increasing use of the *Caixa*'s services, its accounts showing the most activity. Finally, credit to the private sector grew in amount and complexity, naturally accompanying the development of the Portuguese economy and the emergence of new industrial sectors and more complex forms of management. To top it all, another transformation in enterprises' functioning was under way, related to the increasing adoption of mechanised computational methods. The introduction of computing in management began in the largest companies, amongst which were those of the banking sector.[29] The *Caixa* could not ignore this small revolution, which would be the final challenge of the last administration of the *Estado Novo*.

In an equally novel gesture, in 1971 the *Caixa Geral de Depósitos* was visited by a fact-finding mission of the OECD. The assessment was commissioned by the bank's management and carried out within the framework of technical assistance the organisation provided to member countries. The mission had three main objectives. The first was the analysis of information technology (IT) use, with particular attention to the effects the new methods had on the bank's operation and relations with the public. The second goal was to find ways of reducing delays in granting credit. Finally, it aimed to define the IT solutions that would simplify the handling of deposit accounts.[30] The mission was also consulted on the utility of establishing an 'organisation and methods' department and its integration with other departments. The resulting report is extremely interesting as it reveals the impact of the introduction of IT use and presents a unique picture of the *Caixa*'s functioning and problems.

The report starts by describing the *Caixa*'s resources, departments, and the use it made of its funds. The *Caixa* managed the accounts received directly at the institution, as well as through the Treasury and through the *Caixa Económica Postal*. In 1971 there were more than one million current accounts, 223,000 term deposits, 2,000 house purchase savings accounts, 178,000 mandatory deposit accounts, plus 304,000 current accounts at the *Caixa Económica Postal*. This amounted to the extraordinary number of about 1,792,000 accounts, almost one account for every five Portuguese citizens. The funds received amounted to 28 million *contos*, which were invested in loans to industry (8 million *contos*), under various guarantees (4 million), property (3.4 million), corporations (3 million) and administrative bodies (1.5 million). Reserves made up the rest, about 29% of total liabilities. The *Caixa* also managed the *Caixa Geral de Aposentações*, with 311,000 contributors and a current account of about 314,000 contos, and *Montepio dos Servidores do Estado*. However, these bodies had separate accounts from the parent company. The report also refers to an organisational chart in an appendix which, however, was not found, and the mission had to draw its own.[31] It is also said the *Caixa*'s organisation had three 'operational directorates' and 12 'directorates' or 'support departments'.[32]

The absence of an organisational chart makes it difficult to interpret this view of the bank's organisation. However, the *Caixa* had eight service directorates established, namely for Administrative Services, Credit Analysis, Credit Operations, Financial Services, Depository Services, Computer Record and Actuarial Services, Study and Planning, and the National Pension Fund. Most of these directorates had subdivisions, the most important of which were those of the Directorate for Credit Services, which was composed of the Directorate for Credit to the Public Sector (DSC1), Agriculture (DSC2), Industry (DSC3), Property (DSC4) and 'Popular', or pawns (DSC5).[33] In addition to these, the report refers the directorates for legal consultation, litigation, and notary.[34] According to the OECD report, these three services, together with the DSC, DST and DAS, were the top of the institution.

The OECD report mission began by noting that the use of IT within the *Caixa* was minimal and restricted to a part of credit operations, namely in the directorates for the public sector (DSC1), industry (DSC3), and property (DSC4). The improvement of service, therefore, necessitated broadening the application of IT. The report warns this should be done in a coherent, integrated way, which had not always occurred. This analysis, initially meant to advise on the use of information technology, ended up showing the weaknesses in the operations of the *Caixa*, for which there is little information available. One of the problems immediately detected was the significantly reduced number of staff involved in the plan for IT use: an engineer, two analysts, and two programmers. A second part of the report calls for greater interaction between IT managers and heads of department. Further advice reveals a situation seen frequently in institutions which still need to hone their functioning. The report says that the three heads of department should meet with the heads of Litigation and legal consultation and the notary and the IT managers under the aegis of one of the administrators. This indicates that the organisational deficiencies were due not only to the novelty of the problem or to inadequacy of knowledge, but also to a lack of cooperation within the institution.[35]

The proposals regarding the Directorate for Credit Services (DSC) shed further light on the operational problems. Firstly, the report suggested that the departments should be closer, and that their heads should meet regularly, under the supervision of the head of DSC, since it was clear that 'some heads of departments were unaware of the roles and problems of their colleagues'. Secondly, it recommended the rationalisation of forms, since the approximately 300 different types found were excessive; their content needed to be systematised and the information requested in them re-examined. Similarly, the systematic use of carbon copies should replace copies made by hand. The bank was advised to limit the number of times operations were controlled; the mission found the current practice excessive, perhaps motivated by 'distrust of computers'.[36]

The report also called for the restructuring of the entire Directorate for Credit Services, abandoning the classification of creditors by activity. This classification had historical precedent, which went back to the beginnings of credit for economic activity, distinct from credit to the public sector, and divided into credit to agriculture and later to industry and property. This classification caused problems, since the same type of tasks were undertaken in different departments and also because there were customers with different types of credit and others that would not easily fit any of the categories. A change was recommended that would take into account the main stages of loan management instead of the type, namely a single application department, managing a central debtor file sorted and updated by computer. It was also recommended that relations with debtors be decentralised at county, council, subsidiary, and delegation levels, noting the need for a marketing service. In a second level, there should be a loan negotiation department that would follow up each process until the conclusion of the respective contracts. Finally, a third department was recommended to manage contracts 'until payment of the last instalment'.[37] The mission further commented that the *Caixa*'s staff was too specialised in a specific type of credit (industrial, agricultural, etc.), and that this was not necessarily positive nor was it a guarantee of higher departmental efficiency.

The list of recommendations continued with further proposals that can only be interpreted as resulting from the mission having found slow operating conditions stemming from the use of old, bureaucratic practices. Other suggestions pointed to the need to allow some operations to run in parallel. The Directorate for Credit Services only sent the documents to the other departments through which credit applications had to go, namely the Directorates for Administrative Services, Financial Services, and Litigation, after the processes were complete. And this route was taken by every request, without exception. The report further noted that procedures should be designed not from exceptions, but around 'normal' cases. All credit requests were presented to litigation, to legal consultation and to the notary, whatever the amount involved. The report argued this should happen only in exceptional and difficult cases. If introduced, this change would enable the reduction of the number of items per case folder, which averaged 110 in industrial credit and 65 in mortgage loans. Besides, almost everything went through the administration without obvious need. Credit applications required prior authorisation by the administration for their analysis to proceed. In the case of house loans, that permission was granted in 95 per cent of cases, which, according to the mission report, could be done by the head of department. Loan applications were gathered in the litigation department, which requested the necessary documentation from the authorities. The type of documentation depended on the request, an authorisation from the Ministry of Finance, a resolution by the municipal council, or a certificate from the Registry Office. The report advised doing this with computer help and directly by the Directorate for Credit Services, which saved time. As a general principle, procedure should be defined by the rule and not the exception. If litigation no longer had to scrutinise applications and instead could focus on solving actual litigation problems, the whole process would be streamlined. The report notes that in 1970, litigation cases were only one in a thousand in housing credit and seven in a thousand in industrial credit. It also pointed out that only 'more complex dossiers are carefully examined by the head of service, while all others pass through subordinates, who only stamped them without any particular examination'.[38] This bureaucratic procedure also rose security issues, since the documentation was moved between departments and through many hands, as well as of diffusion of responsibilities, since no department could be directly held responsible for the progress of processes.

The report also added two notes on the lack of resources, since in the litigation department, only two out of the 90 employees were legal experts and much of the work had to be handwritten as there were not enough typists. The report went further, showing concern with the way contracts were drawn up. There were too many types of contracts, as many as 25; they would need to be standardised, which would allow them to be computer-generated. This would be a great improvement, since according to the report, 50% were still handwritten. It was further suggested that notarial certification should not be used in cases where the law did not require it, such as loans of less than 20 *contos*. A notary was used 'by tradition, by an illusory concern for security,

170

and perhaps to ensure public reading in case one of those involved could not read'. In addition, contracts had to be signed in Lisbon.[39]

Finally, the OECD mission's report focused on the management of deposit accounts. This assessment reflects some care the *Caixa* had in its relations with depositors; these could not differ substantially from what happened in the rest of the banking sector whilst attracting deposits, with whom the *Caixa* competed. However, it pointed out that, except for some operations in Lisbon, almost everything was done by hand; there was room for improvement with the introduction of operational automation. By 1970 there were approximately 1.8 million accounts, which involved 5 million credit and debit transactions, that is, an average of three account movements per year. This was a normal level of activity for savings deposits, but rather low for current accounts, the most active accounts being mandatory deposits, with 1.5 million transactions for 180 thousand accounts.

Finally, the report defined priority areas for the introduction of IT: firstly, an implementation in deposit departments, where the administrative burden was greater; secondly, in the credit department; and, finally, in the *Caixa de Previdência*. In addition, it recommended a comprehensive medium-term development plan and a plan for the automation of departments, and it noted the need for further decentralising responsibilities within the *Caixa*.

There is no indication of how the report was received by the *Caixa*'s management and the various departments. Still, the fact that it was requested indicates an awareness that the institution's operation needed changes, which implied the departure from old practices of the public administration. Many reforms would be easy to carry out as they involved procedural changes. Others were perhaps more difficult to put into practice, since they implied investment in equipment and facilities, the profitability of which still needed to be assessed. The most difficult reforms, however, were surely those involving better technical and professional qualifications of the *Caixa*'s staff, whose limitations surely reflected the drawbacks that could be seen at national level. There was a great shortage of technical skills regarding typists, computer technicians, lawyers, and economists, and the most important changes entailed recruiting staff with these specialisations.

## Notes

1 Lains (2007).
2 Rosas and Oliveira (eds.) (2004); Fernandes (2006).
3 For *Planos de Fomento*, see Correia (1952) and Almeida (1961).
4 Leitão (2007) and Lains (2007).
5 Amaral (1992), Nunes and Brito (1992), Mateus (2013), J. Lopes (2002) and Lains (2003).
6 Projecto do Plano Intercalar de Fomento (…) (1964), vol. 1, pp. 10–19.
7 Projecto do Plano Intercalar de Fomento (…) (1964), vol. 1, pp. 252–256, 296–297.
8 Projecto do Plano Intercalar de Fomento (…) (1964), vol. 1, pp. 196–207.

9  Relatório e Contas, 1965–1968.
10 (III) Plano de Fomento (…) (1967), vol. 2, p. 41.
11 Ribeiro et al. (1987).
12 Relatório e Contas, 1968–1973.
13 OCDE (1972). *Rapport de la mission d'étude effectuée par le G-CAM auprès de la Caixa Geral de Depósitos,* Paris, OCDE (at the Historical Archive of the Caixa Geral de Depósitos, dactil.)., p. 48.
14 The banks were, in descending order, the *Banco Pinto & Sotto Mayor,* the *Banco Português do Atlântico,* the *Banco Espírito Santo & Comercial de Lisboa,* the *Banco Nacional Ultramarino,* the *Banco Totta & Açores,* the *Banco Borges & Irmão,* and the *Banco Fonsecas & Burnay.* See Martins and Rosa, 1979, p. 16; Ribeiro et al., 1987, pp. 973–974.
15 Relatório e Contas, 1968, pp. 1–15.
16 (III) Plano de Fomento (…) (1967), vol. 1, Table XV and p. 141.
17 Projecto do IV Plano de Fomento (1973), vol. 1, pp. 157–158, 169, 179–180.
18 Correia (1973), pp. 16–18.
19 Livro de Actas do Conselho de Administração, 15 November 1968, 4 March 1969.
20 Decreto-Lei No. 693/70, 31 December, in Correia (1973), pp. 79–87.
21 Decreto-Lei No. 48,953, 5 April 1969.
22 Livro de Actas do Conselho de Administração, 11 April 1969, p. 71v.
23 Relatório e Contas, 1969, pp. 23–24, 43. Livro de Actas do Conselho de Administração, 15 April 1969, p. 73v.
24 Relatório e Contas, 1973, p. 54.
25 Relatório e Contas, 1967, p. 21.
26 Relatório e Contas, 1970, p. 42.
27 Diário de Notícias, 1 November 1970.
28 Relatório e Contas, 1970, pp. 31–33.
29 Mendes (2002).
30 OCDE (1972), p. 1.
31 The first organisational chart in the *Caixa*'s historical archives (*Arquivo Histórico da Caixa Geral de Depósitos*) is dated from the early 1980s.
32 OCDE (1972), p. 3.
33 Ordem de serviço No. 6,794, 30 June 1969, in Ordens de Serviço (AHCaixa).
34 OCDE (1972), p. 19.
35 OCDE (1972), p. 38.
36 OCDE (1972), pp. 40–41.
37 OCDE (1972), p. 42.
38 OCDE (1972), pp. 43–46.
39 OCDE (1972), pp. 45–48.

# 14

# THE NATIONALISATIONS AND BEYOND, 1974–1992

On 25 April 1974, the dictatorship that had ruled the country for almost half a century ended with a pacific military coup that quickly gained widespread popular support and went down in the records of history as the 'Carnation Revolution'. The transition to a democratic regime was complex, with international and domestic repercussions, and ultimately affected all aspects of Portugal's political, economic, and financial landscape. The *Caixa Geral de Depósitos* was not immune to such changes, even more so because, as a public bank, it was closely associated with the deposed regime, run by men appointed by the government and a crucial tool of its economic and financial policies. Yet for a number of reasons that we shall explore below, the *Caixa* managed to survive in good health and gained a position of accrued importance in the banking sector, particularly during the first decades of the new political environment. The successful adaptation was mostly a consequence of the fact that it had a solid financial position and managed to keep its reputation with the public, thus leading to a revival of the activity of the institution. The 1974 coup occurred during the change in the international economy provoked by the demise of the Bretton Woods system, the hike in oil prices, and the sharp increase in inflation across the western world, which would ultimately put an end to the golden age of growth. The two negative forces, from outside and the inside, put pressure on the country's financial equilibrium, both at the domestic and international levels, and a period of financial distress emerged. Yet the *Caixa* surfed those years without major financial problems and would ultimately gain market shares. By 1986, at the time of Portugal's accession to the European Communities, the troubles were somehow resolved and from then to 1992, the institution continued to increase its role in the domestic market, even though with accruing competition from the private sector. After 1992, new problems would appear in a context of declining levels of European financial regulation and increasing informal interference from governments, mostly through informal channels.

## Regime change and the banking sector

By 1974, the Portuguese economy, like other economies across the western world, was about to end three decades of rapid industrialisation and transformation of the service sector, including government and finance, with agriculture struggling with low levels of investment but still occupying a considerable part of the labour force. Low levels of literacy, lack of basic social overhead infrastructure, large emigration flows to Western Europe, and a sizable economic relationship with the Portuguese colonies, which would soon abruptly end, also characterised the economy. Moreover, despite the anti-European stance of the dictatorship's official discourse, Portugal's borders were already considerably open to the forces of international trade and finance stemming from the Bretton Woods system and European integration. The 1973 oil crisis, the related international disturbances, and the 1974 Carnation Revolution and the instauration of a democratic regime forced the economy to make significant readjustments, which included institutional changes in agriculture, industry and services, decolonisation, and changes in the public policy. On 25 April 1974, decades of social repression came to an abrupt end, with paramount economic and financial consequences. In May 1974, soon after the first post-coup civilian government was formed by a coalition of the main democratic political parties, the government sent a clear signal of the direction of the new policies by introducing a minimum wage that affected a large part of the labour force and was well above the existent lower wages.

The two years after the revolution were particularly unstable due to the struggles between the political forces with access to government, which included communists, socialists, and Social and Christian Democratic parties, all under close watch of the military that had delivered the coup with the aim of restoring democracy. Divisions also broke soon with the military with a left-wing section that ultimately seized the control of the government in association with the Communist Party. The political turmoil was particularly important for the financial sector because it was clearly at the top of the conglomerates that controlled large manufacturing and service industries and were closely associated with the deposed regime. On 11 March 1975, a set of complex political and military operations led to a coup (actually a counter-coup) and the ensuing government ended up deciding the nationalisation of all industrial conglomerates, an operation that out-passed any other that had occurred in Western Europe until then, or any that has since occurred. The nationalisation of the banking sector was hastily decided on 11 March 1975 at a meeting of the Armed Forces Movement (*Movimento das Forças Armadas*), which created the Council of the Revolution (*Conselho da Revolução*) on the same day. Before that day, the banking unions had taken control of the banks, to push for the sacking of the boards and their replacement by elements favourable to the new political regime. The government was kept apart. This was done without any role for the government, and the minister of finance, Silva Lopes, resigned because of his total lack of power to appoint the new boards.[1] The nationalisation spree created a number of banks owned and controlled by the state but with statutes that differed from that of the *Caixa*, which remained the only public bank. The nationalisation of a substantial part of the capital and economic activity was poorly planned, but the ultimate consequences were less severe than many expected. The country went back to a reasonable level of normalcy following another coup, this time led by moderate forces, which took place on 25 November 1975. In the meantime, free elections for a Constitutional Assembly took place, symbolically on the first anniversary of the Carnation Revolution, and the first democratic parliament with a socialist and social democratic majority was elected on 25 April 1976.

The new institutional framework ended up favouring the public bank as a degree of uncertainty regarding the health of the nationalised banks led to an increase in the confidence of the depositors on the public institution. Moreover, the democratic governments proceeded with a number of new policies, particularly related to the investment in housing, which favoured the business of the *Caixa*. The flipside of such positive elements was the fact that the public bank was also used to finance a number of other policies, particularly concerning the control of price rises of certain staples and covering the operational deficits of some of the nationalised companies which were running into problems of under-capitalisation.[2]

As a public institution, the *Caixa* was associated, *de jure* and *de facto*, with government policy. The government appointed the administration, and the bank played a major role in pursuing some of the objectives of public financing of private activity and the construction of infrastructure, for example, under the development plans. Also, the financial sector was one of the areas of national economic activity most affected by the revolution. It is, however, difficult to track the connections between the governments and the *Caixa*'s administration in the archives, as they were mostly conducted in meetings between the chief executive and the secretary of state for the Treasury, of which no written records can be found. Amongst the vast body of documentation consulted, there is only one reference to the agenda, but not to the minutes of a meeting between the secretary of state for the Treasury and the president of the *Caixa*.[3] A number of documents kept in the archives refer to 'personal contacts' or 'various contacts in the Ministry of Finance', between the board and the government, revealing the high level of informality with which important matters were dealt with.

The changes in the Portuguese financial system affected more than the banking industry. The breadth of political turbulence meant that a considerable part of the monetary policy management responsibilities passed to the Bank of Portugal and, indirectly, to the financial and banking institutions controlled by the state. This was the third way the revolution influenced the *Caixa*'s operation. Due to its financial power, governments used the *Caixa*'s resources to respond to the large needs of financing, caused by a declining economy, with low export growth, increasing trade and government deficits, and the demand for higher spending in essential subsidies. It was somehow fortunate that, in the context of the downturn of the international economy and domestic political destabilisation, the *Caixa* increased its appeal to the public, and deposits in the institution remained stable and eventually increased to the extent that it gained market shares.[4]

The highly unstable political atmosphere, with the pressure from the parties and the military from the left, namely the Communist Party, and a highly vocal, extreme left with little popular representation, forced governments into wage increases and control of the prices of essential goods, particularly food staples. The outcome of such policies was a rapid increase in the public expenditure and deficit, which helped increase price inflation. Simultaneously, emigrant remittances, a major source of foreign financing of the economy, decreased substantially. It was in this context that the *Caixa* was called upon to contribute to the rise of government intervention. It helped financing imports of essential goods, companies in financial difficulties, costs arising from the nationalisation of enterprises, the agrarian reform, and to cover the deficits of economic coordination bodies, most importantly the fund that subsidised prices (*Fundo de Abastecimento*).[5] All of this constituted a change in the ways the money trusted to the institution by the private and public depositors was invested. And it is possible to track vividly the change.

In fact, by the end of May 1974, soon after the military coup and following the first commemoration of Labour Day for decades, which assembled more than a million people in the streets of the major cities, the national electric company (*Companhia Portuguesa de Electricidade*) applied for a loan of one million *contos*. The loan was aimed at investments in line with previous actions and unrelated to the crisis. The board however refused to concede the amount required on financial grounds and conceded only a fifth of what had been asked for.[6] Less than a year after that event, in February, the *Caixa* had the request of a loan of a similar size (in nominal terms) of 1.1 million *contos* from the sugar and alcohol regulator (*Administração-Geral do Açúcar e do Álcool*) in order to import sugar from no other country than Cuba. The request was made with great urgency, which prevented the *Caixa* from being informed of the main aspects of the operation, but the Ministry of Finance considered it to be in the 'national interest' to carry it out, and the board had to comply with the request.[7]

In April 1975, the *Caixa*'s board submitted an extensive report on the institution's financial situation to the minister of finance. The report was in line with government policy, but still made some remarks on the fact that its financial situation depended mainly on retail deposits, both term and demand deposits, and to a lesser extent the mandatory deposits determined by various state authorities and by the courts.[8] A climate supporting a close link between the *Caixa* and government policy was evident in some left-leaning media.[9] But not everyone agreed, as was the case with Sousa Franco, a social democrat, who resigned as board member in September 1975 because he 'disagree[d] with the credit criteria' followed by the *Caixa*, and above all could not 'accept' the "firefighter" role, which was the *Caixa*'s main job, especially at the end of each month'.[10]

From 1976 on, the *Caixa*'s credit operations were again devoted mostly to medium- and long-term financing. These experienced a 42% rise, compared with a 12% increase in short-term operations. In 1976, short-term operations accounted for 47% of the total contracted throughout the year, down from the 53% in 1974–1975.[11] However, there was still much to be done, particularly with regard to granting loans, and the *Caixa* had to play a greater role as a 'savings mobilising machine', both in credit to the 'large nationalised sector' and to the private sector.[12] In June 1976, Jacinto Nunes took the position of chief executive and left perhaps one of the best reports of the internal situation of the institution. Questioned about his experience, he replied:

> For me [the experience] was not very good. The *Caixa* was mammoth, a very heavy structure. I had as vice-chairman a man extremely dedicated to the *Caixa*, but very devoted to tradition and with a very conservative view. He would not allow me to do much. I even left at one point. Internally, a very conservative spirit ruled. The *Caixa* enjoyed great financial soundness, and that was the tradition. However, I thought that, once that soundness was established, the bank should support economic activity [...] it was hard to introduce some dynamism because everything was ponderous. Moreover, at that time there were many labour problems. At one point, I had over 200 people with labour demands at my door.[13]

By mid-1975, the *Caixa* employed close to 4,000 people.[14] Following the fall of the *Estado Novo*, the bank's employees organised themselves into representative, election-based structures with department delegates and an executive committee, through which they began establishing regular contacts with the administration. However, the difficulty in institutionalising labour movements in the *Caixa*, that is, the impossibility for the workers to organise themselves into trade unions due to the organic structure of the institution, prevented a 'more intense collaboration' between workers and administration. The *Caixa*'s trade union issue put an end to the legal ambiguity regarding its workers' professional situation. Nevertheless, the 1969 reform was not considered outdated by the first constitutional governments. It represented a consensus appearing to be sufficient in the late 1970s, introducing greater liberalisation and distance of the *Caixa* from the state, even if the latter still had instruments of supervision and influence over the bank. The interim government took pains to maintain stability and to ward off the revolution from the *Caixa*. The primary goal was to avoid making hasty decisions that could jeopardise the bank's soundness. In essence, the interim executives chose to take advantage of the *Caixa*'s financial capacities rather than change its organisational structure, which could undermine the institution's stability. This period was marked by strong union activity within the *Caixa Geral de Depósitos* and resulted in the immediate constitution of the workers' executive committee as soon as 30 April 1974. Its aims clearly included obtaining permission to form a union for the employees of the *Caixa* or for their integration into existing unions of bank staff.[15] The unionisation of the *Caixa*'s employees was turbulent. It was soon clear that the workers' commission sought to play a decisive role in the management of the institution.[16] By the end of December 1974, over 80% of the *Caixa* employees had registered in the three banking trade unions, even without the due statutory change.[17] In early December 1974 the *Caixa*'s administration asked the secretary of state for the Treasury for a solution to the problem of unionisation of its employees given the 'anxiety' felt in the bank.[18] In spite of the 'desire of the overwhelming majority' of the *Caixa* workers to join banking trade unions, the Ministry of Finance had some reservations, since there was no certainty as to whether or not the bank's employees were still civil servants.[19] In fact, according to the 1969 charter, the regime and situation of the *Caixa*'s staff were markedly ambivalent. The institution's 'tradition' of applying 'fully' the legal regime of civil service to its employees was kept, as was the principle of keeping the *Caixa*'s regulation 'essentially linked to public law'.[20] The bank's administration was given the liberty to establish the list of ranks and salaries, taking into account those practiced by the banking sector, to avoid making the *Caixa*'s running 'incompatible with the requirements of business management'. The level of education of the *Caixa* employees fit the general context of the country. A document from the *Centro de Formação e Aperfeiçoamento* (Training and Improvement Centre) on the situation of 'external courses' by 1 June 1978 listed as learning subjects 'financial management', 'investment problems', 'project assessment', 'export credit and external trade', 'financial audit', 'small and medium-sized enterprises', 'feasibility contracts', 'housing design', 'urban planning legislation', 'personnel training', 'personnel management', 'documentation techniques', and 'clerking'. The document explained that 'for most of the *Caixa*'s staff it is necessary to start with a basic training, oriented towards organisation of thought rather than accumulation of knowledge: points such as presenting a topic properly orally or in writing, or systematising a subject as a basis for analysis, conveying information or composing within a letter. Such a participatory approach focused on working methods was a superior substitute for encyclopaedic courses on a variety of subjects, of which only a small part was of direct interest to each person and job.[21]

## Remittances and construction

In August 1974, the *Caixa*'s priority fields of action were housing credit and the public sector. Following directives from the government, the *Caixa* would increase coverage 'on construction funding' whilst simultaneously building up 'aid to the public sector', burdened by significant difficulties, given the 'existing shortfalls' were no longer covered by the Treasury. Governments sought to take advantage of the 'encouraging increase in deposits within the institution', mainly due to the large remittances of emigrants, looking to reinvest them in certain key sectors of the Portuguese economy.[22] The *Caixa* would need to therefore take advantage of the increased deposits to finance public and private investment in order to foster the Portuguese economy, which was debilitated by capital flight and a drop in private investment. Essentially, it was a matter of cementing the *Caixa*'s vocation within the Portuguese banking system, defining the purpose of this institution as a 'large deposit bank for the people', with the application of deposits in credit and the funding of investment.[23] With the full understanding that the trust of the 'great mass of depositors' resting on the 'special conditions of the institution' independent from the state, yet strongly connected to it, the government and the bank's administration sought to maintain 'continuity' in the management of the institution. Both realised the 'appropriate' approach was not to split the *Caixa*'s business, 'under penalty of irreparable damage'.[24] Taking advantage of the Portuguese government's 'policy of expanding public credit institutions in the principal destination countries of Portuguese emigrants', the *Caixa* opened a subsidiary in Paris with the aim of 'channelling more directly to Portugal' the remittances sent by local Portuguese emigrants.[25] Similarly, the *Caixa* took part in a mission sent by the Portuguese government to France and Germany to assess the local market conditions with a view towards opening delegations in those countries. The objective was to analyse the recent evolution and the prospects of the movement of emigrant payments, as well as the most important facts influencing the evolution and future prospects for the collection of migrant remittances. The mission ended up making a report strongly based on the situation of Portuguese banking in France. It concluded there were eight Portuguese banks in France, including the *Caixa*, even though this had no agency open to the public, only a representation office. Of these eight banks, the most representative were undoubtedly the *Banque Franco-Portugaise d'Outre-Mer*, with 8 agencies open, and the *Banco Pinto & Sotto Maior*, with 19. Both had survey services for emigrants, even if relatively archaic ones. The activity of the Portuguese commercial banks in France aimed to encourage emigrants to transfer their funds to Portugal through cheque or to open special savings accounts for emigrants with appreciable interest rates. In the particular case of the *Caixa*, the lack of an agency open to the public led the bank to encourage emigrants to make these operations via the *Banque National de Paris*, waiving the transfer fee.

In 1966, the Portuguese government instituted a credit-saving scheme with the main goal of creating a type of credit especially for emigrants, favouring property acquisition. It had three main objectives. Firstly, it sought to encourage emigrant remittances, 'to mitigate balance-of-payments imbalances,' protecting it from monetary erosion in years of very high inflation. Secondly, at a time when the construction industry needed 'incentives', the government deemed it 'propitious' to develop a system that would boost investment in the housing sector. Finally, the new regime also considered the need to 'restructure agriculture in the areas of small-scale farming', creating conditions for them to return to their homelands, contributing to a 'more adequate dimensioning' of farms. Essentially, emigrants' savings could later be reinvested either in construction or in the acquisition of agricultural property.[26] In the same year, the government approved a system for homeowners' credit with subsidised rates, and instituted savings-and-credit accounts for emigrants.[27] The government's goal was to set a 'pace for house construction and refurbishment' capable of responding to the 'failures' of the housing market in Portugal, ensuring it necessary to 'reply to the demands of new households' through repayments and prices that were 'compatible with their income'.[28] State credit bodies, together with the nationalised institutions, began to grant Portuguese emigrants loans based on the value of the houses to be acquired or built.[29] However, the impact of these legislative measures was markedly different. As a result, 2,500 'credit applications [were] submitted' at the *Caixa Geral de Depósitos* during March and April 1976. The *Caixa* was to 'grant greater' facilities in loaning to construction contractors to promote their 'responsiveness' in face of the 'measures promoting own-home purchasing'.[30]

The construction sector played an important role in the Portuguese economy, accounting for around 7.5% of the working population in 1978. The *Caixa*'s investments in the sector reflected the need to capitalise on the remittances of Portuguese emigrants around the world, especially in France and Germany. The state sought to create conditions for Portuguese emigrants to invest their savings in the country, in particular through housing credit, without fear of the revolutionary turbulence, helping construction companies and encouraging the increase of jobs in the sector and related industries. For the *Caixa*, housing credit was a way of developing active operations in the medium- and long-term. These were extremely important to the institution's financial stability at a time when its short-term operations were strangled by Treasury requirements. Housing credit grew quite sharply during the late 1970s and the 1980s. Indeed, the outstanding balances of this sector, which in 1977 represented a total of 25 million *contos*, by 1986 had risen to about 363 million, corresponding to 45.1% of total credit granted by the *Caixa*.[31] In 1974, the *Caixa*'s financing to the sector 'almost doubled' compared with the previous two years, loans being directed especially at 'lower-income housing'.[32]

Thus, between 1976 and 1980, the *Caixa*'s results were closely linked to the high level of liquidity arising from the deposits of emigrant remittances; and to the strong investment in lending to construction and to home ownership, combining the design of the governments and the goals of the bank. Despite its importance, housing credit still ranked second, immediately following credit to the industrial sector, and only in 1980 did housing credit reach the top position.[33]

## Normalisation

By the beginning of the 1980s, Portuguese politics began to catch the first winds of change, following events in the rest of western Europe. Few could have imagined that the international economic crisis of 1973 would be overcome through greater economic and financial integration within the European

Communities. Similarly, few would have expected the Portuguese crisis, which was caused by the combination of international and national political crisis, to be overcome through growing liberalisation of the markets and better organisation of the state, all done in tune with future European partners. In the national financial sector, the most important steps were taken through a series of decrees, published between the end of 1983 and the beginning of 1984, opening up the banking and insurance system to private enterprise, hitherto barred from those activities.

In 1981, the institution's organisation was restructured, improving the *Caixa*'s operation. The effort focused on credit, refining its different types and the vertical integration of the various complementary departments. The *Caixa*'s restructuring also involved the matter of facilities, new spaces being acquired where the departments could be organised in accordance with requirements, namely the IT structure.[34] In 1981, the *Caixa* acquired a plot of land measuring 3.68 hectares (36,800 square meters) in Campo Pequeno, Lisbon, to construct a building containing all central departments.[35] In 1983, the Organisational Structure Manual was published, reorganising several directorates linked to management support. From this came, among others, the Directorates of Management Planning and Control, Personnel Services, Accounting and Treasury and Securities Management Services, and also the Public Relations Office, the Balance and Information Centre, the Documentation and Technical Information Centre, the Office for Codification and Standards Delivery, and the Office for New Facilities for the Central Departments. This restructuring phase was completed in 1985.[36]

A report from the administration points out that throughout 1982 the support of the *Caixa*'s information system available to the branches was consolidated. The mechanisation of all the branches on the continent was concluded and the teleprocessing network launched. This network comprised 419 terminals, corresponding to 238 workstations, processing around 110,000 transactions daily, concerning 1,700,000 customer accounts. According to the report, it should have been one of the largest teleprocessing networks in the country. By the end of 1983 the teleprocessing network had been extended to 80 out-buildings, 702 terminals and 395 workstations.[37] In 1984, housing credit was also computerised, and the teleprocessing network reached central services, allowing the computerisation of various departments, such as personnel, staff shop, assets, and foreign works and operations. In 1985, the same network integrated new applications in the areas of the Balance and Information Centre, subsidiaries and branches, industrial credit and accounting.[38]

## The *Caixa* and the government

The large amount of correspondence exchanged between the *Caixa* and the Ministry was essentially devoted to matters such as the payment of interest subsidies by the state, state guarantees, loans taken abroad by the *Caixa*, issues concerning the situation of companies intervened upon by the state, matters relating to how the *Caixa* should act in the event of default by debtor companies and to the placement of the bank's results. There is little or nothing about medium- or long-term strategic options, a matter one would expect to see discussed from time to time by the administration and shareholders and see reflected in the documentation. A recurrent issue in the dealings between the government and the *Caixa* was the question of the investment of results, namely the participation in the *Caixa*'s profits. Most times, the administration proposed a certain amount, generally 60% of the annual profits, to be paid to the state. However, this was not always the case, and sometimes the state required a higher value than that proposed by the administration.

At the end of March 1982, the chief executive had sent the secretary of state a detailed letter, requesting authorisation to open several branches. He justified the need with the increasing demand for the *Caixa*'s services for deposit and handling of small savings, as well as the increase of new assignments, such as the payment of salaries and pensions and tax collection. The operations most pursued by the *Caixa* were 'almost entirely medium- and long-term', such as home loans, which had very slow turnover. Also, 'the *Caixa*'s pace of granting new loans depended fundamentally on raising new funds, which in turn depended on an adequate network of agencies'. The administration was satisfied as to the agency coverage on a national level, which in many areas of the interior of the country was complemented by the delegations operating in public Treasury offices. However, this was not the case in the larger cities, namely Lisbon, Porto, and Coimbra where, of the large national credit institutions, the *Caixa* had the 'smallest network of agencies'. This put the *Caixa*, 'at a disadvantage compared to commercial banking, regarding the raising of funds'. The fact that many areas of these cities already had agencies of commercial banks should not be seen as 'an impediment to the establishment of the *Caixa*'s branches, given its role in attracting small savings and the purpose and terms of credit on which it applies those resources'.[39] The reply would come only two years later, in 1984, through the Bank of Portugal, to whom the *Caixa*'s administration had also defended its view regarding the need to increase the number of branches.[40] Given it was not in the same situation as commercial banks, the *Caixa* objected to the same restrictions as the rest of the banking system being imposed upon it, following a circular letter from the Bank of Portugal. This letter did not allow the increase in the number of branches, in order to ensure the rationalisation of domestic banking coverage.[41] The *Caixa* had permission to transfer the delegations it held in tax offices on to their own premises, and from 1979, a programme was initiated to turn delegations at council seats into private agencies. By 1984, this had not yet been completed. However, in urban areas, the *Caixa* was bound to the constraints imposed on other credit institutions, thus maintaining the 'severe coverage deficiencies'. It therefore requested, again, authorisation to open the new branches listed in the request of March 1982, again receiving a negative reply.[42] Between 1983 and 1987,

182

the expansion of the bank's agency network resulted almost exclusively from the opening of branches in county seats in rural areas, as many in these four years as in 1982. These were four years of waiting time until the *Caixa* could catch up with the commercial bank rollout in urban areas. Only in the early 1990s would the expansion plan outlined in 1982 be complete.

The disagreements between the state and the administration gained some prominence during the governments of Cavaco Silva. In July 1985 the administration informed the secretary of state that 'without prejudice to full compliance with' his order establishing the amount of 5.5 million *contos* for 1984, it must be noted that the 'personal communications with you on the subject, and the elements then submitted, pointed to a lower participation'. Oliveira Pinto underlined that the situation necessarily raised 'some concern for the executive board' and proceeded to indicate the amounts that, in the board's view, negatively affected the equity–liabilities and equity–deposits ratios, and Pinto suggested that it be ensured that reserves were always set at a level equivalent or higher than the rate of inflation. In conclusion regarding 1985, the chief executive argued for the definition of 'an amount for the participation of the state never higher than the one now delivered'.[43] The request would not be granted. A letter sent by the board to the secretary of state at the end of July 1985 defended that the state's participation for that year should be set at 5.5 million *contos*. It later proposed it be between 6 and 6.5 million *contos*, but 'at the insistence of the secretary of state for the Treasury', the amount was finally set at 7 million *contos*.[44]

It was also established that, given the existing forecasts, information should be sent to the directorate-general for the Treasury that the funds to be entered in the budget for 1986 should be the same as those decided for the previous year. This, however, also failed to occur, since in 1986 the state's share rose from 7 to 7.5 million *contos*. The values for 1987 were not without friction either. Following an order from the secretary of state for the Treasury of September 1988, the *Caixa* was instructed to deliver 12.5 million *contos* to the Treasury corresponding to the participation of the previous year, 'regardless of the higher amount that may come to be fixed'. In view of this position, fearing the state would request further increase of the amount, it was recorded in the minutes that the board 'resolved to present in writing' to the secretary of state 'the concerns raised by this level of participation, considering the need to reinforce the *Caixa*'s equity'.[45] At the subsequent meeting, fearing the administration already found the increase of this amount excessive, it once again expressed its concern at the 'possibility of the amount to be allocated to the state's share of the bank's last year's profits being inflated to an amount even higher than 12.5 million *contos*'.[46] Remarking on the possible increase in the sum of the state's share of profits, the executive board points out that the adequate amount was 10 million *contos*, 12.5 already being 'a considerable increase, to the detriment of the needed bolstering of the *Caixa*'s equity base'. It further noted that, in spite of the *Caixa* controlling only 25% of the banking sector, 'its contribution in recent years to the revenues of the state [...] has been more than four times the amount paid by the other institutions in the sector', and that the bank's reserve growth had not matched the growth of its assets. The administration reminded the secretary of state that the proposed participation would determine a reduction in the limits of credits assigned to the *Caixa*, causing restrictions in the granting of loans, namely to the housing sector.[47] The concerns expressed had an effect, and the value delivered to the state did not exceed 12.5 million. However, this was not the only way for the state to balance its accounts through the *Caixa*. At the end of July 1987, 'following various contacts within the Ministry of Finance, the board resolved to grant financing to the Treasury' to the amount of 80 million *contos* over ten years, at the Bank of Portugal's discount rate, minus 0.25%,[48] 'intended for financing the 1987 budget deficit'.[49] In September, it would be raised to 100 million *contos*, and the amortisation period extended to twelve years.[50]

[Graph 14.1]

In 1988, the Council for the Financial System (*Conselho para o Sistema Financeiro*), an advisory body of the Ministry of Finance, was created, having as its main task the proposal for reforms to be introduced in the financial system.[51] Its work was reflected in the legislation adopted between 1989 and 1992. The new general regime reorganised the banking activity in Portugal, seeking not only to adapt it to European legislation, but also to allow for the definitive normalisation of the sector after the troubled years of democratic transition and consolidation.[52] The financial companies were divided into credit institutions and financial corporations, operating under a free competition regime, and the supervising role of the Bank of Portugal was expanded, both in matters of technical regulations and overseeing authorised activities. The new regime also adopted the principle of supervision by the authorities of the country of origin of the institution concerned, a measure for regulating the activity of foreign institutions in Portugal.[53] The council advised for a better specification of the *Caixa Geral de Depósitos* activities and that it should be subject to the prudential, fiscal, or monetary policy regulations applied to other banks. Yet the *Caixa* would keep its special role as a state-owned bank that would need to follow the policy interests of the state and thus participate in the public credit policy, in particular through its action in operations considered less attractive to private banks, but which were deemed relevant to development of the Portuguese economy. The state would continue to hold the power to define the strategy for the *Caixa*, as would any shareholder of a private company. The council's recommendations on the public bank concluded with a caveat: the *Caixa* should diversify its activity, and thus integrating a universal banking model, 'seeking the profitability of its operations and an overall balance of different activities', which would be in line with its leading position in the Portuguese financial market.[54] These recommendations of the working group for the financial system were heeded and included in the text of the decree-law establishing the general regime, under which the *Caixa* was allowed to carry out all operations permitted to banks 'without prejudice to other responsibilities conferred by the legislation specific [to the institution]'.[55]

## The acquisition of the Banco Nacional Ultramarino

On 12 July 1988, the minister of finance 'invited the bank's administration to acquire a majority holding in the capital of the *Banco Nacional Ultramarino* (BNU) and of the *Fidelidade Grupo Segurador*'. It was agreed that a position on the matter would be dependent upon an evaluation of the institutions in question, and that negotiations would follow later between the *Caixa* and the State Treasury Department.[56] After an analysis of the bank's situation, the *Caixa*'s administration underlined: negative results in the years 1985, 1986, 1987, and 1988 (first semester), amounting to 8.8 million *contos*; the existence of credits acknowledged as irrecoverable, 'to the value of 30 million *contos*, poorly provisioned'; a surplus of personnel caused by the absorption of approximately one-and-a-half thousand employees from the former colonies, whose impact on the income account had been estimated at 13.5 million *contos*. Regarding the portfolio of shares and bonds, the properties and the financial investments that made up the assets of the BNU, it was concluded that, 'despite significant unrealised gain, the net worth was strongly negative'.

In mid-September 1988, the *Caixa* presented the secretary of state with the 'minimum conditions to take a favourable view of the proposal to acquire a holding in the BNU'. These comprised a series of elements, including the payment of the subsidy for the 1985 losses, already assumed by the state but still awaiting effective settlement; the grant by the Treasury to the BNU of subsidies to eliminate the 1986 and 1987 losses from the bank's balance sheet; the achievement of a consensus on the results to be ascertained in 1988 so that it 'may be eliminated by virtue of the reserves shown in the balance sheet'; the assumption by the Treasury of the future costs of the retirement and survivor pensions of the employees from the former colonies already retired and to be retired, in proportion to the length of service; and a consensus on the reconstitution of the BNU's executive board. These requirements being fulfilled, the board was willing to acquire 60% of the bank's capital through a capital increase from 7 to 20 million *contos*, of which the *Caixa* would provide 12 million, and the Treasury 1 million.

Divergence remained, however. The Treasury determined the shareholding base value of 1,000$00 per share would be adjusted based on the evaluation to be made by two independent entities to be chosen with the agreement of the shareholders. From the point of view of the *Caixa*'s administration, this method would leave the bank 'exposed to a commitment of an undetermined amount', and it therefore argued that the definitive price per share should be fixed.[57] The *Caixa*'s demand having been met, the protocol was signed on 31 October 1988.[58] Nine days later, the *Caixa*'s executive board approved the subscription of 7 million BNU shares at a unit price of 1000$00, with a view to increasing the capital from 7 to 14 million *contos*.[59] Two months later, the same board approved the increase of BNU's initial capital to 20 million *contos* 'by issuing at par 6 million registered shares with a nominal value of 1000$00, to be subscribed [as follows:] 5 million by the *Caixa* and 1 million by the Portuguese state; this increase will be carried out in cash until December 30 of this year'.[60] Within two months, the *Caixa* had already injected 12 million *contos* into the BNU.

Capital injections were not sufficient to rebalance the income generation account of the *Banco Nacional Ultramarino*, and in the beginning of February 1989, financial support was requested from the Bank of Portugal. The bank agreed to grant a loan of 5 million *contos* 'for the period of one year and at a symbolic interest rate', on the condition that the *Caixa*, 'as the current majority shareholder of the BNU, grant similar support'. Offered the chance of obtaining funding at a symbolic rate, and considering 'the need of the bank, at this stage of its recovery, to be given the support to balance its income generation account (expecting to obtain its counterpart in the future through the valuation of the respective shareholding position)', the *Caixa* agreed and deposited 5 million *contos* with BNU for a period of one year.[61] Once the acquisition was concluded, the finance minister, who had invoked his competence and experience under the pretext of a potentially great challenge invited the *Caixa*'s chief executive, Oliveira Pinto, to chair the other public credit institution, but the latter refused.[62]

The government's intent for the *Caixa* and the BNU having been made public, and outlining the framework for the future evolution of the banking system, the newly-appointed chairman of the *Caixa*'s board presented the pillars that would guide his management: modernisation, seen as innovation and recycling of human resources; internationalisation, which was required in the context of the future economic and monetary union; decentralisation, to follow 'the regionalisation momentum within the country'; finally, universalism, as a consequence of the evolution and liberalisation of financial markets.'[63]

On 9 July 1990, an order of the secretary of state for finance directed the *Caixa*'s administration to acquire 2,440,000 shares of *Soporcel* from the *Banco de Fomento and Exterior* (BFE).[64] The public bank complied on the date and for the price defined by the government. As of this date, the *Caixa* held 49.895% of *Soporcel*'s capital in its portfolio, with the prospect of acquiring another 50,000 shares to obtain the absolute majority of the company's capital, an operation that required legal changes the government supported. However, that further acquisition had not been possible, keeping the *Caixa* from achieving the desired absolute majority of *Soporcel*'s capital. This negatively affected the profitability of the *Caixa*'s assets, since the tie-up in that company was 38% of the portfolio of financial participation, and the value of this participation in the bank's balance sheet represented about 20% of the volume of its own funds. Besides posing a risk to the *Caixa*, this situation exceeded the limits imposed by law to the holding of stocks. It is in this context that Rui Vilar, pointing to the 'severity of the situation', asserted it was made worse 'by the fact the *Caixa*'s portfolio included other large participations resulting from political decisions and not based on a business strategy of the financial group the *Caixa* heads'. The chairman was referring to the injection of 25.8 million *contos* into the BNU, which, together with the participation in *Soporcel*, 'accounts for about 57% of total financial investments and about 30% of the *Caixa*'s own funds'. The problem was further aggravated by the fact that none of these holdings had provided income to the *Caixa* either in the form of dividends or in the form of actual valuation. On the contrary, Vilar notes that, since the amount on the balance sheet was much higher than the stock market price for *Soporcel* shares, the *Caixa* had to provide 20 million *contos* in provisions for potential capital losses. Taking these facts into account, Vilar warned of the need to 'urgently agree and implement' the guidelines allowing the demobilisation of non-productive assets from the *Caixa*'s balance sheet. The bank's chairman further recalled the *Caixa*'s holdings in IPE and the *Banif*, also 'the result of political decisions', suggesting that they be taken into consideration in a future restructuring of the public sector holdings involving the two financial groups of the state: the *Caixa* and the BFE. Regarding the BNU, Vilar defended the proposal that a new shareholder structure be defined and implemented, so as to allow 'not only a reduction of the excessive weight the participation in this bank represents within the *Caixa*'s fixed assets, but also to provide the institutional conditions for the BNU to pursue autonomous development with its own objectives'. The chairman of the *Caixa* thus made quite clear his disagreement with the forced marriage his institution was 'invited' to make, expressing interest in moving towards friendly divorce proceedings. The secretary of state's response was predictably harsh. Elias da Costa made a brief and concise order in which he argues:

> (1) *Caixa*'s involvement in the BNU and the *Soporcel* resulted from government options or recommendations, taking into account the public interests involved; (2) it should be borne in mind that, for this purpose and in terms of distribution of profits, in recent years the *Caixa* has had an exceptional reinforcement of its capital reserves; (3) the need to rethink the integration of BNU in the *Caixa* group is acknowledged, not for financial reasons, but rather of strategy, competitiveness, and operability of the group ....[65]

In February 1992, the chairman of the *Caixa*'s executive board sent a confidential letter to the secretary of state for finance, where, among other matters, he referred to that of the BNU as a financial participation 'that originated in political decisions', with no 'basis in a business strategy of the financial group the *Caixa* heads'. Rui Vilar, who had been appointed to follow the strategy outlined by Miguel Cadilhe, which included the integration of the BNU in the

*Caixa* group and its conversion into an institution dedicated to supporting small- and medium-sized enterprises, complementing the *Caixa*, now, two years later, criticised the mission that had been assigned to him.

A decision was approved in the Council of Ministers in January 1993, which took effect from 31 December 1992, in which it was argued that the growing interconnection of the various institutions making up the the *Caixa Geral de Depósitos* group, not only at management level, but through 'the clear definition of a true group strategy', justifies and supports 'an increase in the *Caixa*'s shareholding in the BNU'. The *Caixa*, which already held 65% of the BNU, should strengthen its position in order to give 'greater consistency' to the group and allow 'greater flexibility in defining the *Caixa* group's strategy'. Besides allowing 'the reorganisation of the financial situation of the BNU', this reinforcement did not require 'the direct involvement of considerable resources of the state'. From that instance, the state would directly own only 10% of the BNU, and for the sole reason that this bank was a direct agent for the issuance of banknotes and Treasury cashier in Macao.[66] This was the government's response to Vilar's friendly separation request. Once again, the shareholder showed who was in charge. However, contrary to the case of Oliveira Pinto, who had never put his opposition to the integration of the BNU in writing and merely defended the interests of the institution he directed, Rui Vilar, despite having defended a strategy contrary to the government's, would spend two more years implementing a policy with which, at least as far as the BNU was concerned, he did not agree.

## Notes

1 Fernandes (ed.) (2006), pp. 52–53; Nunes (1994), pp. 77–78.
2 The 1975 nationalisation left out foreign banks operating in Portugal, as well as savings banks and mutual agricultural credit banks, which together had little weight. See Nunes et al. (1994), pp. 78–79.
3 Letter No. 6,295 from the State Treasury Department to the *Caixa*'s board, dated 28 September 1983 (ACMF, pastas SETF/gabinete do SET/Caixa).
4 Franco (1994), p. 188.
5 Evolução do Estabelecimento, September 1974 (AHCaixa).
6 'Despacho' no. 74/74 Caixa Geral de Depósitos' 21 May 1974 (AHCaixa, 01AO/2OAD/02CAD/4/2–02). See also Relatório e Contas da Caixa Geral de Depósitos, 1976.
7 Carta No. 51/SCA from the executive board of the *Caixa Geral de Depósitos*, 3 February 1975 (AHCaixa, 01AO/3DAM/1/1/1–20). Ordem No. 40/75 of the executive board of the *Caixa Geral de Depósitos*, 7 February 1975 (AHCaixa, 01AO/2OAD/02CAD/4/2–02).
8 The *Caixa Geral de Depósitos*. Sinopse da Situação em 24 de Abril de 1975 (ACMF, series 29, bobin 3).
9 Diário de Notícias, 13 March 1975.
10 O Tempo, 18 September 1975.
11 Relatório e Contas da Caixa Geral de Depósitos, 1976, 1977.
12 Nunes (1976), pp. 8–9.

13  Fernandes (ed.) (2006), p. 80.
14  The *Caixa Geral de Depósitos*. Sinopse da Situação em 24 de Abril de 1975 (ACMF, série 29, bobin 3).
15  Collective proposal presented and approved in a workers' general meeting on 30 April 1974 (AHCaixa, FG 2093-MS0002).
16  Communiqué No. 4 from the workers' executive committee of 17 May 1974 (AHCaixa, FG 2101-MS0010).
17  Diário de Notícias, 15 July 1974.
18  Carta No. 140 from the board of the *Caixa Geral de Depósitos* of 12 December 1974 (AHCaixa, 01AO/3DAM/1/1/1–20).
19  Diário de Notícias, 23 September 1974.
20  *Decreto-Lei* No. 48,953, 5 April 1969.
21  *Despacho* No. 101/78, Despachos Numerados, 1978, 2.º vol.
22  Expresso, 31 August 1974.
23  The *Caixa Geral de Depósitos*. Sinopse da Situação em 24 de Abril de 1975 (ACMF, series 29, reel 3).
24  Carta No. 249/SCA from Caixa's administration, dated 24 October 1977 (ACMF, series 29, reel 3).
25  Expresso, 24 January 1975.
26  *Decreto-Lei* No. 540/76, 9 July 1976.
27  Relatório e Contas, 1976.
28  Diário de Notícias, 20 April 1976.
29  *Decreto-Lei* No. 540/76, 9 July 1976.
30  Expresso, 3 July 1976.
31  Relatório e Contas, 1986.
32  Relatório e Contas, 1974.
33  Relatório e Contas da Caixa Geral de Depósitos, 1980.
34  *Relatório e Contas da Caixa Geral de Depósitos*, 1979, p. 29. *Despacho* No. 40/81, in Despachos Numerados, 1981, Vol.1.
35  *Relatório e Contas da Caixa Geral de Depósitos*, 1981, p. 30; 1982, p. 38.
36  Despacho No. 80-A/83, in Despachos Numerados, 1983.
37  *Relatório e Contas da Caixa Geral de Depósitos*, 1982, p. 40; 1984, pp. 38, 42.
38  *Relatório e Contas da Caixa Geral de Depósitos*, 1984, p. 38.
39  Letter No. 43/SCA from the chief-executive to the secretary of state for the Treasury, dated 30 March 1982 (AHCaixa, 01AO/3DAM, 1/1/1–27).
40  Carta No. 31 095/DIC, 7 December 1983.
41  Circular No. 911/DIC of 24 October 1984.
42  Letter No. 344/SCA from the chief-executive to the governor of the Bank of Portugal, dated 30 November 1984 (AHCaixa, 01AO/3DAM, 1/1/1–27).
43  Carta No. 1,603/DPG of 31 July 1985 (ACMF, Caixa, microfilm 1,475).
44  Actas do Conselho de Administração, 25 June 1986 (ACaixa, 01AO/20AD/02, folder 24).
45  Actas do Conselho de Administração, 12 October 1988 (ACaixa, 01AO/20AD/02, folder 27).
46  Actas do Conselho de Administração, 12 October 1988 (ACaixa, 01AO/20AD/02, folder 27).
47  Letter No. 154/SCA from the chief-executive to the Secretary of State for the Treasury, dated 13 October 1988 (AHCaixa, 01AO/3DAM, 1/1/1–30).
48  Actas do Conselho de Administração, 29 July 1987 (AHCaixa, 01AO/20AD/02, folder 26).
49  Explanatory note from the secretary of state for the Treasury's office, dated 21 July 1987 (ACMF, Caixa, microfilm 1,475).

50  Actas do Conselho de Administração, 16 September 1987 (AHCaixa, 01AO/20AD/ 02, folder 26).
51  Livro Branco sobre o Sistema Financeiro (1992), p. 2.
52  O Sistema Bancário Português (1994), p. 15.
53  O Sistema Bancário Português, (1994), pp. 27–28.
54  Livro Branco sobre o Sistema Financeiro, 1992, pp. 52–53.
55  Decreto-Lei No, 298/92, 31 December 1992, article 4, No. 2.
56  Despacho No. 154-A/88 of 14 September 1988 (AHCaixa, 01AO/20AD/02CAD, caixa 27, 1/2–123).
57  Despacho No. 190/88, of 31 October 1988 (A C G D, 01AO/20AD/02CAD, box 27, 1/2–123).
58  Despacho No. 190-A/88 of 31 October 1988 (ACaixa, 01AO/20AD/02CAD, caixa 27, 1/2–123).
59  Actas do Conselho de Administração, 9 November 1988 (AHCaixa, 01AO/20AD/ 02CAD, caixa 27, 1/2–126).
60  Actas do Conselho de Administração, 21 December 1988 (AHCaixa, 01AO/20AD/ 02CAD, caixa 27, 1/2–126).
61  Actas do Conselho de Administração, 1 February 1989 (AHCaixa, 01AO/20AD/ 02CAD, caixa 27, 1/2–126).
62  Actas do Conselho de Administração, 21 July 1989 (AHCaixa, 01AO/20AD/02CAD, caixa 27, 1/2–126).
63  Expresso, 28 October 1989.
64  Despacho No. 696/90F-DE.
65  Despacho No. 199/92F-DE from the secretary of state for Finance to the chairman of Caixa, dated 26 February 1992 (AHCaixa, 01AO/3DAM, 1/2/1–07).
66  Carta No.103 from the secretary of state for finance to the director general for the Treasury, dated 14 January 1993 (AHCaixa, 01AO/3DAM, 1/2/1–08).

# 15

# COPING WITH THE MONETARY
# UNION, 1992–2010

In 1992, the Portuguese banking and financial sectors were still largely shaped by the transformations resulting from the 1975 nationalisations and their partial reversal by the privatisations in 1983 and 1989. The *Caixa Geral de Depósitos*, being a public institution, was only indirectly affected by such events, and it overall held well in the different phases of the new environment. Despite that positive side, the *Caixa* remained a relatively backward institution with many structural deficiencies, benefitting from a number of protective legislations.[1] The main factor in its favour was the circumstance that it kept attracting private deposits, on top of all the mandatory deposits that it received as the main public bank. Yet the public bank had to change due to the creation of the European Monetary Union, following the 1992 Maastricht Treaty, which the government strongly endorsed. The new European legislation imposed that all banks, either private or public, were formally barred from state protection. In August 1993, the *Caixa* became a public limited company, which had to cope with the banking legislation for the whole sector. The new statue also created a General Assembly consisting of the members of the executive and supervisory boards, and a state representative, appointed by the minister of finance.[2]

It was in this new international context that, in 1993, the *Caixa* acquired a new statute, becoming a public company fully owned by the state. The new statute would allow the *Caixa* to help the state in stabilising the financial market and preparing for the new monetary union under formation. It was also supposed to contribute to consolidating the position of decision-making centres in Portugal.[3] Overall, the strategy worked, as the *Caixa* managed to increase its competitive levels and its shares in the savings and credit markets. Yet, the institution also suffered from the many problems that affected the banking system, in Portugal and the rest of the Eurozone, in a context of increasing globalisation of financing activity which was not duly accompanied by improvements in banking regulation. The *Caixa* was also affected by its close relationship with the state, which led to deals sponsored by successive governments on political grounds and would eventually incur in heavy losses. Yet, overall, the *Caixa* was certainly one of the Portuguese banks that would better surf the financial crisis that erupted in 2008.

The international activity of most Portuguese banks was traditionally restricted to receiving emigrant remittances originating mostly from Europe, and the financing of Portugal's external trade through a small number of subsidiaries held abroad. As the EMU was on its way, Portuguese banks extended their activity abroad by opening new branches and by acquiring smaller foreign banks, and four new foreign banks began operating in Portugal.[4] The Portuguese banking system needed to adjust with the increase in competition from abroad, given its adverse competitive conditions with regard to labour and overall operating costs. The strategy was also a reaction to the deterioration of the quality of the services provided by the public bank, amidst an increasingly more competitive domestic banking sector.

The projected changes were welcome by the higher levels of the public bank, which, in coordination with the government, announced publicly the guidelines for the new period, thus listing what were the main problems the *Caixa* had to face in the new conjecture. The guidelines were summarised as 'modernisation, decentralisation, universalisation and internationalisation'. This was of course not the first time the institution's administration reacted to changes in the circumstances, and the stakes were probably higher, because competition did not come only from the domestic private sector, but from international competition as well. The *Caixa* still had by 1992 a deficient management structure, its administrative and decision-making services were still too concentrated in Lisbon, it had little diversification in terms of business model, and of course it had a fragile position in the international markets. According to the board, the public bank had to prepare its business model to the opening of the European financial markets and the projected creation of the single currency and thus offer a more comprehensive range of financial services, taking advantage of its size and domestic market share and the many economic sectors, both public and private, where it operated.[5] The government and the board also declared the purpose of increasing operations in the foreign markets.[6] The new phase started from a favourable position, as assets and deposits were on the rise.[7] The changes that the board put in place had positive results in all aspects except one, namely that of the internationalisation, as the *Caixa* failed its strategy of implementation in the external markets, particularly in Spain, as well as in Brazil and the Portuguese-speaking African countries.

The *Caixa*'s annual reports consistently show the concern that increasing its activity abroad implied the improvement of management practices within the institution and what officials termed a deep 'organic consolidation'. But the two movements were also considered as interlinked, as internationalisation could provide an added stimulus to the needed changes in the functioning of the institution. To use the wording of the reports, the contact with foreign markets and their more advanced practices would make a 'decisive contribution' to 'achieve consistent and recurring levels of profitability' through 'dispersion and diversification of risks', thus becoming one of the 'main drivers of the group's growth' and bypassing the 'potential constraints presented by the national market'. That is to say, the Portuguese banking industry not only adopted a more aggressive and complex presence in the foreign markets, no longer catering first and foremost for emigrants, but also sought to move to new areas of the globe. Four markets were then established as relevant and feasible areas of action: Spain, Brazil, Portuguese-speaking African countries, and Macao, through the *Banco Nacional Ultramarino* (BNU). With the exception of Spain, where the results remained 'modest', the *Caixa* favoured the markets of countries with Portuguese emigration and the Portuguese-speaking countries.

The *Caixa*'s international expansion was initially targeted at countries with significant Portuguese emigrant communities. This gave an irregular character to the foreign network, as it was driven by the constraints of migration and not by a coherent internationalisation strategy. The process of internally restructuring the institution, implemented from the 1990s, would reverse this trend. From then on, the internationalisation of the *Caixa* group followed two strands. It persisted in 'strengthening its presence in the markets where the group's banks were already operating' and at the same time advancing 'other markets' where the *Caixa* 'has no presence but where new business opportunities can be identified'.[8]

## The fragile internationalisation

The move towards internationalisation by the *Caixa* was to follow three different forms, namely through organic growth, implying the constitution of a new institution, or the development of operations where the *Caixa* already had a presence; acquisitions of existing banks and mergers; and the establishment of partnerships with other existent institutions. The choice of these strategies varied according to the target markets and the economic environment and were sometimes used in combination. In a first stage, from 1997 to 2003, internationalisation through acquisitions prevailed. In some cases, where the *Caixa* already had its own banks, such as in Spain and Brazil, acquisitions were intended to help the group grow at a quicker pace than through organic growth. However, in these countries the strategy would have limited results. In Spain, the high levels of banking activity in the market and the reduced acquisition opportunities hindered the *Caixa*'s efforts. In Brazil, the acquisition of the *Banco Bandeirantes* in 1998 did not provide the desired projection. The instability of the Brazilian economy at the turn of the millennium and the low return on investment forced the *Caixa* to revise its presence there. Nevertheless, the acquisition option proved more profitable in other markets. In Cape Verde, where the group was already present through the *Banco Interatlântico* (BI), the *Caixa* took advantage of the privatisation in 2000 of the *Banco Comercial do Atlântico* (BCA) to acquire 52% of its shares, becoming the most important institution in the archipelago. Another successful case was the acquisition of 60% of the *Banco Comercial de Investimentos* (BCI) in Mozambique in

1997. The *Caixa*'s organic consolidation process led to the integration of commercial units, promoting articulated management and cross-selling; it sought to establish the dominance of the group's companies, which allowed an 'increase in their competitive capacity', and strengthen internationalisation. The most significant outcomes of these measures were the incorporation of BNU into the *Caixa*; the merger between the *Fidelidade* and the *Mundial-Confiança*; the purchase of minority interests; taking control of group companies; and the acquisition of *Império-Bonança*, reinforcing its leadership in the national market and gaining a prominent position in the Iberian market.

Between roughly 2000 and 2005, the tactic of strategic partnerships prevailed. In 2000, the *Caixa* signed an agreement with *União dos Bancos Brasileiros, S.A.* (UNIBANCO), Brazil's third largest private group, which provided for the exchange of the *Caixa*'s stake in the *Bandeirantes* for 12.3% of the institution's capital. The objective was to support the goals the acquisition of the *Bandeirantes* had failed to realise, strengthen the investment banking segment, acquire a wider presence in the Brazilian market, and to provide a specific channel for Portuguese companies. Another example was the partnership between the *Caixa* and the BPI in Mozambique in 2003, which resulted in the merger of the BCI with the *Banco de Fomento* (BF), giving rise to the *BCI Fomento*, which substantially improved the *Caixa*'s position in that market. In the case of Brazil and Spain, the acquisitions and the partnerships having failed, organic growth became again a priority from 2003. In Spain, the *Caixa* opted for increasing the capital of the *Banco Simeón*. In Brazil, it would create a new bank in 2008, the *Banco Caixa Geral - Brasil, SA*. This strategy took on a sharper form from 2005, when a clear commitment was made towards structural reinforcement and the concentration of services. Concurrently, the corporate identity was redefined, reinforcing the connection of the subsidiaries abroad to the *Caixa* in Portugal. In South Africa, where the *Caixa* had holdings in the Mercantile Lisbon Bank Holdings, it always betted on organic growth, making successive capital increases in spite of the negative results.

In 1999, the Portuguese banking system was in a situation of some vulnerability to possible foreign acquisitions. The mergers that occurred in Spain raised concerns with the national banking sector, which feared becoming of interest to international groups. In this context of uncertainty the *Caixa*'s then-chairman, João Salgueiro, pointed out that the association with partners sharing the *Caixa*'s profile with statutes that protected it from hostile operations provided an alternative for Portuguese banking groups to withstand the 'unstoppable movement of mergers and acquisitions' that would continue to occur in the sector. He further warned that it was not enough to grow in size to ensure protection from a foreign takeover bid, since size could increase interest in national groups.[9] As the *Caixa*'s shareholder, the government announced it could not maintain a passive attitude in face of the wave of mergers with Spanish banks, 'introducing protections conflicting with the logic of market liberalisation', the public financial group was available to support Portuguese banking groups and 'strengthen their position and affirmation in the Iberian space'.[10] The state was signalling what expectations it had from the national banking institutions, namely coordinated efforts for internationalisation. The secretary of state for the Treasury (Teixeira dos Santos) added that the *Caixa* would not be 'a mere spectator' but rather 'an actor'. Within the private sector, many also argued for the state to have a role as guarantor of keeping decision-making centres in Portugal. This sequence of declarations came after the merger between the Spanish banks *Santander* and *Central Hispano* (BSCH), giving rise to the largest financial entity in Spain and reinforcing the idea that the phenomenon of international concentrations would reach Portugal.[11]

The government wanted the *Caixa* to set up a financial group and establish national partnerships, to help the Portuguese financial sector prepare for the increasing foreign competition. This intention was confirmed in May 1999 when the *Caixa*'s general assembly and the finance minister, Sousa Franco, approved the decision to have the institution undertake 'strategic projects developed in partnership with Portuguese groups'. According to a leading newspaper (*Expresso*), the measure would strengthen the *Caixa*'s role in the markets and as a 'political intent of the Portuguese State to defend national financial groups against undesirable incursions by foreign financial groups'.[12] Indeed, the 1999 Strategic Guidelines for the *Caixa* charged the institution with promoting 'market stability' and keeping 'the economic and financial decision-making centres in Portugal'.[13] The pursuit of these goals could only be guaranteed if the process of internal restructuring of the group proceeded, which implied a better management and integration of the different business units.[14]

Fears that Spanish banking would advance on the Portuguese market became a reality when the deal was announced between the group the *Banco Santander Central Hispano* and the Champalimaud group, the series of Portuguese companies owned by António Champalimaud. The chairmen of the *Banco Português de Investimentos*—Artur Santos Silva (*Banco Comercial Português*), Jorge Jardim Gonçalves (*Banco Espírito Santo* (BES)), and Ricardo Salgado (*Banco Mello* (BM))—met in São Bento with the Prime Minister, António Guterres, Finance Minister Sousa Franco, and the *Caixa*'s chairman, João Salgueiro, to discuss the negotiations. The bankers were 'convinced' that the government had 'scope to oppose the operation', even though there was no 'legal basis' for this; they manifested their 'annoyance' over the breach of a 'verbal agreement' they had made with António Champalimaud to 'keep the group in national hands'.[15] After months of deadlock, the terms of the takeover bid for the Champalimaud group were outlined at the end of 1999, implementing a merger strategy that had taken a decade to negotiate, and which accelerated the restructuring of the sector, with consequences on the internal market and the internationalisation process. The final agreement determined that the banks *Totta & Açores* and the *Crédito Predial Português* integrated the BSCH group, that the *Banco Pinto & Sotto Mayor* be integrated into the BCP, and that the *Mundial-Confiança* and the *Banco Chemical* be transferred to the *Caixa*. This distribution, chosen by the

Portuguese government, was not broadly welcomed in the national banking sector. For the then president of BCP, Jardim Gonçalves, the decision of the 'government prevented the creation of a national group with a community dimension'.[16] In spite of this, the merger and acquisition operations around the Champalimaud group led to a significant increase in the concentration of national activity, with the two largest groups now having a market share of around 50%.[17]

When João Salgueiro left the *Caixa*, in February 2000, he expressed his discontent over the role the government had sought to give the bank in the reorganisation of the national banking system. In his view, the conditions for 'consolidating and developing the *Caixa*'s position in the market, reinforcing internationalisation, integrating the group's units, and recovering imbalances' had disappeared. The criticism was extended to the general performance of Guterres' government, in lacking a 'strategy for Portugal in the context of European integration', and for showing resignation towards the European Union.[18] The incorporation of the *Mundial-Confiança* and the *Banco Chemical* reinforced the *Caixa*'s position in investment banking, venture capital, insurance, asset management, and specialised credit.[19] This not only allowed the *Caixa* to consolidate its position in the market segments it led, but also to move into areas of business where its performance had been low-key or nonexistent, providing the group with complementary structures that allowed it to face the increasingly intense competition and to exploit the market's potential to the maximum.

## The Iberian ambition

In 1991, the *Caixa* acquired in Spain the *Banco de Extremadura* and *Chase Manhattan Bank España, SA*, then renamed *Banco Luso-Español*. The official justification of the board, backed by the government, was the need to strengthen the development of trade between Portugal and Spain, which was lagging behind the increase in international trade of the two countries and with an increasing deficit on the side of Portugal. With such acquisition, the *Caixa* would help the government push for higher investment and trade across the border, in both directions, providing a further stimulus to the integration of Portugal's business in the global market.[20] At that stage, the Portuguese economy was increasingly integrated within the European Union, but business within Iberia needed a further stimulus. Thus, the *Caixa* would increase its share in the banking operations of the neighbouring country, providing funds to invest across the border, and Galicia and Extremadura seemed two promising starting grounds.[21] The operation would prove however a wrong one, as the *Caixa* was not able to generate benefits from it, indicating the banks that were purchased may not have been the best choice. In fact, *Chase Manhattan Bank España* had little presence in the border area, as its territorial expansion was mostly in the urban centres across Spain, and it was decaying in terms of deposits. On the other hand, the *Banco de Extremadura* was a regional bank, with its headquarters in Cáceres and 44 agencies in the provinces of Cáceres and Badajoz. Its financial situation was much better, with high profitability and a balanced financial structure. Yet it was dependent on the *Banco de Bilbao y Vizcaya* in its central banking services, namely, all the information technology structures. Moreover, its price tag was high, given the bank's good condition.[22] The administration argued that the two banks complemented each other, as *Chase* was essentially a bank of 'high-income urban' depositors, its credit portfolio focusing on individuals, while the *Banco de Extremadura*'s clients were rural depositors of all strata and its credit operations were turned predominantly towards companies. The solution advocated would thus be the purchase and subsequent merger of the two banks, which would bring commercial, financial, and fiscal advantages.[23] With the integration of the *Banco Luso-Español* and the *Banco de Extremadura*, at the end of 1994, the *Caixa*'s network in Spain was composed of 91 agencies, mostly across the border and in most cities in Spain.[24] But it did not stop there. In 1995, the *Caixa* acquired 99.21% of the *Banco Simeón*, with a network of 59 agencies, 45 of which were in Galicia and the rest in Astúrias and Castilla y León, and branches in Switzerland, Mexico, and Venezuela. By the end of 1995, the *Caixa* group had a network of 146 branches, 126 of which were located along the border with Portugal. In addition, during this year the *Caixa* increased the *Banco Luso-Español*'s capital, making the group the main *escudo* trader in Spain. In addition to the expansion in Spain, the *Caixa* opened representative offices in Geneva and Bonn in 1996, in Luxembourg, where it created the *Caixa Luxemburgo*, and a majority stake in the *Banco Comercial e de Investimentos*, which had two branches in Maputo.[25] In 1994, the *Caixa*'s operations expanded to Brazil with the purchase of 8% of *Banco Itaú* shares, associated with two seats on the bank's executive board.[26] The *Caixa Brasil* was created in 1998, acquiring 80% of *Sistema Financeiro Bandeirantes* (Bandeirantes Financial System) shares, which owned the *Banco Bandeirantes* and other financial companies.[27]

Meanwhile, the partnerships the *Caixa* signed with other national banking groups had two immediate objectives: to increase their operational efficiency and contribute to the good running of the Portuguese banking system, fulfilling the goals established by the state as shareholder. The partnerships focused on the domestic market, insurance, and, above all, the creation of platforms of understanding on international action. In 2000, the *Caixa* and the BES strengthened their shareholding position in the *Portugal Telecom* and considered extending this alliance to Brazil, where the three companies had business. In the same year, the *Caixa* and the BCP, where the *Caixa* owned 8% of the capital, signed an agreement for international expansion, which provided for the establishment of partnerships to strengthen the position of both groups in Eastern European countries. In the following year, the *Caixa* group and the BCP agreed on a joint action for 'opportunities arising in foreign privatisation operations'.[28] These initiatives, which maximised technical and commercial cooperation, boosted the soundness of the institutions and could act as a deterrent to a potential takeover bid, ensuring the continuation of the decision-making centres in Portugal. In the view of Ricardo Salgado, chairman of BES, the *Caixa* was in a 'unique institution' with an 'important role to play in Portuguese society', and therefore keeping it in the hands of the state was 'a matter of national strategic prudence'.[29]

The high growth rates of the Spanish economy in the late 1990s contributed to making this market a priority for the *Caixa*'s internationalisation strategy.[30] In 2000 the *Caixa* group had 163 agencies distributed throughout the main cities of Spain and along the border.[31] Despite the slowdown in the Spanish economy in the beginning of the new millennium, the *Caixa* continued to strengthen its presence with the expansion of its number of branches. In 2002, the group completed its Spanish restructuring process, with the merger of the three banks with which it operated—the *Simeón*, the *Extremadura*, and the *Luso-Español*—giving rise to a new corporate institution, the *Banco Simeón*.[32]

It was at this moment that the *Caixa* revised its strategy in Spain, opting for organic growth to the detriment of acquisitions. In 2003, the *Banco Simeón* had its internal restructuring completed and its capital reinforced. Despite the effort to optimise its activities, the consolidated net result did not show significant evolution. The priority was now to 'rethink' the group's presence in Spain and to consider the use of the *Simeón* as a 'bargaining chip' in a hypothetical acquisition that would allow the group to expand in that market. The option for organic growth was a contingency in the face of failed attempts at acquisition in Spain, namely that of the *Banco Atlántico*. The ineffectiveness of both internationalisation strategies resulted from the same fundamental source—the *Caixa*'s inability to undertake the 'reinforcement of its capitals, to an amount currently beyond its capacity'.[33] According to another president, it would have been difficult to 'gain a foothold' in a market with such a high level of bank activity, and where 'the *Caixa*'s operation is too small'. The result was that the final accounts were 'always around zero: some years we gain, others we lose'.[34]

After two failed attempts at acquisitions in 2003, activity in Spain turned again to the organic growth of the *Simeón*. The *Caixa* reinforced its capital and started the 'process of strategic relaunching and internal restructuring', seeking to counter 'the very aggressive competition' in Spain.[35] In 2005, the *Simeón*'s administration implemented a recovery plan with two objectives: to ensure commercial development and to extend the agency network, considering the opportunities available in Spain.[36] According to Carlos Costa, a member of the *Caixa*'s administration and former interim chairman of the *Simeón*, 'Spain is not an easy market for acquisitions', and the *Caixa* had therefore decided 'not to wait for an opportunity to arise', but instead to take the 'organic growth route'. Spain had become the chief market for Portuguese investment and its main trading partner. Priority was being given to 'applying the organic growth strategy' to reverse the trend of the *Simeón*'s successive negative results.[37] This would only be achieved in 2006, by which time the bank was already called the *Banco Caixa Geral*.[38] In the view of the bank's chairman,

Faria de Oliveira, the *Simeón* 'was not able to grow because the strategy focused more on new acquisitions than on reinforcing organic growth and human technical resources', and the objective was to 'not remain dependent on an acquisition, but rather focus on growth'.[39]

## Following the language

In 2000, taking advantage of the Cape Verdean privatisation process, a consortium comprising the *Caixa* and the *Banco Interatlântico* acquired a 58.24% stake in the *Banco Comercial do Atlântico*, the largest Cape Verdean bank, 64.27% of the *Garantia - Companhia de Seguros de Cabo Verde* (Cape Verde Insurance Company) and 50.93% of the *Promotora - Sociedade de Capital de Risco* (Venture Capital Company). In February 2006, the *Caixa* acquired 50%, with an option to purchase a further 1%, of the *Banco Totta de Angola*, hitherto 100% controlled by the *Banco Santander Totta*. This operation allowed the *Caixa* to enter the Angolan market, at a time when the five largest Portuguese banks were already active there. The public bank was now present in the markets of all the Portuguese-speaking countries. Despite the agreement between the *Caixa* and the BST, the deal was suspended by the Angolan government, making their authorisation dependent on national investors taking part in the transaction. That government had for some time been pressuring Portuguese banks in the country to release up to 50% of their capital to local partners, a figure that caused some discomfort to the administrations of *Santander* and the *Caixa*.[40]

The delegations of the *Banco Ultramarino* in London, Macao, Zuhai (China), Hong Kong, Timor, Cape Verde, India, and South Africa took on a special role in the internationalisation of the *Caixa*, while competing to take advantage of the group's synergies. BNU became a 'strategic reference' for the 'development' of the *Caixa*'s activities in the 'markets' where it was established. It enabled the *Caixa* to open new 'commercial lines' to support 'exporters of Portuguese products and services'. At the time of the handover to China, in 1999, the BNU was the largest Portuguese bank operating in Macao, and it came fourth in the ranking of the 21 banking institutions present in the territory. It was also the only Portuguese bank licensed to operate throughout China without having to open subsidiaries. Since for many years the BNU was the only banking institution working in Macao, it left the *Caixa* in an excellent position with the industrial and export sector, as well as a good network of correspondents.[41]

Its integration within the *Caixa* group accelerated the process of internal restructuring of the *Banco Nacional Ultramarino* and gave rise to a new bank in Macao, the *BNU-Oriente*, with capital from the BNU, the *Caixa*, the *Fidelidade*, and the *Caixa-BI*. The purpose of this new institution was to provide the 'development of business in the surrounding Asian markets' to the *Caixa* group.[42] The conclusion of the merger between the *Caixa Geral de Depósitos* and the *Banco Nacional Ultramarino* in 2001 allowed the full integration of the activities of the two institutions into *BNU-Oriente*, which, together with BNU's offices in London and Timor, integrated the network of the *Caixa's* international branches.

In 2000, the *Caixa* acquired 9% of the share capital of the *Banque Franco-Portugaise* (BFP) from BNU, from which time it directly controlled its entire capital, with a view to its integration into the French subsidiary. Finally, during 2001 the integration of the two institutions was completed, with the BFP's assets being absorbed by the subsidiary in France, an important step in restructuring the *Caixa's* presence in France.[43]

During the period analysed in this chapter, subsidiaries played an important role in the growth of banking institutions and in strengthening the group's presence abroad. Together with the *Banque Franco-Portugaise* and the French subsidiary of the *Fidelidade Seguros*, the Parisian subsidiary of the *Caixa* continued throughout 1998 to promote its image with the emigrant community and the reinforcement of its presence in the country, using the expedient of cross-selling. The second half of 2000 saw the start of the integration of the banking operations of the *Caixa* group in France, resulting in the merger of the BFP with the Paris subsidiary. The Luxembourg subsidiary, established in 1997, focused on investment banking and private banking, aiming to form a significant customer base built on the resident Portuguese community. The *Caixa's* presence in Luxembourg had been improving, benefiting from the 'articulation with the other commercial units of the group and the high business dynamism with the local customers'.[44] Since 1998, the Madeira subsidiary had tightened its relationship with the *Caixa's* offices and affiliated banks abroad, particularly with the *Banco Bandeirantes*, the *Simeón*, and the representative office in Venezuela, which resulted in an increased volume of business, contributing to the *Caixa's* strengthening in these markets. In the following years, the subsidiary registered a favourable evolution. In 1998, the opening of the New York subsidiary was approved, which started operating in 1999. As a strategic vehicle for USD-denominated operations, the New York subsidiary would play an important role for the *Caixa* in attracting and diversifying liabilities, granting credit, and promoting the image and services among the communities of Portuguese emigrants. Pursuing its internationalisation strategy in the United States market, in October 2001 the *Caixa* signed an agreement with Crown Bank, N.A. in which it acquired 51%.[45]

The subsidiary in Timor was created at the end of 1999, and by 2000, it was already acting as the bank of the territory's administration.[46] This is the unit of the group specialised in high-risk and trade-finance operations with Latin America and other emerging markets. It is a tool for supporting the internationalisation of the *Caixa's* clients, presenting proposals appropriate to the target market. The subsidiary served the clients of the group in the region, most of whom had connections to the Macao Administrative Region.

The *Caixa Internacional*, 90% owned by *Caixa-Participações*, is responsible for the management of shareholdings of the *Caixa* group in companies domiciled outside the national territory, managing since 1998 the group's interest in the share capital of the *Banco Comercial e de Investimentos* (BCI) in Mozambique (60% of the total).[47] In 1998, the *Caixa - Brasil* was set up (whose capital was 90% held by the *Caixa* group and 10% by the *Caixa Geral*), whose purpose is the management of shareholdings in other companies.[48]

In 2008 the *Caixa* group had a network of eight representative offices located in Germany, Belgium, Brazil, Switzerland, Venezuela, Mexico, India, and Shanghai, in addition to a branch for Portuguese nationals residing in the United Kingdom, located in the subsidiary of London. This international network works with Portuguese communities residing abroad, as well as with clients of foreign nationalities with interests in Portugal.

## Notes

1  Cunha (2002), pp. 190–192.
2  Evolução do Grupo Caixa no Triénio, 1996–1998, n.d., p. 1 (ACMF, 0005-0024-2315-2324).
3  'Orientações Estratégicas para o Grupo Caixa de 27 de Maio de 1999', pp. 1–3 (ACMF, 0005-0023-2294-2302).
4  Vilar (1996), pp. 460–461.
5  'Orientações Estratégicas para o Grupo Caixa de 2 de Novembro de 1993', pp. 2–5 (ACMF, 0001-0004-0694-0713); see also E. R.Vilar (1996), pp. 466–467.
6  'Principais Orientações Estratégicas para o Grupo Caixa de 10 de Janeiro de 1998', p. 2 (ACMF, 0002-0008-1184-1187). Relatório e Contas da Caixa Geral de Depósitos, 1998, pp. 59, 82.
7  Diário Económico, 29 January 1994.
8  Relatório e Contas da Caixa Geral de Depósitos, 2000, p. 14.
9  Público, 11 February 1999.
10  Expresso; Caderno 2, 13 February 1999.
11  Público, 28 January 1999.
12  Expresso; Caderno 2, 29 May 1999.
13  *Orientações Estratégicas para o Grupo Caixa*, 27 de Maio de 1999, pp. 2–3 (ACMF, 0005-0023-2294-2302).
14  Relatório e Contas da Caixa Geral de Depósitos, 2000, pp. 12–13.
15  Público, 12 June and 15 October 1999.
16  Público, 13 November 1999.
17  Relatório e Contas do Banco de Portugal, 2001, p. 212.
18  Público, 23 February 2000.
19  Relatório e Contas da Caixa Geral de Depósitos, 1999, pp. 18–19.
20  Relatório e Contas da Caixa Geral de Depósitos, 1991.
21  Memorando da Caixa sobre a Aquisição de Duas Instituições Bancárias em Espanha, 10 April 1991 (ACMF/arquivo/GMF/29, microfilm 1475-C4).
22  Cunha (2002), p. 191.
23  Carta de Rui Vilar, administrator of *Caixa*, to the Minister of Finance, dated 28 May 1991 (ACMF/arquivo/GMF/29, microfilm 1475-C4).
24  Relatório e Contas da Caixa Geral de Depósitos, 1994, p. 56. *O Desenvolvimento da Rede Caixa em Espanha*, May 1994 (ACMF/arquivo/GMF/29, microfilm 1476-C4).
25  Relatório e Contas da Caixa Geral de Depósitos, 1995, p. 55 and 85.
26  Presentation to Rating Agencies on Caixa Geral de Depósitos, October 1998 (AHCaixa, gestão financeira). Expresso, 28 June 1997.

27 Relatório e Contas da Caixa Geral de Depósitos, 1998, pp. 82–83.
28 Expresso; Caderno 2, 20 January 2001.
29 Expresso; Caderno 2, 19 January 2002.
30 Expresso; Caderno 2, 13 February 1999.
31 Relatório e Contas da Caixa Geral de Depósitos, 2000, p. 28.
32 Relatório e Contas da Caixa Geral de Depósitos, 2002, p. 42.
33 Público, 20 February 2003.
34 Expresso; Caderno 2, 4 February 2004.
35 Relatório e Contas da Caixa Geral de Depósitos, 1999, pp. 62; 2004, p. 92.
36 Relatório e Contas da Caixa Geral de Depósitos, 2005, pp. 87–88.
37 Público, 5 October 2005.
38 Relatório e Contas da Caixa Geral de Depósitos, 2005, p. 23, 2006; pp. 23 and 90.
39 Público, 28, 29 June 2006.
40 Expresso; Caderno 2, 18 June 2007.
41 Expresso; Caderno 2, 24 April 1999.
42 Relatório e Contas da Caixa Geral de Depósitos, 1999, p. 72.
43 Relatório e Contas da Caixa Geral de Depósitos, 1998–2006.
44 Relatório e Contas da Caixa Geral de Depósitos, 2003, p. 64.
45 Relatório e Contas da Caixa Geral de Depósitos, 2001, p. 39.
46 Relatório e Contas da Caixa Geral de Depósitos, 2005, p. 98.
47 Relatório e Contas da Caixa Geral de Depósitos, 1998, p. 100.
48 Relatório e Contas da Caixa Geral de Depósitos, 1999, p. 158.

# CONCLUSION

The history of the *Caixa Geral de Depósitos* (*Caixa*) is an exceptional source of information for the analysis of state intervention in national economy and finances. Given that it was owned by the state, and therefore administered, directly or indirectly, following policies issued from the government, the *Caixa* must necessarily reflect the state's position on the economic and financial issues in which the institution was involved. The bank was one of the main instruments of the Portuguese state for conducting economic policy, a role that increased in significance over the period traversing the republic and the *Estado Novo*. This growing importance was due to the privileged place the state granted the institution, as well as the ability of the public bank to thrive in the market. The *Caixa* would not have developed as well as it did until 1974 had it not been able to raise deposits from individuals and manage its loan portfolio properly.

Opportunities to examine this aspect of the country's institutional history are scarce—analysis typically focuses on institutions of public administration rather than private ones. The symbiosis of public and private within the *Caixa* thus becomes a special field of observation showing the circumstances in which the State can make practical, pragmatic interventions. With the advent of democracy, and after that European integration, the Portuguese state became more complex. Concurrently, the diversity of sources of information increased, for which reason the history of the *Caixa* for this period is not as revealing of the evolution of the state as it was in the preceding eras.

When the law that constituted the *Caixa* was passed in 1876, little importance was given to it. At a time when government acts were scrutinised in Parliament and in the newspapers, often to an unjustified degree, the fact that the *Caixa* arose amid relative silence can only denote the existence of a certain consensus among those most interested in financial issues. Despite all the troubles the bank faced throughout its history, occasions when politicians and financiers agreed on important decisions about the institution were frequent. In spite of the disorder permeating Portuguese politics of the constitutional monarchy, there seemed to be a consensus regarding the dangers that excessive prominence could bring to the financial institution.

At points, it was not convenient to the state to interfere with the banking interests of the *Caixa Geral de Depósitos*. This was due to an increasingly important element of deposits, that is, retail deposits in the *Caixa Económica Portuguesa* (CEP), being sensitive to the way the institution was managed. Excessive government intervention could lead to withdrawal of deposits from the public. Despite criticism in periodicals at the time, the image of the state as debtor was not overly negative in Portugal. In addition, there were still few alternative investment opportunities for savings, and these may entail greater risk. These two factors ensured deposits at the *Caixa Económica* continued to grow over the period, even if they faced some setbacks along the way. The state, however, could not abuse citizens' trust in its bank or exceed certain limits of arbitrary action. The *Caixa* developed precisely in search for a balance between meeting the needs of the state and satisfying the basic interests of the individuals who entrusted it with their deposits. This was clearly an unequal game, given the state's dominance of the financial markets and the lack of alternative investment sources for the institution's funds.

However, from the mid-1890s, deposits in the *Caixa Económica* experienced further development. Public deposits showed some growth, but this evolution was more gradual, mainly because the *Caixa*'s responsibility in managing central and local government funds was successively expanded. With the growth of retail and public deposits, the *Caixa Geral de Depósitos* reached the final days of the monarchy holding a prominent position within the Portuguese financial system.

In 1896, the *Caixa*'s first executive board was created, presided over by the chairman of the Public Credit Board. The other members were the heads of the four departments into which the *Caixa* was then reorganised. This period of relative autonomy ended in 1898, when the administration was placed under the control of a new supervisory board, this time made up of members of the public administration and the president of the Chamber of Commerce and Industry of Lisbon. However, this body had a hard life, since the only member not in the public service refused to take part in the travails. In fact, the hardships faced by the board reflected the financial problems of the country and the *Caixa*.

The constant legislative changes in the *Caixa*'s history contrasted with the relative security of its administration. Over the period leading to the end of the monarchy, the *Caixa* had only four directors or chief executives, two of whom remained for long periods. The supervision over the *Caixa* also presented different forms. Until 1893, this task fell to the Public Credit Board, then passing to the supervisory board, created that year. This too maintained remarkable stability: the chairman of the Public Credit Board, responsible for supervising the *Caixa*'s running, became the chairman of the supervisory board in 1893. After an interregnum between 1893 and 1896, the same man moved to the now renamed fiscal council, holding the position until his death in 1902. This council would be abolished in 1909.

The appointment of the heads of the *Caixa*'s administration and fiscal council sometimes met with protest from the opposition parties in Parliament. Indeed, when senior officers had to be appointed, the government chose men within its political trust. Yet, once sworn in, the directors and chairmen of the executive board and the fiscal council were generally confirmed in their positions. This inevitably conferred stability to the *Caixa*, allowing the bank to overcome any problems the successive reforms to its legislation may have posed.

The consecutive changes to the bank's legal framework were generally aimed at extending its powers regarding both liability and credit operations. Thus, a model clearly emerges, which will eventually result in the 1909 reform; it is also clear that this model was followed by successive governments, regardless of party tendencies. None of the legislative changes brought any reversion in the role the government wanted the *Caixa* to perform within the country's financial system. On the contrary, sometimes the legislator entrusted the *Caixa Geral de Depósitos* with operations it was not able to perform satisfactorily. This regime consensus on the *Caixa*'s development, however, did not go far enough to allow it to develop faster. Indeed, observations were recurrently made on the restraints the legislation imposed on the number of staff or their remunerations.

Integrating the study of the *Caixa* in the context of relations between the state and the financial system also helps understand the way in which governments in Portugal acted on fundamental financial issues. In the historiography of the constitutional monarchy there is recurrent reference to the poor performance of the state's financial administration, which possibly underlay the imbalance of public accounts. This view is based mostly on the analysis of opinions of key actors in contemporaneous political life and of a few analysts, less directly involved in either governance or opposition. Apart from that, merely scrutinising the evolution of public account balances and realising there were effectively moments when the state was hard-pressed to fulfil its financial commitments clearly shows there were major problems in this area. In situations of greater financial distress, decisions may even have been taken without due respect for established practices: after all, the government was sovereign and the *Caixa* was a public institution. The most important lesson to take from this narrative is that the mode of action of governments and public finance administrators was, above all, circumstantially determined.

Criticism of the *Caixa*'s departments worsened as the institution grew. However, despite the deficient services and the difficulties resulting from its institutional connection with the state, the *Caixa* remained dominant in the small deposit market. In addition, in times of greater political and financial instability in the country—many of which saw runs on deposits, even if never very serious, the *Caixa* was able to keep the confidence of its clients and even benefit from some new customers and new deposits.

The Republican revolution of 1910 was a source of great political instability for the country. This was yet another change of regime, not just government, undertaken by people with a distinctly ideological programme and who sometimes lacked directive consistency. The revolution did not have immediate impact on the composition of the *Caixa*'s executive board, which was only altered in October 1917, even then keeping some members from the period of monarchy. Yet, it did have important consequences for the institution's management, forcing the *Caixa* to take less profitable paths. The aim was to promote the expansion of the *Caixa Económica Portuguesa* through the creation of a large number of branches in the main urban centres of the country. This programme, which marked the bank's activity for some years, was clearly inspired by the Republican populist spirit and based on an incorrect assumption. In fact, the designers behind the strategy believed the less affluent classes needed a greater and more varied offering of financial services, and that the *Caixa* had an obligation or even a 'moral duty' to meet the needs of these potential clients.

The actions of the first Republican governments showed a desire for arguably excessive change, which came to undermine some of the principles guiding the country's financial sphere. Governments felt that, given the *Caixa* was a public bank, they could use it to pursue political or social ambitions, which, though perhaps legitimate, were often not sufficiently anchored in fiscal reality. This interference had two main facets. The first was a careless replacement of the administration, a process that was even preceded by an inquiry, something until then unheard of. It should be borne in mind that government officials with responsibilities in public finance handled sensitive matters diligently to minimise impact on markets and institutions.

The second aspect of the Republican governments' behaviour was their obsession with making the *Caixa* a bank for the working class, something it had never been, and would never become. In fact, the *Caixa*'s main clientele was the middle class, civil servants, merchants, and the urban populations. Portugal was too poor for the working classes to access banking services. Republicans were merely following a mythos that was disseminated in many circles, including some of the *Caixa*'s own documents. The problem was that they sought to change reality, and during the first governments of the regime the bank's administration was forced to open delegations across the country to get closer to this 'public' that persisted in failing to appear at its branches.

Salazar's rise, first to the finance portfolio and then as president of the council, brought a new order that pleased a large majority of those heading the country's public and private finances. However, as far as the *Caixa* was concerned, the new governments had a cautious attitude, markedly different from the Republican activity and more in tune with that of monarchical times. The most significant example of this was Salazar having preferred to allow Daniel Rodrigues, a Republican and chief executive of the *Caixa*, to finish his term rather than replace him (which, however, did not prevent the dictator from having him arrested for a time). Also symptomatic of this new approach was the dictator's major concern in personally leading the *Caixa*'s reform process. This would culminate in the law of 1929, which improved the institution's running and clarified its areas of action, in accordance with the directives that, one way or another, emanated from the government.

Salazar's reorganisation of the state's financial, and increasingly economic, management later brought the Economic Reconstitution Act (*Lei de Recon-stituição Económica*), which between 1935 and 1950 provided a reasonably efficient framework for the state's programmes of public investment and expenditure. By the end of World War II, this legislative framework was already obsolete, and an extended period of indecision followed.

A little over a decade of equilibrium rolled by between the *Caixa* and the government, during which the latter determined what the bank could and could not do. This was generally a peaceful relationship, given that the *Caixa* was interested in financial investments in the public sphere, and the state wanted this funding to be made in the professional and relatively efficient manner the *Caixa* was able to provide.

However, the less positive side of the *Estado Novo* in terms of the state's finances and the economy was beginning to materialise and create problems that to some extent hindered the development of the country's most important financial institution. This was not necessarily detrimental overall, as it provided private banking with the room it needed to develop. Specifically, for a long time the government held on to the characteristics given to the institution by the 1929 law and did not allow the *Caixa* to gain greater administrative autonomy in order to cope with the growing competition from private banks, which were growing strongly. The *Caixa*'s evolution throughout the 1960s was thus limited by this institutional restraint. While concern for controlling the country's major financial institutions was crucial to the state's financial reorganisation at the beginning of Salazar's regime, that control eventually became counterproductive.

In 1968, Marcelo Caetano replaced the regime's founder as head of the government. As early as 1969, the *Caixa* was turned into a public company, which gave it some managerial autonomy. This would prove crucial for changing its operation in the last years of the dictatorship. These years were also marked by the beginning of another important transformation: the introduction of automatic computing systems. This technological change would allow for productivity gains in the workforce, and it would also require the reorganisation of services. Indeed, 'mechanography', as it was then known, would force changes in the routines within the *Caixa*, particularly in relations between workers, heads of department, and the administration. However, this process would be difficult and time consuming. Symptomatically, these changes were more important for the internal functioning of the *Caixa* than to the exterior, and more relevant for borrowers than for depositors. In fact, the functioning of the deposit services does not seem to have limited the growth of the funds delivered to the bank's branches despite their somewhat tarnished image. This is shown by the important report made by an outside consultancy team in the early 1970s.

The 1974 coup d'état and the ensuing revolution hit the *Caixa Geral de Depósitos* just as it was adapting to the new institutional regime and new technologies. New problems arose from then on, related to the management of staff, now restless as a result of the end of years of union and political repression. The democratisation of the country had consequences on the behaviour of governments towards the *Caixa*, a time-consuming change.

Despite the strong connection between the institution and the state, the successive governments eventually lifted the *Caixa* to a level that allowed it to compete on an equal footing with the rest of the national banking system, and likewise in an increasingly open and competitive international economy, especially after the constitution of the European single market in 1992. Probing into how this came about invariably leads to a conclusion that diverts attention from the possibility of long-term poor national governance. The steps that led to this positive outcome were not always safe and secure, however, with some faltering, and the necessity of weathering difficult periods. Moreover, ideal results were never met, and there was always room to think they could have gone further.

Today, the *Caixa* receives deposits from individuals who implicitly trust the institution's investments and its ability to generate profits and offer financial services; an institution that provides loans to the state, companies and individuals following profitability criteria, which requires in-depth knowledge and consistent ability to assess the potential of its clients to meet the respective costs. In addition, the *Caixa Geral de Depósitos* expanded to fulfil increasingly sophisticated roles, following the rest of the national banking system, and moved beyond borders, an area where it even showed some pioneering initiative. Tradition, consolidation of existing practices, and reputation are important elements of the *Caixa*'s fundament. But so are innovation, learning, and exploring new sources of business. Perhaps the period since 1992 was that in which the public bank most broadened its business skills and innovated. This happened out of necessity, but also because the institution was able to respond to that need.

The place the *Caixa Geral de Depósitos* has held in the Portuguese financial system is related to specific characteristics of Portuguese economy and, in particular, to being an underdeveloped economy relative to its main trading partners. This meant, among other things, that some institutional models could be imported from the most developed countries, which happened recurrently, with necessary adjustments. From early on, the *Caixa* became a savings bank, to which was added the role of a public deposit; that is, the safekeeping of valuables belonging to the public administration, such as the courts, because the development of banking focused on the collection of segmented individual savings did not have the vigour in Portugal as was shown in other parts of western Europe. The role of a savings bank quickly provided the *Caixa* with the instrument for growth in the decades that followed, up to this day: retail deposits. Reliance on deposits gave a particular character to the *Caixa* as a public institution: as governments successively acknowledged, depositors' interests must be taken into account. This was paramount so as to avoid weakening an important instrument of political action, firstly financial, then economical, and once again, since 1974, with a focus on the financial world and internationalisation.

This backdrop to governments' behaviour was marked by variations, which in the period of democracy accompanied the fluctuations of national politics and, perhaps for the first time, of European politics. Immediately following the 1974 revolution, the *Caixa* suffered some setbacks in its financial integrity. However, the course was promptly corrected, even if with great difficulty. As the country entered democratic normalisation following the first constitutional government of 1976, the *Caixa* gradually recovered its ability to manage itself without direct intervention from the state or from the other sources of power that marked the revolutionary period. This transformation was indicated by the administration's recovery of some power, which was in its turn a consequence of the relative normalisation of the country's political life. However, the change was also the result of the institution's own internal dynamics, since it continued to run its various departments, deposits continued to come in, and loans were still being requested. The institution's age and its deep roots in the economy and national financial system allowed no outcome other than to proceed with operations, serving as a driving force for the institution's development.

The *Caixa* entered the 1980s with its business restored to some extent, even having to respond to growing demand in one area: mortgage loans. However, efficiency levels and the ability to compete in more dynamic markets did not develop as quickly as the balance in business; as such, action was required. One of the problems the *Caixa* was facing concerned the structure of its internal organisation and, in particular, the dispersion of its facilities in Lisbon. Thus, the institution's administration decided to build a new headquarters where all the departments were gathered, eventually leading to the reorganisation of the *Caixa*'s structure. The building of the new headquarters subsequently put the *Caixa*'s running in the political spotlight, not always from the best angles, and revealed the difficulties in the relationship between the administration, governments, opposition parties, and the media.

The 1980s were marked by the consolidation of the *Caixa*'s role in three sectors of major importance for the life of the institution and for the national economy or, at least, for the welfare of the population: mortgage loans, credit to public bodies, and deposits in the country from remittances of the thousands of emigrants mainly living in Europe. Throughout that decade, the *Caixa* experienced a marked development in all three areas, which would lead the bank to new growth by gaining market shares. The *Caixa* continued to enjoy some privileges with the state and markets, while the rest of the banking sector remained nationalised under the same ministry, meaning competition was necessarily low.

In the meantime, the growth of the institution, coupled with the inertia of structural changes and investment levels, put the need to internally reform the *Caixa*'s operation on the agenda, as well as the necessity to build a new headquarters to reorganise the departments. Interestingly, the construction of the new headquarters turned out to be the most prominent and controversial episode in the *Caixa*'s history in the period covered by this volume.

The reaction to the opening up to Europe, and in particular to the single market and the Euro, was positive in all respects. The *Caixa* distinguished itself in this area, thanks to having some prior experience of internationalisation in relation to the other banks in the country. The *Caixa*'s successive phases of adapting to the changes in the national and international contexts produced results that can be assessed in a positive way. It can also be said that this success was due to the responsiveness of an institution that had developed competences over many years of existence. Clearly, the *Caixa* has been in the business of attracting deposits from individuals and lending to public institutions, companies, and individuals for many decades, having acquired technical and administrative competences, in some cases before its most direct competitors. The prospects of making gains from the development of these activities were surely a reason to pursue them, allowing the institution to reach the dimension it has today. Even if sometimes limited by legislation hindering complete freedom of action, the work of a few generations of bank staff and administrators consistently overcame the various obstacles the institution faced. When conditions are favourable, such institutions can more easily follow equally favourable strategies, despite setbacks arising either from the country's political situation or from less favourable decisions by governments. In this regard, European integration was also one of the main factors for the positive development the institution experienced, since it allowed some respite in the pressure from the Lisbon governments.

Understanding how the path the *Caixa Geral de Depósitos* followed brought it to the place it holds today in the national banking and financial system is the main purpose of this book. It also tries to understand the motives for the Portuguese state to have interacted with the *Caixa* in a way that allowed it to follow this favourable development. This element of analysis is not deep enough to obtain a more thorough understanding of the motivations that led successive governments to this positive role. Even if incomplete, one answer is that governments did not want to negatively affect a major source of revenue and an important business for the state and for the national economy.

The study also shows that European integration played a positive role, with the new rules it brought regarding the oversight of the activity of national governments and the implications on the management of institutions. However, the specific motives of each senior official in the country's governments and in the *Caixa*'s administration are yet to be fully grasped to understand this result. This is all the more important given that the future of the institution is not necessarily secure, as the world will continue to be increasingly competitive and demanding, and new problems will require new answers.

Given that good decisions are those framed by institutional forms that lead those responsible towards the right paths and with them, all the other parts involved in the business, it must be considered whether the institutional framework (particularly that established in 1993) may not need to be rethought. It is interesting to note that all the chairpersons since 1976 have been opposed to the possible privatisation of the *Caixa*, complete or partial. Privatisation recurs in Portuguese public opinion as a measure that would help the *Caixa* overcome what is sometimes seen as an obstacle to its business. This idea is championed by those who think the *Caixa* still suffers from excessive interference from governments and should therefore be given further autonomy.

Yet, it must be questioned whether privatisation would indeed give the *Caixa* more independence or autonomy from the state. The *Caixa*'s business portfolio and the state's demand for banking services require a relationship of some dependency between the state and the banking system. Privatising the *Caixa* would not change that—it would merely provide another institutional format to the relationship of dependency. This is not to say that the general framework in which the state and the *Caixa* operate has reached an optimal format, as more can be done to improve the system's functioning. It could be argued that reading the history of the *Caixa*, from its earliest moments to the most recent, does not, in fact, help clarify what more can be done and what route can be taken. However, the institution's history is a very important part of its form, as there is much that is inherently intangible, and so many of its operating baselines are rooted in decades-old practices and the reputation it has achieved over the years.

However, its history shows that privatisation, though obviously a legitimate political option, is not a pressing necessity of the institution itself. Several institutional changes in the past have given the *Caixa* more autonomy and less dependence on the state, but without actual separation. Such separation would surely not have allowed the *Caixa* to get where it is today. This was especially true in 1909, 1969, and 1993. The reform of 1929, though also very important, followed a different path. The question now is whether it is time to take another important step, as these were. If this new step is taken within the current framework, this will be a crucial moment of modernisation of the functioning of the Portuguese state. This, by all accounts, would be a bolder decision than privatisation, which could be seen as a headlong rush without guarantee that the essentials would change. Interpretations tell more about the past than opinions, but these can also be given on the future, even in a history book. The one offered here, however, is grounded in the history of the *Caixa Geral de Depósitos*, which shows how the institution has been able to transform itself over time towards greater autonomy from the state's potential arbitrariness.

The transformation of a state-owned bank, working almost like a public office, into a bank of public capital with an autonomous administration, operating in a competitive sector at national and international level, is part of the pattern revealed by the *Caixa*'s history. The drive for this transformation came, inevitably, from within the institution itself, since it was effectively changing financial functions with a considerable degree of specialisation and a link to the country's economic and financial activity. In other words, in 1974 there were few institutions in the country that performed the same role, and that knew the financial markets of the country so well, as the *Caixa*, on the sides of both depositors and investors, public and private. This level of expertise was revealed, for instance, by the recurring problem of outflow of staff from the *Caixa* to other national financial institutions. That was facilitated precisely by the *Caixa* being, until very late, constrained by the restrictions of public administration. But such a straitjacket must not hide the fact that the *Caixa* does fulfil the role of financial intermediary with relative efficacy. However, in terms of efficiency, the *Caixa Geral de Depósitos* would not compare well with the rest of the banking system, let alone with the banking systems of more developed countries.

# REFERENCES

## Newspapers

*A Capital; Diário de Notícias; Diário Económico; Expresso; Diário Popular; Jornal do Comércio [e das Colónias]; O Tempo; Público.*

## Official papers

*Actas da Câmara Corporativa*, 1954–1974.
*Diário da Assembleia Nacional e da Câmara Corporativa*, 1935–1952.
*Diário da Assembleia Nacional*, 1953–1974.
*Diário da Câmara dos Deputados*, 1870–1910.
*Diário da Câmara dos Deputados*, 1910–1926.
*Diário do Governo*, 1881–1913.
*Diário do Senado*, 1910–1926.

## Legislation

*Carta Orgânica do Banco de Portugal* (1857). Lisboa: Imprensa Nacional.
*Colecção de leis, decretos e regulamentos da ditadura*, s. l., Arquivo Jurídico, 1887, 2 vols.
*Diplomas orgânicos regulamentares*, Lisbon: Banco de Portugal, 1946.
Flores, João [1937], *Legislação que rege a Caixa Geral de Depósitos e Instituições de Previdência. E ainda a que se relaciona com os seus serviços*. Lisbon: Caixa Geral de Depósitos.
*Legislação do Banco de Portugal* (1946). Lisbon: Banco de Portugal, 6 vols.
*Parecer sobre as Contas Gerais do Estado*, Lisbon: Assembleia Nacional, 1935–1952.
*Regulamento definitivo da Caixa Geral de Depósitos*, 17 August 1881.
*Regulamento Provisório da Caixa Geral de Depósitos*, 12 December 1876.
*Reforma bancária (Decreto n.º 10 474), parecer da comissão encarregada de fundamentar a inexiquibilidade do Decreto n.º 10 474, unanimemente votada pela assembleia geral de 26 de Janeiro de 1925 de bancos e casas bancárias*, Lisbon: Tipografia do Banco Lisboa e Açores, 1925.

## Financial reports

*Actas do Conselho de Administração da Caixa Geral de Depósitos*, 1912.
*Actas do Conselho de Fiscalização da Caixa Geral de Depósitos e Económica Portuguesa*, 1893.
*Actas do Conselho Fiscal da Caixa Geral de Depósitos*, 1909–1932.
*Administração e Parecer do Conselho Fiscal*, 1953–1973.

Caixa Económica Portuguesa, *Relatório do Ano de 1936*.
Caixa Geral de Depósitos e Instituições de Previdência (1908–1930/31), *Relatório e Contas e Parecer do Conselho Fiscal*.
Caixa Geral de Depósitos e Instituições de Previdência (1925/26–1933/34), *Relatório da Casa de Crédito Popular*.
Caixa Geral de Depósitos e Instituições de Previdência, *Declarações Apresentadas em Conselho e Respectivas Resoluções*, vol. 1, 3–10–1929 to 15–13–1935.
Caixa Geral de Depósitos e Instituições de Previdência, *Relatório da Repartição de Operações Financeiras e Bancárias*, 1925/26–1934/35.
Caixa Geral de Depósitos e Instituições de Previdência, *Relatório da Secretaria da Administração*, 1960–1973.
Caixa Geral de Depósitos e Instituições de Previdência, *Relatório e Contas (1907/8–1916/17)*, 1909–1918.
Caixa Geral de Depósitos, *Actas do Conselho de Administração*, 1909–1974.
Caixa Geral de Depósitos, Crédito e Previdência, *Copiadores e Ofícios do Conselho de Administração*, 1935–1959.
Caixa Geral de Depósitos, Crédito e Previdência, *Informações, Pareceres e Relatórios*, 1931–1932 and 1953–1957.
Caixa Geral de Depósitos, Crédito e Previdência, *Relatório do Conselho de Administração e Parecer do Conselho Fiscal*, 1953–1973.
Caixa Geral de Depósitos, *Relatório e Contas (1917/18–1920/21)*.
Caixa Geral de Depósitos, *Relatório e Contas (1921/22–1930/31)*.
Caixa Geral de Depósitos, *Relatório e Contas*, 1973–2009.
Caixa Nacional de Crédito, 1.ª Repartição, *Normas de Serviço*, vols 1 and 2.
Caixa Nacional de Crédito, *Actas do Conselho de Gerência*, vols 1 and 2.
Caixa Nacional de Crédito, *Boletim de Crédito, 1.º relatório do Conselho Nacional de Crédito, ano 1959*, no. 1, 1961.
Caixa Nacional de Crédito, *Crédito Agrícola Mútuo, Relatórios da Inspecção*.
Caixa Nacional de Crédito, *Processos de Crédito*.
Fundo de Fomento da Habitação, *Relatório de Actividades*, 1978.
Junta do Crédito Público, *Relatório e Contas da Sua Gerência*, 1840–1913.
Junta do Crédito Público, *Relatório e Propostas sobre a Administração da Caixa Geral de Depósitos (1876/77–1890/91)*, Crédito e Previdência, 1878–1892.

### Books and articles

Aguirre Bellver, Manuel, et al. (1971). *Función de las Cajas de Ahorros en las Relaciones Económicas con el Exterior*. Madrid: Confederación Española de Cajas de Ahorros.
Allinne, Jean-Pierre (1976). 'La Caisse des dépôts et consignations. Son rôle, ses opérations. De 1816 a 1895', in *Travaux et recherches de l'Université de Droit, d'Économie et des Sciences Sociales de Paris* (series 'Sciences historiques', no. 8), Paris: Presses Universitaires de France pp. 63–175.
Almeida, J. A. Simões de (1961). *O II Plano de Fomento: Financiamento do Desenvolvimento Económico*. Lisbon: ISCEF.
Almeida, Pedro Tavares de (1991). *Eleições e Caciquismo no Portugal Oitocentista, 1868–1890*. Lisbon: Difel.

Amaral, Luciano (1992). 'O plano inclinado do socialismo: sobre o intervencionismo económico do Estado Novo', in J. L. Cardoso and A. Almodovar (eds.) *Actas do Encontro Ibérico sobre História do Pensamento Económico.* Lisbon: CISEP pp. 373–394.

Amaral, Luciano (2019). *The Modern Portuguese Economy in the Twentieth and Twenty-First Centuries.* Springer.

Anonymous (1877). *A reorganização do Banco de Portugal.* Porto: Tipografia Ocidental.

Antão, P., Boucinha, M., Farinha, L., Lacerda, A., Leal, A. C., and Ribeiro, N. (2009). 'Integração financeira, estruturas financeiras e as decisões das famílias e das empresas', in *A Economia Portuguesa no Contexto da Integração Económica, Financeira e Monetária.* Lisbon: Banco de Portugal, pp. 423–561.

Ballardini, Achille (1956). *Le Casse di risparmio.* Rocca San Casciano: Cappelli.

Barbosa, António Pinto (1959). *O Banco de Fomento Nacional, Factor Basilar de Desenvolvimento da Economia Portuguesa.* Lisbon (no pub.).

Barbosa, António Pinto (ed.) (1999). *O Impacto do Euro na Economia Portuguesa.* Lisbon: Dom Quixote.

Barbosa, Daniel (1972). *Banco de Fomento Nacional. Discurso do Governador Prof. Eng.° Daniel Barbosa na Assembleia Geral de 31 de Maio de 1972.* Lisbon (no pub.).

Barros, Pedro Pita and Pinho, Paulo (1995). *Estudos sobre o Sistema Bancário Português.* Lisbon: Banco Mello.

Belo, Agostinho Simões (1952). *Notas sobre a Caixa Geral de Depósitos, Crédito e Previdência* (dactil. Caixa Geral de Depósitos Historical Archive).

Brito, J. M. Brandão de (1989). *A Industrialização Portuguesa no Pós-Guerra, 1948-1965.* O Condicionamento Industrial. Lisbon: Dom Quixote.

Bruck, C., et al (1995). Les caisses d'Épargne en Europe, t. 1, *Les 12 pays de l'Union Européenne.* Paris: Les Éditions de l'Épargne.

Bulhões, Miguel de (1884). *A Fazenda Pública de Portugal. Práticas Vigentes e Várias Utopias do Autor.* Lisbon: Imprensa Nacional.

Burnay, Comte de (1897). *Quelques considérations sur la situation financière du Portugal.* Paris: Imprimerie Chaix.

Carvalho, Filipe de (1887), *À memória de António Maria de Fontes Pereira de Melo.* Lisbon: Imprensa Nacional.

Carvalho, Mariano Cyrilo de (1889). *A Questão dos Tabacos. Discursos Proferidos na Câmara dos Senhores Deputados nas Sessões de 12, 13 e 15 de Abril de 1889.* Lisbon: Imprensa Nacional.

Cassies, Youssef (ed.) (1992). *Finance and Financiers in European History, 1880–1960.* Cambridge: Cambridge University Press.

Castro, Armando (1978 [1947]), *A Revolução Industrial em Portugal no Século XIX.* Porto: Limiar.

Coelho, F. J. Pinto (1877), "*António Maria de Fontes Pereira de Melo*", in *Contemporâneos Ilustres,* vol. 1. Lisbon: Tipografia Rua dos Calafates.

Comín, Francisco (1988). *Hacienda y Economía en la España Contemporánea, 1800–1936.* Madrid: Ministerio de Economía y Hacienda, 2 vols.

Cordeiro, J. A. da Silva (1999 [1896]). *A Crise em seus Aspectos Morais. Introdução a Uma Biblioteca de Psicologia Individual e Colectiva.* Lisbon: Edições Cosmos.

Correia, José Dias de Araújo (1938). *Portugal Económico e Financeiro.* Lisbon: Imprensa Nacional, 2 vols.

Correia, José Dias de Araújo (1952). *Elementos de Planificação Económica.* Lisbon: Imprensa Nacional.

Cunha, António da Silva (2002). *Internacionalização da banca portuguesa. Opções estratégicas.* Lisbon: Universidade Autónoma de Lisboa.

Duet, Daniel (1991). *Les caisses d'épargne.* Paris: Presses Universitaires de France.

Esteves, Rui Pedro (2000). 'O crowding-out em Portugal, 1879-1910', *Análise Social,* vol. 34, 2000, pp. 573–618.

Faria, Miguel Figueira de (2001). *Banco Comercial Português. A Primeira Década, 1985–1995.* Lisbon: Edições Inapa.

Farinha, António Dias Farinha (1994). 'O primeiro banco português', Estudos em homenagem a Jorge Borges de Macedo, offprint n. 235. Lisbon: Centro de Estudos de História e Cartografia Antiga, Instituto de Investigação Científica Tropical.

Fernandes, Filipe S. (ed.) (2006). *Memórias de Economistas.* Lisbon: Biblioteca Exame.

Fernandes, Tiago (2006). *Nem Ditadura Nem Revolução. A Ala Liberal e o Marcelismo, 1968–1974.* Lisbon: Dom Quixote.

Figueiredo, Afonso (1973). *Le Portugal: considérations sur l'état de l'administration, des finances, de l'industrie et du commerce de ce royaume et de ses colonies.* Lisbon : Lallement Fréres.

Fishlow, A. (1961). 'The trustee savings banks, 1817–1861', *Journal of Economic History,* 21: 26–40.

Fortuna (1877), João António Freitas. *O Projecto de Reconstituição do Banco de Portugal e o Comércio.* Porto: Tipografia de Freitas Fortuna.

Franco, António de Sousa (1982). 'Ensaio sobre as transformações estruturais das finanças públicas portuguesas, 1900–1980', *Análise Social,* 18, pp. 1105–1138.

Fuschini, Augusto (1896). *Liquidações Políticas. Vermelhos e Azuis.* Lisbon: Companhia Tipográfica.

Fuschini, Augusto (1899). *O Presente e o Futuro de Portugal.* Lisbon: Companhia Tipográfica.

Gonzalo y González, Leopoldo (1981). *El Tesoro Publico y la Caja General de Depósitos, 1852–1868. Un Estudio sobre la Deuda Flotante en España a Mediados del Siglo XIX.* Madrid: Instituto de Estudios Fiscales.

Gueslin, André (1992). 'Banks and state in France from the 1880s to the 1930s: the impossible advance of the banks', in Youssef Cassis (ed.) *Finance and Financiers in European History, 1880–1960.* Cambridge: Cambridge University Press, 63–91.

Herculano, Alexandre (1983 [1844]), 'Da instituição das caixas económicas', *in Opúsculos,* vol. 1. Lisbon: Presença, pp. 107–119.

Horne, H. Oliver (1974). *A History of Savings Banks.* London: Oxford University Press.

Justino, David (1994). *História da Bolsa de Lisboa.* Lisbon: Bolsa de Valores de Lisboa.

Lains, Pedro (1995). *A economia portuguesa no século XIX: crescimento económico e comércio externo, 1851–1913.* Lisbon: Imprensa Nacional Casa da Moeda.

Lains, Pedro (1997), 'Savings banks in Portuguese banking, 1880–1930. The rise of Caixa Económica Portuguesa', in *Conference on Finance and the Making of the Modern Capitalist World.* Berkeley: University of Califórnia.

Lains, Pedro (2002), *Os Progressos do Atraso. Uma Nova História Económica de Portugal, 1842–1992.* Lisbon: Imprensa de Ciências Sociais.

Lains, Pedro (2003). *Os progressos do atraso. Uma nova história económica de Portugal, 1942–1992.* Lisbon: Imprensa de Ciências Sociais.

Lains, Pedro and Silva, Álvaro Ferreira da (eds.) (2005). *História Económica de Portugal, 1700–2000.* Lisbon: Imprensa de Ciências Sociais, 3 vols.

Lança, Ariósto da Gama (1948). *Caixas Económicas.* Lisbon: Gráfica Lisbonense.

Laranjo, José Frederico (1903). *Câmara dos Dignos Pares do Reino. As Ditaduras Políticas e Financeiras e os Amigos das Instituições. Discursos Pronunciados nas Sessões de 8 de Abril de 1902 e 10 de Junho de 1903.* Lisbon: Imprensa Nacional

Laurent, H. (1892). *Les caisses d'épargne et de prévoyance depuis leurs origines jusqu'à nos jours.* Pithiviers: Imprimerie des Caisses d'Épargnes.

*Le Casse di risparmio nel mondo* (1959). Roma: Associazione fra le Casse di risparmio italiane.

Leitão, Nicolau Andresen (2007). *Estado Novo, democracia e Europa, 1947–1986.* Lisbon: Imprensa de Ciências Sociais.

Leite, João Pinto da Costa (1926). *Organização Bancária Portuguesa.* Coimbra: Coimbra Editora.

*Livro Branco sobre o Sistema Financeiro* (1992). Lisbon: Ministério das Finanças.

Lopes, José da Silva (2002). *A economia portuguesa desde 1960.* Lisbon: Gradiva.

Macedo, Jorge Borges de (1963). *Elementos para a História Bancária de Portugal, 1797–1820.* Lisbon: Faculdade de Letras da Universidade de Lisboa.

Malvé, Philippe and Thiveaud, Jean-Marie (eds.) (1991). *La Caisse des dépôts et consignations. 175 ans. Revue d'économie financière. Hors-série.* Paris: Edition Le Monde.

Marques, A. H. de Oliveira (1989). *Crédito Predial Português. 125 anos de História.* Lisbon: Crédito Predial Português.

Marreca, António de Oliveira (1983), *Obra económica 1835–1853.* Lisbon: Instituto Português de Ensino à Distância.

Martins, Guilherme de Oliveira (1988). *O Ministério das Finanças. Subsídios para a Sua História no Bicentenário da Criação da Secretaria de Estado dos Negócios da Fazenda.* Lisbon: Ministério das Finanças.

Martins, Joaquim Pedro de Oliveira (1954). *Política e Economia nacional.* Lisbon: Guimarães Editores.

Martins, Joaquim Pedro de Oliveira (1956). *Estudos de Economia e Finanças.* Lisbon: Guimarães Editores.

Martins, M. Belmira and Rosa, J. Chaves (1979). *O Grupo Estado. Análise e Listagem Completa das Sociedades do Sector Público Empresarial.* Lisbon: Edições Jornal Expresso.

Mata, Eugénia (1986). 'A dívida pública externa fundada de Portugal da guerra civil à Regeneração'. *Revista de História Económica e Social* 18: 75–90.

Mata, Eugénia (1993). *As finanças públicas portuguesas da Regeneração à Primeira Guerra Mundial.* Lisbon: Banco de Portugal.

Mata, Eugénia and Valério, Nuno (1982). 'O Banco de Portugal, único banco emissor, 1891–1931'. *Revista de História Económica e Social,* 10: 49–69.

Mata, Eugénia and Valério, Nuno (1988). 'O Fundo Especial de Amortização e o caminhode-ferro do Norte, 1846–1860'. *Revista de História Económica e Social,* 24: 77–87.

Mata, Eugénia and Valério, Nuno (1991). 'Foreign public debt and economic growth in Portugal, 1830–1985'. *Estudos de Economia* 11: 421–432.

Mata, Eugénia and Valério, Nuno (1996). 'Monetary stability, fiscal discipline and economic performance. The experience of Portugal since 1854', in J. B. de Macedo, B. Eichengreen and J. Reis (eds.). *Currency Convertibility. The Gold Standard and Beyond.* London: Routledge, pp. 204–227.

Mateus, Abel (2013), *Economia portuguesa: crescimento no contexto internacional (1910–2013).* Parede: Principia.

Menezes, Tomás Eugénio Mascarenhas de (1904). *Dívida pública portuguesa. Repertório de legislação*. Lisbon.

Mónica, Maria Filomena (1992). *O Tabaco e o Poder. Cem Anos da Companhia dos Tabacos de Portugal*. Lisbon: Quetzal.

Mónica, Maria Filomena (1994), 'A lenta morte da Câmara dos Pares, 1876–1896', in *Análise Social*, 29, pp. 121–152.

Mónica, Maria Filomena (1996). 'As reformas eleitorais no constitucionalismo monárquico, 1852–1910', *Análise Social*, 31, pp. 1039–1084.

Mónica, Maria Filomena (1999). *Fontes Pereira de Melo*. Porto: Edições Afrontamento.

Mura, Jurgen (ed.) (1996). *History of European Savings Banks*. Stuttgart: WS.

Nadal, Jordi and Sudrià, Carlos (1983). *Historia de la Caja de Pensiones. La 'Caixa' dentro del Sistema Financiero Catalán*. Barcelona: Edicions 62.

Nunes, Ana Bela, e Brito, J.M. Brandão de (1992). 'Política económica, industrialização e crescimento', in F. Rosas, org., *Portugal e o Estado Novo, 1930–1960. Nova História de Portugal* (dir. J. Serrão e A. H. Oliveira Marques), vol. 12. Lisbon: Editorial Presença, pp. 306–351.

Nunes, Ana Bela, Bastien, Carlos and Valério, Nuno (1994). *Caixa Económica do Montepio Geral. 150 Anos de História, 1844–1994*. Lisbon: Montepio Geral.

Nunes, Ana Bela and Valério, Nuno (2005). 'Moeda e bancos', in P. Lains and A. Ferreira da Silva (eds.) *História Económica de Portugal, 1700–2000*. Lisbon: Imprensa de Ciências Sociais, vol. 3, pp. 227–263.

Nunes, Manuel Jacinto (1976). *O Caminho do Futuro. Palavras. Proferidas na Posse de Administrador-Geral da Caixa*. Lisbon: Caixa Geral de Depósitos.

Nunes, Manuel Jacinto (2009). *Memórias Soltas*. Lisbon: Aletheia.

O Sistema Bancário Português (1994). *Estudos e Documentos*, 8. Lisbon: Caixa Geral de Depósitos.

OCDE (1972). *Rapport de la mission d'étude effectuée par le G-CAM auprès de la Caixa Geral de Depósitos*. Paris: OCDE (at Historical Archive of the Caixa Geral de Depósitos, dactil.)

Oliveira, Carlos (1866). *Considerações sobre a Liberdade do Bancos*. Lisbon: Tipografia da Gazeta de Portugal.

Oliveira, Mathieu de (1991) 'La *Caixa Geral de Depósitos*, origines, fondation et évolution', *Revue d'économie financière*, Numéro spécial hors-série: La Caisse des dépôts et consignations 175 ans (NOVEMBRE 1991): 327–343.

Palacios Bañuelos, Luis (1985). *Sociedad y Economía Andaluzas en el Siglo XIX. Montes de Piedad y Cajas de Ahorros*. Córdoba: Monte de Piedad y Caja de Ahorros de Córdoba.

Pereira, A. Ramos (1956), 'O mercado monetário em Portugal no período de 1931–1955', in *Estudos de Economia*, 9 (1),, pp. 5–34.

Pereira, A. Ramos (1969). *O Sistema de Crédito e a Estrutura Bancária em Portugal*. Lisbon: ISCEF.

Pereira, Miriam Halpern (1983 [1971]). *Livre–Câmbio e Desenvolvimento Económico. Portugal na Segunda Metade do Século XIX*. Lisbon: Sá da Costa Editora.

Pereira, Miriam Halpern (1993). *Das Revoluções Liberais ao Estado Novo*. Lisbon: Editorial Presença.

Pereira, Miriam Halpern, org. (1989). *Obras de Mouzinho da Silveira*. Lisbon: Fundação Calouste Gulbenkian, 2 vols.

Pereira, Raul da Silva (2007). *História da Caixa Geral de Depósitos*. Lisbon: Edição do autor.

Peres, Damião (1971). *História do Banco de Portugal, 1821–1846.* Lisbon: Banco de Portugal.

Pina, Mariano (1893). *Os Planos Financeiros do Sr. Mariano de Carvalho.* Lisbon: Companhia Nacional Editora.

Pinheiro, Magda (1983). 'Reflexões sobre a história das finanças públicas no século XIX'. *Ler História* 1: 47–67.

Pinheiro, Magda (1987). 'Portugal e Espanha: integração e ruptura. Os caminhos-de-ferro, 1850–1890'. *Ler História,* 11: 47–75.

Pix, Manfred, and Pohl, Hans (1993). La diffusion de l'idée de caisses d'épargne au xix siècle, t. 2, *L'Histoire des caisses d'épargne européennes.* Paris: Les Éditions de l'Épargne.

Portugal, Presidência do Conselho. *Projecto de Plano de Fomento para 1959–1964* (1958). Lisbon: Presidência do Conselho 5 vols.

Portugal, Presidência do Conselho (1959). *Plano de Fomento, 1959–1964.* Lisbon: Imprensa Nacional.

Portugal, Presidência do Conselho (1968). *III Plano de Fomento para 1968–1973* (1967). Lisbon: Imprensa Nacional, 3 vols.

Portugal, Secretaria Geral da Assembleia da República e da Câmara Corporativa (1973–1974). *Projecto do IV Plano de Fomento* (1973). *Lisbon: Secretaria-Geral da Assembleia Nacional e da Câmara Corporativa,* 3 vols.

*Projecto de Plano Intercalar de Fomento para 1965–1967* (1964). Lisbon: Imprensa Nacional, 2 vols.

Ramos, Rui (1994). *A Segunda Fundação, 1890–1926. História de Portugal* (ed. by José Mattoso), Lisbon: Círculo de Leitores, vol. 6.

Ramos, Rui; Monteiro, Nuno and Sousa, Bernardo V. (2009). *História de Portugal.* Lisbon: Esfera dos Livros.

Reis, Jaime (1991). *A evolução da oferta monetária portuguesa, 1854–1912.* Lisbon: Banco de Portugal, vol. 3.

Reis, Jaime (1993), 'Os bancos portugueses, 1850–1913', in *Anais da Conferência Internacional de História de Empresas.* Rio de Janeiro: Universidade Federal do Rio de Janeiro, pp. 43–91.

Reis, Jaime (1994). 'Portuguese banking', in M. Pohl e S. Freitag (eds.) *Handbook on the History of European Banks.* Hants: Edward Elgar, pp. 821–826.

Reis, Jaime (1995a). 'The National Savings Bank as an instrument of economic policy: Portugal in the interwar period', in Y. Cassis, G. D. Feldman and U. Olsson (eds.) *The Evolution of Financial Institutions and Markets in Twentieth Century Europe.* London: Scholar Press, pp. 163–183.

Reis, Jaime (1995b). 'Portuguese banking in the inter-war period', in C. H. Feinstein (ed.) *Banking, Currency and Finance in Europe between the Wars,* Oxford: Clarendon Press, 1995, pp. 472–501.

Reis, Jaime (1996a). *O Banco de Portugal das Origens a 1914.* Lisbon: Banco de Portugal, vol. 1.

Reis, Jaime (1996b) 'First to join the gold standard, 1854', in J. B. de Macedo, B. Eichengreen, e J. Reis (eds.) *Currency Convertibility. The Gold Standard and Beyond,* London: Routledge, pp. 159–181.

Reis, Jaime (2000). 'The gold standard in Portugal, 1854–1933', in P. Martin Aceña and J. Reis (eds.), *Monetary Standards in the Periphery. Paper, Silver and Gold, 1854–1933.* London: Macmillan, pp. 69–111.

Relvas, José (1977–1978). *Memórias Políticas.* Lisbon: Terra Livre, 2 vols (ed. João Medina).

Ribeiro, Hintze (1896), *Relatório, Propostas de Lei e Documentos Apresentados na Câmara dos Senhores Deputados na Sessão de 16 de Março de 1896 pelo Ministro e Secretário de Estado dos Negócios da Fazenda*. Lisbon: Imprensa Nacional.

Ribeiro, J. M. Félix, Fernandes, L. Gomes, e Ramos, M. M. Carreira (1987). 'Grande indústria, banca e grupos financeiros, 1953–1973', *Análise Social*, 23 (99): 945–1018.

Rocha, Maria Manuela (1996), 'Actividade creditícia em Lisboa, 1775–1830', *Análise Social*, 31, pp. 579–598.

Rocha, Maria Manuela (1998), 'Crédito privado em Lisboa numa perspectiva comparada (séculos XVII–XIX)', *Análise Social*, 33, pp. 91–115.

Rollo, Maria Fernanda (2007). *Portugal e a reconstrução económica do pós-guerra. O plano Marshall e a economia portuguesa dos anos 50*. Lisbon: MNE-Instituto Diplomático.

Rosas, Fernando (1994). *O Estado Novo, 1926–1974. História de Portugal* (ed. by José Mattoso), vol. 7, Lisbon: Círculo de Leitores.

Rosas, Fernando, and Oliveira, Pedro Aires (eds.) (2004). *A Transição Falhada. O Marcelismo e o Fim do Estado Novo, 1968–1974*. Lisbon: Editorial Notícias.

Rosas, Fernando, Carvalho, Rita Almeida de, e Oliveira, Pedro Aires (2002). *Daniel Barbosa, Salazar e Caetano. Correspondência política, 1945–1974*. Lisbon: Círculo de Leitores, 2 vols.

Rouquet, Jean (1896). *Les caisses d'épargne. Leur régime ancien et nouveau*. Paris: Marchal et Billard.

Salazar, António de Oliveira (1930). *Reorganização Financeira. Dois Anos no Ministério das Finanças, 1928–1930*. Coimbra: Coimbra Editora.

Salazar, António de Oliveira (1997). *O Ágio do Ouro e Outros Textos Económicos, 1916–1918*. Lisbon: Banco de Portugal.

Santos, Henrique Mateus dos (1901). *O Banco Emissor e Suas Relações com o Estado e com a Economia Nacional*. Lisbon: Banco de Portugal.

Santos, Raul Esteves dos (1974). *Os Tabacos. Sua Influência na Vida da Nação*. Lisbon: Seara Nova, 2 vols.

Seixas, António José de (1882). *A Junta de Crédito Público e as Caixas de Depósitos e Económica Portuguesa*. Lisbon: Tipografia Universal.

Sérgio, Anabela (1995). *O Sistema Bancário e a Expansão da Economia Portuguesa, 1947–1959. História Económica*. Lisbon: Banco de Portugal.

Silva, Aníbal Cavaco (1966). 'O mercado de capitais português no período 1961–1965', *Economia e Finanças* 34 (1): 7–90.

Silva, António Martins da (1997). *Nacionalizações e Privatizações em Portugal. A Desamortização Oitocentista*. Coimbra: Minerva.

Silveira, Luís Espinha da (1987). 'Aspectos da evolução das finanças públicas portuguesas nas primeiras décadas do século XIX, 1800–1827', *Análise Social*, 23, pp. 505–529.

Simões, Raul Humberto de Lima (1930). *Crédito Bancário. Os Bancos, o Financiamento do Comércio e da Indústria e os Riscos da Insolvência*. Lisbon: Instituto Superior de Comércio de Lisboa.

Sousa, Carlos Hermenegildo de (1960). *Política económica bancária*. Lisbon: Livraria Portugal.

Sousa, Fernando Freire de and Cruz, Ricardo (1995). *O Processo de Privatizações em Portugal*. Porto: Associação Industrial Portuense.

Straus, A. (1975). 'Trésor public et marché financier. Les emprunts d'État par souscription publique, 1878–1901', *Revue historique*, 541: pp. 65–112.

Tedde Lorca, Pedro (1991). 'La naturaleza de las cajas de ahorros: sus raíces históricas', *Papeles de Economía Española*, 46: 2–11.

Teles, Basílio (1992). *O livro de Job*, Porto, Lello & Irmão.

Telo, António José (1994), 'A obra financeira de Salazar: a 'ditadura financeira' como caminho para a unidade política, 1928–1932', *Análise Social*, 29, pp. 779–800.

Titos Martinez, Manuel (1989). 'La Caja de Madrid en el siglo XIX: actividad asistencial o financiera?', *Revista de Historia Económica*, 7 (3): 557–587.

Titos Martinez, Manuel, and Samos, Javier Piñar (1993). *Ahorro Popular e Inversión Privilegiada. Las Cajas de Ahorros en España, 1939–1975*. Madrid: Caja de Madrid.

Ulrich, Rui Ennes (1902). *Crises Económicas Portuguesas*. Coimbra: Imprensa da Universidade.

Ulrich, Rui (1946). *História do Banco de Portugal, 1846–1890*. Lisbon: Banco de Portugal, 3 vols. (mimeo).

Valente, Vasco Pulido (1997). *Os Militares e a Política, 1826–1856*. Lisbon: Imprensa Nacional.

Valente, Vasco Pulido (1999). *O Poder e o Povo. A Revolução de 1910*. Lisbon: Gradiva.

Valério, Nuno (1984). 'A Companhia Confiança Nacional'. *Revista de História Económica e Social*, 13: 67–92.

Valério, Nuno (1984). *A Moeda em Portugal, 1913–1947*. Lisbon: Sá da Costa.

Valério, Nuno (1986). 'Expectativas dos credores externos sobre a solvabilidade do Estado português, 1891–1910', in *Revista de História Económica e Social*, 18, pp. 1–8.

Valério, Nuno (1988). 'A dívida pública externa de Portugal, 1890–1950'. *Estudos de Economia*, 9: 21–32.

Valério, Nuno (1994). *As Finanças Públicas Portuguesas entre as Duas Guerras Mundiais*. Lisbon: Edições Cosmos.

Valério, Nuno (ed.) (2006–2010). *História do Sistema Bancário Português*. Lisbon: Banco de Portugal, 2 vols.

Valério, Nuno, et al. (2001). *As Finanças Públicas no Parlamento Português. Estudos Preliminares*. Lisbon: Afrontamento.

Vieira, Anselmo (1905). *A Questão Fiscal e as Finanças Portuguesas*. Lisbon: Ferreira e Oliveira.

Vilar, Emílio (1996). 'Grupos financeiros em Portugal, o mercado interno e UEM', in João Ferreira do Amaral *et al.* (eds.) *Ensaios de Homenagem a Manuel Jacinto Nunes*, Lisbon: ISEG, pp. 457–469.

Vilhena, Júlio de (1916). *Antes da República. Notas Autobiográficas*. Coimbra: França e Arménio, 2 vols.

Vogler, Bernard (ed.) (1991). L'histoire des caisses d'épargnes européennes, t. 1, *Les origines des caisses d'épargnes, 1815–1848*. Paris: Les Éditions de l'Épargne.

Voltes Bou, Pedro (1965). *Las Cajas de Ahorro Barcelonesas. Su Pasado, Su Presente, Su Porvenir*. Barcelona: Caja de Ahorro Provincial de la Diputación de Barcelona.

Wallich, Henry C. (1951). *O Sistema Financeiro Português*. Lisbon: Banco de Portugal.

# INDEX

Administrative Code 145, 148
agricultural credit 48, 98, 122, 188n2;
from 1926 to 1929 105, 108, 109; from
1968 to 1974 165, 166; *see also* industrial credit
Aguiar, Joaquim António de 49
Almeida, Ferreira de 62
Amortisation Fund (*Fundo Especial de
Amortização*) 7–8; nationalisation of 8–9
Angolan crisis (1929–1930) 122–125; *see
also* Bank of Angola (*Banco de Angola*)
annual reports, *Caixa* 33, 35, 36, 78, 84,
86, 89, 94–96, 132, 192–193; of 1912
95; of 1916 96; of 1928 119; of 1940
134; of 1950 143; of 1951 145; of
1952 146
armed forces xiii; Armed Forces Movement (Movimento das Forças Armadas)
174
autonomy: administrative 91, 104, 111,
121, 157, 163, 207; *of Caixa Económica
Portuguesa* 96; of *Caixa Geral de Depósitos* xii, xiii, 60, 102, 103, 107, 110,
111, 143, 157, 163–165, 204, 207,
211; colonial 124; financial 2, 104,
111, 124; formal 103; French model
37; limited/partial 110, 143; managerial
207; operational 96; Public Credit
Board x, 3, 37, 45, 46; state 2
Ávila, António José de 8

balance of payments 55
*Banco Caixa Geral* 198
*Banco Comercial de Investimentos* (BCI)
193–194, 201
*Banco Comercial Português* (BCP) 195,
196, 197
*Banco de Extremadura* 196–197

*Banco de Fomento* (BF): *Banco de Portugal
Colonial* 125, 126; *Banco de Portugal
Nacional* 152–154, 161, 163; merger of
BCI with 194
*Banco de Portugal see* Bank of Portugal
(*Banco de Portugal*)
*Banco Luso-Español* 197
*Banco Mercantil do Porto* 11
*Banco Nacional Ultramarino* (BNU) ix, 20,
35, 121, 122, 193, 194, 199; acquisi-
tion (1988) 185–188; *BNU-Oriente* 200
Bandeirantes Financial System (*Sistema
Financeiro Bandeirantes*) 197
Bank of Angola (*Banco de Angola*) 122,
125, 152
Bank of Commerce and Overseas (*Banco
do Comércio e Ultramar*) 123
Bank of Lisbon (*Banco de Lisboa*) 5; borrowing from 4; decades following
creation 3; and financial crisis of 1846
5; foundation (1821) viii, 1, 2; merger
with *Companhia Confiança Nacional* 5–6;
predecessor of Bank of Portugal 13;
and Public Credit Board (1821–1846)
2–5
Bank of Portugal (*Banco de Portugal*) viii,
ix, xi, 1, 7, 26, 53, 73, 105, 141, 151;
agreement with state (1931) 150;
banknotes issued by 53, 55, 59, 66,
70–71; bonds 60, 77; and *Caixa Geral
de Depósitos* 58–59, 151, 152; as central
bank 12, 53, 54, 57, 92, 99, 197;
charter 10, 28; contract with state
(1887) 79; *Crédito Móvel Português*
(pawn loan bank) created by 11; and
crisis of 1876 19; deposits 6–7, 162;
executive board 49–50; general assembly 4; loans to government 12; new

statute for 10; and Public Credit Board 9, 53; public debt securities 59, 60; public deposits 10, 11, 30, 31; reforms 59; role in public administration 9; statutes xi, 3, 6, 7, 10, 56–59; treasurer general of the state 57
Banking Council 100
banking crises *see* financial crises
banknotes, issue of viii, 1, 2, 6, 11, 20, 35, 115, 121, 188; by Bank of Lisbon 5, 7; by Bank of Portugal 53, 55, 59, 66, 70–71; financial reforms (1886–1890) 56, 59
banks *see Caixa Económica Portuguesa* (CEP, Portuguese Savings Bank); *Caixa Geral de Depósitos* (public deposit bank and state-owned banking corporation); commercial banks; deposit banks/houses; investment banks; private banks; savings banks
*Banque Franco-Portugaise* (BFP) 200
Barbosa, Daniel 136, 137, 151, 152
Barbosa, Pinto 151
Baring Brothers 66, 68
Barros Gomes, Henrique de 39, 41, 57, 63, 64, 67
Basto, Eduardo Pinto 87
Basto, Júlio Ferreira Pinto 36, 78, 86, 87
Beirão, Veiga 70
Belo, João 121
BFC *see* Colonial Development Bank (*Banco de Fomento*)
bonds viii, 10, 14, 63, 73, 185; Bank of Portugal 60, 77; bearer 6, 74; *Caixa Nacional de Crédito* 124, 125, 137; *Companhia do Crédito Predial* 34, 35, 39, 77; consolidated 85; interest paid by 81, 86, 88; mortgage 115–116, 124; public 4, 16, 89; Public Credit Board 22, 23, 123, 151; state x, 43, 106, 151; Treasury 8, 17, 18, 23, 34, 40, 44, 46, 72, 88
Braamcamp, Anselmo José 28, 67, 83
Brazil: banks 193, 194; Financial Agency of Rio de Janeiro 100, 103, 111; recognised by Portugal as a separate state (1825) 4
Bretton Woods system xiii, 150, 173, 174
budgets, state 39, 47, 55, 63
Burnay, Eduardo (brother of financier Henry) 61, 84
Burnay, Henry (financier and Count) 64, 66, 71, 76; tobacco deal (1891) 68–69, 70, 73

Caetano, Marcelo (President of Council of Ministers) 207; as dictator xiii, 156, 157
*Caixa Económica Portuguesa* (CEP, Portuguese Savings Bank) xi, xvi, 60, 96, 102; Annual Report 1917–1918 98; autonomy 96; charter 45–46; debate 39–41; delegations 94; deposit ceiling 74, 77; deposits and depositors 43, 46, 51, 58, 74, 77, 95, 96, 98, 99, 105, 106, 116, 204; establishment (1880–1886) 28, 39–52; falsification of documents 96; financial reforms (1885–1886) 45–52; headquarters 51; interest rates 105, 115; investment *see* investment; legal limits on deposits with 51; legislation concerning foundation of 40, 51; management 98; merger with the *Caixa Geral de Depósitos* (1896) 86–87; negative balance (1910–1911) 95; plan for establishment of 41–45; premises 82; and Public Credit Board 46; reform 46–47, 77, 85; Republic (1910–1926) 98; staff/workforce 50; yield of debt securities 43–44; *see also Caixa Geral de Depósitos* (public deposit bank and state-owned banking corporation); savings banks
*Caixa Geral de Depósitos* (public deposit bank and state-owned banking corporation) xvi, 89; in the 1980s 209–210; accounts 89, 115, 134; annual reports *see* annual reports, *Caixa*; assessment by the OECD (report mission of 1971) 167–171; autonomy of xii, xiii, 60, 102, 103, 107, 110, 111, 143, 157, 163–165; and Bank of Portugal 58–59, 151, 152; bookkeeping 36, 165; charters 28, 33, 164, 165, 166, 178; creation of *see Caixa Geral de Depósitos*, creation (1876); deposits *see* deposits, of the *Caixa Geral de Depósitos*; public deposits; Directorate for Credit Services (DSC) 168–170; directors-general 60, 62, 78, 86; early period 29–37; ending Public Credit Board's control over 78; executive board 35, 37, 60, 124, 136, 144, 164, 185, 187, 191, 206; expenses 27; fiscal council 60, 61, 62, 122, 135, 204, 205; functions 27, 30–31; funding 29–30; governor, creation of post for life 60, 61;

growth/expansion xiv, 26, 29, 33, 50, 94–96, 99, 111, 165–166, 193, 197, 198, 208, 210; information technology use 167–168, 171; internationalisation 141, 193–196; investment *see* investment; lending operations *see* Caixa Geral de Depósitos, credit activity and lending operations; investment; management 42, 78, 89, 192; merger with the *Caixa Económica Portuguesa* (1896) 86–87; and monetary union 191; National Pensions Fund linked to 39, 57; Old and New Accounts 30–32, 34; parliamentary debate 25–29; profits 45, 56, 60, 82, 83, 94, 98, 111, 116, 125, 134, 135, 138, 182, 183, 208; public bodies financed by 143–144; as a public company xiii, xv, 157, 163–165, 191, 207; Public Credit Board, under administration of ix–x, 2, 28–29, 31, 32, 34–36, 37, 39, 53, 57, 59, 62, 82; reforms *see* Caixa Geral de Depósitos, reforms; regime change, politics of 112–113; Republic (1910–1926), impact on 91, 94–97; reserves 34, 83, 85, 99, 132, 152, 162–163, 168; service directorates 168; significance 129–130; staff/workforce 35–37, 42, 96, 110, 111, 154, 164, 165, 169, 171; state borrowing 33–34; supervisory board x, 77, 78, 86–88, 97, 98, 144, 204; vertical integration of departments 181; workload 37, 42, 49; *see also Caixa Económica Portuguesa* (CEP, Portuguese Savings Bank)

*Caixa Geral de Depósitos,* credit activity and lending operations 59, 79, 116, 165; development plans *see* development plans; Interim Plan (1963–1965); Interim Plan (1965–1967); and establishment of the *Caixa Geral de Depósitos* 26–27, 28; growth 166; loans to private sector 166–167; nationalisations and post-nationalisation period (1974–1992) 180–182; and new order (1926–1929) 104, 106; state and market (1950–1968) 143, 146–148, 150, 153, 154

*Caixa Geral de Depósitos,* creation (1876) viii–ix, xv–xvi, 1, 13, 25–38, 39; legislation 25, 26, 35, 36, 203; motivations for ix, 18, 27

*Caixa Geral de Depósitos,* reforms 59, 60, 61, 93, 207; of 1896 85–90; of 1929 108–113; enlargement of duties 46, 47, 48; reform of 1929 108–113, 211; replacement of outdated practices 30–31; report of 1877 37; Republic (1910–1926), impact on the *Caixa* 91, 94–97; restructuring 85, 181, 193, 200; statutes xi, xii, xiii, 27, 85, 91, 94, 102, 108–110, 112, 114, 156, 164, 174, 191, 194

*Caixa Internacional* 200–201

*Caixa Nacional de Aposentações see* National Pensions Fund (*Caixa Nacional de Aposentações*)

*Caixa Nacional de Crédito see* National Credit Fund (*Caixa Nacional de Crédito*)

Camacho, Inocêncio 92

Cameira, Eurico Máximo 97

capital: investing 21, 32, 132, 138, 146; investing x, xi, 68, 109, 111, 115; markets 144, 146, 151; raising 1, 159, 160, 182; share capital 125, 134, 200, 2201; venture capital 196; *see also* investment

Carlos, King D. 71, 81, 92

Carmo e Cunha, Raul 104–106, 112, 119, 126

Carnation Revolution xiv

Carrilho, António Maria Pereira 78

Carvalho, Alberto António Morais de 84

Carvalho, Mariano de x, 6, 55–57, 59, 60, 83; draft bill of 1887 77; and financial crisis of 1890–1892 66, 68–71, 74, 77; removal from office 63–64

Carvalho, Pedro Augusto de 36

Cassequel Agricultural Society (*Sociedade Agrícola do Cassequel*) 126

Castro, José Luciano de 64; head of Progressive Party 54, 61, 87, 88

CEP *see Caixa Económica Portuguesa* (CEP, Portuguese Savings Bank)

Chagas, Manuel Pinheiro 83, 84

Champalimaud, António/Champalimaud group 195

*Chase Manhattan Bank España* 196, 197

Chaves, Joaquim Alves 84

Civil Code (1868) ix

civil war (1846–1847) 5

Coelho, Manuel Maria 104

Colonial Development Bank (*Banco de Fomento*) 124, 126, 152

colonialism xiii, 123–126; colonial economy 123, 126; companies 123, 125; credit 122, 123, 130, 138; goods/products 81, 118, 121, 122
commercial banks 16, 19, 89, 138, 151; from 1968 to 1974 162–163; from 1974 to 1992 179, 182
commissioners (judges) 40
*Companhia Colonial de Navegação* 123, 126
*Companhia Confiança Nacional* (financial syndicate) 5, 7, 10; merger with Bank of Lisbon 5–6
*Companhia de Obras Públicas de Portugal* 7, 8
*Companhia do Crédito Predial Português* 18, 20, 39, 60; bonds 34, 35, 39, 77
*Companhia Geral de Angola* 124–127
construction sector 105, 135, 148, 150, 175; civil construction 136, 138, 149; credit/investment in 98, 102, 106, 119, 166, 178–180, 181; housing/economic housing 98, 119, 120, 130, 133, 139, 149, 150, 167, 180; railways 8, 9, 17, 64; roads 27, 50, 63, 97; urban 166
consumer tax 12
Cordeiro, Silva 73
Cordes, General Sinel de 103, 104, 112, 121
Corporate Chamber (*Câmara Corporativa*) 131, 151, 156–157
Correia, José Araújo 111, 112, 117, 120, 124, 143; and public investment 130–131, 136–137
Corvo, Andrade 49
Costa, Afonso 92, 95, 97
Costa, Carlos 198
Court of Auditors 3, 85, 164
Coutinho, Sousa 43
credit expansion 117, 138, 145, 151, 153, 160; *see also* agricultural credit; industrial credit; mortgage credit
*Crédito Móvel Português* (pawn loan bank) 11
Cristóstomo, João 67, 70
Cunha, Augusto José da 64, 67, 68, 92
Cunha, Carmo e *see* Carmo e Cunha, Raul

Dawes Plan (1924) 99
Decree-Law Numbers: 15,086, of 1928 105; 16,665, of 1929 112; 17,252, of 1929 117; 23,052, of 1933 120;

33,853, of 1944 139; 34,486, of 1945 149; 35,669, of 1946 136; 41.403, of 1957 151, 152; 42,641, of 1959 151; 42,951, of 1960 150; 46,305, of 1965 154; 48, 953, of 1969 164
deflation 121, 138–139, 160; *see also* inflation
deposit banks/houses ix, x, 47; *see also* Caixa Geral de Depósitos (public deposit bank and state-owned banking corporation)
*Depósito Público de Lisboa see* Public Deposit of Lisbon (*Depósito Público de Lisboa*)
*Depósito Público do Porto see* Public Deposit of Porto (*Depósito Público do Porto*)
depositors xiv, 21, 27, 30, 43, 60, 93, 95, 99, 110, 141, 171, 175, 179, 207, 209, 212; *Caixa Económica Portuguesa* 43, 46, 51, 58, 74, 77, 96; higher-income 197; interest paid to 26, 27, 43, 58, 116; judicial 14; medium- and low-income xi, 102, 116, 161; private xi, 26, 166, 176; public 176; rural 197; withdrawals by 152
deposits, of the *Caixa Geral de Depósitos*: amount 30, 32; balances 89; ceilings for 28; growth 166; interest on 33; mandatory 30, 58, 87, 136; small and medium-sized savers 129
development plans 147–148; First (1953–1958) 142, 147, 149; Second (1959–1964) 153, 158; Interim (1963–1965) 159; Interim (1965–1967) 159, 160; Third (1968–1973) 159, 161, 162; Fourth (1974–1979) 159; five-year 158–159, 161, 162
*Diário de Notícias* (newspaper) 108
Dias Ferreira, José 81, 83–84; and financial crisis of 1890–1892 69, 70, 71, 75–77
dictatorships 92, 129; of Caetano xiii, 156, 157; fascist xii, xvi, 102; military 97, 100, 113, 120, 121; of Salazar xii, xiii, 100, 108, 156; technocratic 157–163
Directorate for Credit Services (DSC) 168–170
Directorate-General of Public Debt 59, 60

economic growth xiv, 16, 100, 129, 151, 157; golden years xiii, xvi, 158

Economic Reconstitution Law (*Lei de Reconstituição Económica*) 130, 131, 137, 139, 142, 207
economy notes 115, 116
*Estado Novo* regime xvi, 113, 130, 158, 164, 167, 207; *Caixa* and the empire 121–127; changes in 156; consolidation (1929–1935) 115–128; credit to the economy 116–119; financial stability 115–116; progress xii–xiii; social housing 119–121; urban improvements 119–121; Wheat Campaign (1929–1930) 116–118, 123
euro xiv, xv
European Coal and Steel Community (ECSC) 142
European Community: integration of Portugal into (1986) xiii, xiv, 142; *see also* integration, European
European Economic Communities (EEC) 142, 157
European Free Trade Association (EFTA) 141, 158
European Monetary System (EMS)/European Monetary Union (EMU) xiv, xvi, 191, 192
European Payments Union 150
Eurozone xv, 191
exchange rates 63, 73, 93, 103, 118

farming 117, 138, 179
Ferreira, José Dias *see* Dias Ferreira, José
Finance Committee 40, 41, 50, 69, 74, 75, 79n24
Finance Ministry *see* Ministry of Finance
Financial and Banking Operations Office (*Repartição de Operações Financeiras e Bancárias*) 130
Financial Committee for the Colonies (*Comissão Financeira para as Colónias*) 126
financial crises 13; *see also* financial crisis of 1846; financial crisis of 1876; financial crisis of 1890–1892
financial crisis of 1846 5–9
financial crisis of 1876 ix, 16, 17, 19–22, 40, 56
financial crisis of 1890–1892 x, xi, xvi, 59, 66–80; debt, high levels 66; fall in value of wine 66; origins 67–71; progressive government 77–79; radical solution 71–77

financial reforms xvi; of 1885 to 1886 42–52; of 1886 to 1890 53–65; of 1891 70–71; Bank of Portugal 56–59; government control 59–65; Progressive government (1886) 54–56; *see also* reforms
First Development Plan (1953) 142, 147, 149
floating debt 19, 33, 47, 49, 57, 67–69; domestic and external 55; and establishment of the *Caixa Económica Portuguesa* 40; government control 62, 63; interest rates 55; Treasury 17, 26, 28, 72–73, 98
Fontes Pereira de Melo, António Maria de 9, 10, 12, 17; and *Caixa Económica Portuguesa* 41, 45; and financial crisis of 1890–1892 76; and financial reforms of 1886 to 1890 53, 55, 57, 63, 64; head of Progressive Party 41, 45, 53, 61, 63, 67, 76
*fontismo* policy 53
foreign exchange reserves 99, 103, 134, 151
Fourth Development Plan (1974–1979) 159
France: *Caisse de dépôts et consignations* 35, 37, 42, 50; subsidiary companies 200
Franco, Francisco 157
Franco, João 66, 67, 69, 70, 75, 81, 92
Franco, Pedro Augusto *see* Restelo, Count of (Pedro Augusto Franco)
Franco, Sousa 195
Franzini, Marino 9
*Fundo Especial de Amortização see* Amortisation Fund (*Fundo Especial de Amortização*)
Fuschini, Augusto 69, 72–74, 75; as finance minister 81, 83–84

Gama, José Augusto da 84
General Agreement on Tariffs and Trade (GATT) 150
gold standard ix, 71
Gomes *see* Barros Gomes, Henrique de
Gonçalves, Jardim 195
Gouveia, Melo 67, 69
government control 59–65
Guterres, António 195

High Court of Tax Litigation 92
historical periods *see* nineteenth century; twentieth century

housing: constructing 98, 119, 120, 130, 133, 139, 149, 150, 167, 180; economic programme 120–121; investment in 119, 149, 159, 175, 180; lending operations 167, 170, 180, 182, 184, 209; savings accounts 167; social 119–121

industrial credit 48, 138, 145, 181; from 1926 to 1929 105, 106, 107, 109; from 1929 to 1935 118, 119; from 1968 to 1974 163, 165, 166, 170; see also agricultural credit
inflation xi–xii, xiii, 133, 150, 151, 173, 176, 183; high 100, 129, 179; inflationary pressure 142, 143; see also deflation
instability, financial and political viii–ix, xiii, 5
integration, European xiii, xiv, xv, 161, 174, 196, 203, 210; economic 142, 158, 159, 180–181; financial 180–181; political 142
interest rates xiii, 10, 11, 18, 24n30, 86, 131; annual 34, 43; average 58, 78; Caixa Económica Portuguesa 105, 115; Caixa Geral de Depósitos 27, 33, 36; changes in 40–41; decreasing/reducing 51, 55, 104–106, 108, 116, 120, 122, 123, 126, 130, 135; differentials 43, 44; domestic 75; effective 52, 55, 69; Estado Novo 115, 118, 119; floating debt 55; high 105, 129; increasing/rising 55, 75, 115, 143, 166; new order (1926–1929) 102, 112; nominal interest 75; real 43
Interim Plan (1963–1965) 159
Interim Plan (1965–1967) 159, 160
International Monetary Fund (IMF) xiv, 150
internationalisation 141, 186, 192, 198–200, 210; fragile 193–196
investment: the Caixa 26, 33, 34, 43, 85, 87, 106, 107, 116, 160, 180, 193, 208; of capital 21, 32, 132, 138, 146; in companies/enterprises 96, 138, 149; construction sector 98, 102, 106, 119, 166, 178–180, 181; financial 19, 20, 44, 115, 143, 147, 185, 187, 207; in housing 119, 149, 159, 175, 180; in infrastructure 131, 159, 160; levels of 162, 174, 210; policies xi, 141, 158;

portfolios 21, 102; prioritising 139, 159; private xiii, 18, 153, 158, 160, 179; public see public investment; returns on 29, 58; and savings 151, 204
investment banks xii, xiii, 21, 58, 86, 152, 194, 196, 200

Janeirinha (revolt) 12
Jornal de Comércio 43, 47, 60–62, 84, 87; aligned with Regeneration Party 78, 82
Junta do Crédito Público see Public Credit Board (Junta do Crédito Público)

Keynesianism 129, 151, 160

Laranjo, José Frederico 49, 70
Law of Means (1891) 70
Leal, Cunha 122
Liberal League (Liga Liberal) 81
liberalism viii–ix, 1, 17, 91
liquidation 125, 135, 136
liquidity 9, 23, 25, 46, 76; liquid assets 121, 136; liquidity boom (1870–1876) xv, 16–19; risks 152; Spanish 17
Lisbon: Public Deposit see Public Deposit of Lisbon
Lisbon City Council 132, 133, 145
Lisbon Stock Exchange 19, 72
loans: to administrative bodies 144–147; and Caixa Geral de Depósitos 146–148, 150, 154, 165, 180–182; debenture 21; home/housing sector 167, 170, 180, 182, 184, 209; to individuals 11, 21; long-term 148; mortgage-backed 108; new 74, 107, 144, 145, 182; notaries 170–171; on pawns 11; private sector 18, 153, 163, 166; public sector 166; Public Treasury 26; refusal of loans to the state 7; revocable 33; short-term 27; to the state 34, 35, 42, 58, 68, 96, 123, 134, 135, 136, 166, 208; to welfare institutions 149; to workers 149; see also Caixa Geral de Depósitos, credit activity and lending operations

Maastricht Treaty (1992) xiv, 191
Machado, Bernardino 92
Mamede, Joaquim Gonçalves 41
map, rose-coloured 64, 67
Marshall Plan 142, 150
Martins, Oliveira 46, 57, 67, 81, 84; and financial crisis of 1890–1892 71–75, 79n24

Means Law 149
Mello e Sousa, José Adolfo de 92
Melo, Fontes Pereira de *see* Fontes Pereira de Melo, António Maria de
Melo Sampaio, Tomás Pizarro de 87, 88
Mendes, José Luís Teixeira 43
Miguel, D. 4
military coups: of 1823 4; of 1842 4–5; of 1910 91, 92; of 1926 xii, 91, 103, 107; of 1974 208; of 1975 xiii
Ministry of Agriculture 109, 117, 118
Ministry of Finance ix, 37, 54, 78, 85, 141, 146–147; from 1910 to 1926 92, 96, 99; from 1926 to 1929 109, 110; memorandum sent to (1929) 109–111
Ministry of Public Works 54, 82, 97, 137, 145–146
*misericórdias* (district road funds), transfer of funds 48–50
monetary depreciation xi–xii
monetary policy xiv, 129, 151, 160, 175, 184; *see also* Keynesianism
monetary union (1992–2010) xiv, xv, 186, 191–202; acquisition of Spanish institutions 196–199; fragile internationalisation 193–196; internationalisation of the *Caixa* 199; privatisation, Cape Verdean (2000) 199; *see also* European Monetary System (EMS)/European Monetary Union (EMU)
*Monte de Piedade* (pawn credit) 85
*Montepio Geral*, savings bank xi, 18, 19, 21, 50, 87; and financial crisis of 1890–1892 67–68
Morais, Paulo de 112
Moreira, Guilherme Alves xii, 112–113, 120, 125–126, 143, 144–146
mortgage credit 11, 98, 108, 135
Motta Veiga, António da 161, 164, 167
Municipal Council of Setúbal 121

National Assembly (*Assembleia Nacional*), 130, 131, 143, 149, 150, 153
National Credit Council (*Conselho Nacional de Crédito*) 152
National Credit Fund (*Caixa Nacional de Crédito*) 108–110, 145, 165; bonds 124, 125, 137; creation of (1929) 150; *Estado Novo*, consolidation in 116–119, 123–125; public investment 134–135

National Development Fund (*Fundo de Fomento Nacional*) 152
National Federation of Wheat Producers (FNPT) (*Federação dos Produtores de Trigo*) 118
national guild (*Montepio Nacional*) 85
National Pensions Fund (*Caixa Nacional de Aposentações*) 39, 47, 48, 57, 84, 85, 108
National Press (*Imprensa Nacional*) 96
nationalisations and post-nationalisation period (1974–1992) 173–190; *Caixa* and the government 181–185; normalisation 180–181; regime change and banking sector 173–178; remittances and construction 178–180
Navarro, André Severiano Roman 87
Neto, Amaral 149
new order (1853) 9–14
new order (1926–1929) 102–114; bond transactions 106; industrial credit 107; lending to agriculture, manufacturing and construction 106; memorandum sent to Ministry of Finance (1929) 109–111; military coup of 1926 xii, 107; mortgage-backed loans 108; prior to Salazar 102–104; reforms of 1929 108–112; regime change at the *Caixa* 112–113; Salaza as finance minister 104–106; suspension of activities in 1926 107; Treasury Bills, discount of 106; warrant system 106
nineteenth century: public finance, rise of (1820–1870) 1–15; new financial order (1853) 9–14; liquidity boom (1870–1876) xv, 16–19; crisis of 1876 19–22; financial reforms (1886–1890) 53–65; financial and banking sector changes ix; instability, financial and political viii–ix, xiii, 5; unclear boundaries, financial sector xiii
Noronha, António Caetano do Carmo 84
notaries 170–171

oil crises of 1973 and 1979 xiv, 174
Old and New Accounts 32, 34
old order, return to (1892–1910) 81–90; *Partido Regenerador* government 82–85; reform of 1896 85–90
Oliveira, Faria de 199
Organisation for Economic Cooperation and Development (OECD) 156, 160;

assessment of the *Caixa* (report mission of 1971) 167–171
Organisation for European Economic Cooperation (OEEC) 142, 150

Pacheco, Duarte 130
Pais, Sidónio 97, 98
Parliament: chambers 36, 41; debate regarding proposed public deposit bank 25–29; draft bill on transfer of *misericórdias' funds* 48–50; Financial Committee 28, 41; state budgets submitted to 39, 47, 55, 63; *see also Caixa Geral de Depósitos* (public deposit bank and state-owned banking corporation)
*Partido Progressista see* Progressive Party (*Partido Progressista*)
*Partido Regenderador see* Regeneration Party (*Partido Regenderador*)
*Partido Republicano see* Republican Party (*Partido Republicano*)
pawns 28, 59; *Casa de Crédito Popular* 99; *Crédito Móvel Português* (pawn loan bank) 11; *see also Monte de Piedade* (pawn credit)
Pedro, King D. 4
pensions *see* National Pensions Fund
Pereira de Melo *see* Fontes Pereira de Melo, António Maria de
Pimentel, Eduardo Serpa 92
Pinto, Gabriel 104, 105–106, 119–120, 122
political parties *see Partido Progressista* government; *Partido Regenderador* government
Porto: Public Deposit *see* Public Deposit of Porto;
Porto riots (1888) 62
Portuguese Financial Agency (*Agência Financial de Portugal*) 23
Post Office Savings Bank, England 51
postal services 164
*Praça do Comércio*, Lisbon x
prerogatives: Bank of Portugal 6, 7, 10–12, 14, 20, 28, 56; government 94; note issuance 1, 7, 20, 56; over mortgage credit 11; state 2, 91
private banks xi, xiii, 89, 141, 148, 161–163, 207
Progressive Party (*Partido Progressista*) x, 53, 59, 61–65; and financial crisis of 1890–1892 66, 67, 69, 70, 76;

governments/in power 54–56, 60, 66, 76, 87
promissory notes 5, 115
public companies: growth of *Caixa* activity 165–166; operational problems 166
Public Credit Board (*Junta do Crédito Público*) viii, 3, 5, 8, 16, 18, 25; accountancy department 48, 51–52, 60; autonomy x, 3, 37, 45, 46; and Bank of Lisbon (1821–1846) 2–5; and Bank of Portugal 9, 53; bonds 22, 23, 123, 151; and *Caixa Económica Portuguesa* 44, 46; *Caixa Geral de Depósitos* under administration of ix–x, 2, 28–29, 31, 32, 34–36, 37, 39, 53, 57, 59, 62, 82; chairman 60, 61, 86; composition 3–4, 83, 86; ending of control over the *Caixa* 78; and financial crisis of 1890–1892 72; financial intermediation 44; governmental interference, alleged 42–43; liquidity boom (1870–1876) 17; membership 3–4, 60; proposal for the *Caixa Económica Portuguesa* 41–42; and provisional regulation 35–36; public debt securities 30; reconstitution 83, 84; reforms 22–23, 43, 59, 78, 82–84, 87, 88; role 1, 59, 60, 62, 87, 88, 89; segmentation 60
public debt ix, x, xii, 1, 2, 7, 13, 88; from 1870 to 1876 16, 17; from 1880 to 1886 40, 44; from 1886 to 1890 56, 62; from 1890 to 1892 67, 68, 70, 75, 77; bonds 14, 16; domestic 53, 75, 76, 79n24; external 53, 56, 83; funded 55, 69; nominal 52n2, 56; Portuguese 4, 6, 18, 20–22, 55, 76, 84, 87
public debt securities 5, 8, 98, 102, 152; from 1870 to 1876 19, 21, 22, 23, 24n30; from 1876 to 1880 25, 30, 34, 37; from 1880 to 1886 39, 41, 42, 43, 46, 49, 51; from 1886 to 1890 55, 58; from 1890 to 1892 66, 72, 77, 78, 79; acquiring 60, 72, 86, 89; of the Bank of Portugal 59, 60; and *Caixa* 26–27, 28; domestic 73; pawned 59, 79; Public Credit Board, held by 30; *see also Caixa Geral de Depósitos* (public deposit bank and state-owned banking corporation)
Public Deposit of Lisbon (*Depósito Público de Lisboa*) ix, 6, 14; and *Caixa Geral de*

*Depósitos* 26, 29, 30, 31, 32; founding of (1821) 3, 7; reform (1868) 13

Public Deposit of Porto (*Depósito Público do Porto*) ix, 3, 6, 7, 13; and *Caixa Geral de Depósitos* 26, 29, 30

public deposits ix, xiii, 2, 13, 165, 204; administration 31; Bank of Portugal 10, 11, 30, 31; and *Caixa Geral de Depósitos* 26, 27, 29–31; as financial intermediaries 31; reforms 14, 25, 32; *see also* Public Deposit of Lisbon (*Depósito Público de Lisboa*); Public Deposit of Porto (*Depósito Público do Porto*)

public finance, rise of (1820–1870) xv, 1–15

public investment xiii, 106, 141, 142, 147, 157–160, 179, 207; from 1935 to 1950 129–140; new state and the economy 130–132; World War II xvi, 132–135; post-World War II 135–139

Public Treasury 2, 3; from 1870 to 1876 17, 20, 21, 23; administration of state finance 55; and *Caixa Económica Portuguesa* 44; issues 74; loans 26; *see also* Treasury

railways, extension of 64

*real de água* (tax on some consumer goods) 12

reconstruction: economic 142; financial 132; material 144

reforms xi, xii, 41; of 1929 108–112; of *Caixa Económica Portuguesa* 46–47, 77, 85; development plans 147–148, 158–159, 161, 162; and establishment of the *Caixa Geral de Depósitos* 26; financial (1885–1886) 45–52; financial (1886–1890) 53–65; financial (1957 and 1959) 162; outdated practices, replacing 30–31; public companies 163–165; Public Credit Board 22–23, 43, 59, 78, 82, 83, 87, 88; railways, extension of 64; regime change and banking sector 173–178; reserves 162–163; Second Republican 97–100; state/Bank of Portugal agreement (1876) 26; Treasury restructure viii, 77; *see also Caixa Geral de Depósitos*, reforms; new order (1853); new order (1926–1929)

Regeneration of 1851 9, 12

Regeneration Party (*Partido Regenerador*) 25, 53, 59; division of 47, 55, 63; and

financial crisis of 1890–1892 66, 71; governments/in power 77, 81, 82–85, 93; *Jornal de Comércio* aligned with 78, 82

Relvas, José 93

Republic (1910–1926) xvi, 91–101; governments, relations with the *Caixa* xii; impact on the *Caixa* 94–97; new political regime 92–94; 'New Republic' 97; Republican Revolution (1910) xi, 66, 91, 206; Second Republican reform 97–100

Republican Party (*Partido Republicano*) 75, 91, 92, 93, 95, 97, 129, 206

reserves 68, 99, 142, 152, 162, 183, 185; of the *Caixa* 34, 83, 85, 99, 132, 152, 162–163, 168; capital 187; cash 34, 58, 83, 132; foreign exchange 99, 103, 134, 151; gold 19, 71, 76

Restelo, Count of (Pedro Augusto Franco) 41, 46, 62–63, 77, 78, 87; member and head of Public Credit Board 45, 60, 64, 83, 86

Ribeiro, Hintze 46, 48, 53, 64; as finance minister 47, 84, 85; and financial crisis of 1890–1892 67, 72, 75, 76; head of Regeneration Party 64, 72, 81, 82, 84

Rio, Manuel Alves do 43

Rio de Janeiro, Financial Agency 100, 103, 111

Rodrigues, Daniel José xii, 97, 98, 104, 106, 109–113, 117, 122, 206

Rodrigues, Inocêncio Joaquim Camacho 92

Rosa, Morais 112

Salamanca syndicate 64, 72

Salazar, António de Oliveira 117, 123, 129, 137, 154, 206; as dictator xii, xiii, 100, 108, 156; as finance minister xii, 103, 104–106, 108, 112, 113, 117, 164; journey to power xii–xiii; as prime minister xii, 130, 142, 151; prior to rule of 102–104; propaganda 112; regime of xiii

Salgado, Ricardo 195

Salgueiro, João 195, 196

Sampaio, Rodrigues 41, 64; leader of Regeneration Party 39

Santos, Rodrigues dos 82

São Vicente, Madeira: municipal council 144

savings banks x, 7, 17–19, 26, 84, 105, 148; and *Caixa Económica Portuguesa* 40, 44, 46, 51; deposits 19, 28, 58, 105; limits 19, 28; nationalisations 188n2; new 6, 7, 10–12; private x, 50; role 17–18; *see also Caixa Económica Portuguesa* (Portuguese Savings Bank); *Montepio Geral*, savings bank; Public Credit Board (*Junta do Crédito Público*)

Second Development Plan (1959–1964) 153, 158

Seixas, António José de 37, 41, 42–43, 45

Serpa, António de 25, 39; as finance minister 21, 56; and financial crisis of 1890–1892 67, 76; head of Regeneration Party 61, 64, 76, 81; replacement as president of council by Crisóstomo 67

Silva, Artur Santos Silva 195

Silva, Cavaco xiv

Simões, Augusto 153, 154

Soares, Mário xiv

social housing 119–121; *see also* housing

Social Security Fund (*Caixa Nacional de Previdência*) 108, 109, 110

Sousa, António Teixeira de 92

South Africa 194

Spain 21, 193; acquisition of Spanish institutions 194–199; joining the European Community (1986) xiv; railways 64; Salamanca syndicate 64, 72

Special Mission of the United States Economic Cooperation Authority (Marshall Plan) 142, 150

state 33–34; budgets, submission to Parliament 39, 47, 55, 63; contract with Bank of Portugal (1887) 79; expansion of role viii; interest rates of loans taken out by 18; loans to 34, 35, 42, 58, 68, 96, 123, 134–136, 166, 208; and market *see* state and market (1950–1968); powers to control financial sector 3

state and market (1950–1968) 141–155; development plans 147–148; financial concerns 142–147; housing 149–150; new banking framework 150–154

subsidiary companies 28, 95–96, 98, 99, 111, 192, 199; *Caixa Económica Portuguesa* xi, xvi, 39–52, 96, 102; foreign 192, 194, 200, 201

syndicates xiii, 5, 19, 27, 69; Salamanca 64, 72

Tavares, Carlos Bessa 112, 116

Telefones de Lisboa e Porto (TLP), telephone company 164

Tenreiro, Henrique 149–150

Third Development Plan (1968–1973) 159, 161, 162

tobacco industry: deal of 1891 68–69, 70, 73; imports 66, 81; loan 72, 73, 83; monopoly viii, 54, 62, 68, 69, 132; nationalisation of 66; reestablishment of monopoly (1888) 62; revenues 68

Treasury x, 2, 3, 17, 111; bonds 8, 17, 18, 23, 34, 40, 44, 46, 72, 88; and *Caixa* 26, 27; discount of Treasury Bills 55, 106; and financial crisis of 1890–1892 72–73, 76; floating debt 17, 26, 28, 72–73, 98; General Accounts 131, 143; restructuring viii, 77; *see also* Public Treasury

Treasury Directorate-General 55, 103

twentieth century: Republic (1910–1926) 91–101; new order (1926–1929) 102–114; Estado Novo, consolidation (1929–1935) 115–128; public investment (1935 to 1950) 129–140; state and market (1950–1968) 141–155; from 1968 to 1974 157–172; monetary union (1992–2010) 191–202

Ulrich, Fernando Enes 131

Ulrich, José Frederico 144

unemployment 119, 138

UNIBANCO (*União dos Bancos Brasileiros*) 194

urban improvements 119–121

Vasconcelos, Estêvão de 93, 94, 96

Vasconcelos, Luís Augusto Perestrelo de 78, 87

Vaz, Lopo 41, 45, 64, 67, 70, 71

Vieria, Anselmo 79n24

Vieria, Silveira 43

Vilaça, António Eduardo 87

Vilhena, Júlio de 70

Wallich, Henry C. 150–151

war economy 142

Wheat Campaign (1929–1930) 116–118, 123

wine production 55, 66, 148
World Bank 150
World War I, Portugal's entry into
  xi, 93

World War II xvi, 132–135; post-war
  period 135–139

Xavier, Alberto 99

Printed in the United States
by Baker & Taylor Publisher Services